The DREAM HOUSE Encyclopedia

THE
DREAM
HOUSE
ENCYCLOPEDIA

By Hubbard H. Cobb

Peter H. Wyden, Inc. / Publisher / New York

THE DREAM HOUSE ENCYCLOPEDIA

LIBRARY OF CONGRESS CATALOG CARD NUMBER: 73–110352

TYPOGRAPHY BY SOPHIE ADLER

MANUFACTURED IN THE UNITED STATES OF AMERICA

TO BETSY

Acknowledgments

I would like to thank the many individuals and organizations who were helpful in furnishing me with information and source material that went into this project. Without their help it would be today what it was about one year ago—a blank piece of paper in a typewriter.

I am especially grateful to William Ward of Sigman-Ward for his help in developing the Space Planner and putting it into drawings; also to Mr. Charles Rieger for his floor plans and detailed drawings. My thanks to the National Forest Product Association for use of their detailed drawings of wood framing and construction and to Mr. Robert Brann of Shoreline Homes, Inc., to the Window Shade Manufacturer's Association, the Ponderosa Pine Woodwork, and the Andersen Corporation.

Mrs. Alma McCardle, Mrs. Lois Rea, Mrs. Jo-Anne Simpson, Miss Jessie Walker and Mrs. Joanne Young merit special thanks for their scouting and help in developing the case histories, as do the photographers who took the many pictures shown in the case histories.

Thanks also to Mrs. Sophie Adler for the attractive book design and layouts, and to Mrs. Grace Shaw and the staff of Peter H. Wyden, Inc. for all their work, patience and understanding that were required to put this book together.

HUBBARD H. COBB

Table of Contents

House. Interior Wall Surfaces. Windows. Fireplaces. Interior Layout. Non-Dwelling Structures. Foundations. Woodwork. What You Will Need. Detailed House-Inspection Form.

terior of an Existing House, Studying Traffic Patterns. Allowing Sufficient Space for Comfortable Use of Furnishings. Standard Specifications for House Interiors: Bathrooms; Kitchens; Dining Areas; Bedrooms; Closets; Living Rooms.

Awning Windows. Bay Windows and Bow Windows. Sliding Windows. Reconditioning Existing Windows. The Sash. Metal Windows. Special Money-Saving Tips.

**THEIR DREAM HOUSES
CAME TRUE:**

*The Step-by-Step Case Histories of 20 Families and
How They Got the Job Done. Text and Photographs.*

List of Illustrations

The DREAM HOUSE Encyclopedia

The Offbeat
Dream House 1

This book is about finding, buying, and fixing up the Offbeat Dream House. What is an Offbeat Dream House? Well, often it is not a house at all. It may be a barn, it may be a beached barge, or a deserted mill that's just been sitting quietly in some little town since the railroad went the other way. Maybe it's a monster Victorian house draped with Steamboat Gothic carpentry, or an abandoned farmhouse sitting alone surrounded by empty fields. It might be one of those bungalows with an impossible floor plan, built half a century ago, or its descendant built right after World War II, with an equally impossible floor plan. It might be a town house found along almost any city block, where the area has deteriorated along with the dwellings. It might also be the house that you already own and are now ready to renovate.

An Offbeat Dream House can be a chicken coop without chickens but on a nice piece of land, or the gasoline filling station that went under when the highway was moved.

The OB Dream House is the one that the real estate broker shows you only after he has given up trying to find you anything else, and even then he is often ashamed to show it because some OB Dream Houses can look very odd indeed. The OB Dream House is one with true possibilities—the one that needs the right people with the right amount of imagination, the proper amount of courage, and a tremendous amount of faith, patience, and endurance.

No, the OB House is not for everyone. It's for those who are too imaginative to want a more conventional house, too broke to afford one or, to paraphrase Mr. Rat in *The Wind in the Willows,* who find that there is "nothing half so much worth doing as simply messing about with houses." The OB House is truly a dream house, but it's a possible dream. You can make this kind of house into precisely what you want it to be. Many people think of their dream home as if it were a doll house in the sky, or an unattainable castle. Your OB Dream House *is* attainable, and this book will show you how, every step of the way.

If you already own a house, now is the time to take a second look at it and see how it can be made into the house of your dreams. Skip over the chapters on finding and buying a house and settle right down to business. The chapter on planning can help you get your ideas on paper, and the chapter on estimating costs can help you determine in advance how much renovations will cost. And the remainder of this book can help you get the work done with the least amount of fuss and bother and at the least cost, whether you have all the work done by professionals or do all or some of it yourself.

If you don't want to become completely involved in a house but simply need a comfortable place in which to eat, sleep, and entertain, the woods are full of such places. You can buy them new or you can buy them slightly used. The conventional house may have drawbacks, such as a certain repetitiveness of design and/or being located a little too close to too many neighbors, but it does make adequate and often attractive shelter. The plumbing system works, the heating system works, the kitchen is fully equipped with all the modern conveniences, and you can move into it the same day that you buy it. You don't have to bring a thing to such a house but your personal possessions and yourself, and some builders will even arrange to decorate and furnish the place for you so that you don't even have to worry about these matters.

The OB Dream House is something else again. You have to provide almost everything, including vast amounts of love, inspiration, effort, and—naturally enough—money. It will, perhaps, also require some physical work.

Incidentally, throughout this book we will use the terms "money" and "work" quite often. When used in connection with an OB Dream House these two words are interchangeable. When someone says, "This old barn is a perfect piece of property but it will take a little work to fix it up," it means that it will take a lot of work unless you pay someone to do the work for you. With few exceptions there is no such thing as a "little" when it comes to the OB Dream House. That's part of the challenge and part of the game, and if you can't take this sort of sport, then, as Mr. Truman said, "Get out of the kitchen."

There are many good reasons for searching out the OB Dream House. Some big families need one just because the family is so very big. If you have a huge collection of children, you probably don't need to be reminded that you are going to have trouble finding the amount of space you need in a new or relatively new house. The vast majority of houses built since World War II contain only three bedrooms. Today, four- and five-bedroom houses are being built, but you've no doubt noticed that their builders get a whale of a lot of money for them. And even so, under the $75,000 mark these houses usually do not encompass enough living space in which to handle comfortably a family consisting of eight or more persons, especially if six of them are children.

So, if this describes your family, your best bet probably is one of those big old Victorian jobs where you have room on room, attic on attic, a tower, a huge basement, even outbuildings, and the children not only won't be heard but often not seen for days on end except at feeding time. You can frequently pick these behemoths up at a reasonable price, because aside from holding you and your brood, the only other uses to which they lend themselves are as rooming houses, apartments, and funeral parlors, and often the local zoning ordinances prohibit the use of these places for commercial purposes.

If you have more taste than money, or if you have money plus taste, the OB Dream House is for you. Some people have so much taste that they would rather live in a tent than in a typical "Colonial-style" house. Not authentic Colonial but "Colonial-style." With taste plus time and/ or money, an old barn can be transformed into a handsome and exciting dwelling, but very little can be done with a poorly designed, new, pseudo-something development house.

There are, of course, many definitions of taste, but, for our purposes, let's also think of taste as integrity—the honest approach. A barn made into a house is still a barn but it has been redesigned to contain humans rather than cattle or horses. A split-level dumped onto a flat piece of ground with only the trappings of Colonial design, is pretending to be something it isn't. It is shelter and little else.

The OB Dream House can also be for those who are perhaps disenchanted with the stock market and are looking for a good place to live plus a good investment. Here the town house—a house in the center or close to the center of urban areas—can work to your advantage. Whether the area is in San Francisco, Chicago, Brooklyn, or New Haven, it is still possible to find an old town house in a deteriorated (but hopefully soon to improve) neighborhood for a relatively moderate price. We'll show you how to remodel such a place so that the finished house includes one or more rental units.

Assuming that the price of the house is not too great and that the cost of remodeling is not too high, you can end up with an extremely comfortable place for your own occupancy, and the rent you collect will often take care of the carrying charges on the entire property— taxes, mortgage payments, and maybe insurance.

Even if you don't live rent free, you are getting excellent living quarters for far less than you would have to pay elsewhere, and you increase your equity in the property each month. If, as is often the case, other houses on the block go through the same transformation, the property values increase considerably, and if you ever wish to sell, you can come off with a handsome profit.

The not-so-urban house also may lend itself to some sort of income-producing property. You may pick up an old farmhouse with a barn or other outbuilding. Fix up that second building for rental, even a summer rental, and you have a modest income plus the tax advantages that go along with this sort of arrangement.

It is amazing how quickly property increases in value once something is done to it. Usually it's an addition, but sometimes a subtraction does the trick. Some years ago we bought a large old summer house near the water in Connecticut. The house had a name, "The Sandpiper," and at one time it had been used as a combination gift shop and summer rooming house. It had a beat-up two-story houseboat in the back yard. The yard wasn't very large and the houseboat—54 feet long, with an 18-foot beam—was almost as big as the yard.

The boat had been there for thirty-odd years and was in dreadful condition, but not so dreadful that it was willing to fall apart. It had given "The Sandpiper" a somewhat ludicrous image. When we went into town to do some shopping and gave our address, the clerks would smile and say "Oh, 'The Sandpiper'—that's the one with the houseboat instead of a back yard." This sort of thing got to us after a while, but it's not easy to get rid of a houseboat in your back yard. I spent a few weekends working at it with a wrecking bar and ax but didn't make much of a dent. We tried to get a house-wrecker, but none was interested in such a small job. Finally my wife charmed some of the boys at the local garage into coming over nights and ripping the boat apart with the help of the garage's wrecker. They did a nice clean job (they almost wrecked the wrecker, which belonged to their boss), and the removal of the houseboat not only decreased our taxes (a substructure had been removed) but immediately added about $1,000 in appearance value to the property. We paid the boys $500 for the job.

Some people simply take everything at face value. If the property has a houseboat in the backyard, that's it. If they don't want a houseboat in their backyard, they aren't interested in the property. It does not occur to them that they could remove the houseboat. The same holds true right down the line. People will pass up a perfectly good house because the outside paint is in bad condition, the house has a strange front porch, the roof leaks, or the grounds are covered with weeds and brush. Paint the house, remove the front porch, fix the roof, and cut down the brush, and you've made the house come alive. It often does not take a lot of imagination to see what can be done with an OB Dream House. Just a little imagination, plus tidying up, will do the trick.

The OB house has a great attraction for artists. I don't know whether that's because this group is less inclined to conform to stereotype and wants something less conventional than the standard dwelling. Or because artists know how to use their imagination on real estate as well as on their art. Or because artists need the space that only the OB Dream House can provide. Maybe all these factors hold true. Certainly, for a sculptor working with large pieces of stone, or with metal, or for an artist working on a large canvas, a standard two-story house isn't going to make the ideal home and workshop. These people need a barn or a warehouse.

We were brought up in and around Westport, Connecticut, which is now pretty suburban, but in the early twenties it was an artists' and writers' colony.

Poets, writers, sculptors, painters, and illustrators moved to Connecticut from Greenwich Village in New York City because living in the Village was becoming too expensive. They made their new homes and studios out of barns, factories, mills, and just about anything else they could get their hands on that was inexpensive. Many of these places are now almost collector's items and are probably worth more than the artist who first made it into a house earned in his entire life.

The well-known American painter Arthur Dove, for years lived on a yawl that was bogged down in a bay off Long Island Sound. The yawl didn't sail because the hull was not sound, so the vessel just sat in the mud, but it was the right sort of place for Mr. Dove. Perhaps what attracts the artist to the OB House is that it isn't a house in the conventional sense—it doesn't always look like a house, doesn't always act like a house, and therefore does not confine like a house. Well nigh perfection after you've thrown in a few creature comforts.

Of course, you don't have to be an artist to like an OB House, but an OB House is for the adventurous who dare to dream. No doubt about that. The whole operation is a grand adventure from the time you start to hunt one down to the time you buy it, decide what must and should be done to it, raise the money to do the work, and get the work done. As the young are usually more adventurous and more likely than their elders to believe in the attainment of dreams, you'll find many of the younger set hunting for OB Houses. But there are a good many people with gray hair who have lived for years in conventional houses who will suddenly kick over the traces and go on the prowl for the OB Dream House that they probably would have preferred in the first place.

The OB Dream House is not necessarily for those with a limited amount of money, but dollar for dollar, you can get more for your money buying something that doesn't appeal to everyone than you can for something that appeals to many. The whole game of supply and demand is in operation here. Obviously, a "nice" conventional house in good condition in a "nice" neighborhood is going to appeal to many. An old run-down farmhouse on a back road is going to appeal to relatively few.

The run-down farmhouse may sit there for years with a not-too anxious owner holding fast to a high price, but one day he may need some money and if a firm and reasonable offer is made, you've got a house. We don't like to generalize, but as a rule you'll get more house (it may not be in great condition) and more land (and this is something worth having) in the OB Dream House than in something along more conventional lines.

If you are working on a thin budget, you may pick up a barn, outbuilding, or house without any modern conveniences. This means no inside plumbing, heat, or electricity—nothing. But you can get it pretty cheaply, you've got a structure that you can probably camp in, you've got land, so you're in business. Now it's just a matter of time and work until the project is done, and if you have a lot more time than money, we'll show you how to master even the most formidable construction problems without too much outside assistance.

Assuming that you purchased this book because you are an OB House nut, we hope that we've not taken too much time trying to convince you of something that you already knew—that you want an OB House. The publisher of this book asked me to write it because I happen to be an OB House nut myself. I was practically born in one and it wasn't until I was about ten years old that I can recall ever seeing a new, conventional house. I love OB Houses. I've fixed up quite a few myself and have known and talked to at least a couple of hundred people, and maybe more, who feel the same way and have done the same thing.

The consensus among those who have fixed up an OB House is that at the beginning all is just wonderful. Then as more and more problems arise and the work seems to just drag along, there comes a period of discouragement and that "how did we ever get into this mess?" feeling. Finally one day things begin to fall into place and you start feeling that you are making progress and the progress you are making is good, and that means you are over the hump and probably won't have any more fits of deep depression.

Fixing up anything old takes work. But it can be rewarding, both spiritually and financially. It can give you a nice, warm, inner glow to know that you have saved something from perhaps complete ruin or have transformed a nondescript nothing into an attractive dwelling—the house you've always dreamed of.

Stalking the OB Dream House 2

The first move in finding an OB Dream House is to know what you are after. This is not always as easy as it seems. Sometimes, of course, certain situations can make the decision less difficult. If you are the family with seven or eight or more children, then it is quite clear to you that what you want, in fact, what you must have, is a big house with a good many rooms. You will be tempted perhaps, but you won't fall for a cozy old barn way off in left field, a chicken coop with lots of potential oomph, or a houseboat tucked away in a quiet little bay. You not only need a big house but you need one in a moderately good neighborhood where there are schools, convenient shopping facilities, and all the other things required by large families with small children. What's more, if for business or other reasons you have to move into it in a hurry, you want a house that, while perhaps unusual, is not going to require extensive work to make it livable. A few experiences in life should be avoided assiduously, and one of these is living in a house with a number of children while that house is being systematically ripped apart and put together over the course of many months.

Urbanites, too, don't have a difficult decision to make. If the city is what you want or what you have to take because of your profession, or if you would rather go to jail than commute, you've got no problem. All you have to do is to start looking in the city for property you like and can afford. And your search doesn't have to cover a wide area. If you have to live in Chicago, then Chicago is where you look.

But now how about the rest of you? What do you want?

First, let's decide just what you are going to use the place for, because until you make this decision you can't really do any intelligent looking. Do you want something just for weekends and summer vacations? Are you looking for a house to live in all year round? Are you planning to start out with something that is just for weekends and vacations but that you can eventually turn into your principal residence?

Do you want a house that is off the beaten path, where you can enjoy a high degree of privacy, or do you want something close to a busy community, where you can look forward to an active social life? Do you want a lot of land or as little as possible? Do you love the woods or do they give you the creeps? What about rolling meadows, old orchards, the lakes, or the shore? Or don't you really care about any of these as long as the place strikes your fancy?

Do you want an old house to fix up, a barn to transform, or will any structure do as long as it is interesting? We might at this point suggest that it is best never to get your heart completely set on any particular type of structure, for if you do that is exactly what you will never find—until you've bought something else. On many occasions we have gone out to find an old barn and an old barn is the one thing that we were never able to find. We have even tried to pretend that we were not looking for an old barn, that we were looking for anything in the world except an old barn. But it didn't work. So keep in mind that the minute your heart is set on a certain kind of OB Dream House, that kind just disappears from the market and won't return until you have purchased something else.

The best advice we can give you is to know pretty much what you want in a general way but to stay very loose. Keep your mind open so that you can switch from an old gatehouse to a barn, from a barn to a charming old house in the middle of the village, from the charming old house to a chicken coop, and from a chicken coop back to a barn.

If you are working through a broker, impress him with the fact that you are interested in almost anything that is a bit unusual. If you don't, but say instead that you want an old farmhouse, old farmhouses are what you are going to see—if any are available. If none are available you may not see anything at all.

The amount of time you can allow plays a major role in helping to decide what you want. How soon must the place be livable? Obviously, it takes more time to make certain structures livable than others. An old house can be suitable for occupancy the day you take title. Even if it lacks modern equipment it can make a comfortable, if rustic, spot where you can camp for the summer or weekends. An old barn, a chicken coop, or warehouse is not going to even make a camp for most people until certain work is done. If you need a livable place immediately, then your horizons are considerably less broad than if you are in no particular rush.

Since we are on the subject of time, we should bring up something else in that respect. The greatest single handicap to a successful renovation of the OB Dream House is a shortage of time. It can be an even worse handicap than a shortage of money. You should *never* rush into a remodeling job. Don't allow yourself to rush and don't allow others to rush you. You need to give yourself time to get the feel of the place, to become aware of all the options available to you. You then need to take the time to go over these options carefully, one by one, and select the plan that best suits your purpose and your purse.

The ideal would be to live in a place for at least six months before you did anything to it other than the most obvious repairs—patching a leaky roof, nailing loose boards, and replacing broken window glass. If you don't have a lot of time to fool with the place, time to experiment with ideas about what you might do to it, and then the time to have the work done properly, stay away from anything that is going to take extensive planning and work. Look for a house that might require interior and exterior decorating but not much else. Leave the house that requires major structural changes to your more leisurely neighbor.

Because you are looking for an OB House, many of the rules that go for a new house don't apply. When you buy a new house, you are really buying space. You get plumbing, wiring, heating, a kitchen, and all the rest, but what you are paying for is square footage. You can almost compute the cost of a new house—minus land—by the number of square feet it contains. The larger the house, the more it will cost. A builder will often offer two similar houses built in the same manner with the same materials but one larger than the other. The smaller one will cost proportionately less than the larger. This rule doesn't apply to an OB House. You may easily find a huge house costing far less than a tiny one. You cannot determine the value of an OB House by the number of square feet it contains.

A similar distinction applies to the land accompanying an OB Dream House and the land accompanying a conventional one. Newer houses are built on plots that, while undoubtedly costly, are usually not very large. A quarter of an acre, half an acre, or a full acre are probably the most common sizes in most areas. But in most parts of the country, even in that big state of California, you can find many lots that will just about take a house, a carport, and some flowering shrubs. With an OB Dream House you can expect almost anything in the way of land. You may be buying practically all house, as we did with "The Sandpiper," or it may be 25 acres. Some years ago an old friend of ours moved from Connecticut to Cleveland. Instead of buying one of the more conventional houses in a popular suburb, he headed for a small town, about forty-five minutes driving time from downtown Cleveland. He picked up an OB farmhouse with 15 acres of woods and meadows for $22,500. He had a pond full of bass, meadows full of pheasant, room for a pet Nubian goat to gambol, and space for his daughters to keep and ride horses. Our friend considered the half-hour's extra drive into the city well worth the difference, in contrast to the $35,000 he would have had to pay for a house close to work but with only a small amount of land. So, if you enjoy having a great deal of land around you, if you like the idea of ponds, meadows, and woods all your own, then the only place you can get them, unless you are very, very rich, is with an OB Dream House.

We have known people who have gone out and bought an OB House even when what they really wanted was a new house. That's because it is often possible to get a large piece of land with an OB House on it for *less* than you would pay for the land alone. These people then divide the land, sell off the portion with the house on it, and keep the remainder or part of it for their new house. A run-down house or building often reduces the value of property in spite of the fact that the property is probably worth more with something on it than with nothing on it.

You can't determine the value of the OB House by its size and you can't determine it by the amount of land involved. Only the seller determines its value. If the owner is anxious to sell, he'll eventually put a price on it that will sell the house. If he would only like to sell provided he can make a real killing, then he'll put a killing price on it and just sit back and wait.

Where the OB Dream House is concerned, there are no general price ranges. Barns don't fall into any general price category, nor do chicken coops, nor strange and wonderful houses. It's just a matter of how badly the seller wants to get rid of the place.

You have to take a rather tolerant view of your fellow man when you go out hunting for the OB Dream House, or at least you should be prepared for what you may find and what you don't find. What you are probably not going to find is what you hope to end up with—a lovely, charming place with all the modern conveniences. A typical OB Dream House often has a minimum of modern conveniences, and where they exist they may not work too well. Don't be shocked to find that even in this day and age there are people who get along without inside plumbing or electricity. You will also, even in cold climates, find houses without central heat, or if there is central heat the fireplaces have been closed up to keep out drafts or because "fireplaces dirty the place up."

An OB House can sometimes have much of the character of a barn or outbuilding and not a very clean one at that. It's a great big beautiful world, but not everybody has the same ideas of good housekeeping. Sometimes a house is not just dirty, it's plain filthy—kitchen, bedrooms, bathroom (if any), the whole works, including the yard, which has obviously been used for the past fifty years as a garbage dump. Filth and rubbish, however, while not the most pleasant things to deal with, are about the least expensive, and once they have been removed you'll experience a feeling of genuine accomplishment. So don't be thrown by all the mess you may find in and around the house.

THE TIME TO LOOK

It is obvious that the time to look for an OB Dream House is when you decide you want one, but we have always favored the late fall. In most sections of the country, property looks its worst after the leaves have fallen and before the snow sets in. It is uphill work for the seller or broker to paint a rosy picture of a house on a dreary, drizzly November afternoon. There you stand in the unheated living room, looking out on grounds strewn with leaves and bare stalks, with maybe a scraggly evergreen or so providing the only relief from the overall gray. You start watching the little trickle of water from a leaky roof run down on the inside wall and you get a feeling that any reasonable offer will be accepted. You can be pretty sure that you are really seeing the place at its worst. No distracting your attention with colorful flowers, green grass, and warm and sparkling sunshine. No, sir, you are seeing the bare bones of the matter, and it takes all your imagination to add the trimmings. That is, if you don't lose heart yourself and wonder if you really do want to buy a house. One other point in favor of this time of year: you probably won't have much competition.

Fall is also the time when many elderly people, who often own OB Houses, decide that they've had it and want to move to some nice, warm climate or into a garden apartment where they won't have to worry about trying to keep the place from falling apart, shoveling snow, icy roads, or just trying to keep warm. Fall is when many of them say "Oh, the heck with it, Agatha. Let's get rid of this old place and move into a nice cozy condominium in Florida." Or southern California.

Winter is a good time for hunting the OB House, but not as good as fall, for a blanket of snow can cover many sins, including a roof that needs drastic action, grassless lawns, and loosened shingles. Almost anything, even a junk yard, looks good if one piles enough snow over it.

Of course, if you are looking in areas where there is no snow, then fall or winter are about the same.

Spring is a lovely time of the year to go house hunting, if you don't mind plenty of company. Of course, everybody and his brother are also hunting because it's so nice to be out and almost everybody decides at this time of the year that it would be nice to have a little place of their own. A good many of them are not really serious but they do get underfoot and if several prospective buyers are snooping about a piece of property and showing even a moderate interest, the seller is probably not too interested in an offer below his asking price. Spring, like snow, makes things look much better than they are. All those green shoots can hide a multitude of flaws, and a field of daffodils might just distract you enough so that you don't even seen the junk yard directly in back of the property. Spring is, of course, an ideal time to take title because it gives you all summer and fall to work on your new acquisition.

If you are house hunting in an area with a large summer population, be cautious about looking for your OB Dream House in the springtime because prices are likely to be high. Then too, anyone planning to put property on the market is apt to hold off until the end of the season so that they can get one more well-paid summer rental out of it. Fall is the best time to look for summer property because that's when the owner, faced with the prospect of having to pay taxes and upkeep during the winter months, may decide to get rid of it.

In urban areas, one time is as good as another to hunt. Town houses go on the market when someone decides to sell. And, a house in an urban area is going to look essentially the same in spring as in winter.

WHERE TO LOOK

OB Dream Houses are everywhere, but "everywhere" is a rather vague concept and there are certain factors you will want to consider when you decide where to start your hunt. Again, for those of you who want a town house, the obvious place for you to look is in the town where you live. For those who want a place for weekends and summer vacations only, you must first decide on how much time you are willing to devote to getting there and getting back.

Some people don't mind a three- or four-hour drive each way on a weekend to get to their little hideaway. Others find that two hours of driving each way is about all they can take. If your heart is set on finding something by the shore, on a lake or pond, or in the mountains, you are probably going to have to travel farther to find something at a reasonable cost than if you are willing to settle for something just "out in the country." But there are exceptions. In many metropolitan areas you can find small communities that, for one reason or another, never caught on or became fashionable, or if once fashionable became passé. You can often find attractive property in these locations. There are also bargains to be found in even the very fashionable summer resort areas. We have some friends who picked up an OB Dream House in East Hampton, Long Island, and East Hampton is a most desirable community. Our friends paid $55,000 for a big old place with a carriage house and several acres. They sold the carriage house and one acre of land for $35,000 almost the minute after they took title to the property, leaving them a big house with lovely grounds, including a private beach, acquired for only $20,000. This is quite a feat almost anywhere, especially in East Hampton, Long Island.

Before you start hunting for a weekend place it's a good idea to decide the maximum amount of time you'll want to spend traveling back and forth. Then draw a circle on a map of the area to include all the communities that fall into this time-travel zone. If you plan to drive out each weekend, a standard road map will give you the mileage and you can work out a rough idea of the time involved. If you wish to travel by public transportation, make a careful check of train and bus schedules covering the communities within your circle. Keep in mind that today distance is not as important as time. On good, uncrowded highways you can do a hundred miles as easily and in less time than you can cover fifty miles on crowded or less-direct roads. Good bus or train schedules may allow you to reach a distant area more quickly than one relatively close to urban centers. Many people travel back and forth to their weekend places by plane. This is expensive and

weather is sometimes a factor, but if you have the money and are willing to put up with some of the inconvenience of air travel to remote
areas, it certainly increases your options as to where you can look for
a vacation house.

For year-round living, you must obviously take into consideration
where you have to go to work. If you aren't chained to an office and are
fortunate enough to be able to work at home, then it's just a question
of where you would most like to live. Most people, though, have to
work outside their homes and this means travel. Figure out how much
time you are willing or able to spend in daily travel. Decide if you'd
rather drive back and forth each day or prefer public transportation.
Decide how much you can afford to spend on public transportation,
not only in time but in money. Commuting can be expensive if you live
far from your office. Draw the circle on the map as was suggested for
summer houses and work within this area. Check highways and bus and
train timetables to get an idea of the facilities and the time involved.

Once you have determined the areas in which you wish to look, make
a list of them in order of preference. If you would like to know more
about these communities before you pay them a visit, you might wish
to order some geological survey maps that will show in detail items
such as the ponds, lakes, brooks, hills, and mountains. You can order
these by writing to Topographical Division, U.S. Geographical Survey,
1009 North Highland Street, Arlington, Virginia 2210. The maps are
priced at 50 cents and up.

HOW TO LOOK

Probably the best, as well as the easiest way to find an OB Dream
House is through a real estate broker. If you have had no experience
with real estate brokers, you should know certain facts about them.
First, to be a broker in real estate an individual must have a license
issued by the state in which he works. To obtain the license he must
meet certain requirements and pass an examination. Some of the salesmen who take you out to look for your OB Dream House may not be
licensed brokers but they will be working for a licensed broker and he

must take responsibility for their actions. If a licensed broker does something that is not correct, the state can take away his license. If a licensed broker joins the National Association of Real Estate Boards he can call himself a "realtor."

When someone has property he wishes to sell, he puts it in the hands of a broker unless he wishes to handle the selling himself. He may give the property listing to just one broker and this is called an "exclusive listing." If you want to buy that property, you will have to go through the broker who has the exclusive. Many brokers prefer or insist on an exclusive because they don't have to split or share the commission on it with other brokers. They feel that they can then afford to advertise the property more widely and push harder than if they were only going to get part of the commission. When property goes into so-called "multiple" listing, all the brokers who belong to the multiple-listing service are notified that the property is for sale and each of them can show it. When the property is sold the commission is split between the broker with whom the listing was originally placed and the broker who actually made the sale. The listing service also gets a small percentage of the fee. This can be a good arrangement for the buyer because it usually means that each broker will have many more offerings to show than if he had only exclusive listings.

Most brokers today have card listings on each piece of property. These show a photograph of the house and give details as to acreage, cost, assessed valuation, general condition, number of rooms, type of heating, and the like.

A licensed broker knows a great deal about the business of buying and selling houses. He is also well informed about mortgages, land and housing costs in his area, what the fair market price for a piece of property ought to be, and how to write up a sales contract. But he does not necessarily know much about house construction or what it costs to renovate a place. Because he represents the seller and not the buyer he may say, for example, "It would be easy to add a second bathroom right here in this old closet." Well, it might be easy to add and then again it might be darned near impossible. Once we were somewhat interested in an old farmhouse but it had a number of things wrong with it. In the space of half an hour the broker had transformed the place into a palace. "Rip out this wall, add the fireplace here, move the kitchen over to there, raise the ceiling in the living room, move the porch around to get a better view, and give the place a fresh coat of paint. We figured roughly that all this was going to cost in the vicinity of $15,000 so we dropped the house. Brokers, especially lady brokers, frequently use the expression "great possibilities." This means that fixing up the property is going to cost you a lot of money.

Always remember that the broker represents the seller, and while he will want to protect your interests so that you don't get stuck with a complete lemon, his first loyalty is to the seller. Also remember that he isn't going to stress the shortcomings and that he can't tell you about the major flaws unless he has been told about them by the seller or has seen them with his own eyes and is able to evaluate just how serious they may be.

It is not hard to find real estate brokers. Most of them are not overly modest and so you'll find their advertisements in local papers, on billboards, and in the yellow pages of the telephone book. You should make up a list of several brokers in the area where you are looking and make an appointment with each or perhaps just drop in for a chat. You need a very special type of broker to help you with an OB Dream House. Once when we were out hunting an OB Dream House we dropped into the office of a broker and the next thing we knew he was putting down our vital statistics so he could run them through a computer that would tell him and us what kind of house we wanted. He didn't seem to understand that getting the right OB House is not dependent on the university you attended, the quality of the clubs you belong to, your religion, or your social life. We left the office before we found out what the computer said about us. It probably said "GIGO" (see the chapter on "Painting and Finishing" if you don't know what this means).

What you need is a broker who understands at once what you are after—an OB Dream House. Some brokers have an extremely warm spot in their heart for OB Dream Houses. They watch for them to come on the market and often they will lend a hand to get them on the market.

We know one lady who is a tremendous OB Dream House broker. She knows every OB structure within miles and miles. She knows the owners because she has visited them. And even if they don't wish to sell at the moment, when and if they do, she will be the first to know about it. This is the sort of broker you want—someone who knows not only what is available right now but what might be coming up in the months ahead.

If you can't find out how much a broker knows about OB Houses from the files of property for sale in his office and by talking to him, go out with him and see what he shows you. If all he turns up are conventional houses and he doesn't seem to understand that you'd like to see an old warehouse, barn, or wreck of a farmhouse, forget him and try another broker. Keep trying until you find a broker who gets the message.

You don't, by the way, have to lock yourself up with one broker. Use as many as you wish but tell them that this is what you are doing. If they feel that you are seriously interested in buying and that there is a little competition in the field, they might work a lot harder to find something that you will like. Some brokers will really beat the bushes to make a sale and even go so far as trying to talk the owner of property in which you might have expressed interest into putting it up for sale.

Not every piece of property, especially OB property, goes through the hands of a broker. Many owners prefer to sell the property themselves so that they can save the commission payable to a broker if he makes the sale. This is especially true if the owner isn't in any great rush to sell. Property of this nature is offered in the local papers and even by a "For Sale" sign on the front lawn. Buy the local papers for the real estate listings. If you are on a long-term house hunt, subscribe to these papers so you can keep a close watch on what's happening. If you are familiar with the area and know that East State Street is pretty tacky but that Burro Hill area is a delight, it will help you a great deal in determining which of these listings may be of interest.

If you are working through a broker or have made a few trips with a broker you will soon get a pretty good idea of property values in the area. Real estate ads in the local paper will do the same—give you an idea of price. Many metropolitan papers have real estate listings that cover areas some distance away from the urban center, but it has been our experience that most of these are for the fairly conventional and high-priced house. Someone who wants to sell a chicken coop is probably not going to place an ad in the *New York Times,* the *Chicago Tribune,* or the *Los Angeles Times.*

If you have friends in the area where you are looking, put them to work. If they are close friends they may be anxious to get you up into their area and will make a real effort to try and find something that is of interest to you.

You might also stir up a little action yourself by running an ad in the local paper—"Wanted to Buy: Old run-down house," or something on that order.

The time element is important in finding the OB Dream House. If you can afford to play a waiting game you've got a far better chance of getting something close to your heart's desire than if you have to move in a hurry. Property comes on the real estate market almost daily and you can never tell just when the place that will be ideal for you is going to make its debut. You don't, of course, want to wait away your life in the hope that just the perfect place will turn up, but you stand a better chance of getting something good if you can bide your time a bit. Assuming, of course, that you have made the necessary contacts with brokers and friends so that when something of interest does appear, you'll be among the first to hear about it.

Keep communications open with friends and especially with your broker or brokers. If you just go off and they don't hear from you, they assume that you have found something else and neglected to inform them or that you have decided you didn't want an OB House after all. Keep calling them every week or two so that they will know you are very definitely in the market.

You should establish contact with brokers and friends and read the newspapers in all regions that you decide are worth exploring. Get as many irons in the fire as you can and keep them hot until you find something you want. Don't become so enchanted with one community that you could never think of living in any other place. Who knows, the community on the other side of the ridge might be just as pleasant. It might, in fact, be the place where your OB Dream House is waiting for you.

► *Check List: Short Form for House Stalking*

1. Location
2. Name of owner
3. Name of broker
4. Asking price
5. Assessed valuation
6. Taxes per year
7. Amount of existing mortgage
8. Size of lot
9. Description of lot
10. Type of structure
    A. Dwelling
    B. Non-dwelling
    C. Number of rooms
11. Construction
    A. Wood frame
    B. Masonry
    C. Other

12. Condition of structure
    A. Good
    B. Fair
    C. Poor
    D. Needs extensive repairs
    E. Needs extensive alterations and/or additions
    F. Needs conversion into dwelling
13. Source of water supply
14. Type of heating
15. Type of sewage system
16. Electricity
17. Fireplaces
18. Garage
19. Other out buildings
20. General comments.

Real Estate Terms and Their Meaning

3

Setting out to look for an OB Dream House (or any kind of house for that matter) requires more on your part than just spotting what you want and trying to determine what sort of shape it is in. You should know not only something about construction but also something about certain terms used in real estate transactions—and what they really mean.

Acre. A unit of land measurement. An acre is a chunk of land that is 43,560 square feet or 4,840 square yards in area. Many lots in housing developments are measured in a fraction of an acre—½ acre, ¼ acre, and so on, and city lots are so small that they are generally measured in feet —so many feet wide and so many feet deep.

If you go house shopping in rural areas where land is relatively inexpensive, you will hear the expression, "an acre more or less." This, believe it or not, means exactly what it says. It means that no one knows exactly how much land is involved but it looks as if it might be around an acre.

My family once traded a mean old horse for "an acre more or less" and a few years later sold the land for $100. The new owner had a

23

survey made and the property turned out to consist of almost five acres. This was some years ago and chances are that today the acreage in such estimates will be less rather than more. If you want to know how much land there actually is when no survey exists, you can measure it off yourself. All you need is a 100-foot steel tape. Get the width and the length of the lot in feet, multiply them together and see how the sum compares with 43,560 square feet. The most accurate way of determining the exact size of a lot is to have a survey made but this is expensive and you would certainly not want to have one made on land that you did not as yet own and perhaps never would.

Assessed Valuation. This is the value put on property by a unit of government for purposes of taxation. The amount of the assessed valuation does not necessarily reflect the true market value of the property. It may be that the market value of a house is $20,000, but it may be assessed for only $12,000. Sometimes assessed valuations will be low and the mill rate, the amount of money you have to pay on each one hundred dollars of assessed valuation, will be high. In some cases it will be just the other way around, with high assessments and a low mill rate.

When you buy a house that is going to need extensive improvements, you can expect the assessed valuation to go up when the renovation is finished. If you file for a building permit, the tax assessor will hear about the improvements involved and eventually he will pay you a visit to determine how much to increase the assessments. Even if you don't file for a building permit, the tax assessor will eventually hear about the work you have done and will drop over to see what it is all about. On run-down property you should look for a very low assessment because you can be pretty certain that when you have finished with the improvements, the assessed valuation will go up considerably. Before your plans for improvements are too well developed, you might check with your local tax assessor to see if there are any ways to keep the assessed valuation down. We know of at least one section of the country where many people use gravel rather than concrete for basement floors because it gives them a small break in assessed valuation.

If you are interested in a piece of property where the assessed valuation seems unnecessarily high, you might be able to get a reduction from the tax assessor. A friend of ours with a large family was very interested in a big, run-down house in an old, well-established neighborhood. The house was in poor condition but was assessed for a whopping amount. The buyer went to the tax assessor, said he wanted to buy and fix up the place but he couldn't take the high real estate tax. The tax people were extremely agreeable and cut the assessed valuation way down for him. It seems that they had been raising the assessed valuation in the hope that the previous owner, who had allowed the place to run down, would sell and get out. So you can never tell what might be possible on this score.

Building Codes.   Local ordinances that regulate the construction of buildings. In most areas they also regulate renovation and remodeling work to one degree or another. They are discussed in detail in this chapter under "Zoning Ordinances and Building Codes."

Deed.   The document used to transfer real estate. There are two basic types of deeds, the *warranty deed* and the *quit claim deed*. If you buy property, you want the seller to deliver a warranty deed, which means that you are protected against any claimant. A quit claim deed means just that. The grantor, or seller, has relinquished any possible interest in the property that might cloud the title. You will find more on the subject of deeds in the chapter entitled "Buying the House."

Easement.   The granting of certain property rights to others than the owner. For example, an easement can give someone other than the owner the right to pass through the property, put in a road, and maintain it. A utility company might have an easement to install power lines across a piece of property and to send men over the property to maintain the lines and equipment. As an easement becomes part of the deed, it is transferred to the new owner each time the land is sold. If someone has an easement on the property you wish to buy, you will have to accept it. If the easement is held by a private individual who no longer needs it—perhaps it was for a road and he has made other arrangements to reach his property—he may agree to have it removed from the deed. But if he won't, then you are stuck with it.

If there are easements on a piece of property, they will turn up during the title search made by your attorney.

Easements, of course, can also work in your favor. You might be interested in a piece of property accessible only via a road running through the property but owned by someone else. If you have an easement in the deed, then you have the right to use and maintain the road, and when and if you sell the property, the new owner will have these same rights. If you buy a large piece of land and sell off the back portion, you would give the buyer an easement to put the road through your property if this were the only way he could reach his land.

Unless an easement covers the situation, never buy a piece of property where the only practical way to reach it requires passing through property owned by someone else. If there is no easement at the present time, the agreement of sale should be written in such a way that the deal is contingent on your being able to get an easement before the time of closing. Don't fall for that old line, "Oh, Mr. Brown owns that land and he doesn't care if you use the road across it to get to your place." One day Mr. Brown might just change his mind and tell you to stay off his property or he might sell the land to Mr. Jones who doesn't care a hill of beans about any of Mr. Brown's oral agreements. If there is no easement, no dice on the property.

Eminent Domain.   This is the little hooker that means the right of the people or government to take over all or part of your property for public use upon payment of compensation. A water company, for example, might exercise its right of eminent domain to take over private property for use as a reservoir. A utility company might exercise its right of eminent domain to put a power line across the property. The worst troublemakers today in this respect are the highway people. When a decision is reached to build a major highway, the matter of eminent domain grows to major proportions for it involves not only land but houses, forests of redwoods, or anything else that happens to be in the way of the projected route.

Condemnation is the method of taking private property under the right of eminent domain. Compensation is involved but it is seldom adequate.

It is very difficult to find out which property might, in the future, be condemned under eminent domain. One of the best information sources to check, however, is the editor of the local newspaper. These individuals usually have a pretty good idea of what is afoot at the town hall, the county seat, the state capital, and even in Washington, that might affect their general area.

Encumbrances. Claims or liens that may exist against the property, such as unpaid real estate taxes, easements, or judgments. They will show up during the title search, and before taking title to the property you should discuss each one with your attorney to determine which ones will be removed. Unpaid taxes and judgments must be removed before you take title. An easement cannot be removed except as previously discussed in this chapter.

Fixture. An article of personal property which, because it is fixed to the property, becomes a part of the property. You can best determine whether an item in the house is a fixture by analyzing whether it can be removed without causing damage to the house. A free-standing kitchen range could be considered not a fixture because it can easily be disconnected and removed without extensive damage. A built-in range, on the other hand, could only be removed by doing some harm. A refrigerator can be removed easily, but an air-conditioning unit set into the wall below a window cannot be removed without leaving a large hole in the wall. It would therefore be considered a fixture. A window-unit air conditioner would not be a fixture, however. If you want to play it perfectly safe, you will have included in the agreement of sale an itemized list of all the items that could possibly be considered personal property.

Lien. A type of encumbrance. It is a claim against the property and is recorded by the town clerk; it remains a claim until it is cleared—by paying the amount of money involved. The most familiar lien is the *mechanic's lien.* This is designed to protect those who have performed work or provided materials for the improvement of the property. If a contractor does work on your house and you don't pay him, he might slap a lien on your property. If you did not pay the contractor by the time you sold the property, the lien would be paid off out of the money you received for the property. The money would not come to you first so that you could pay it to the contractor but would go directly to him. If you decided that you preferred to go bankrupt rather than pay the contractor (and you might get so angry at a contractor that you would), he has the legal right to force you to sell the property so that he can get his money. If you fail to keep up your mortgage payments and the lender has to foreclose, the holder of the lien gets his money before the lender gets his. For this reason, lenders hate to see a lien on any property on which they hold the mortgage.

Liens can be very tricky and they differ from state to state. In some areas even if you pay a contractor in full you can be liable for a lien if he does not pay off one or more of his subcontractors or does not pay for the materials used on your job.

Mill. One-tenth of one cent. It is the standard measurement for real estate taxes. You can find out the amount you will have to pay in taxes by getting the assessed valuation of the property and multiplying this by the mill rate that is current in your area. If your property is assessed at $8,000 and the mill rate is 30 mills on each one hundred dollars of assessed valuation, your property tax will be $240. The seller, the broker, or the town clerk can tell you for how much the property is assessed and the mill rate.

Restrictions. Regulations written into a deed that restrict the use of the property in one way or another. These should not be confused with zoning or building codes, which are a type of restriction set up by a unit of local government. Restrictions are private regulations put into the deed by the previous owners or by the developer. Until the courts knocked them out, many restrictions were designed to prevent the sale of property to certain ethnic or religious groups. Many restrictions that exist today are designed to maintain a certain character in a neighborhood. They may prevent building fences along the front lawn or they may state that you have to keep your lawn cut and that if you don't the developer or home-owners' association may have it done and can charge you for the work involved.

Right of Way. An easement that gives someone other than the owner the right to pass through the property. Sometimes a right of way is given in the form of an oral agreement but this oral agreement isn't worth anything. A right of way should always be in the form of an easement.

Zoning Ordinances and Building Codes. Local regulations that govern the use of property and the construction of buildings. It is very important that you become fully acquainted with the regulations in your area before you sign an agreement of sale on a piece of property, for these regulations can affect what you can and cannot do with the property. Let's start out with zoning.

Zoning. These local regulations establish the manner in which property can be used and for what purpose. Just about every community has some form of zoning. The regulations are drawn up and enforced by a zoning board or zoning commission. The idea behind zoning is to protect property values and to promote an orderly growth of the community.

In a typical small community you might find that some areas are zoned exclusively for single-family houses, which means that unless and until the regulations are modified, no structure other than a single-family residence can be built and no existing structure can be used except as a single-family residence. Other areas in the community may be zoned to allow multi-family as well as single-family dwellings. Another area may be zoned for commercial buildings. Generally speaking, the downtown area will be zoned for commercial as well as multi-family and single-family houses. As you move out from the downtown area there will be zones for multi-family and single-family housing and finally those areas that are for use exclusively as single-family residences.

The zones in any community may be scattered about. Your broker, the town clerk, or the zoning board can give you a map of the area showing the locations of the various zones, as well as a detailed description of the sort of building permitted in each zone. With this information you can easily see what the regulations are in areas in which you are interested. This may be quite a factor in whether you buy or don't buy. You may find that the property you want happens to fall into an area that is zoned for commercial use. Someone could come along and put up a factory, a garage, filling station, or something else right next to your property. If you buy a house on a street that is zoned for multi-family housing you may find that one by one the existing single-family houses on the block will be converted into apartments.

You should study the relationship of the property you want to buy to the adjoining zones. For example, if you are right on the line between two zones, one day a motel may go up across the street or down the road a bit.

Zoning ordinances also determine how much land must be used in connection with a dwelling or building—the minimum amount of land, that is. In a residential zone the requirements may be that a house must have one acre or so many feet fronting on a public road. This is important information to have in advance of any agreement of sale if you have plans for the property other than keeping it as is. If you buy a large piece of land with the idea of selling off some of it, you may find that you don't have enough to meet the zoning requirements. If you have a little less than two acres and the zoning calls for a minimum of one acre, you can't sell off that land unless you can talk the zoning board into granting a variance which will allow you to do so.

Zoning ordinances may also determine how you may use the property. You may be buying a large house with the idea of turning part of it into a rental apartment. If you are in a single-family zone, forget it.

Some of these regulations can be pretty tough. A friend of ours recently built a house for himself and wanted to include a wing with a bedroom-living room, bath, and kitchenette for his parents. The zoning people would not allow him to install the kitchenette because they considered that this made the house into a two-family residence and the area was zoned exclusively for single-family houses.

If you plan to use your house for some type of commercial purpose, the zoning regulations may have something to say about this. Some areas zoned for single-family houses will allow "cottage industries" that are family affairs and where no paid outside help is involved. Some will allow professional offices for attorneys, doctors, and dentists but not a gift shop or antiques shop.

Variance. An adjustment of a local regulation permitting use of your property for some purpose that the zoning ordinance prohibits. Getting a variance involves a hearing before the zoning board, where you explain what you want to do and why it won't affect the character of the neighborhood or decrease property values. The owners of the adjoining property are usually consulted and there is just no way of knowing in advance whether you will or will not get the variance. You are taking a considerable risk in buying property with only the hope that you will get a variance to use the property as you wish. If you run into a situation of this sort, the best approach would be to find out from the zoning board when you can get a hearing and a final decision. Have the agreement of sale written so that the sale is contingent on your getting the variance and so that the closing date on the property is set far enough ahead to give you time to have the hearing and get the decision.

Zoning regulations are subject to change. Most communities are growing in population and commercial activity. Most communities are anxious to attract more and more industry because industry helps produce tax money for schools and recreational facilities, and helps hold down real estate taxes on residential property. In many semi-rural areas the fight over changes in zoning is between the local people and those who have moved there from the cities. The local people want to change the zoning regulations to allow more industries to come in so that there will be more jobs and more tax money, and the city people want to see the community left as it is. These matters come up from time to time and the only way that you as a property holder can have a say in what is going to be done in the zone where you live is to become active in local affairs and get to the zoning meetings and speak your piece.

Building Codes.   Ordinances that regulate construction. These take over where the zoning ordinances leave off. They not only regulate new construction but in most areas they will have something to say about major renovation work. They will certainly become involved if you are making changes in the exterior of the structure, such as adding a wing, deck, or porch.

Building codes in major cities are extremely strict. They not only specify the manner in which the work is to be done but also specify certain materials that are to be used and who will do the work. Some communities even insist that before work begins plans drawn up or approved by a registered architect must be approved by the building inspector. An inspector will come around from time to time to see how the work is being done and if he doesn't approve it, it will have to be corrected.

When you are out in the country the codes are much less strict. Almost every community will require that you or your contractor get a building permit before any extensive work is done but that may be about as far as they go. A friend and former associate of ours who had done considerable new construction in Westchester County, New York, where building codes are rather strict, recently purchased some property in Maine. One day he stopped by the office of the local building inspector in his new town to find out what sort of building requirements he would have to meet. All the building inspector had to say about construction requirements was "Build it sturdy, son." Unfortunately, there are not many places like that left.

In some areas the building codes will state how close to property lines a building can be placed; this becomes important if you have a house close to the property line and wish to add a wing. This matter may also be included in the zoning ordinances.

Building codes are also an element to consider if you plan to put in a rental apartment. They may specify the minimum number of square feet of space required for the various rooms, the use of fire-resistant materials at certain points and other factors that could possibly affect the health and general welfare of the tenants.

You should find out about the local building codes at the same time you are checking into the zoning ordinances. These codes are usually available through the office of the town clerk, the building inspector, or the local department of housing.

If the renovation work on your house is going to be handled by an architect or general contractor, you don't have to know every last detail of the code. They will be familiar with it and will see that the work done meets local standards, but before you agree to buy the property you should make it your business to ascertain that nothing in the code will prevent your doing what you plan to do with either the structure or the property.

Caveat Emptor is a phrase that you probably learned in school and the idea behind it can make you or break you when you buy property. It means "Let the buyer beware"; that is—it is up to you to make sure that you get what you are led to believe you are getting. In other words, if you come out on the short end of the deal, it's your fault and your loss.

Caveat emptor is the single most important phrase in any transaction where there is an exchange of goods or property, but it is not put into any sales contract.

It is very easy to be led to believe that something is the case which is not so. Sometimes it is the seller, the broker, the lender, or even your own attorney who may uncalculatingly or not lead you to believe something that is not correct. Often you, yourself, by wishful thinking or carelessness, assume that something is just fine when it is not and never will be. Don't assume anything.

In the purchase of real estate, there are many areas where you can be "led to believe." Here is just a sample:

1. The house is basically sound and needs only a few minor repairs.
2. The roof is sound and free from leaks.
3. You can put the place in tip-top condition for under $5,000.
4. Certain non-fixtures such as the kitchen range, the refrigerator, and the pile of old boards out by the barn are included in the deal.
5. You will be able to get a right of way from the owner of the adjoining property.
6. You won't have any trouble getting a variance from the zoning board so you can fix up and rent the garage as an apartment.
7. The town plans to take over the road, fix it up, and maintain it.
8. You will have no trouble getting a good mortgage on this particular piece of property.
9. When you are ready to take title, the lender will provide you with the required amount of money at the interest rates that were prevailing at the time you made your loan application.
10. The way property values are going in this area you could sell this place a year from now and make a profit of over $4,000.

This list could go on forever. Many of the things that you are led to believe may actually come true, but if you want to play safe you will ask questions and get matters in writing before you sign anything or hand over any money.

The seller is under no obligation to point out to you the flaws in his property. If you ask him, however, and he tells you something that he knows is not true, he could be held responsible for misrepresentation and you would have grounds for legal action. If you ask the seller if the roof is sound and doesn't leak and he says that it is sound and if you find out this isn't the case, that is misrepresentation. If he says that he "believes" the roof is sound and you accept this, you don't have much of a case if you end up with a leaky roof. If you don't even ask him, you have no grounds for anything.

So it is up to you to ask the questions and try to get a straight answer rather than an "I believe." Sometimes when the questions get too tough the seller may try to move you off to something else. Stay with it. If you are using a broker, get the broker to get the answers from the seller.

If the seller or the broker says that he "believes" you could fix the place up for under $5,000, take it with a grain of salt. It may be true, but all they are doing is expressing an opinion. If you want to know exactly how much it will cost, call in a contractor and have him give you a firm bid.

The seller and his broker can only express their opinions about matters such as getting a variance from the zoning board, the town taking over the road near your property, projected increases in property values, and obtaining satisfactory financing. If you want the answers—the straight dope—to these questions, go to the correct source: the zoning board, the lender, and the others who can give specific answers. And whether or not you can make a profit of $4,000 if you sell the place in a year depends on just one thing—finding someone who will pay what you ask for it.

There are many questions to ask and much checking to be done before you get satisfactory answers from all the various sources. You don't have to do all this yourself. Your attorney can handle a good bit of the work and so can the broker. But you are the one who must ask the questions, demand a straightforward answer and insist on getting things in writing before you hand over any money or sign any agreements. Always keep this in mind. While others may be involved in this transaction, you are the only one who is spending money. You are the only one who can get hurt if what you were led to believe doesn't come out quite the way you thought it would.

What Is It
4 and
What Is It Called?

Life is going to be a lot simpler while looking for your Offbeat Dream House if you know something about how a house or structure is put together and what the various parts are called. You need this knowledge before you go shopping for property, so that when you find something of interest you will be in a position to evaluate it. And when you get into renovation work you will certainly want to know as much about house construction and building terms as possible.

First, let's cover the basic components of an average sort of house.

Footing. The lowest point of any structure. A footing is a large mass of concrete set into the ground below the frost line; its function is to support the foundation walls of the house. A footing will have a broader base than the foundations in order to eliminate any chance that the foundation might sink. This, of course, would throw the house out of alignment. A sunken foundation is one of the primary reasons for windows sticking, doors sticking, cracked plaster and uneven floors. The foundation may have sunk just a fraction of an inch—but that is enough to throw things out of kilter. Footings are required for any structure that has considerable weight. If you wish to build a brick garden wall, there should be a footing. If you build an outdoor fireplace or barbeque, you need a footing to support the masonry.

Foundations. The walls of masonry that rest on the footings and on which the house proper sits. Foundations may be of brick, masonry block, stone, or poured concrete. If the house has a basement, the foundation walls serve as the basement walls.

Many houses and structures do not have basements. If the structure has a wood floor, there will be a space between the floor and the ground underneath, and this area is called *crawl space.* You will also find *attic crawl space,* and this occurs when there are only a few feet between the top floor of the house and the roof—enough to crawl around in but not enough to use as living space. You will often find houses and structures with concrete floors. These are called *concrete slabs;* with these there is no space between the slab and the ground, and the foundation walls are low.

Sills. The wood members that rest on top of the foundations and serve as a base for the house structure. In relatively new construction—houses less than a hundred years old—the sills are made of rather light materials—2 inches by 6 inches, 2 inches by 8 inches, and so forth. In older houses you will find sills made of heavier stock. In many farm structures you find a *mud sill,* a heavy beam often resting directly on the ground. Here, there will be little, if any, foundation and no footing. This may be a satisfactory arrangement for a barn but not for a livable structure. In very high-quality construction a sheet of metal, usually copper, is placed on top of the foundation wall directly under the wood sill. The metal extends beyond the foundation wall for about 4 inches and is bent at a 45-degree angle. This is called a *termite shield* and its purpose is to prevent termites from using the foundation wall to reach the woodwork portion of the house.

Floor Joists. The beams that support the floor. The joists for the first floor of the house will be supported at the ends by the sills. The joists for the other floors in the house will be supported by the outside walls and by some of the interior walls or partitions. Joists are usually 2 inches by 8 inches or 2 inches by 10 inches. The size of the joists will be determined by their length and by how far apart they are spaced.

Girders.   Heavy wood or steel beams that are installed where added support is required. A girder is usually installed to give added support to floor joists and will be placed at about midpoint under the joists. The ends will be supported by the foundation wall, and if the girders are of considerable length, there will be additional support in the form of posts at various intervals. These posts may be of wood or metal and will rest on a concrete footing. Girders are also used in other areas of the house, for example to carry the load when a large section of exterior wall is to be removed to accommodate a sliding glass door or large window. They also are used when an interior partition that carries a load is removed.

Bridging.   Usually an X formed by two pieces of wood or metal and installed between the floor joists at about 8-foot intervals. It helps provide added rigidity and helps distribute a concentrated load over several joists.

Subflooring.   A rough floor beneath the main floor structure. In conventional house construction there are two layers of flooring. These are the subfloor, or rough floor, which is nailed directly to the floor joists, and the finish flooring, which is nailed to this. In many older houses as well as nonresidential buildings, there will be only one layer of flooring.

Exterior Wall Framing.   Most houses built within the past hundred years utilize a type of construction known as *balloon framing* (a modification of this method is *platform frame construction*). In this method of construction the house framework is made of relatively lightweight materials. The walls are framed with 2-inch-by-4-inch stock, and the roof and joists of somewhat heavier material. The vertical pieces that frame the walls are called *studs*, or *studding*. They will be supported at the base either by the sill or by a *plate* nailed to the subfloor. They will be tied together at the top by a similar plate called the *top plate*. The corners of the framework will often be braced with wood.

This method of construction utilizes many relatively lightweight members to produce the required strength. Maximum strength and rigidity are not achieved until all the framing is in place and the outside surface of the walls has been covered with sheathing.

Balloon framing came into being when it became possible to produce steel nails at a relatively low cost. Before that time most structures were put together with *timber-frame construction.* This method of building utilizes relatively few pieces of lumber but they are very heavy and the framework provides all the strength. This kind of construction is much the same as that used today for commercial construction, where a framework of steel or reinforced concrete provides all the strength and the exterior walls of glass or masonry are there only to keep out the weather. If you pick up a very old house the chances are that it will be put together in this manner and you will also find that barns and out-buildings, some relatively new, are of this construction.

A modified form of timber frame construction is also used occasionally today. It is called *plank-and-beam framing,* but the size of the timbers used and the manner in which they are fastened together is not quite the same as you find in a timber-frame structure. Timber framing is an art that is almost extinct, and it is a shame for there are few things in the world of construction as beautiful as a fine job of this kind of framing. The heavy timbers, 6 inches by 6 inches or larger, were not fastened together with nails or bolts but were fitted together in such fashion that all that was needed for fastening was a wood peg or two. Some years ago we watched a barn being built in this manner in Lancaster County, Pennsylvania, where the Amish still have the skills and patience to do this kind of work. An entire wall would be assembled on the ground with each joint as nice and clean as you could ask, and when the wall was complete a group of neighbors came around and hoisted the wall into place and then fitted and pegged it into the adjoining wall. It was a beautiful thing to see.

Sheathing.   The rough covering applied to the outside walls. Sheathing is also often applied to the roof. In conventional framing the sheathing provides additional rigidity to the wall as well as serving as a base for the exterior-finish siding. Sheathing may be of boards applied horizontally or diagonally to the studding, or it may be made out of large sheets of plywood or composition board.

Rafters.   Parallel beams that make up the framework for the roof. Rafters are usually made of 2-by-6-inch stock or 2-by-8-inch stock. Sheathing is applied over the rafters and except in the case of wood shingles, the sheathing will be a completely solid covering. When wood shingles are to be used as roofing, a solid deck of sheathing is often omitted and individual boards with several inches of space between them are nailed to the rafters as a base for the shingles. This method is often used in warm and humid climates for it allows the underside of the shingles to get ample ventilation and thus helps reduce the chance of decay.

Roofing.   The material used to provide the top for a structure and to keep out the weather. There is a wide range of roofing material, which is discussed in some detail in the chapter on "Roofs."

Flashing.   Sheet metal used to make a watertight joint where two different planes of the roof join to form a *valley*. Flashing is also used around the chimney where it joins the roof, to make a watertight joint, and also to make a watertight joint between the top of window and door frames and the house siding. Flashing is made of copper or aluminum.

Interior Partitions.   Walls used to divide the space within a structure into rooms. They are built with studding, in much the same fashion as the walls of the exterior of the house if it is made with balloon framing. Some partitions also serve to carry some of the weight of the floor above. This framing consists of ceiling joists and is much the same as the construction used for framing the first floor. When a partition or wall helps to support the floor above, it is called a *load-bearing partition*. Those that don't carry any weight other than the finish-wall surface applied over the framing are called *non-load-bearing*. You can move or eliminate a non-load-bearing partition pretty much at will, but if you remove one that is providing support for the floor above, something else, usually a girder, must be installed to carry the weight. All the exterior or outside walls of a house should be considered to be load-bearing.

Rough Opening for Doors and Windows. Apertures framed with double studding on each side to provide additional support to compensate for the fact that the window or door itself will not provide any strength to the wall. The tops of these openings are usually made with a heavy material that serves as a short girder; these are called *lintels* or *headers*. The bottom horizontal piece of the rough opening for a window is called the *rough sill*.

Exterior Siding. This is the finish covering that is applied over the exterior wall and is usually nailed to the sheathing. Its primary purpose is to keep out the weather.

Insulation. Material used on exterior walls, the roof, or ceiling of the house, and often under the first floor to reduce heat loss in winter and heat gain in summer. Some interior walls, such as bathrooms, are also often insulated to reduce sound transmission.

Interior Wall Surfaces. The materials that are applied to the inside surfaces of all walls and partitions. See the chapter on "Interior Walls and Ceilings."

Solid Masonry Construction. A solid masonry house will be different in basic construction from one that is framed with wood. Masonry walls provide the strength, and woodwork is used only for such items as floor and ceiling joists, rafters, and interior walls. A masonry house may be of brick, stone, or concrete masonry block. You don't find too many solid brick or stone houses being built today, because they are extremely expensive. Many that are seemingly built of brick or stone are not actually solid masonry but have a veneer of brick or stone over a conventional wood-framed house. Solid-masonry-block construction is used in the warmer climates such as Florida and the Southwest. It is also used extensively in commercial construction, for such structures as gasoline stations and warehouses.

We know of a crazy story that involves a masonry house. This house is a big, beautiful Victorian place, a real mansion that has everything you could ask for in gingerbread, turrets, and cupolas, all done on a grand scale. The last time we saw the place it was in prime condition—it just sparkled. The gentleman for whom the house was built came from a region where solid brick was what you used for a house and that was what he wanted his house to be built of. He just didn't believe that wood was as solid as brick and he wanted a solid house. His architect explained that no one in that area built solid brick houses, that a house of solid brick would be out of place and maybe a laughing-stock among the people who count. But the owner insisted on brick, so the architect came up with an ideal solution. He built a solid brick house and then he covered it with wood. He covered it with wood siding, wood gingerbread, wood anywhere he could find a place for it, with the result that everyone was happy.

Interior Trim. The woodwork around windows, doors, and other inside portions of the house.

These are the basic elements of a house. There are, of course, other items with which you should be familiar and these are listed in the "Glossary of Building Terms" at the back of this book.

A PORTFOLIO OF HOUSE-CONSTRUCTION DETAILS

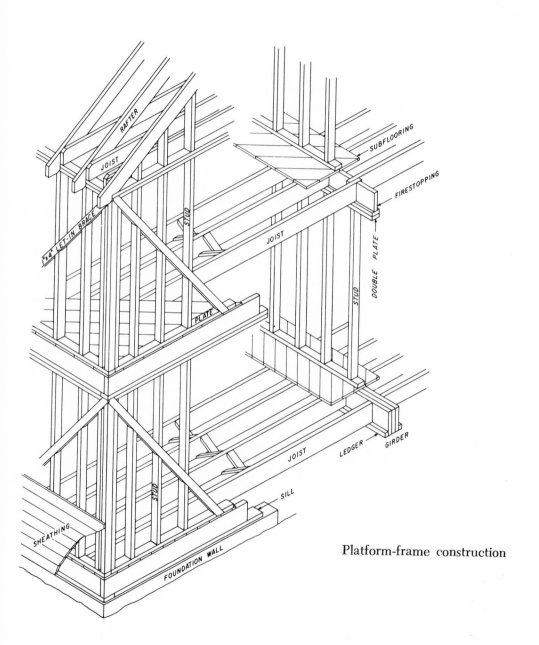

Platform-frame construction

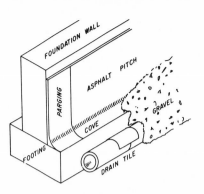

Continuous foundation
wall and footing

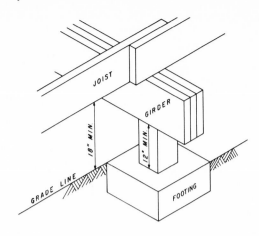

Clearance between earth and floor framing

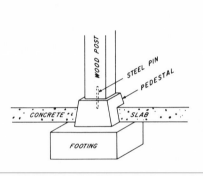

Support for basement
or cellar post

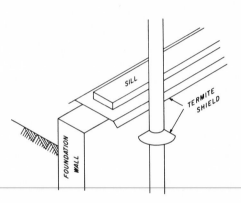

Installation of termite shields on exterior wall

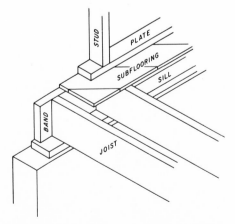

First-floor framing at exterior wall
platform-frame construction

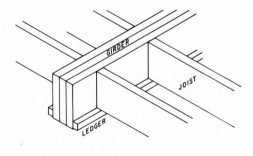

Joists framing into
girder on ledger strip

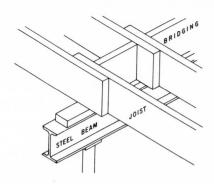

Joists resting on steel beam

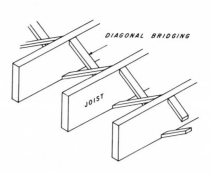

Diagonal bridging of floor joists

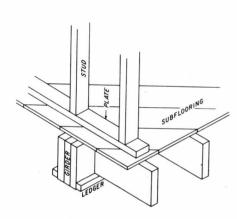

Framing under
non-bearing positions

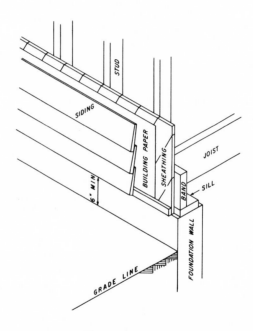

Clearance between
exterior siding and ground

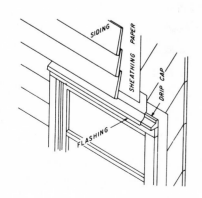

Application of bevel siding
over wood sheathing

5 Inspecting the House

Offbeat Dream Houses seldom if ever come in pairs. When you find one that seems just about perfect for you, move fast, for, like a pretty girl, it may not sit around waiting for you to make up your mind. And once it's gone, you'll never find another exactly like it. Remember that no matter what sort of shape it is in, if it is of interest to you then somewhere in this world there must be someone else who may also be interested in it, and there is no telling when he will show up. At the same time, you should know what you are getting into. After all, it is your money and you should know exactly how you are about to spend it. You can do this in a matter of hours if you know what to look for and have some idea of the costs involved in putting things right.

You will need a little special equipment for judging property. Bring along some old clothes or coveralls, because you'll not only want to tramp about the property but also do a little crawling about inside the house. You should have a flashlight, a penknife, or, even better, an ice pick—if you can locate one—and a pair of binoculars. A steel tape 8 feet or longer is useful and you should also have handy some ¼-inch graph paper, a pad, and a pencil.

When you make your inspection, the first thing to do is to go over the land with the broker or the owner and see precisely what you are

46

getting. You want to know not only how much land is involved—an acre, a half acre, ten acres, or more—but what it looks like and how it is laid out. Find out where the rough boundaries are and what is and what is not included in the transaction. If there is a brook, find out if it is part of the parcel that goes with the house. If there is a little outbuilding, find out if that is included. Boundaries on urban property are well defined but when it comes to rural property, especially if a considerable quantity is involved, boundaries can be very vague. Property lines may be fixed on fences or trees that disappeared at about the same time the Indians did. If you are working with a broker and he is not sure of the dimensions or items included, have him check with the seller. Sometimes it may be necessary to check with the owner of the adjoining property to see if he knows where the boundaries fall.

If a large amount of land containing several acres is involved you can be a bit more casual at this time about the exact location of the boundaries than if you are dealing with a relatively small plot of an acre or so, because with a small plot, a few feet one way or another can make a lot of difference. They may, for example, mean the difference between being able to add a wing to the structure or just not having enough land to add anything.

Once you have inspected the property and found it satisfactory, your next move is to see what you are getting besides the land, in what condition it is, and about how much money and time it will take to put it in order. It would be ideal if you could go over the building with an architect or a contractor but it is doubtful that you can line up either on short notice, so you should be prepared to inspect and judge the structure yourself. In the next chapter you will find a list of costs—how much it will cost to apply 10 square feet of asphalt shingles to a roof, how much for a bathroom with 3 fixtures, how much for each electric outlet, and so on. These are extremely rough costs. They may vary in either direction, depending on the quality of materials used, the amount of labor required, and the cost of local labor, but they will give you an idea of what it is going to cost you to put the place into shape.

As you inspect the house, make a note of every item you find that will require work and then refer to the cost table so that you can figure out the approximate costs. The resulting list of costs will not only help you to decide if this is the place you want, but will tell you about how much it is going to cost to fix up the place—information you'll need when you go shopping for a mortgage.

ACCESS

You must have a way of getting to the house. Usually there will be a driveway or a road that leads to it, but not always. If the property has just been divided it may be that no road or driveway exists, and in this case you will have to put one in. Measure off how long a driveway or road will be necessary and add this to your list of costs.

WATER

An adequate water supply is a must, so find out what, if anything, the house has in the way of a water supply. Houses in built-up areas usually have town water and that's a big help, so you can stop worrying if such is the case. It is when you're in the country or semi-rural areas where there is no city water that you need to check carefully. Private water supplies come in all shapes and forms. We've seen farm houses out in the country that still depend on a cistern—a large container filled from rainwater off the roof—as the primary water supply. Cisterns aren't much good unless you have plenty of rain and don't use much water. Sometimes the water supply comes from a spring that "never runs dry," or even a pond or a lake. Springs can produce delicious water but they do run dry; ponds and small lakes usually provide adequate water, but they are not always ideal as a source of drinking water because their water can get a bit gamey around August. We were brought up in a house that got its water supply from a large pond, and while the grown-ups drank only bottled water and we were supposed to, the stuff from the lake never seemed to hurt any of us young ones.

The best kind of private water supply comes from a well. Wells are of two kinds—shallow or "dug" wells, and drilled wells. The drilled well is better than the shallow well because it seldom goes dry.

Shallow wells, as you may have guessed, are shallow. They are dug by hand by someone who figures that if he digs deep enough in one spot he'll hit water. One of the great drawbacks of having a shallow well is that during a long dry spell they often do go dry because they depend on water that is fairly close to ground surface. Even if you are told that the well on the property has never gone dry within the memory of living man, that may be because there was no inside plumbing or the residents never took many baths or did much washing.

The shallow well that comfortably served your grandparents might not do the same for you because you probably bathe a good deal more frequently than they did and you have a great many more water-consuming devices, such as an automatic washing machine, a dishwasher, a garbage disposer, and maybe even a swimming pool. There is no way to make a quick inspection to determine how good a shallow well is—you will have to take the word of the owner. The other disadvantage of a shallow well is that it can be contaminated from a nearby cesspool or a septic tank. You can determine the condition of the water by taking a sample to a laboratory or to the county agent.

If a shallow well has abundant water that is pure, the well may be fine for a weekend place, but if you are thinking about year-round living and have a sizable family, you should realize that eventually you will probably have to put in a drilled well.

A drilled well is a deep well going many feet down to underground water. If you have one on the property, then your water problems are over. If you have to drill one, the cost will probably be considerable, especially if you have to drill very deep to hit water. It is best to check with the local people about cost per foot, as the rate varies, depending on what area you're in.

SEWAGE

After you have found out about the water supply, check the sewage system. Again, houses in town are usually connected into a main sewage system but this is not always the case. You will find that in many built-up areas there is no sewage system and each house has its own cesspool or septic tank. In rural areas you will find only cesspools or septic tanks. Cesspools are simply large holes dug into the ground, lined with stone or masonry block, and provided with a cover. The sewage flows into the cesspool and is absorbed by the surrounding soil. Eventually the soil around the cesspool may become so saturated with grease that it can no longer absorb water and the cesspool overflows. Pumping it out will help for a time but eventually it will fill up again. The only real solution is to dig another cesspool some distance from the old one or put in a septic tank. If the house has a cesspool, figure that in the future, hopefully the distant future, you will need a septic tank.

The septic tank is the best way, short of a city sewer main, to handle sewage. If you have the tank checked once a year by a firm that cleans septic tanks—they are listed in the yellow pages of the telephone book under "Septic Tanks"—and have it cleaned when the inspection so indicates, it won't give you any trouble.

STRUCTURE

It is now time to move inside the house and see what the situation is. Start with the mechanical elements—electricity, plumbing, and heating.

Electricity is taken so much for granted these days that you probably will be surprised if you have fallen for a house that doesn't have it. There are still, however, quite a few farms off the beaten path that don't have electricity, and many remote summer cabins are in the same condition.

If your place doesn't have electricity, the best way to get it is through your local power company. But even the most friendly power company will show a surprising lack of enthusiasm at the suggestion that it bring power to your place if said place happens to be some distance from the road where its lines are strung. What the power company will ask you to do is to pay for the necessary number of poles to carry the wires across your land to your house. Since you will be charged around $45 for each pole and since the poles will have to be spaced 200 feet apart, this can mount up if the main electric lines running along the road are a good distance away from your property. The same, of course, goes for a telephone. If you want a telephone and electricity you had better measure off the distance from your house to the nearest lines and then as soon as you reach the nearest telephone, check with the telephone people to see what they will do about it. Needless to say, once the poles are up to carry electricity the phone company will utilize these same poles.

You don't, of course, absolutely have to have electricity and this is certainly true if you just want a summer weekend place. You can cook, refrigerate, and even heat on bottled gas and you can buy your own gasoline-powered generator and be pretty self-sufficient. We lived with this setup for several years right after World War II and it wasn't too bad. The stove, hot-water heater, and refrigerator all ran on bottled gas. We used kerosene lamps for lighting and the generator to run the water pump. We could have used it for light but it was rather noisy so we preferred the quiet of the kerosene lamps. But this is still pretty much like camping, and we'd just as soon not do it again.

HOUSE WIRING

Much of the wiring inside the house is concealed in walls and ceilings but some of it will be exposed in the basement or in the attic or attic crawl space. You can get some idea of the condition of the interior wiring by looking at the *service entrance,* where the electric wires connect to the house and where the fuse box is located. If the fuse box seems relatively new and the electric cables coming out of it are covered with a flexible metal or plastic covering you can assume that the wiring was installed fairly recently. Your main concern will be to determine how many additional outlets you will require. If, on the other hand, the service entrance looks as if it had been put together out of odds and ends from a junk yard, if the wires that are exposed to view are single strands covered with fabric, then the place may require extensive re-wiring, along with the additional outlets. This is not a major expense in the average house but it can run to around $500, including a decent service entrance and additional outlets. Be sure to check each room to see how many outlets you will need. These cost around $7.00 apiece and there are many structures where there aren't any—just a cord hanging down from the ceiling to supply the lighting.

PLUMBING

While reworking the existing wiring or installing a new electrical system is relatively inexpensive, plumbing is something else again. Extensive plumbing can run up to a lot of money, $750, $1,000, $2,000, even more, depending on what you start with and what you want, so if there is existing plumbing in the house, check it out carefully to determine how much of it you will be able to live with—happily. As with electricity, the best place to start inspecting the plumbing system is in the basement, where there are usually exposed pipes. If the pipes are made out of copper (and you can tell this because they have a copper color) you are in luck. Copper lasts almost indefinitely, and as it has only been used in residential work for a relatively short time, its presence means that the plumbing system is relatively modern—or at least the pipes are. If the pipes are made of galvanized iron—a sort of silvery color—you've got problems, because this type of pipe will rust on the inside and leak, or the inside will become so coated with rust or mineral deposits that only a trickle of water will be able to get through. Galvanized pipe means that you have an old plumbing system and that the cold-water and hot-water lines will have to be replaced. The time to replace them is when you do the renovation work, so add this to your list of items along with the approximate cost.

Plumbing fixtures seldom if ever wear out but they do become outdated and pretty dilapidated looking, what with rust spots where the enamel has been chipped and cracks repaired with white lead or even friction tape. If you feel that you don't want to live with the existing fixtures, put down the number of new ones you'll need along with the approximate cost. You may, of course, be dealing with a structure that has no plumbing at all, so you should allow at least $1,000 for a basic system, including a kitchen and bathroom.

One other item that should concern you during your inspection is the hot-water heater. If the structure contains a relatively new electric, gas, or oil unit, you are probably safe. The same holds true to a lesser degree if the hot water comes from the boiler that provides heat for the house. If you have only an old-fashioned kerosene heater, forget it and add a hot-water heater to your list.

HEATING

You don't often find a modern heating system in an OB house. The best you can hope for is that whatever is there works and that with a small investment it can be made to function adequately to serve your needs. Aside from fireplaces and oil or wood stoves, you will find one of three types of heating system. In older houses one of the most common is the gravity warm-air system. This consists of a basement furnace fired by coal, oil, or gas. If the house is out in the country the furnace will usually be fired by oil or coal because there won't be any gas mains in the vicinity, and heating a house on bottled gas is expensive. The heat from the furnace comes into the house by means of a large register, usually located in the floor of a centrally located room. When the furnace is going, a hot blast comes up through that big register, bringing with it a considerable quantity of dust.

The general idea is that because warm air rises, the upstairs of the house will eventually become warm. It's an extremely primitive system and unless you are very tight for money you should put in something else. Another type of warm-air heat is the forced system, where the heated air is pushed through the ducts by a fan and the ducts open into various rooms in the house. This is a pretty fair system and unless the furnace is in very bad shape from rust and corrosion it should be possible to bring the system up to date.

Another type of central heating, found mostly in New England and the Atlantic states, is steam. Steam heating is an old system that isn't being used much today except in commercial work. This kind of system consists of a boiler fired by gas or oil and rather massive radiators usually set just where you don't want them. The system works. We know because we happen to be living with one right now. Unless the proper valves are installed, however, the radiators are either very hot or stone cold and the system can do a lot of rumbling, gurgling, and wheezing, but it works and will probably last for another hundred years. We don't intend to replace it until we have money to spend that has no other place to go, and that time will probably be a long way off.

If you are in luck, you'll find the house is equipped with a hot-water heating system. This is a very good system and is fairly new compared with gravity warm air and steam. What's more, even if it is a very early system it can be modernized and the large radiators replaced with units recessed into the walls or with baseboard units along the walls.

To sum up what you may have found in the way of heating systems: if you have a gravity warm-air system or if you have no system, then you will need a new heating system. If you have steam you can live with it, but it's not ideal. If you have forced warm air or forced hot water and they appear—and that's the only way you can judge at this point—to be in good condition, you probably don't have to be too concerned about central heating as a major item of expense. For those of you who will need a new heating system, see the chapter on "Heating."

THE ROOF

As this is an important item that is often overlooked by people inspecting a house, let's do it first so that it won't get lost in the shuffle. The ideal way to look at a roof is to climb up a ladder so that you can see it up close. If this isn't possible and you can't reach the roof easily from a window or dormer, try a pair of binoculars from a short distance. Naturally you'll ask the broker or seller what the roofing is made of. Slate is great if the shingles are in good condition and none is missing or has pulled out of place. The one trouble with a slate roof is that it is not easy to repair. You need an expert slate man to do the job, because stomping about on a slate roof in the wrong way can really mess things up. But a slate roof is very beautiful and will last forever if it was properly installed to begin with. Asbestos shingles are another long-lasting type of roofing, and if this is what you find on the roof and you can live with the color and texture, you probably don't have to worry about your roof.

A large percentage of roofs throughout the country are covered with asphalt shingles and you can determine the condition of these shingles by whether or not they are still covered with mineral granules. If many of the shingles have no granules so that the asphalt-treated black felt is exposed, you will need a new roof. If the shingles are still in fairly good condition you may have to make some small repairs from time to time but there are probably a good many years of life left in them, and you can cross this item off your list. Wood shingles, also, don't last forever. After a number of years they will start to come loose, curl up at the edges, and look awfully tired. If the wood shingles on the roof are in this state, make a note. For those of you with roofing problems, see the chapter on "Roofs."

While you are up on the ladder or viewing the roof through your binoculars, check a couple of other items. Take a look at the exposed portion of the chimney to see if the mortar between the bricks is sound or has begun to crumble. Also look at the top of the chimney. This is usually covered with a concrete or tile cap and if the concrete is badly cracked or some of the tiles are missing you will want to make a note of it. This repair work doesn't involve a lot of money—probably less than $50, but it's still money. Another thing to look at is the flashing around the chimney and in the roof valleys. If this is copper or aluminum, fine. If it is galvanized iron it will be rusty, or if it is just asphalt roofing paper it should be replaced even if the roofing itself is sound. The flashing is the weakest point of any roof and if this isn't right, there will be leaks even if you have the best roofing material in the world.

OUTSIDE WALLS

After you have finished checking the roof, check the outside walls. Is the exterior siding something you like or is it something that you honestly feel will have to be replaced? What is the condition of the siding? If it is of wood, is the wood sound, or are the ends or pieces near the ground soft from decay? A nice little tool for checking on the condition of woodwork, by the way, is an old-fashioned ice pick. Jab at a piece of wood with this and if the pick goes in easily it may mean either rot or termites.

If the woodwork is painted, inspect the condition of the paint. If you find many areas where the paint is peeling it may mean a leak in the roof or in the siding. If the paint is covered with deep cracks it means that all that old paint will have to come off before repainting. With a large house this can be expensive or time consuming. Give the siding a couple of good slaps just to see how solid it sounds and feels. Check the condition of porches, stoops, and steps around the outside of the house. If you have a porch or stoop made out of wood, try to get in under it with your ice pick and flashlight to examine the condition of the wood framing. Any wooden outside structure such as a porch is apt to have problems from decay or termites, so check carefully.

Masonry structures made of stone, brick, or block aren't damaged by decay or insects but you should inspect them carefully just the same. Look for crumbling mortar and more important, cracks running from top to bottom of the wall. This can indicate a condition where the wall has settled more than the normal amount, and while such cracks may never grow any larger, they might. If you find indications of such a condition, the walls should be checked out by a contractor.

Other items you should check while inspecting the outside of the house are the roof gutters and the leaders that run from the gutters to the ground. If the gutters are sagging, if you notice holes in them or an area on the ground directly under the gutter where the soil has obviously been disturbed by a stream of water, make a note that the gutters may have to be replaced. Look at the condition of the windows on the outside to see if the putty around the glass panes is sound or has cracked and fallen away. It might take a man the best part of an hour to replace the putty on one window, and if you have 20 windows and you pay him $5 an hour, you can see what these repairs could cost.

THE UNDERSIDE OF THE HOUSE

This is one of the best places to go to look for trouble. If the house has a basement, do it here. First examine the interior of the foundation walls to see if you can find any discoloration caused by water leaking through the walls. Also look for damp spots on the walls and floors. A nice dry basement is usually a good sign in more ways than one because it means that there is little chance that the woodwork that you view from this location is damaged by rot or decay. Just the same you had better check it, and the place to do this is along the sills where the woodwork joins the top of the foundation wall. Use your ice pick here to determine if any of the wood seems softer than the rest. Also check for little earthen tunnels about ⅜ of an inch wide on the outside as well as the inside of the foundation wall. These are made by termites so that they can reach the woodwork from their nests in the ground without being exposed to light, which they don't like. If you find these tunnels you'll know there are termites about. How many and how much damage they have done is difficult for the amateur to determine. But in any case, termites are a negative factor and you should certainly ask the seller to pay the cost of getting rid of them and to repair any damages made by them. He may not go along with this but you should certainly ask.

In many very old buildings you will find that there is a type of decay on the outside of the beams. Sometimes it's so soft that you can cut into it with your fingernail. This isn't too serious because it is just on the outside, and the major portion of the beam below this outer covering is still sound and tough. Here is another place for you to use your ice pick.

You can get a very good idea of just how solid the joists, beams, and girders are that support the first floor, or other floors for that matter, by jumping up and down on the floor. If it bounces, if windows rattle along with any objects that might be on the floor, the framing is weak. The situation may not be too serious; perhaps the framing can be made solid by the addition of posts or a girder but some money will have to be spent in this area, so make another note.

INTERIOR WALL SURFACES

Examine the condition of the interior wall surfaces carefully. If they are plaster, look for cracks, an excessive number of bulges, damp spots, and areas where the plaster has fallen out and the lath is exposed. Plaster in this condition is probably so far gone that it cannot be salvaged and will have to be removed and replaced with something else, usually gypsum wallboard. Measure the area of all the walls and ceilings that will require extensive work and add this figure to your list. Often you will find walls and ceilings covered with one of the many types of inexpensive wallboard where the joints between panels are covered with woodlath. If you don't care for this kind of covering, it too will have to be replaced with gypsum wallboard.

WINDOWS

Test windows by opening and closing. The sash should fit tightly in the frame but should move easily. Ask if there are screens and storm sashes for all the units. Screens are required in almost all the areas during the warm months, and storm sashes are required if the house is to be heated in winter and you want to keep the heating costs low. A combination screen and storm sash for the average window will cost about $20. If you have a good many windows and you have to buy screens and storm sashes you have a fair-sized item of expense.

FIREPLACES

If the house has a fireplace or fireplaces, make sure that they are working fireplaces. Friends of ours once bought a place and only after they moved in did they find, to their dismay, that the fireplace did not work. The flue had been blocked off some years before so that the furnace connected into the same flue would operate properly. It cost them several hundred dollars to have a separate chimney made for the furnace and to remove the obstruction from the fireplace flue.

Ask the seller to tell you what he thinks you should know about the fireplace. You can check on it yourself by looking up into the flue with the aid of your flashlight. If you don't see any obstruction or if you can see daylight coming from the top of the chimney, the flue is clear. Ashes and accumulations of soot in the fireplace opening also indicate that it is a working fireplace. By the way, if the paint or stone above the fireplace is badly discolored, it may mean that the fireplace doesn't work too well and allows a great deal of smoke to come into the room. This condition can often be corrected by adding a few feet or so to the top of the chimney, putting a cap on the chimney top to eliminate downdrafts or changing the interior dimensions of the fireplace just a little by the addition of a few more bricks. None of this is very expensive but it might cost you $100 or so to stop the fireplace from smoking.

INTERIOR LAYOUT

You should go over the room arrangement quite carefully and make note of any interior partitions that you might have to remove to make the interior space more suitable for your needs. Many older houses have lots and lots of little rooms, and to make one big room out of two or more means ripping down partitions. Some partitions can be removed with ease, but load-bearing partitions cannot. If a load-bearing partition is removed, a large header or girder will have to be installed to carry the weight formerly carried by the partition and this will add considerably to your costs. Determine as best you can, how many load-bearing partitions may have to be removed. See the chapter on "What Is It and What Is It Called?"

NON-DWELLING STRUCTURES

In some respects it is a lot easier to check on the condition of a non-dwelling structure such as a barn, warehouse, or garage, because fewer items are involved. You will probably not have to be concerned with the condition of the plumbing, heating, or even the wiring because there just isn't any. What you are buying is a relatively empty structure and if the structure is sound and if you can get water and electric power in, then you know about all that there is to be known.

FOUNDATIONS

You will not always find conventional foundations on non-dwelling structures. They may rest on wood posts driven into the ground or on masonry-block piers. Many farm buildings rest on "mud sills," heavy beams that rest directly on the ground. In many sections of the country the foundation walls are often made of stone laid up without mortar.

Masonry or wood piers, if they are in good condition and in sufficient number, can provide adequate support for a structure, but if the place is to be heated in winter the area under the house should be enclosed to keep the floors from being chilled and to prevent pipes from freezing. These walls around the foundation can be made of masonry block. Measure off the length of the four walls to determine how many feet of wall you will need. Also get the height from the house sill to the ground. Check on the condition of the piers, especially the wood ones. Use your ice pick to test the base for softness caused by decay or insects. Check the masonry piers to see if they have shifted position so that they are on a slant. Go up to the floor above and do a little jumping to see just how solid the floor is. If it bounces, it means that there are not enough piers or that some of the piers have sunk so that they aren't providing adequate support.

If the structure rests on "mud sills" you are going to have to do better than this. The usual treatment here is to jack the structure up so that a masonry foundation can be installed. This can be a fairly expensive proposition. Of course, if all you want is a rustic summer place and don't plan to put more than a few dollars into it, you can get along with the mud sills, but if you are really going to fix the place over you will want a foundation that not only will get the structure away from the ground but can't be damaged by decay or insects.

A dry stone-wall foundation is perfectly adequate for supporting the structure. It isn't airtight or watertight but it can be made reasonably so by covering it on the inside with mortar.

WOODWORK

You should examine very carefully all the woodwork that is close to or in direct contact with the ground. Lack of maintenance or poor construction provides ample opportunity for rot and/or termites to do considerable damage. So take your ice pick and prod all that woodwork. Check the siding as well as the structural framing members. Also pay particular attention to all woodwork that is close to dense vegetation. Often trees and bushes have grown so close to the structure that the woodwork near them gets no sun or ventilation and will often start to decay in spite of the fact that it may be some distance from the ground.

Examine the outside walls to see the condition of the siding. You may have picked up an old barn that is covered with lovely weathered vertical siding. This you will no doubt want to keep, but to get a perfectly weathertight wall it may be necessary to remove all the siding, apply sheathing to the barn framework, and then reapply the old siding.

WHAT YOU WILL NEED

After you have inspected the structure but before you leave it, sit down and make a list of all the basic items that will be needed to make the place livable—new foundations, plumbing, heating, wiring, windows, interior partitions, new roof, insulation, interior wall surfaces, flooring, a kitchen, and so on. Make this list as complete as you can and when you have finished it, take another look at the place. Knowing the amount of work that will be required and the rough cost will make it easier for you to decide whether this place is a good buy for you or not. At the end of this chapter, we've provided a detailed check list to help you remember all the items you will want to find out about in making your inspection.

SUMMING UP

If you know what to look for, if you are willing to take the time to inspect every element in the house that you can, and if you continually ask questions directed to the broker or the seller and insist on an answer, you will end this inspection with a very good idea of what you are getting. Always remember that the seller or his representative are not required to point out all the faults of the structure. But they are required to give an honest answer to a question directed to them, so it is up to you to ask the questions and wait until you get the answer.

► *Detailed House-Inspection Form*

1. Type of dwelling or structure
   A. House
   B. Barn
   C. Other

2. General appearance and condition
   A. Good
   B. Fair
   C. Poor

3. Condition of lot
   A. Good
   B. Fair
   C. Poor
   D. Needs extensive landscaping and planting

4. Driveway and/or road
   A. Blacktop or concrete
   B. Gravel
   C. Dirt
   D. None

5. Exterior of structure
   A. Type of siding or exterior walls
   B. Condition
      a. Good
      b. Fair
      c. Poor
   C. Condition of outside paint
      a. Good
      b. Fair
      c. Poor

6. Roof
   A. Type of roofing material
   B. Condition
      a. Good
      b. Fair
      c. Poor

7. Roof flashing
   A. Good
   B. Poor

8. Foundations
   A. Type
   B. Condition
      a. Good
      b. Poor

9. Exposed structural wood members
   A. Good
   B. Fair
   C. Poor. Indications of termites and/or decay

10. Basement or crawl space
    A. Dry and clean
    B. Damp, wet, or musty

11. Floors
    A. Firm, solid, and level
    B. Weak and/or sagging

12. Flooring and floor coverings
    A. Type
    B. Condition
       a. Good
       b. Fair
       c. Poor

13. Exposed portion of chimney
    A. Good
    B. Fair
    C. Poor

14. Insulation
    A. Roof or ceiling
    B. Walls
    C. Floors
    D. None

15. Interior walls, partitions, and ceilings
    A. Type of materials used
    B. Conditions of surfaces, excluding paint and paper
       a. Good
       b. Fair
       c. Poor

16. Wall and ceiling finishes
    A. Types
    B. Condition
       a. Good
       b. Fair
       c. Poor

17. Windows
    A. Type
    B. Condition
       a. Good
       b. Poor

18. Window screens and storm sashes
    A. Yes
    B. No

19. Electric wiring
    A. Capacity of service entrance
       a. 30 amperes
       b. 100 amperes
       c. 200 amperes
       d. None
    B. Electric outlets and fixtures
       a. Adequate
       b. Need some additions
       c. Require complete rewiring

20. Water Supply
    A. City
    B. Drilled well
    C. Shallow well

D. Other

E. None

21. Sewage system
    A. City
    B. Septic tank
    C. Cesspool
    D. None

22. Water pipes
    A. Copper
    B. Galvanized iron

23. Hot water heater
    A. Type
    B. Age
    C. Condition
    D. None

24. Bathrooms
    A. Number
    B. None
    C. Condition of fixtures
       a. Good
       b. Usable
       c. Not usable

25. Heating

A. Type of heating system

B. Condition

C. Age

D. None

26. Kitchen
    A. Cabinets and counters
       a. Adequate
       b. Additional units required
       c. None, or not serviceable

27. Interior paint and finishes
    A. Condition
       a. Good
       b. Fair
       c. Poor
       d. None

28. Garage and/or outbuildings
    A. General condition
       a. Usable
       b. Require repairs
       c. Not usable

29. Other comments

Estimating the Cost of Renovation Work 6

You can save yourself a good deal of time and disappointment, not to mention money, if, when you go out to inspect property, you are able to figure out approximately how much renovation work will cost.

Few people aside from architects, builders, and contractors have any concept of building costs. The average individual engaged in buying or selling a house, be he seller, buyer, or broker, will invariably under-estimate the cost of renovation work. Of course, the best way to get a true picture of the cost of a renovation project is to have a builder or contractor come in and make a firm bid on the job. But when you are out shopping, there isn't time for this. Therefore, when you go house hunting you should go out armed with enough knowledge of building costs so that you can inspect the property and then estimate roughly what the work is going to cost. We are now going to tell you how to estimate these renovation costs.

Naturally enough, the information we are about to give you is for purposes of rough estimating. Many factors involved in a renovation job just can't be figured out in advance except by a professional, but if you use our guide carefully and thoroughly you will arrive at a pretty fair estimate of what the renovation work will cost.

These costs for labor and material were figured out for us by a very fine and competent builder and his job superintendent—the man who is responsible for getting a job done in the right way at the right price and on time. Material costs were based on the prices in effect at the time these costs were drawn up, winter, 1970. Labor costs were based on the prevailing rate at that time, which are fairly representative of the rate across the country except in large cities, where the labor rate is higher, and in rural areas, where it may be considerably less.

Following the general description of various projects and the cost for materials and labors, you will find check lists covering the various rooms and areas of the house. We suggest that you make several copies of these check lists and take them with you, along with the price list, when you inspect a house. In this way you can rather quickly figure out your renovation costs at the same time that you make your inspection.

THE COST FINDER

Forced Warm-Air Heating.   You will need two outlets per room and each outlet will cost about $65 installed. The average cost of an oil-fired furnace for a house with 1,500 square feet, will be about $600. The average cost for a six-room house would be $1,380. If you wish to have the system designed to cool the house in summer, double this figure.

Circulating-Hot-Water Heating.   The boiler for this type of system will run between $700 and $900, depending on the size of the house. Each radiator or equivalent piece of radiation equipment will come to about $50. For a small, compact house, a complete circulating-hot-water system can be installed for about $1,500.

Chimney.   A single-flue chimney for an oil or gas heating system will cost $275 if made of masonry block, and $375 if made of brick. This would be for a two-story house. For a one-story house, knock about $100 off the price given.

Electricity

Utility Poles. If it is necessary for the utility company to install poles on your property to bring electric power to the house, you will have to pay $45 for each pole installed. Poles will have to be spaced not more than 200 feet apart. If guy wires are required, add $25 for each pole and $25 for each 100 feet of wire beyond the first pole.

Electric Wiring. A 100-ampere service entrance will cost about $175 installed, and a 200-ampere service entrance will be $300.

Allow $7 for each electrical outlet—wall outlets, outlets for ceiling and wall fixtures, and switches. If you plan to install more than one switch at any one location, each one will cost $7 installed, even though they are placed side by side.

The cost of wiring for an electric range will be about $50. A dishwasher will run $40. Wiring for a water pump will run $25, and the electrical connections for a forced-warm-air furnace will be about $50.

Electric Heat. The cost here for the 200-ampere service entrance will be $300, but this, of course will also furnish power for the house electrical system and for heavy-duty electrical equipment such as the kitchen range and hot-water heater. The installation of the actual heating system will cost about 70 cents for each square feet of floor space that is to be heated. The cost of installing electric heat in a house with 2,000 square feet would be around $1,700—$300 for the service entrance, and $1,400 for the installation of the heating equipment and controls.

Insulation for Electric Heat. Figure these costs as follows: For ceilings that require 6-inch thick insulation, it will cost 20 cents a square foot installed. For the walls where 4-inch thick insulation is adequate, figure 12 cents installed, and for floors where 3-inch thick insulation is used, 10 cents a square foot.

Additions—Exterior

Additions to the House.   The basic cost of adding a wing, bedroom, family room, or the like, one story high, will run about $25 a square foot for average construction. This will include the foundations, framing, roof, floor, walls, and electrical wiring. It would not include plumbing, a fireplace, or cabinet work. This figure is also based on using conventional materials. You must always keep in mind that adding to a structure will cost more per square foot than new construction because of the additional labor involved in connecting the addition to the existing structure. A 12-foot by 20-foot addition will cost about $5,000.

Garages.   A frame one-car garage with overhead door and a concrete slab floor will cost about $1,500. A 24-foot by 24-foot two-car garage will cost $2,600.

Outside Decks.   A wood deck will cost about $2.50 a square foot.

Additions—Interior

Interior Partitions.   Partitions 8 feet high will cost about $10 per lineal or running foot. This price includes the cost of framing and the application and taping of gypsum wallboard. It does not include the cost of removing an existing partition or decorating.

Gypsum Wallboard.   The cost of material and applying it to walls and ceilings will be 17 cents a square foot. This price also includes taping. It assumes that the existing framework is adequate for the proper application of wallboard.

Ceramic Tile.   The cost of installing ceramic tile over a suitable base will be $2 a square foot. This includes material and installation.

Insulation.   For a house that is to be heated with forced warm air or circulating hot water, a 3-inch-thick insulation for ceiling and 2 inches for walls is adequate. Figure this cost at 8 or 10 cents a square foot respectively.

Closets. A closet 2 feet deep and 4 feet wide will cost about $100, including door and hardware. To find the cost of a larger closet, use $10 for each lineal foot of wall, plus the cost of an interior door.

Doors. Interior doors installed will run about $85 each. This price includes the rough opening, the installation of the door, and the hardware. An exterior door will cost about $150 installed.

Windows. The average-sized double-hung window will cost around $100 to install. This price includes making the rough opening in the wall, installing the window and patching the exterior siding. A fixed window of equal size will cost about the same.

Stairs. A standard flight of wood stairs will cost about $185 installed. A flight of custom-made spiral stairs will run around $800, but stock prefabricated units that can be adjusted for height will run about $500 installed.

Flooring. Building a floor that will include the framing and the subflooring will cost about $1.25 a square foot.

Underlayment applied over a subfloor to provide a suitable base for resilient materials and carpeting will cost 30 cents a square foot installed.

A prefinished hardwood floor will cost 40 cents a square foot installed. Other types of hardwood flooring will run up to 65 cents a square foot installed.

Vinyl asbestos tile will cost 50 cents a square foot installed. Vinyl tile will run $1 a square foot installed, and sheet linoleum will cost $7 a square yard installed.

Kitchen Cabinets. Labor and materials for standard wood kitchen cabinets and work counters should be figured at running about $40 per lineal foot for each. If you have a total of 20 lineal feet of cabinets and counters, the cost will be $800.

Painting. Interior and exterior painting on new work will be around $1 per square foot, and this includes the paint as well as labor.

Fireplace. A brick fireplace with a chimney adequate for a story-and-a-half structure will cost around $800. A metal prefabricated fireplace with prefabricated metal chimney will run around $450 installed.

Plumbing Costs

Wells. The cost of drilling a well will be around $5.50 per foot and you will hope to get water at 100 feet. You may get water before you reach this depth, but you may not. There is no way to be absolutely certain in this matter. The cost of a pump for a well 100 feet deep will be about $350 installed. A pump for a well 200 feet deep will be $450, and for a 300-foot-deep well you will need a pump costing $550. Figure the minimum cost of a well and pump at $1100.

Septic Tank. Where soil conditions are average, a tank suitable for a three-bedroom house will have a 1,000-gallon capacity and will cost about $650 installed.

House Plumbing System. On new work or on a major renovation project where the plumbing can be installed with relative ease, figure $1,450 for a complete system consisting of a full bathroom, a half bath or lavatory, and the kitchen sink. A full bathroom will cost about $800, and a lavatory with two fixtures about $375. Cost of kitchen sink and installation will be around $150. Plumbing fixtures in this price range would be standard but not luxurious.

For a complete water system consisting of a well, sewage system, and plumbing system you should allow at least $3,150.

Roads, Driveways, and Grading

Roads. If you have to put a road through your property to get to your house, figure that a gravel road 10 feet wide will cost $2 a lineal or running foot. This price is based on a road running through a clear field where no trees or rocks must be removed. If you wish a blacktop road rather than gravel, figure this as costing about $4.50 a lineal foot for a 10-foot-wide road. This same price range would hold true for driveways.

Blacktop. If you want to cover an existing road or driveway with blacktop, figure this as costing about $2.35 per square yard.

Fill for Grading. Gravel for fill that may be required for grading roads and property will cost delivered between $1.50 and $2.50 per cubic yard.

Rental of Bulldozer. Depending on the size, the hourly rate for this equipment plus the operator will run from $12 to $22.

Installing Foundations. If an existing structure requires foundations, the cost of the labor and materials to jack the place up and install the foundations can be figured at around $2 for each square foot of floor area. This needs to be figured on the first-floor area only. A building 20 by 30 feet will contain 600 square feet of floor space, so the cost of the foundation work will be around $1,200. If you want a 4-inch-thick concrete slab poured over the earth, this will cost an additional 50 cents a square foot.

Roofing. The cost of applying asphalt shingles plus the materials will be $15.50 a square. A square is an area 10 feet by 10 feet, or 100 square feet. Wood shingles will cost installed about $51 a square. Both these figures are based on the assumption that the surface is suitable for direct application of the new material. If the old roofing must be removed or if the roof, framing, or sheathing is not adequate, the costs will naturally be higher.

Siding. Wood clapboard or aluminum siding will cost about $50 per square. Red-cedar shingles will be in this general price range, but white-cedar shingles will be around $45, and wood shakes, which are the rough-textured, hand-split shingles, will cost about $56 a square installed.

Gutters.   The cost of gutters and downspouts will be around $1.10 per lineal foot installed.

Concrete Terraces and Patios.   Figure these with a 4-inch-thick concrete slab at around 45 cents a square foot.

► *Check Lists: Cost Estimates*

	REQUIRE (Yes or No)	QUANTITY	ESTIMATED COST
Bathroom			
1. Partitions			
2. Doors			
3. Windows			
4. Gypsum wallboard			
5. Flooring			
6. Electric outlets and fixtures			
7. Heat			
8. Tile for walls			
9. Tile for floor			
10. Built-in cabinets			
11. Painting and decorating			
12. Electric fixtures			
Kitchen			
1. Partitions			
2. Doors			
3. Windows			
4. Gypsum wallboard			
5. Flooring			
6. Electric outlets			
7. Cabinets and work counters			
8. Range			
9. Dishwasher			
10. Refrigerator			
11. Painting and decorating			

Continued on following page

	REQUIRE (Yes or No)	QUANTITY	ESTIMATED COST

Bedroom

1. Partitions
2. Doors
3. Windows
4. Closet
5. Gypsum wallboard
6. Flooring
7. Electric outlets
8. Electric fixtures
9. Painting and decorating

Halls and Foyers

1. Partitions
2. Doors
3. Windows
4. Gypsum wallboard
5. Flooring
6. Electric outlets
7. Electric fixtures
8. Painting and decorating

Service and Utilities

1. Road or driveway
2. Utility poles required
3. Service entrance for electricity
4. Well
5. Pump
6. Septic tank
7. Plumbing system for house

Exterior

1. Roof
2. Siding
3. Painting
4. Gutters and leaders
5. Garage
6. Deck or terrace
7. Windows

Continued on following page

	REQUIRE (Yes or No)	QUANTITY	ESTIMATED COST
8. Window screens and storm sashes			
9. Doors			
Heat			
1. Electric			
2. Forced warm air			
3. Circulating hot water			
4. Chimney			
Basic Structure			
1. Installation of foundations			
2. Construction of floors			
3. Concrete slab			
4. Additions			
5. Garage			

Buying the House 7

You have found something you want, you have inspected it, and you not only know what condition it is in, but have more than just a vague idea of how much it is going to cost to put the place into decent shape. The next step is to make an offer, and that's when things begin to get a little tense. How much to offer?

Let's say the asking price is $16,000. Ordinarily, if you have visited several properties in the vicinity with the same broker, you have established some kind of relationship with him in your travels around together. You will have asked the broker: How long has the property been on the market? How anxious is the owner to sell? How firm does the broker believe the seller's asking price to be? You will note, too, that the "asking" price is $16,000. That does not necessarily mean that the "taking," or selling, price will be that same amount.

Most sellers, but not all, generally ask for somewhat more than they expect to get, in order to leave themselves some room for dickering. Naturally, they want to get as much as they possibly can for the property, but, on the other hand, if they really want or need to sell, they will give sober consideration to what they think is a fair offer. Much depends, too, on whether other people are also interested in the property.

They may perhaps be represented by the same broker you are using or by another broker in the area.

How much do you want the place? How much can you afford to pay for it, keeping in mind the amount you now believe—after your thorough inspection—it will cost you to fix it up according to your taste? Is the place in bad shape? Fair? Good? Has it obviously been unoccupied for a considerable length of time? How are the roof, the plumbing —if any, the heating system? Does the place need a new exterior paint job?

The broker and the seller are no doubt pretty much aware of all the negative aspects of the property, but it does no harm, and it is often helpful, to point them out to the broker, or to the seller if you are not working through a broker.

If the place has obviously been "prettied up," with fresh paint applied to the most conspicuous areas, a freshly cut lawn, and pink geraniums in the window boxes or around the front entry way, you can let the broker and/or seller know that while you appreciate the effort, you realize that this is all part of the "psychology of selling" a house and hasn't distracted your attention one whit from the fact that the place needs a new roof. You are too smart a buyer to be influenced by "curb appeals."

Keep in mind, that while the broker represents the seller, he is also anxious to make the sale, and if you make a reasonable offer, he can often talk the seller into accepting it, especially if both are aware that you are a knowledgeable prospect and have taken a realistic look at the whole setup.

If the asking price is $16,000, you might set your original offer to the broker at perhaps $13,500. If he feels that there is no chance that this will be accepted, he will probably tell you so but may came up with a clue as to the figure he feels the seller will accept, say $14,250. If the broker feels that $14,250 is a reasonable offer, he will take it to the seller, and there is a good chance that it will be accepted. If it is not accepted, the seller may come up with a counterproposal—$14,750, which may be acceptable to you. This sort of wheeling and dealing directly is much easier if you work through a broker. If you are dealing directly with the seller, you may find that it is easier to bargain over the telephone than in person unless you are expert at maintaining a poker face.

EARNEST MONEY

If the offer you have made is accepted, the conventional next step is for you to put down a *binder,* or *earnest money,* or *hand money,* as it is sometimes called. It signifies your serious interest in the place but should be the smallest sum that will be acceptable to the seller. It may be $50, or a few hundred dollars, but keep it as small as you can.

The reason you want to keep this amount small is that there are a good many steps before you finally take title to the property at the closing, and there is always a chance that something may go wrong that prevents you from taking title. Most sellers will refund this earnest money if the deal fails to materialize through no fault of yours. There are instances, however, where the seller might feel justified in keeping the money. So make this amount as small as possible and get a receipt from the seller or broker stating that this amount represents an initial payment on such and such property. Earnest money may be given to the broker or the seller but whoever receives it should give the receipt.

AGREEMENT OF SALE

This is sometimes called a *contract of sale,* or a *sales contract.* It is the most important element in the purchase of property because it spells out the details of the transaction. Once you and the seller have signed this agreement, you have entered into a legal agreement, and if either of you fails to live up to the terms of the agreement, the other party could institute legal proceedings for breach of contract.

When you sign the agreement of sale you will have to make a down payment and this, as a rule, will be 10 per cent of the selling price. If you have previously put down earnest money as a binder, that sum will be deducted from the amount of the down payment.

The agreement of sale is drawn up by the seller or by his broker.

Before it is drawn up you should discuss the terms in detail so that it will protect you as well as the seller.

The agreement of sale will describe the property, the selling price, the amount you will make as a down payment, the time and place for the closing and other related information. For your protection, here are some of the points that you should make sure are included.

1. The date of the closing should be specified, and you should make sure that this date is one that is convenient for you. If you are going to have to shop around for a mortgage and if you want to get one or more contractors to give you estimates on the cost of the renovation work, you'll need as much time as possible before title closing. Thirty days between signing of the agreement and the date of the closing may be a little too tight for you, so ask for sixty days. The date for the closing as specified in the agreement can be deferred by either party for a few days or even a week if there is a valid reason. Nevertheless, you should get the closing set far enough in advance so that you won't feel pressured.

2. The agreement should include a clause that allows you or your architect and contractor to enter the premises to determine the work that has to be done.

3. The agreement should state that at the closing the seller will deliver to you a warranty deed and not a quit claim deed on the property.

4. The agreement should list any items other than fixtures that are to be included in the transaction. As was described in "Real Estate Terms and Their Meaning," a fixture is an article of personal property so attached to the premises that its removal would cause harm to the property. A kitchen sink or a built-in bookcase is a fixture. A kitchen range, refrigerator, wall-to-wall carpeting, or a pile of old lumber in back of the house are not fixtures, and the seller can remove them unless the agreement states that they are to be included.

5. The agreement should state that the sale is contingent on your

being able to get adequate financing. This is an item about which you want to be especially careful. The agreement should state the amount of mortgage money you will require, the length of time that the mortgage will run, and the interest rate. If you are going to need additional money in the form of a construction loan, this amount should be included in the total mortgage as specified in the agreement. See the chapter on "Financing."

Unless all the points noted regarding your mortgage are clearly spelled out in the agreement of sale, you can get into trouble. For example if the agreement simply states that you will require a $15,000 mortgage and 7½ per cent interest, and you are not able to get this on your own, the seller can take back the mortgage himself but he may only give you a 15-year mortgage. The monthly payments on this would be far greater than on a 25-year mortgage, and this might be a hardship for you. So be sure that the length of time you want for the mortgage is stated clearly. The agreement should make it perfectly clear that if you are unable to get a suitable mortgage, you will get back any money you have given to the seller, the agreement will be terminated, and the seller will have no cause for legal action against you.

Many of the problems that might arise over an agreement of sale can be eliminated if the buyer states his requirements to the seller or to his broker before the agreement is drawn.

After you receive the agreement, look it over. If it appears to be satisfactory to you, you can give oral approval, but with the understanding that you wish to go over it in detail with your attorney before you sign it. Your attorney can examine the agreement for legal pitfalls, but you too should study it carefully to make sure that it states clearly all the items that are of concern to you. The agreement may stipulate that if you default and fail to go through with the transaction, the seller may retain your down payment as damages; it should also stipulate that if he does so he will have no further claim on you. If this clause is not part of the agreement and you can't go through with the deal, the seller can not only keep your down payment but also may possibly sue you for additional damages resulting in your breach of the agreement.

In short, an agreement of sale is no small matter. It is the most important element in the purchase of property, and you want to make certain that you are well protected before you sign it.

The agreement is not in force until it is signed by the seller as well as by you. You will receive a copy with both signatures and it is only then that the deal is under way.

TITLE SEARCH

Once the agreement has been executed, your next move is to start trying to get a suitable mortgage. In the meantime, your attorney should make a title search on the property. It is usually best to use a local attorney for this job unless your own attorney lives in the general area. A title search involves going down to the city or town hall and examining the property records to determine the legal condition of the property. Does the description of the property that is on file agree with that in agreement of sale? If there is some minor difference or if the boundaries do not seem clear, your attorney may wish to inspect the property with the seller or his broker and get these matters straightened out. Are there any others besides the seller who have legal claim on the property? Are there any outstanding judgments or liens against the property? Unpaid real estate or school taxes? Are there any easements and, if so, what is the nature of these easements? All these matters will come up, if these situations exist, during the title search. Your attorney will advise you as to which ones may create a problem.

We suggest using a local attorney for this work because he will know the area, perhaps some of the principals involved, and can usually do a title search faster and for less money than someone from out of town. You should find out in advance what the attorney's fee will be for the title search and also for representing you at the closing. Many attorneys have a more or less fixed fee for this type of service—usually about $100. But sometimes they have to spend more time than usual on a title search and this might run up the cost a bit. We had one title search made that cost only $35 because the property had been in the same family since 1755 and the title was free and clear and easily checked out.

Do not try to do a title search yourself. You need an attorney who is familiar with real estate matters to handle this job.

TITLE INSURANCE

Even if a title search is made by your attorney, many lenders will require that you take out title insurance so that if there are any flaws in the title, the lender will be protected. This is a special type of insurance; only one premium is paid, usually at the time of closing, by you, the buyer. It insures the lender for the amount of the mortgage for as long as the mortgage is in force. It does not protect you as the owner. If you wish your own title-insurance protection, then you must take out *owner's title insurance*. The total cost of these two policies will be around $200.

FIRE INSURANCE

The lender will insist that the property be covered against loss by fire. You will therefore have to take out fire insurance to take effect at the time of closing, when you take legal possession of the property. The lender will probably request the original of the policy at the time of the closing and he will keep this until you have paid off the mortgage or have sold the house. Naturally, you pay the premiums. Keep in mind that the lender is only interested in a policy that will protect him for the amount of money he has invested. In other words, he will ask only for a policy equal to the amount of the mortgage. You want to make sure that the policy covers the true value of the house and also that it includes personal property that would be of no concern to the lender. Discuss you renovation and occupancy plans with your insurance broker so that he can make arrangements to have you adequately covered not only against fire, but against theft, storm damage, liability, and whatever else he may believe is vital in your case. After you move in, a so-called *home owner's policy* gives you excellent protection at moderate cost. And don't forget that you should increase the amount of coverage as the renovation work progresses.

CLOSING STATEMENT

At some point preceding the time of closing, your attorney should prepare a closing statement and send it to you. He will have been in communication with all the parties involved in the transaction, including your lender, so that the closing statement will be a rather accurate summation of the financial end of the deal. It will stipulate the selling price, the amount you have made as down payment, and the amount and source of the mortgage money. It will or should also include the other items that you will have to pay for at the time of closing. There may be a charge from the lender for making a credit check on you and for other costs in drawing up the mortgage and loan agreement. If you are required to take out title insurance, the cost of the premium should be listed in the closing statement. The attorney may also include in this statement his fee for the title search and representing you at the closing. This cost can vary considerably depending on your attorney and the time he spent. There may also be a charge for real estate, school, and other forms of property tax that may have been paid by the previous owner and will have to be refunded to him.

After you have had a chance to go over the closing statement, check it over with your attorney so that you fully understand what you are being charged for, by whom, and for what. He should also tell you how the various checks should be drawn. As a general rule, when sizable amounts are involved, you will need certified checks or cashier's checks made payable to you. At the time of closing these can be endorsed over to the proper party. You should also check with your lender to find out whether he will require any sizable amount of money at the closing that might not be listed on the closing statement. At one closing, we had to pay our lender some $500 in advance interest, because we had a construction mortgage and it was easier for him to handle the matter in this fashion than to adjust his bookkeeping. It is nice to know about these things in advance so that they don't come as a shock at the last minute.

Even with an extremely detailed and exact closing statement, some minor items probably won't be included but will come up and will have to be paid by you at the closing. It may be just a few dollars for fuel oil that is in the oil-storage tank or some slight adjustment on the electric bill. You may have asked that the seller put a new lock on the front and back doors, and he will want to be paid for this at the closing. But if you have discussed the closing statement fully with your attorney, lender, and the broker, you should not be in for any major surprises that will require you to pay out large amounts of money.

TITLE CLOSING

This is the big day. You've got your mortgage and whatever additional sums you will need, your attorney has checked over the title and has examined the deed, and everything should go smoothly.

While the day of the closing is specified in the agreement of sale, this can be changed, as we mentioned earlier, at the request of any of the parties involved, for a valid reason. There may be some problem in working out the final papers, someone has to go out of town, or someone gets sick. We know of one closing that was postponed week after week because each week someone else involved came down with flu.

The closing can take place at the office of one of the attorneys involved or at the office of the lender. The cast of characters will usually include the seller and his attorney, you and your attorney, the lender, and the broker, if one is involved in the transaction. A closing can, of course, take place without the seller or buyer being present. The entire operation is handled by their respective attorneys. But as it is you who are buying the property, you should certainly make every effort to be on hand for the event.

At the closing the principal business consists of checking over the closing statement to see that everything is in order, and making sure that everyone understands who gets what money and the amount. Checks are handed about, papers are signed, small problems come up that always seem to be solved, and that's about it. Everyone but you comes away with something. You don't even get the deed to the property at this time. It will be sent over to the town clerk to be recorded and then sent on to you. But, of course, you do end up with something—you end up with a house.

Financing 8

Most people in this country who buy a house of any type finance the major part of the purchase with a mortgage. The common form of mortgage in use today is the *regular,* or *amortized,* mortgage. This type of mortgage is written for a certain number of years, most often 20, 25, or 30, and regular monthly payments are made, based on the length of the mortgage and the interest rate. These monthly payments cover the interest on the mortgage loan and also reduce the principal. The longer the life of the mortgage loan, the lower are the monthly payments, but over the years you will have paid out a lot more money in interest than if you had a mortgage with a shorter life. Some lenders will also set up monthly payments so that they include payments toward real estate taxes.

When you get a mortgage you sign a note that puts the property up as security for the loan. Until the mortgage loan has been paid in full, the mortgagee (you, as the borrower are the mortgagor) has certain legal rights to the property to insure that nothing is done to it to reduce its value.

TYPES OF MORTGAGES

Mortgages fall into two basic types: the conventional mortgage and the government-insured Federal Housing Administration (FHA) and Veterans Administration (VA), or GI, mortgage. You apply for either type through the same lending institutions. The difference between the conventional mortgage and the government-insured mortgages is that with the FHA and VA, the government insures the mortgage loan so that if you default the government rather than the lender takes the loss. Government-insured loans have rather strict requirements covering minimum standards of design and construction and so your chances of getting one of these with an OB Dream House are rather slim. When you go shopping for a mortgage you can ask your lender about these loans, but you should be prepared to accept the conventional mortgage, which is a little more flexible as to the condition and type of property.

You will never get a mortgage loan to cover the full purchase price of the property. Even FHA and VA will not go this far. With an OB Dream House you should think in terms of a mortgage for about two-thirds of the purchase price and if you get a 70-per-cent mortgage you are in luck. Most lenders have a maximum amount that they will lend on any piece of property regardless of size and quality. We were talking to a lender a few months ago and he told us that the policy of his bank was not to lend more than $30,000 on anything—"even the White House."

The amount of money a lender will allow you on a piece of property depends not only on the particular policy of the lender and the value of the property involved, but also on your financial condition. If your income is high and the source appears relatively stable, if you do not have a lot of outstanding debts but have liquid assets such as a savings account and stocks, you have a much better chance of getting a good-sized mortgage on a house than if you are on shaky financial ground. There are, however, exceptions to this rule. A few years ago a friend of ours who is a successful writer and not on shaky financial grounds, wanted to get a mortgage for about $12,000 on a house he was buying for $26,000. He presented his lender with income-tax returns that indicated that his income for the past 10 years had never been less than $40,000 but the lender gave him a very hard time because he had never borrowed any money and had paid cash for everything. He paid cash for his car, cash at the department stores, at the grocery store, and for travel and entertainment. But because he had never needed credit, he had no credit rating, and it took a lot of talking before he was able to get the loan he needed.

WHERE TO GET A MORTGAGE

A mortgage loan can be obtained through savings and loan associations, commercial banks, mutual savings banks, insurance companies, and mortgage brokers. If you are buying a house through a real estate broker, he may be able to suggest a good local source for a mortgage. A local attorney can also be helpful in directing you to a good source for a loan.

When mortgage money is "tight," your own bank is often the best place to go for a mortgage, if it is not too far from the property involved. Some banks and savings and loan associations won't lend money unless you happen to be a customer with a savings account or a checking account. A short while back we read a little item about an official of a bank who granted a loan to a man who had a savings account there. The man was given the loan and promptly withdrew his savings, which, it turned out, had been deposited only a few weeks before he had applied for the loan. The bank has since changed its policy and now stipulates how long an account must have been with the bank before the bank grants a loan.

If a mortgage on the property already exists, you may be able to assume this, or the seller may be willing to take back a mortgage so that you can purchase the property. The various drawbacks to this arrangement are discussed later on in this chapter.

HOW BIG A MORTGAGE DO YOU NEED?

Before you go out to look for property you should determine how much money you can put into the deal and how large a mortgage you can comfortably carry. This comes down to a matter of monthly payments. If you decide that $100 a month is your limit, use this as your guide. Go to the mortgage-loan department of your bank or any lender who writes mortgage loans and ask them to tell you the amount of the mortgage you can carry for $100, based on the length of the mortgage and the prevailing interest rates. Figure that the mortgage will cover only two-thirds of the purchase price and that you will have to come across with the remaining one-third in cash. When you take all these factors into account, you should have a pretty good idea of the price range of property at which you can look.

One other important factor to consider as far as financing goes is the matter of the money needed to make the necessary improvements. When you buy a new or conventional used house, all that you usually need is a mortgage to cover the purchase of the property, but with an OB Dream House you may need a considerable sum of money to do the renovation work. The best way to get this is with a *construction loan*, which is included with the loan to purchase the property.

SHOPPING FOR A MORTGAGE

You can't shop for a mortgage until you have found a piece of property that you want to buy. And because you are dealing with an OB Dream House, you should not try to get a mortgage until you have figured out, more or less, what you are going to do in the way of renovation to make your dreams come true and how much it will cost. Here is why: A lender can take a look at that 1967 split-level house on Rosewood Lane—a house that is surrounded by very similar houses in the same general price range—houses that sold for $22,500 in 1967. The lender can refer to his little black book and find out how much the last house on Rosewood Lane went for, he can take a quick look at the property to see if it has been well maintained, and right then and there he can tell you how much he will lend on it. Tell the same lender that you want to borrow money to buy and improve a chicken coop that has great possibilities and he is going to give you a very dim look. He may be able to figure out the value of the land that the chicken coop sits on, and he can probably figure that the value of the structure, less chickens, is around $50 but he is going to have trouble visualizing it as the place into which you plan to transform it, unless you have some definite plans to show him. He will also want to know how much money you are going to need to fix it up. Also he will want to know how long it is going to take to transform the place into a habitable dwelling.

Remember that while to you that chicken coop is the future home of your dreams, to the lender it's just a run-down chicken coop that is only worth about $50 and won't be worth more than this until the renovation work has been completed. So before you go shopping for a mortgage, have your rough plans on paper, have an estimate of how much money will be required to do the renovation work and also one of how long the work will take before completion.

You may have to shop around for a mortgage on an OB Dream House. (Indeed, it is a good idea to shop around for a mortgage on any house in this era of tight money and high interest rates.) It may be that the first lender you approach is·not one bit interested. Don't let that discourage you. Some lenders have more imagination than others, and it sometimes requires a lot of imagination when dealing with an OB Dream House. Some lenders like to take a little chance on a deal and some only play it very safe. Some lenders are OB Dream House enthusiasts and some just don't see them at all. We know of some who get tremendous delight out of taking part in the restoration of a beat-up old house, and we know of others who would say, "burn the wreck down."

You will also want to shop around to see which lender will give you the best deal. There may be only a fraction of a per cent difference in the interest rates between two lenders, but that fraction can add up to a lot of money when it is spread over twenty-five years or more. One lender might give you a larger loan than another. Lenders don't have the same policy on the amount of money they will lend on an OB Dream House, or any other house for that matter. Sometimes the amount will be based on a firm policy of the lender and sometimes it will depend on you and the property you wish to purchase. If a lender thinks you are getting a tremendous buy and that if you skipped the country he could get his money back almost overnight, he may be more interested in giving you a larger mortgage than on a property at the same selling price that no one could ever love but you.

If you are in good shape financially, if you have definite plans and costs on renovation work, and if what you intend to do in the way of improvements will make the property more attractive to others beside yourself, you are in a better position to get a satisfactory mortgage than if this were not the case.

YOU MAY NEED A CONSTRUCTION LOAN

If you are going to need considerable money to finance the renovation work as well as to purchase the house, this, as stated before, is best managed by obtaining a package mortgage that includes money toward the purchase of the house as well as money to fix it up. Arranging this kind of mortgage can be somewhat tricky. Here is a rather typical example of what you might run into in this situation. Let's say that the property is going to cost $15,000 and you figure, based on your rough plans and an estimate from a contractor, that it will take $8,000 more to fix it up. You feel that you can put $5,000 of your own money into the deal. You need an $18,000 mortgage—$10,000 for the purchase and $8,000 for the renovation work. Your friendly lender likes your plans and the estimated cost of the renovation work, and he does some quick figuring. "Here's what we'll do," he says. "The total amount of money involved is $23,000. That's $15,000 for the house and $8,000 for the improvements. I think you have a pretty good deal here. We'll go for 70 per cent—that's a $16,000 mortgage loan."

Now your problem is that when you add your $5,000 to the $16,000 from your lender you don't get $23,000. You get $21,000. And that isn't enough. You might put in more of your own money—another $1,900, or you can modify the plans for the renovation work in order to reduce some of the cost. The lender, however, may have something to say about how you shave these costs. Lenders like improvements that in their opinion will increase the value of the property and also make it easier to sell if they have to take it over. The lender might prefer that you keep the projected second bathroom and not rip out a wall to make a big country kitchen. He might prefer that you install central heating and eliminate the proposed fireplace in the downstairs bedroom.

Suppose that you are able to shave $2,000 from the cost of the renovation work. If the lender agrees with your plans and will go for that 70-per-cent loan he will give you a mortgage of $14,700 on the total of $21,000. You are still short $1,300. You will have to cut the cost of the renovation work down from $8,000 to about $2,000 before you can swing the deal with just $5,000 of your own money. If you don't believe this, figure it for yourself. Surprising, but true.

If $5,000 is your limit, you might be able to get a 70-per-cent mortgage to purchase the house at $15,000 and arrange to make the improvements out of current income or by doing a lot of the work yourself. You might be able to handle the renovation on a home-improvement loan, which is discussed later on in this chapter, but your best bet would be to find a way to raise the extra $1,900 so that you could go ahead with the complete renovation work by means of a package mortgage, which is the least expensive way to get the money and be able to get the work done the way you had originally planned and in the least amount of time.

If you get a construction loan for the renovation work, before you sign the note you should find out the manner in which this money will be made available to you. As this loan is part of the overall mortgage, it goes into effect at the time that you take title to the property. But that doesn't mean that the lender is going to hand you a fistful of money. The portion of the mortgage money that is applied to the purchase of the property will be turned over to the seller or his representative. The lender will hold onto the money for the renovation work and parcel it out to you as the work progresses. Find out if you are going to pay interest on this money from the time of the closing or only as it is used, and how much time, if any, you have to use it before you will have to pay interest on it. Some lenders will specify that at the end of a certain number of months, interest on the entire amount will be charged, even if they still have some of the money. One of the best deals we ever had was with a lender who gave us $13,000 construction mortgage and didn't seem to be in any hurry to have us use it up, or to charge us interest on anything except what had been advanced to us. This was a good arrangement, especially on a renovation job, because we didn't feel that we had to rush the work and use the money in order to avoid paying interest on money still in someone else's pocket.

When you get a satisfactory arrangement for a mortgage, ask the lender to give you a written commitment to the effect that a certain sum of money at a certain rate of interest and for a certain number of years will be available to you at the time you take title to the property. This will protect you should there be a sudden tightening of mortgage money or an increase in interest rates between the time you apply for a mortgage and the closing.

As you can see, you may need quite a lot of time to find a satisfactory mortgage for your OB Dream House.

But suppose that for all your shopping about you still can't get a satisfactory mortgage. What happens then? In such a case, the seller can, if he wishes, take back a mortgage from you to cover the purchase of the property. All he has to do is to fulfill the terms of the mortgage requirements as detailed in the agreement of sale. If the agreement is carelessly drawn from your standpoint, it might state only that the "sale is contingent on buyer obtaining a $15,000 mortgage at no more than 7½ per cent interest." In this event the seller could offer a 15-year mortgage instead of a 20- or 25-year mortgage and you would have to take it or break the agreement. Meeting the monthly payments on a short-term mortgage might be quite a hardship and, of course, with this arrangement you won't be able to get a construction loan to handle the cost of the renovation work.

We have had only one experience with a seller attempting to take back the mortgage, and it was not a pleasant one. All went well for a number of years until we decided to sell the place. The lady who held our mortgage (she was the former owner) agreed to allow the buyer to assume our mortgage under the same terms as we had had. This was a little surprising because she was a very smart cookie and our mortgage was at a far smaller interest rate than was currently available. The logical thing for her to have done was to write a new mortgage for the new buyer at the current interest rate, but she didn't do this. Instead she gave the new buyer a written commitment. Apparently she regretted her decision somewhere along the line because on the day of closing she suddenly claimed that she had not received our last payment and that we were, therefore, in default and she was going to foreclose. The buyer was in a twit, we were in even a worse twit, and our attorney was almost out of his mind. Fortunately, we had been sending the monthly payment to her bank. Our attorney rushed over to the bank and, after spending a good deal of time there, found that sure enough, our check had arrived and had been properly credited to her account.

What bothers us about this incident is that if the checks had been sent directly to this lady, she could have destroyed the final one and then, at just the right moment, could have started foreclosure proceedings. The case could have been taken to court, of course, but this would require time and money and would certainly have put the sale in limbo for a good many months. Different states have different laws regarding this sort of thing, but you are probably better off getting a mortgage through an institution than through a private individual.

If the property you want to purchase has a mortgage on it, you may be able to assume it. This means that you just take over the existing mortgage with perhaps a more favorable interest rate than you would get with a new mortgage. One drawback to this arrangement is that you still have to get money for the renovation work. Then too the existing mortgage may not be sufficient to cover your needs.

OTHER WAYS TO FINANCE RENOVATION WORK

The construction mortgage is without doubt the best and least expensive way to finance your renovation work, but it is not the only way. A second mortgage is another possibility. This is a short-term affair, usually running one, two, or five years, and has a much higher rate of interest than the first mortgage. The interest here is higher because if the holder of the first mortgage had to take over the property and sell it, he would be paid off first in full and the holder of the second mortgage would have to satisfy himself with whatever was left over. Because of the high interest rates and short term of a second mortgage, the monthly payments can play havoc with your budget.

On the other hand, if you expect to come into some money that would enable you to pay off a short-term second mortgage in the near future, such an arrangement would probably not be a bad deal.

Many banks and lending institutions have "home improvement" loans, which, while running for a much shorter term and at a higher interest rate than a construction mortgage, are good if you don't require a very extensive loan and can handle the monthly payments.

Some contracting firms have their own financing arrangements but before you get into one of these, you should study the terms of the agreement carefully to see just how much interest you are going to pay and what other carrying charges are added to the original amount required for the work. Some of these outfits can afford to do the work at near cost and make their real money out of interest and carrying charges.

FINANCING THE DOWN PAYMENT

You have now learned, we hope, that you are going to need some cash of your own to buy a house. No lender is going to give you a mortgage for 100 per cent of the selling price on any piece of property. You will need several thousand dollars to buy an OB Dream House and some of it you will need just as soon as you sign the agreement of sale. This usually calls for a 10-per-cent down payment.

You will also need a certain amount of ready cash to cover some of the items that come up with the purchase of property. You should have a cushion of several hundred dollars just for the closing. With that protection you will not be caught short by such items as the fee for your attorney, a charge perhaps by the lender for making a credit check, insurance premiums, or real estate taxes.

Some buyers have arranged to get the necessary money for the down payment through a second mortgage, but as discussed above, this is an expensive way to raise money. It may also make it difficult for you to get a primary or first mortgage because if the lender finds out that you will need a second mortgage to raise money for the down payment, he may easily come to the conclusion that you are getting in over your head and will not give you a mortgage. And you can be sure that any good lender is going to ask you where you are going to get the money for the down payment, especially if he can't find such a sizable amount itemized in your credit report. But again, if you have immediate prospects of coming into a sizable amount of money from an estate or the sale of stocks or bonds, he may decide that you are safe to play with.

Borrowing on your life insurance is one way of getting your down payment, and it's a good way because the interest rate on these loans is relatively low. If you have a sizable amount in a savings account, you can also borrow against this, or borrow against stocks and bonds.

DON'T STRETCH YOURSELF TOO THIN

Transforming any house, even a new one, into a comfortable home, costs money. There are hundreds of small items—window shades, telephone installation, drapery hardware, garden furniture, tools for outdoor work and many more—that you will have to purchase for cash or through charge accounts at local stores. If you purchase a house that is the maximum you can afford, you may have trouble getting it in really perfect shape because you just don't have the money. We suggest that in purchasing the house you do not go the limit but rather somewhat under your limit. Then you will not be strained financially and will not feel that your OB Dream House is a giant leech that leaves you constantly anemic financially.

9 Planning

Planning an OB Dream House involves two stages. If the house is going to require a considerable amount of alteration and improvement and you are going to need a construction loan as well as a loan to purchase the property, then stage-one planning should be done before you sign any sales contract. We have given the reasons for this in the chapter on "Buying the House." If you are going to finance the alterations and improvements out of your own funds but will need a mortgage to purchase the property, then you can do stage-one planning after you have signed the sales agreement. In any event, before you go out shopping for a mortgage you should have mapped out a basic plan of work to be done.

You'll need a rough idea of what you plan for the house so that you can show it to the lender and you'll need plans to show contractors so that they can give you an estimate of the amount of money required to put the house in shape.

Stage one is a rough-planning stage. You may change things around quite a lot before you get to stage two, which is the final plan, but stage one should contain all the basic essentials. For example, if heating and/or plumbing are required, they should be included in stage one. If a wing or addition has to go, or one is to be added, include this in stage

96

one. If partitions are required or existing ones must be moved, figure these also as part of stage one. If all you have bought is an exterior shell, then you'll need partitions, ceilings, heat, electricity, plumbing, kitchens—all the essentials—and these are part of stage one. This rough planning is going to take a little time and thought, but when you're shopping for a mortgage you are going to do much better if you are prepared to show what you plan in the way of improvements on the property.

Your first need is a floor plan of what you have, and this will have to be drawn up, because you seldom find existing plans for OB Houses. If you are working with an architect and he is there at the very beginning, he will draw up the plan and charge you for it. If you are alone at this stage of the game, you draw up your own floor plan. You'll need some sheets of ¼-inch graph paper, which you can get at a stationery store, and you'll also need a rule and some sharp pencils. If you expect to do most if not all of the final stage-two planning yourself, treat yourself to a triangular rule with calibrations of ⅛, ⅜, ¼, ½, ¾ of an inch and 1 inch. This is the standard rule used for architectural work and with it you can detail just about everything that is required for final working drawings. You will also need a steel measuring tape. You can get along with an 8-foot tape but if you have a big house you may also want to get a 50-foot or 100-foot tape just to save a little time.

Now draw up a plan of the entire house. As you need only a rough plan at this point, you can make your measurements on either the outside or the inside of the house, whichever seems the easiest. Get each dimension in feet and inches and don't worry about fractions of inches. After you have the dimensions, draw the plan out on your graph paper. As you have ¼-inch paper, let each square represent one foot. If a wall measures 18 feet, 6 inches, draw a line through 18½ squares.

Include as much as possible in this rough floor plan—the location and sizes of doors and windows, setbacks, and all such refinements. Once all the outside walls are on paper, measure off the rooms and put these on your plan. Include all the basic essentials in these plans. Bathrooms, if existent, should be indicated as such, along with the location of the fixtures. If there is a fireplace, draw this in, or at least indicate where it is located and its approximate size. If the building includes a second floor, indicate the location of the stairs and measure off the second floor in the same manner as you did the first. You will find in the next chapter, "The Space Planner," some of the more common symbols used in architecture and these will be helpful to you in drawing up your plans. Even if you don't have to draw up plans you might study these symbols, because these are the marks that will appear on plans drawn up by an architect or by your contractor and you should know how to read and understand their plans.

It may easily be that you have a structure for which you can make a floor plan without much time and effort. All you will probably get out of an empty barn is a drawing that shows the outside dimensions and locations of the doors and a few windows. A silo or sizable wine-storage tank is a cinch to measure. You need only find the diameter and the height.

Once you have drawn the floor plan, you are ready to make some elevations. Elevations show height, and you will need them in those areas where you plan to do extensive alterations. Your elevations give you the heights of the structure, the height of the interior walls from ceiling to floor, the height of windows and their distance from ceiling and from floor and similar information.

Now that you have the floor plan and some elevations you are almost ready to sit down and see what has to be done. But first, since you have probably already made some tentative decisions and you will want to try variations of most of them, have a dozen or more copies Photostatted or photocopied. Making these copies doesn't cost much and is well worth the effort, since you don't want to go through the whole measuring routine again and your potential lender as well as any contractor you call in will probably want to look over a set.

Now, start with the overall floor plan and see what has to be done. Get a sharp red pencil and use this to indicate changes. You can then see at a glance what is original and what is going to be removed, added, or switched about. Are you going to add space to what you have? If so, where is the addition going to go and how large is it going to be? If you are taking something off, a useless wing for instance, indicate that on the floor plan. If you are working with an open space where there are few if any partitions, start planning rooms, their size, and location. Indicate where bathrooms and kitchens are to go. If you have many changes, sketch them out roughly on plain paper and then when they're satisfactory, draw them to scale in your plan. There are established minimum dimensions for every room in the house and we list these in "The Space Planner." Remember that these are minimum dimensions. You can have a bathroom just as big as you want, but it can be only just so small.

In this stage-one planning you want to achieve a fairly comprehensive idea on paper of what is going to be required in the way of alterations. As we said before, this does not need to be the final plan. If later on you decide you prefer to install the kitchen on the west end of the structure instead of at the east end, it probably won't make a big difference in the cost of the kitchen. You do need to know now, however, that there is going to be a kitchen of approximately such and such size and that it will have roughly so many feet of cabinets and work surfaces. When these facts are established, it is not too difficult to figure out what the kitchen is going to cost.

If you are starting out with a more or less empty structure such as a warehouse or a barn, you should indicate whether a floor or floors are to be installed, where the stairs are to go, and how the empty space is to be divided into rooms. Planning to open one wall with sliding glass doors? Put that down on your plans. Need a fireplace, chimney for a heating system, some place to shelter a car, or would you like a nice big deck? Now is the time to put it all down on paper, even if you haven't worked out the exact dimensions or style.

It seems a good idea at this point to mention that with a really major remodeling or restoration job an architect is almost a must. He can save you money and time and heartaches. All of the matters pertaining to working with an architect are discussed in the following chapter on "Who Will Do the Work." Still, even with an architect, it is up to you to figure out what you want. He can help you decide and he can pull the whole project together but he can't read your mind. Therefore, although you may intend to use an architect, go through this rough planning so that you get your thoughts down on paper.

The plan itself need not necessarily detail everything you need for your renovation project. A list is sufficient for such items as a new roof, a well, a road, new exterior siding, wiring, plumbing, and painting.

Once you have your plans and your handy little list, you can talk with a few general contractors and go over the house with them so that you can get an estimate as to the cost of the work you intend to do. You can then go to the bank or lender with your plans and list, plus the estimate, and hope for the best. This is assuming that you need money to make the improvements as well as to buy the house. The banker or lender will look over what you plan to do in the way of improvements and you can tell him from the estimates about how much this will cost. He'll want to know how much money you want to borrow to purchase the property and naturally he is going to look into your financial state quite carefully. The chances are awfully good that he won't give you all the money you need to do everything you have planned to do.

Perhaps you have found a piece of property that you can get for $15,000; you can put $5,000 of your own money up so you need a $10,000 mortgage. The place needs a lot done to it and the estimate based on your rough plan comes to about $9,000. What you need is $19,000 from the lender. He doesn't want to go that far. He'll go for $15,000 and that's all. As described earlier, in such situations you have a choice of putting up more of your own money or reworking your plans and eliminating some items to reduce the cost of restoration—in this case from $9,000 to $5,000. But you will still have to keep the lender in mind, because lenders consider some improvements more essential than others. Lenders consider a second bathroom more essential than something else you may have set your heart on, such as a wine cellar or an outdoor enclosure for nude sunbathing. They may consider a modern, fully equipped kitchen more desirable than a sunken tub or a little cottage for weekend guests. They think more kindly about sinking money into a modern heating system than about putting their cash into teakwood cabinets, so that "John will at last have the right place to put his shell collection."

If you've kept pace with us up to this point, you have just about covered stage one in planning. It has taken time but you have begun to get your thoughts pulled together. You have enough information to have worked out a fairly realistic estimate of how much the work is going to cost so that you can arrange to get all or part of the money required. When you take title to the property you'll know the general direction in which you are going, will have a good idea of what the cost, and, last but not least, you'll have floor plans and elevations to work from. Now you get into planning—"stage two."

This is the point at which you don't want to hurry. You want to study every option that there may be. You want all the ideas you can get, because only by playing with them and discarding will you eventually come up with something quite special for yourself and your family.

Here's where those extra copies of the floor plans are going to come in handy, because you are going to want to fool around with a lot of ideas on paper. Draw your ideas out on the plans, walk around the areas and try to visualize how that wall would look there, how that door would be if it were moved over to here, what sort of traffic pattern you would have if the stairs were moved or built here and the kitchen moved over to there. This is a nice time to have an architect around, for he is trained to visualize easily. For some people it's hard work, and others just can't visualize at all. But the longer you spend fooling around with the plan and trying to apply it to the actual house, the better off you'll be.

We heartily suggest that you live in the place if you can and just as long as possible before you actually get down to work doing anything of a major nature. In "What to Do First" we will tell you how you can even camp on your property for a time until you get your plans set. It is extremely important for you to spend a lot of time in the place before you begin remodeling. You'll find that suddenly someone will come up with a smashing and most practical solution to a problem that until that minute appeared insoluble.

We had some friends who picked up a large two-story garage on a big estate that was being divided. The structure was set into a hill and was not too far away from a busy road, which created a problem because a living room would look out onto the road or the hill and neither offered a very desirable view. Our friends spent days moving their living room all around but no matter where they put it, it didn't work; and then one day the answer came to them: They put the living room and kitchen upstairs, where there was a great view, and the bedrooms and baths downstairs, where a view wasn't all that essential.

Keep an open mind when planning the renovation of an OB House. Talk out every conceivable solution to a problem no matter how far out and crazy some of the ideas may seem. And don't keep gnawing away at the same old bone. When something isn't right and you can't seem to find the right solution, get away from that problem for a few days. Let your subconscious do a little work. Perhaps the next time you come back to that problem you'll have a new and perfect solution. This is a sort of "new think" and it works.

Don't hesitate to pick up ideas from anyone who has a good one. Get your friends, and even relatives, to come out and view the place; see what they suggest. Friends with a keen sense of form and design are very good friends to have at a time like this. Artists, photographers, designers—interior, industrial, or fashion, it doesn't matter—all can make most interesting contributions in the way of original ideas. And once you own an OB Dream House you are in the market for ideas. Even if you plan to have an architect, you'll want to contribute some ideas of your own or it will be his house rather than yours when it is finished.

You can get some great ideas from seeing what others have done. We don't mean that you want to copy others, but seeing what someone else has done can often spark your imagination and get your creative juices flowing. Study pictures of houses. Pictures of the outside of houses and the inside of houses. Pictures of big houses and little houses, of barns, stairs, windows, kitchens, bathrooms, fences, cupboards and closets, terraces, and just about everything else you can get your hands on that is related to housing. You should start looking through the home-service magazines that devote so much space to houses, rooms, and decorating. When you find something of interest, tear it out and file it for future reference. Libraries, too, have fine reference books. You might also want to purchase some of the excellent books that are published from time to time showing outstanding houses—traditional as well as contemporary. Pay attention to the home or real estate section of your newspaper. Many of the companies that make products for the home offer booklets that contain worthwhile ideas; write in for these for they are worth mulling over.

Set up a file of the various categories in which you expect to be involved. A file for kitchen ideas, one for bathrooms, others for windows, flooring, hardware, stairs, additions, fireplaces. These files will not only help you in planning but will be of great help when you sit down with an architect or with a contractor. It's easier to show a picture of what you have in mind than to try to explain it in words. And if you plan to do the whole job yourself, it helps if you have a picture in front of you, showing the general idea.

You are going to need product ideas as well as creative ideas. Residential construction is a huge field, with as many people making different manufactured parts as there are individual items in the house. There are, in fact, so many different products, with new ones coming on the market all the time, that no one, not even a busy architect, can keep up with them all, although architects are much more apt to be innovative than contractors. The contractor will usually stick with those products with which he is familiar and which have given him good results in the past. This is certainly sensible but it may mean that he is not likely to use something available that would be just right for your particular needs. It is up to you to know what is available and ask for it.

So, once again, go back to your home-service magazines and to your newspapers, read the sections carrying advertisements for building products and materials and write in for more information and booklets. It may be a skylight, a spiral staircase, a new color or texture in flooring, bathroom fixtures, or stain for woodwork—whatever catches your fancy or seems practical. Some of these items, of course, can be seen at local lumberyards or building-supply houses, but you should visit various ones because each handles certain lines exclusively and it is difficult to get information from them on competitive products. Contractors usually deal with a particular lumberyard where they have long-established credit and tend to use the products handled by that yard. So visit a number of lumberyards and building-supply houses to see what is available. If you live in or near a large city you may find that there is an architect's or designer's display building where a variety of products can be seen. These centers usually also have on hand a great deal of literature on building products. If you can't find such a center listed in your telephone book, call any architect or interior decorator and they can probably tell you where one is located.

It is most important that you learn as much as you can about what products are available, because unless you do and then insist on getting what you want, you will get what the architect, the general contractor, or the subcontractor decides to use. This is particularly true with plumbing, because the plumbing subcontractor is often the retailer for a certain brand of fixtures and that brand is what he will give you unless you specify that you wish to use something else. He may rumble a little because he may not get the same markup using the brand that you want but that's his problem, not yours. We go into a considerable detail on the subject of plumbing fixtures in the chapter "Plumbing."

All this collecting of ideas and products takes time, and you really should get at this chore the minute you become serious about acquiring an Offbeat Dream House. Many people collect ideas for years before they purchase or build a house. By the time they are ready to go out to look and to buy, they have a complete file on everything they want.

Let's get back to "stage two"—making the final, or working, plan that includes all the basics, plus product and materials specifications. If you are working with an architect, stage two is part of his job, so it doesn't have to concern you. If you don't have an architect, you'll have to handle it yourself. You'll have to draw up your own plans in sufficient detail so as to include all the essentials, plus specifications. This is not the easiest thing for an amateur to do, and if you make a mistake it's on your head, not the contractor's. But even if your plans and specifications are not perfect, the chances of not getting what you want will be fewer than if there are no plans and specifications at all and you are just playing the job by ear. No matter how you plan to do the job, whether working through a general contractor, individual subcontractors working under your supervision, or doing the job yourself, the more detailed your plans are, the better for you.

You are going to have several sets of plans. The first set is the overall plan you have already made, showing room dimensions, location and size of windows and doors, and the like. Say you have an empty space that is to be made into a living room. Your plan shows the room size and the location of the doors and windows. Very good, so far. If there is to be a fireplace, where does it go and what sort of fireplace are you planning. Is it to be of brick or stone or is it to be a free-standing metal fireplace? If it is to be of masonry, do you want the masonry exposed to the ceiling or covered above the mantel? What sort of mantel is to be used? What size and what material for the hearth? You indicate windows on the plan but what type of window? Double hung, casement, awning, or sliding? What materials are to be used for the walls? Gypsum wallboard, plywood, or wood paneling? As you can see, a great many decisions must be made and put on paper, either on the plan or on the specifications, but it's really not all that difficult a task because at this stage of the game, if you have done your homework you should have an excellent idea of just about every item you want to include in your project. But to make sure that you don't forget anything, at the end of this chapter we've placed a check list of items that you should specify. Just remember that if you don't, they may not be included.

Most of this information doesn't have to be drawn on the plan—just write down the specifications. Pick the style of door you wish to use from a catalogue provided by the manufacturer, contractor, or building-supply house and write down, "so and so's door No. 10036B. Use YCH brand hardware, style No. 194–36B," and that's that. The paper with all this information should be attached to the plans. Keep a copy for yourself, so that as the work progresses you can make sure that your decisions are being carried out and that someone is not going off on his own. By the way, watch for substitutions over the telephone. You may get a call one day from the contractor telling you that it will take three weeks to get delivery on the item you wanted because of a trucking strike. The same item is made by another outfit and the lumberyard has this in stock, the contractor reports, so it could be picked up immediately. Well, maybe it's exactly the same as the item you specified and maybe it's not.

On one house I renovated I had a problem of this sort involving a door. I had ordered two panel doors to match the existing ones but something went wrong and they never arrived. The carpenter called me to say he could pick up a couple of doors that were almost an exact match with the ones I had specified. I said, "Go ahead," and now have two doors that do not match the rest of the doors in the house. There are, indeed, panel doors, but the size and design of the panels are not the same as that of the old ones. Close but not the same. The carpenter had said that they were "almost an exact match," but I should have listened to the "almost." His idea of exact was one thing and my idea was something else again.

Go over every room, every hall, every corner, and cranny, putting down as much detailed information as you possibly can. Of course, a good contractor or carpenter will help you, because once he realizes that you want it done just right and done your way, he'll start asking what you want here and what you want there, and if you use the check list we have provided you should be in good shape.

You'll need to go into just as much detail if you plan to do the work yourself. Don't try to play it by ear, because it's going to take much longer and will be much more difficult and probably far more expensive even though your labor is free. We had friends who bought an old icehouse and went to work fixing it up themselves. Maybe you don't know much about icehouses but among the things they don't have, for obvious reasons, are windows. So one of the first things our friends did was to make openings in the walls for windows. They framed the openings just right and then went out to get some window units. The only trouble was that no one made a window unit that came even close to fitting the openings they had made. You can do one of two things in such a case. Either get custom-made window units that cost a whale of a lot more than standard units, or rework the openings so that they would take a standard unit. As our friends with the icehouse were doing the job on a tight budget, they went to work and reframed the openings, which incidentally also involved patching the siding. A little planning and checking ahead would have saved them a lot of extra work.

This brings us to another element that involves careful planning: manufacturers' specifications. A great many of the products that you will use are manufactured items. Plumbing fixtures, kitchen sinks, dishwashers, heating plants, kitchen ranges, refrigerators, washing machines, doors, windows, and exhaust fans all are manufactured and therefore come only in certain sizes. There may be a range of sizes but the range isn't all that great. Before you can plan in great detail you have to know the exact size of the unit to be used, or you will find that you have allowed too little or too much space. After you have determined the products you plan to use, get the specification sheets for that particular unit from your local dealer or distributor, or from the manufacturer. These will tell you exactly how much space is required. We're giving you a check list on this too so you'll have the information on hand when you need it and won't forget anything.

▶ *Check List: Manufactured Items*

Here is a list of the principal manufactured items that may be included in a restoration. You should look around to see what is available and make your selection as to the brand, style, and color you wish to use in your house.

Bathrooms
1. Fixtures: bathtub, lavatory, water closet, and shower stall
2. Accessories: towel rods, soap dishes
3. Wall tile or wall covering
4. Flooring
5. Lighting fixtures
6. Exhaust fan

Kitchen
1. Range
2. Sink
3. Refrigerator and/or freezer
4. Dishwasher
5. Counter tops
6. Cabinets
7. Hardware
8. Flooring
9. Exhaust fan
10. Lighting fixtures

General

1. Doors
2. Fireplace and fireplace equipment
3. Flooring
4. Hardware: interior and exterior
5. Heating system
6. Hot-water heater
7. Interior woodwork
8. Laundry equipment
9. Lighting fixtures: inside and outside
10. Ornamental ironwork
11. Paints and finishes: interior and exterior
12. Roofing
13. Shutters
14. Siding
15. Skylight
16. Wall systems
17. Windows

You should also have a separate set of plans for the electrical wiring, the heating, and the plumbing. Detailed instructions for working these out are given in the chapters on "Heating," "Plumbing," and "Wiring" because they involve a great deal of background information you should have. This chapter would become rather lengthy if we tried to include it all here, however.

To sum up: Take your time to pull your ideas and thoughts together and make your plans as clear and as detailed as you possibly can. Put everything down on paper that isn't included in the plans. Refer to the minimum-room-size chart at the end of this chapter so that you don't waste your time trying to fit a kitchen into a space where a kitchen can't be fitted.

Use the check lists we've provided and don't be afraid to add items to them in the event that we've left something out that applies to your special situation. The late Mies Van der Rohe once said, "God is in the detail." Let this be your watchword in planning your OB renovation.

The Space Planner 10

The Space Planner will help you achieve both maximum and efficient use of the interior space you now have or are planning to create. Achieving the perfect floor plan is usually the result of experimenting with many different approaches and concepts until you finally arrive at the one that is the most attractive and the most suitable for you. Even an experienced architect does not expect to come up with the perfect floor plan on the first attempt. He will make many rough sketches of various approaches to the problem, discard some ideas, modify others, until he finally comes up with a solution that pleases him. This is exactly the procedure you should follow in working up plans for your own house. Even if you intend to consult an architect, you will be wise to take the time to go through some of these preliminary planning steps first. If you have carefully thought out your basic requirements and have these on paper, it will make your discussions with the architect more productive.

The first stage of planning is, in a way, the most difficult, because you are dealing with concepts only. You, too, will want to make a great many rough sketches because only by putting a concept down on paper can you tell if it is really good.

Begin with a rough floor plan of the house. If you don't have several copies of the plan, use tracing paper so that you can overlay on the existing plan and draw your ideas on the tracing paper.

If you are working with an empty shell, such as a barn, your basic floor plan has to show only the primary dimensions—width and length of the area involved—and the location of any doors and windows that might be or are definitely to be retained.

If you are renovating a house that is not a shell, then the basic floor plan should contain not only the location of any exterior doors and windows that are to be retained, but also the location of existing interior partitions. Indicate which partitions are load bearing, if you have that information at this stage. The location of these load-bearing walls will have some control over how you can rearrange the space. Also indicate the position of any items that can be moved only at considerable expense, such as bathrooms, kitchen, fireplace, and chimney.

Begin the rough-planning operation by drawing freehand circles on the plan to indicate the general areas you wish to have. If you want a large living area, draw a large circle to indicate the location and general size of the living room in its relationship to the other areas or other rooms. Draw another circle to indicate the general size and location of the kitchen, the dining area, the bathroom, and bedrooms. Keep the sizes of your circles more or less in relationship to the actual size of all the rooms involved. A living room or family room are usually considerably larger than the average kitchen or bedroom. A bathroom will be smaller than a bedroom and a lavatory will be smaller than a full bathroom. You don't have to worry about exact dimensions at this point—that will come later on.

Once you have drawn up a few of these very rough sketches you will begin to get a good idea of just how many rooms you can get into a given space. If you have a relatively small area with which to work and you take a large chunk for the living area, then you probably won't have much room for anything except basics—a kitchen, lavatory, and possibly a dining area. You will need to discard the idea of a first-floor master bedroom suite unless you want to reduce the size of the living area quite drastically.

As you sketch out these general areas, keep in mind their location in respect to the structure and the land. If one area of the house offers a lovely view, this might be the obvious place to put the living room. And while it is nice to have a pleasant view from a bedroom, the primary consideration here is quiet and privacy. The kitchen should be located so that it offers easy access to the garage or parking area. If you have a nice view here, so much the better.

Again, if you are working with a shell, you have a good deal of freedom as to where to place your areas to best advantage. With an existing structure that is finished on the inside, your placement of various areas is often controlled not only by the location of the load-bearing partitions but also by existing facilities. The decision to move an existing kitchen to another area rests between you and your budget. To move a living room from the east side to the west side may not be much of a problem but moving a kitchen or bathroom can become expensive because of the plumbing lines involved. Unless you intend to gut the entire inside of the house and start off from scratch, rearranging the existing floor plan requires certain compromises between what you want and what already exists.

As you try these rough sketches, keep in mind also the relationship between the various areas. Try to imagine how people can move from one area to another without having to take a 5-mile hike. At the same time, try to plan the traffic flow so that no one has to walk through the seating area in the living room to get from the kitchen to a bedroom or bath. The ideal arrangement is a plan that permits you to reach any area of the house without disturbing others to get there. This can be achieved, but it takes careful planning.

Play around with the circles until you arrive at an area relationship that is harmonious and pleasant. When you have it, go on to the next stage, which involves translating these freehand drawings into actual room sizes on the basic floor plan. These room dimensions do not have to be exact, but you should use a scale ruler or ¼-inch graph paper so that they measure out in feet. Indicate the location of windows, doors, and other breaks in walls, and then see what you have. Now you should be able to get an excellent picture of how much space you can allot to the various rooms. Perhaps you were a little too optimistic about the amount of space you actually have available and you will have to eliminate something, or a particular area will have to be reduced. If this is the case, go back to your circles again and come up with another concept.

You will also now have a chance to study the traffic pattern more closely to see exactly how it will work. If you have a front door opening into the living room, it could create an impossible traffic pattern and cut down the usable space in the living room considerably, not to mention the drafts that might be a part of the arrangement. You may find that the only way to get out the back door is to go straight through the kitchen, which is not good if there are children, dogs, and cats in the family. Do you really have a dining room or a dining area, or do you just have a dining room table set up in an oversized hall? Is the downstairs bathroom or lavatory located so that someone can gracefully disappear into it or does it open right onto the dining area or the living room? Can you reach all bedrooms without having to pass through an adjoining bedroom or bath?

Take your pencil and draw little traffic lanes on the plan. Try to visualize how the various members of the household will move about not only inside the house but from the house to the outdoors. Don't be dismayed if your first attempts are not ideal. They seldom are—even those in the final drawings of outstanding houses.

Some years ago we went to a press party to be on hand at the unveiling of a scale model of an extremely expensive modern house that had been commissioned by a leading manufacturer of building materials and designed by a well-known architectural firm. The roof had been removed from the model of the house so that everyone could study the interior, and there was a good deal of "oohing" and "aahing" and comments about "brilliant concept" and "total living environment." Then, for a second, the chatter died down and a young lady who obviously didn't know a thing about architecture queried in a plaintive voice, "How do you take the garbage out of the kitchen without having to walk across the entire living room?" She had a good point. Not only was there no way to do it without going through the living room, but it would be necessary also to go through the front entry, through the front door, and then around to the side of the house where one might hope after all this walking to find a garbage can.

If you are working with an existing house, you must also study your plan to see how many partitions you are going to have to remove to achieve the results you wish. If you have kept those load-bearing partitions in mind during the circle-planning operation, you should not have a problem, but, if you neglected to take them into account, review the contractor's bid. You may want to make some drastic adjustments to avoid having to remove any more of these partitions than is absolutely necessary.

Next, study the plan to see just how much usable space you have in each room, or area, and whether it is sufficient to make the room functional. Remember that you can never get total use out of the entire square footage in any given area. Every room in a house must have a means of access and egress, which means a door, an archway, or an opening of some sort, and any one of these will remove a certain number of square footage from the area involved. A hinged or swinging door is going to take up more space than a sliding door, but, as you can see, you lose space where there is any opening in a room. Windows, too, unless placed high on a wall, take away floor space as well as wall space.

You must also allow sufficient space for people to move around in a room and make comfortable use of the furnishings. There should, for example, be enough space in front of a chest of drawers so that drawers can be pulled out to their complete depth. A room for pleasant living will not and should not be as compact as the interior of a submarine. There must be breathing space and people space.

Now comes the moment of truth. Is this dream home you have created on paper really going to work? Will these rooms hold standard-sized people and accommodate standard-sized furnishings?

Fortunately, most of the equipment that goes into a house comes in more or less standard sizes. Even people, who come in many sizes and shapes, do conform to certain standards for human beings just as a kitten or an elephant conforms to certain standards for kittens and elephants. Because the human adult is a standard, it is possible to set up standards for the objects we use. A kitchen counter, for example, will be 36 inches high because this is a comfortable working height for most people. The counter will be about 25 inches wide because this is a comfortable reach for most people. The standard-sized bed is 72 inches long. If you install a pole in a closet at a height that is 50 inches from the floor, it will be at about the right height for holding the garments of most adults. All manufactured items that go into a house come in standard sizes.

STANDARD SPECIFICATIONS FOR HOUSE INTERIORS

So that you can check your planning in advance here are some of the standards that have been developed.

Bathrooms.   The minimum area required for a bathroom with three fixtures is 7 feet, 3 inches, by 4 feet, 9 inches, or 5 feet, 7 inches, by 5 feet, 8 inches. There are, of course, variations of these dimensions but if you have less space than the square footage indicated, you won't have space for a full bath. It will help you to determine the usability of the space you have allotted if you draw in the fixtures to scale. The average water closet will be about 29½ inches deep, and the width of the tank, which is the widest part of the unit, will be about 22½ inches. Bathtubs run from 4 feet to 5 feet, 6 inches, in length and are 2 feet, 7 inches wide. The minimum size for a stall shower is about 30 inches square, and a small lavatory or wash basin will run about 12 inches square. You will also need at least 1 foot, 6 inches, from the outside edge of the water closet to the nearest wall or fixture, and you will need this same minimum distance between the outside edge of the lavatory and the nearest wall or fixture. A two-fixture lavatory will have to be at least 4 feet by 4 feet, 7 inches. In short, you not only must have space to accommodate the fixtures but some left over for you.

In planning a bathroom you must take into consideration the location of windows, doors, medicine cabinets, towel rods, and general storage space. All these require space.

Kitchens. Here we have a situation similar to that in the bathroom in that most of the equipment is fixed and it is all necessary. You may be able to dispense with a grand piano in the living room if you find that you are short of space, but you can't very well have a kitchen without a sink or a range.

Most of the equipment that goes into a kitchen will run about 25 inches in depth. This includes base cabinets, counters, ranges, built-in ovens, dishwashers, and sinks. Refrigerators and freezers will usually run a little more than this. A range will run from 24 inches to 48 inches in width, and a dishwasher about 24 inches.

The average-sized family will require about 40 square feet of storage space in the kitchen for cooking utensils, china, and glassware.

While your kitchen will no doubt be carefully planned down to the last personal detail, the general information given here will get you off to the right start. Sketch in these general dimensions, then see if you have enough space for anything else that you may wish to include.

Dining Areas. Too many dining rooms and dining areas are planned around the idea that the chairs are always going to be placed up against the table, and this doesn't allow much room for anyone to sit on the chairs. You need an area at least 10 feet square for a dining room that will accommodate 6 people and this does not allow any space for any furniture other than the table and chairs. If you want to plan a more spacious dining area, figure a 2-foot minimum distance when a chair is pulled out from the table to the wall. This is tight but it does mean that someone can move around the table to serve or get something out of a cabinet without having everyone pull their chairs and tummies up against the edge of the table.

Bedrooms. If you want a bedroom for sleeping and not much else, you can get along with a space 12 feet by 8 feet for a single bed. This will allow for a very minimum amount of furniture and a little closet space. For a double bed, the overall size of the room should be 12 feet by 13 feet—minimum.

Figure that you need at least 3 feet of clearance between one side of the bed and the wall, the closet, or a piece of furniture—and this is tight. We can remember only one bedroom we ever slept in that met this miserable minimum requirement and that was a hotel bedroom in Chicago that cost us $26.50 for the night. Grand larceny.

If you don't want to have twin beds side by side, they should be at least 18 inches apart, which allows just enough room for a thin person to get between them to make them up. A standard bedroom chest of drawers is about 21 inches deep, and if a closet is going to be built into the room rather than recessed in the wall, figure that it will be about 24 inches deep.

Closets.   You can get along with a closet that is only 20 inches deep, but it will be extremely tight. We prefer 24 inches as a minimum depth, and 30 inches is even better, if you can afford the space. If a closet is going to have a single hinged door, keep the closet not much more than 48 inches wide. If the closet is going to be wider than this, then use two hinged doors, folding doors, or sliding doors so that you will be able to reach all the articles in the closet without making it a major production.

Living Rooms.   Living rooms involve so many variables that it is impossible to give a minimum size. The only way to determine whether or not you have sufficient space for your living room is to figure out what furniture you are going to put into it and then see how the situation works for space. Most upholstered furniture—chairs and sofas—will be about 32 inches deep. A large chair will be about 40 inches wide, a love seat about 54 inches, and a sofa about 80 inches. Figure that you need at least 3 feet of space to be able to walk comfortably between, around, or in back of most furniture.

If you apply these minimum standards to the plans you have drawn, you will know if your allotment of space is feasible. The next step is to take your plans to the house and start the business of trying to visualize how well they work in actuality.

HOW TO GO ABOUT IT

Stretch your creative-design muscles and see how many different approaches to these three examples—a vacation house, a farm house, and a barn—you can develop.

■ VACATION HOUSE

What is the best way to enlarge a typical two-bedroom vacation house **or** cottage into a comfortable year-round house?

RIGHT: An inexpensive approach to renovation would be to make the additions at the rear to provide space for another bedroom and to install a second bath adjoining the existing one, leaving the kitchen-dining-living-room area alone.

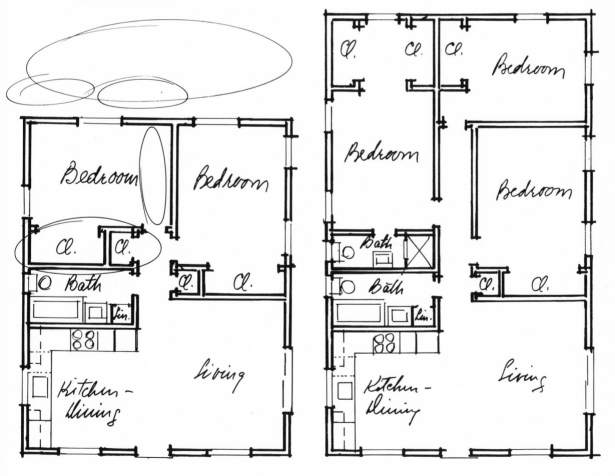

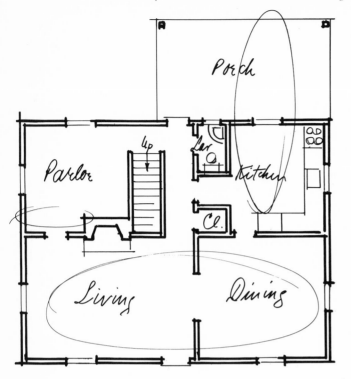

■ FARMHOUSE

Here is the first-floor plan of a rather typical farmhouse. The problem centers on how to utilize the space at the least cost to provide a more spacious and contemporary feeling.

One solution here involves removing the partition between living and dining rooms to create one large room. Door from living room into old parlor was closed up to provide more wall space around fireplace. Part of existing outside porch was enclosed to provide additional space for large kitchen. Note that the only major structural change beside enclosing some of porch was removal of load-bearing partition between living room and dining room. Fireplace, stairs, lavatory, and kitchen plumbing were not disturbed. How would you rework the space?

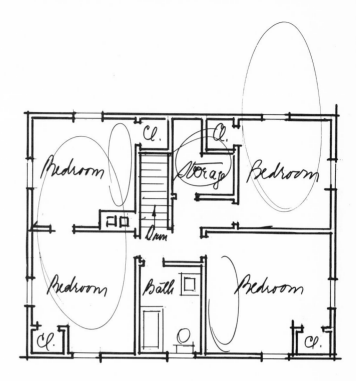

Second floor of house had four small bedrooms and only one bath. How could this space be put to better use?

One approach would be elimination of one bedroom because the old parlor on the first floor has been converted into a bedroom. With one bedroom out of the way, a master bedroom adjoining a bath was possible. Rear bedroom was enlarged by adding to it over the space that was added to the kitchen directly below. Rearrangement of closets and storage space created area for second bathroom.

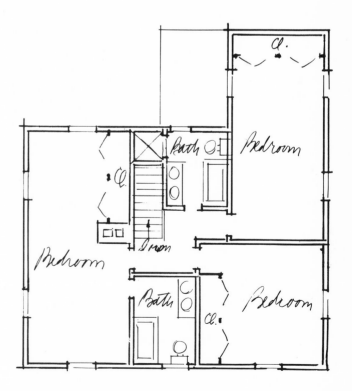

■ BARNS

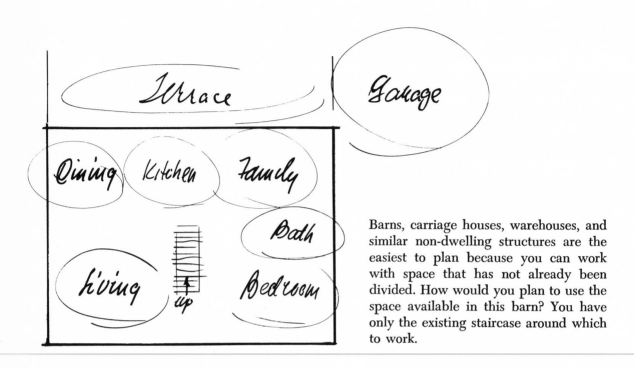

Barns, carriage houses, warehouses, and similar non-dwelling structures are the easiest to plan because you can work with space that has not already been divided. How would you plan to use the space available in this barn? You have only the existing staircase around which to work.

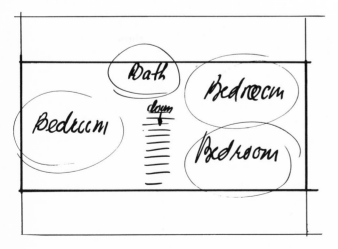

Second floor of barn is somewhat smaller than first floor; stairs divide the area into two equal parts.

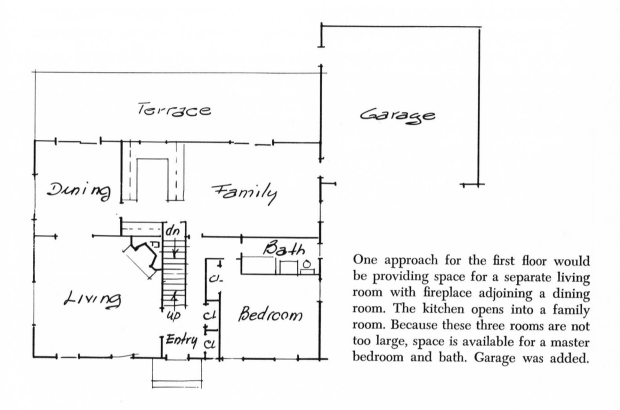

One approach for the first floor would be providing space for a separate living room with fireplace adjoining a dining room. The kitchen opens into a family room. Because these three rooms are not too large, space is available for a master bedroom and bath. Garage was added.

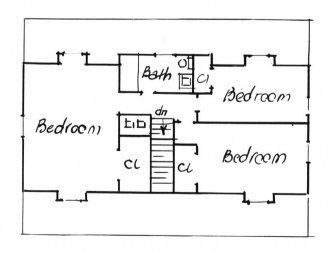

Existing space on second floor works out to provide areas for three bedrooms and a bath. This floor can be used for children and guests as there is the master bedroom on the first floor.

DETAILED ROOM PLANNER

These illustrations give you the minimum requirements for various rooms in the house. If your plan concept does not provide the necessary space, go back to the drawing board.

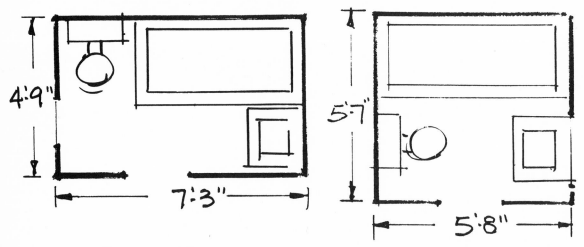

■ BATHROOMS

A full bath can be installed in a space 4 feet, 9 inches, by 7 feet, 3 inches or 5 feet, 7 inches, by 5 feet, 8 inches. These are minimum dimensions, and placement of doors and windows is an important factor in determining whether spaces with these dimensions will do the trick.

■ LAVATORY

A lavatory or powder room can fit into a space 4 feet by 4 feet, 7 inches, or 3 feet by 6 feet. It may be necessary to use the more compact fixtures, especially the lavatory, or it may be necessary to use fixtures designed for corner installation.

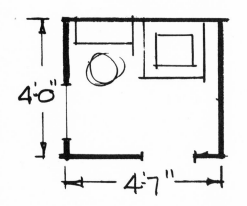

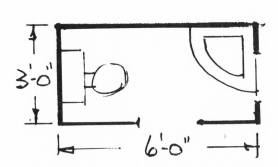

■ KITCHENS

Kitchens come in a wide variety of sizes and shapes, but the kitchen must be sufficient to accommodate the basic equipment, such as ranges, sinks, and work counters. It should also provide space in which to move about. Dimensions of kitchen plans shown are minimum and consequently cannot be reduced without eliminating an essential item or creating a kitchen so compact that it is impossible to work in it with any degree of comfort.

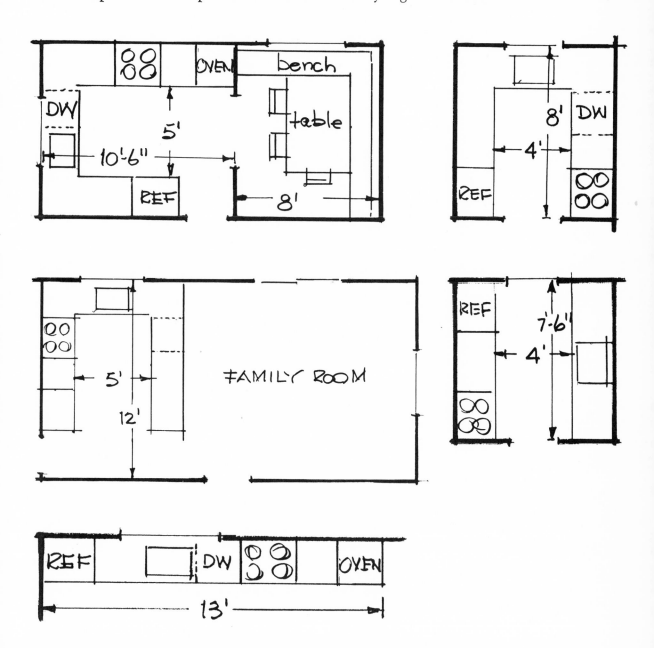

■ DINING ROOMS

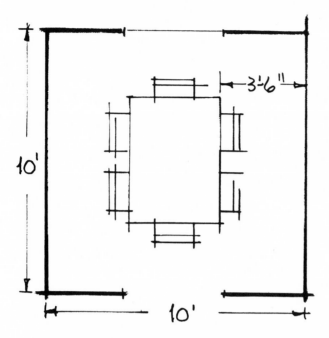

Plan the size of the dining room according to the maximum number of people who will be at the table. Illustration shows minimum-sized room that can accommodate 6 persons. Space between the table and walls or pieces of furniture set against walls should measure at least 3 feet, 6 inches. This will provide 2 feet of clearance between chair and wall when chair is occupied.

■ CLOSETS

Closets with single hinged door should not be wider than 4 feet, or reaching garments at either end of closet will be difficult. For closets more than 4 feet in width, use folding or sliding doors or two hinged doors. While the minimum depth of a closet is 1 foot, 6 inches, a 2-foot depth is more desirable.

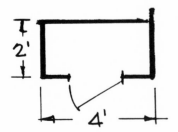
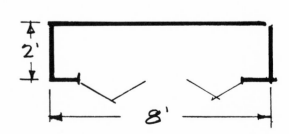

■ BEDROOMS

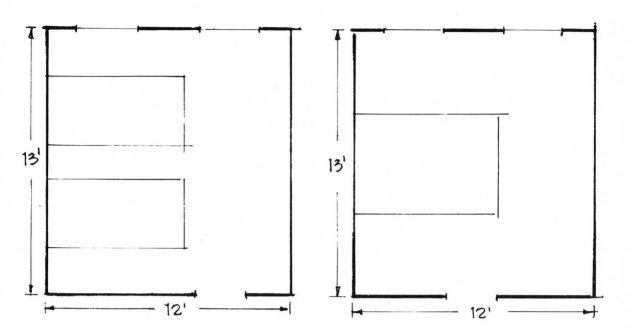

Minimum dimensions are shown for bedroom with twin beds, double bed, and single bed. These minimum dimensions will allow space for closets and also for bedroom furniture.

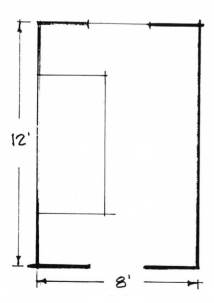

■ LIVING ROOMS

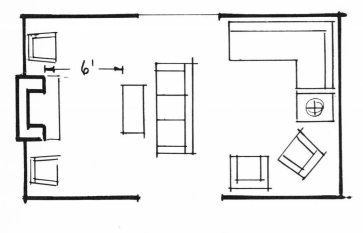

In planning the amount of space for a living room or family room with a fireplace, figure that you need at least 6 feet from the fireplace hearth to the nearest piece of furniture that is to be placed before the fireplace. If less space is provided, the heat from the fireplace will be too great for the person sitting on the chair or couch.

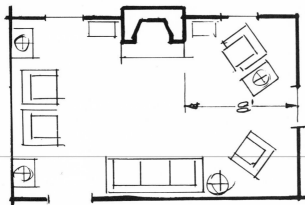

If you wish to have furniture set off to one or both sides of the fireplace, then you need 8 feet between the side or sides of the fireplace and the wall.

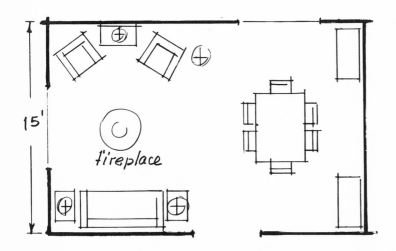

fireplace

If there is to be a free-standing fireplace in the center, a room must be at least 15 feet in width to allow for furniture to be placed around the fireplace.

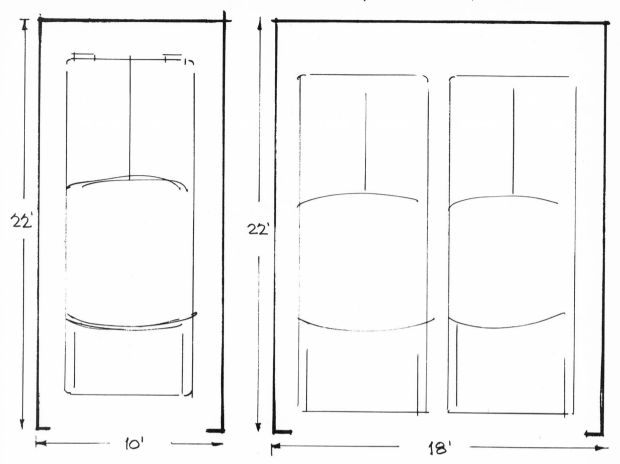

■ GARAGES

A standard-sized car will fit into a garage that is 22 feet by 10 feet. Two cars require a space 22 feet by 18 feet. These dimensions provide no space for storage in the garage, and getting in and out of cars when they are in garage is a tight squeeze.

11 Who is Going to Do the Work?

Who does the work of renovating a house depends on how much and what type of work is to be done, how much money and time are available, and how much of the work you can and are willing to do yourself.

You may, of course, be among the lucky few who pick up an OB Dream House that doesn't require any work whatsoever except perhaps a little interior painting or wallpapering. There are some of these about, but not many. Some years back we became interested in a lovely Victorian house owned by an engineer who was being transferred to another state. This place was in beautiful condition, mint condition, if you please. You would have been hard pressed to spend $10 on that house. We have always regretted not having bought this place, but it was just a little too expensive for us, because among the many assets was a heating system with controls designed for United States destroyers, impressive and very sensitive. It was lovely to think that you could change the inside temperature from 70.34 degrees to 70.86 degrees. But houses like these are exceptional and you should, therefore, assume that anything you buy is going to require work. Let us explore some of the ways that this work can be done and by whom.

THE ARCHITECT

The easiest, fastest, and probably the best way to restore a house is to commission an architect to handle the job for you. It can also be, but not always, the most expensive approach. You and your architect go over the place and you tell him what you have in mind. If you don't know what you have in mind, if you have no idea as to what to do with the place, he'll work up various approaches and eventually he'll come up with something that suits your precise needs. Even if you do have very definite ideas as to what you want done, he'll make suggestions and very likely improve on what you had in mind. If he is good, he will come up with some new thoughts that might be even less expensive than your original ideas. After some general discussions, the architect will make rough drawings and after you and he have pulled these apart and then come to a final agreement, he will produce finished working drawings on the work to be done. The architect will also help you in the selection of materials to be used, colors, and so forth.

Once the final plans have been approved by you, the architect will ask various contractors to bid on the job and he will help you determine which bid to accept. It may not always be the lowest bid because the architect is also interested in the quality of the workmanship and the reliability of the contractor. The architect will supervise the work and handle all dealings with the contractor. Once you have approved the plans you can take off for Europe or Asia and you can stay away until the job in finished and the place is ready for you to move in. An architect will charge you about 20 per cent of the total construction costs as his fee. In other words, if the cost of the construction is $10,000, you will have to pay the architect about $2,000 for his services.

If you have the money and considerable work needs to be done in terms of concept and planning, using an architect has definite advantages. The first is that he has a trained eye and mind and can see solutions to problems that you or even a good contractor can't visualize. He will see the big picture as well as the little picture and see that they both come together and in harmony. He'll be able to suggest new materials and methods that your contractor may not know about, and because you will have seen the final working drawings, you will know in advance just what the finished job will look like.

An architect will also help make the job go along smoothly and quickly, especially if the contractor selected is one with whom the architect has worked in the past. An architect can apply subtle pressure on a contractor that an ordinary individual cannot. The architect will have other jobs coming up that the contractor may be interested in; therefore the contractor is going to try to keep that architect happy. This is no small consideration, especially when time is a factor, for contractors, like so many of us, have a habit of starting a job and then letting it drag along while they become involved in other projects.

An architect will make sure that the work is done according to his plans and specifications. On any sizable undertaking, mistakes can happen and plans are not always followed to the exact letter. To correct these mistakes costs money, and the contractor is usually not too anxious to redo the work if he can avoid it. He may be able to talk the individual out of insisting on the change but he can't do the same with the architect.

Of course, you don't have to use the total services of the architect. You can make an arrangement with him only to draw up the plans, and then you carry on from there, either selecting your own contractor and supervising his work yourself or doing all or part of the job yourself. Here we are talking about a lot less money than if the architect supervised the entire job. You may be able to get just what you require for a few hundred dollars or so. And this is certainly worth spending if you have a problem place and just can't seem to come up with the right concept or design yourself.

The great trouble with using an architect, other than the money involved, is finding one who is good and who is interested in restoration work. Your residential architect is somewhat like your general practitioner of medicine, a dying breed because there just doesn't seem to be enough money in it for the amount of skills and training involved. Just as young doctors are becoming specialists in certain fields of medicine, young architects are turning to commercial work. Commercial work is where the money is and that is what it takes to pay for all that training, pay for the overhead on the shop, and get all those good things life has to offer. So you may have a bit of trouble finding an architect who is interested in your project. First, of course, you find out if anyone you know has worked with a local architect or knows of someone who has. Local brokers can often come up with some good recommendations. If there is a university or college in the general area and it has a school of architecture, check with the dean of the architectural school. He may know of one of his former students who is doing residential work in your area. You might also keep an eye on the real estate pages of your local paper to see if any of the houses shown were done by local architects. And then, of course, there are always the "yellow pages."

You should know a few things about architects before you hunt one up. First, one can't call oneself an architect unless he has met certain requirements set by the state. This usually includes having gone to an approved school of architecture, passing the required courses, and then taking a state examination. One then becomes a "registered architect" and can go out and practice architecture in the state where he has been registered.

There is a professional association known as the American Institute of Architects, or A.I.A. This group is composed of registered architects who have set up certain codes of professional standards and ethics, and if you are a member you use A.I.A. after your name. You have to be a registered architect to become a member, but just because an architect is not a member does not necessarily mean anything other than that he, for one reason or another, does not wish to join.

Something new in this area of house design is the individual who calls himself a "designer." He may or may not have completed a formal course in architecture. He may be an interior designer who has branched off into exterior design work or he may even be a contractor who has had a certain amount of training in the area of house design. Some designers are very good and it may be that you'll have less trouble latching on to one of these than to an architect, but don't confuse the two; an architect is a highly trained man or woman, and a designer may have more talent than training.

Trying to tell someone how to pick an architect is like trying to tell someone how to pick a doctor—it is almost impossible. When you get in touch with an architect, your approach should be to pay him a visit and see what sort of work he has done in the past. He can show you photographs and drawings and tell you the location of some of his work or even drive you around and show the houses to you himself. These preliminaries enable you to find out whether the sort of thing he does and likes is compatible with your taste. If all he thinks and likes is ultramodern and what you want is something a bit cosier and more traditional, you had better find this out right now and go off and look for another architect who thinks more or less along the same lines as you do.

If you are going to utilize the full services of an architect then it is important that you get along well together. He should be someone with whom you feel comfortable talking and one to whom you can express your ideas without feeling embarrassed by your lack of knowledge in certain areas. If the architect scares you, then you are in for trouble because you'll end up getting just what he wants, which might not be at all what you want. On the other hand, if he accepts everything you say as the final word, you may be wasting your money. There should be a free and easy exchange of ideas and viewpoints between the architect and the client, and you as the client should do a lot of talking because the more the architect knows about you, your family, the way you like to live, and your tastes, the easier it will be for him to design something that will be right for you.

WORKING WITH AN ARCHITECT

The very first thing you want to establish with the architect you have selected is the matter of his fee. He may bring this subject up himself at an early stage in your conversation but if he doesn't, you should, so you'll not be in for any unpleasant surprises later.

An architect can base his fee on a percentage of the total cost of the project, or he can base it on an hourly rate, perhaps $20 per hour. If he is going to handle the entire operation, design, selection of contractor and materials, and supervision of the work, he'll probably want to work on a straight commission and this would be best from your point of view as well as his. If you just want him to work up designs and help you with the selection of materials, then the hourly rate would be the most intelligent approach. You must remember, however, that these $20 hours can pile up rather quickly. If an architect is going to survive in this cold, hard world he has to be something of a business-man and he will keep pretty accurate records of how much time goes into your job. Each time you ask him to revise the plans it will mean several hours of work, not just on the part of the architect but of the draftsmen and other employees in his shop who turn out those beautiful detailed drawings and plans.

If you have a limited amount of money to apply to design, talk the matter over frankly with your architect. Tell him exactly how much money you have for this creative work and he will then be in a better position to know how best to use his talents and time to give you the most for your money. Some time back we ran into a problem with a house and we called in an architect. What we really wanted to know was whether or not our solution to the problem at hand was sound, or, if not, what other options were available. But apparently we did not state our case clearly, nor did we indicate how much we were willing to spend on finding a solution to the problem, because pretty soon the architect had put a lot of time and money into a set of very complete drawings which did not solve our problem and were also very costly.

When an architect is going to handle the entire operation, design, and supervision of the work, it is even more essential that you clarify the money situation early, because a considerable amount of money is involved. First, you want to know what percentage of the construction costs he charges, and also exactly what costs are included. If the archi-tect is going to handle everything, down to the final landscaping, it is obvious that he will base his fee upon the total amount of all the work that is done under his supervision. You might run into a situation, how-ever, where the architect draws up complete plans for everything, but only supervises certain areas of the work. Suppose, for example, that his plans call for a deck but you decide that you will build this deck yourself, after the contractor and the architect are out of the picture. Or suppose that you find you can reduce the cost of a job considerably if you do all the interior and exterior painting and finishing. When this amount is deducted from the total cost of the renovation it obviously reduces the architect's fee.

You should level with the architect and tell him exactly how much money you are prepared to put into the renovation. Don't be coy about this money business because if you do it can be expensive. Here is what can and often does happen. June and Joe get hold of a wonderful OB Dream House and they find a sweet, attractive young architect full of wonderful ideas. Our three new friends have a wonderful time discussing all the things that can be done to the property and along with a few drinks the ideas flow like water. The young architect retires to his drafting table and in time comes up with a set of drawings filled with exciting, kicky, groovy, wild, and simply mad ideas that will transform the structure into something worthy of attention in any magazine you wish to name.

Needless to say, June and Joe are thrilled and can hardly wait until they get the bids from the various contractors. The bids come in and the low one is for $27,638.57, which is just about $20,638.57 more than June and Joe can afford to put into the property. June and Joe decide that they really don't want a house full of exciting, kicky, groovy, wild, and simply mad ideas that much. They decide they don't want a house that might be featured in any magazine they can name. They decide to put in a second bathroom, paint the front bedroom, and use the rest of their money to take a trip to Central Europe. This change in direction comes as quite a shock to the architect, who has a lot of money in time already tied up on the job. He sends Joe and June a bill covering the time he has put into the job, and his bill comes as quite a shock to them. He was so nice, wasn't he? They pay the bill and forget the trip to Central Europe.

June and Joe should have told the nice young architect at the very beginning that they had exactly so much money to put into the house and that this sum would have to include the architect's fee.

The problem is, "What can we do to this place for this amount of money?" The answer might have been, "Put in a second bathroom, paint the front bedroom, and use the rest of the money you have for a trip to Central Europe," or it might have been something else, but unless the architect knows the financial limits under which he is working, he can't do much except come up with what he believes to be the ideal solution to the problem.

You should not mention the subject of money just once and then forget it. Make constant mention in your conversations with the architect of the amount you have to spend. Architects sometimes get as carried away with an interesting project as the owner, and pretty soon the architect and the owner overstimulate each other and the ideas and money start flying about. If the money just isn't there, this is wasted motion and often leads to disappointments.

While you are having this talk with your architect about money, find out how his payments are to be arranged. Will he want a partial payment after he has put in a certain amount of work on the plans, with other payments to follow as the work progresses, or will he wait until the entire job is completed before totaling up the fee? Get this matter straightened out right at the beginning, because you may find that the payment for the architect is going to have to come out of your own private piggy bank and will not be included in the construction mortgage, if this is the way you are financing the project. Time was when most lenders would consider the architect's fee as part of the construction costs and therefore it could be paid out of this money, but today with money very tight things are different. You may have a little trouble convincing your friendly lender that the fee paid to the architect is going to be reflected in a higher property value and therefore is more than a justified construction expense. Your friendly lender might just think that a good honest contractor can do anything that an architect can, only better, and that the money you wish to spend on an architect would be better spent on a three-car garage, a bigger and better kitchen, or a rumpus room. If you are not prepared to pay the architect out of your own money, consult your lender before you get in over your head.

If you have decided to let the architect do the whole project, remember this bit of advice: Once you have approved the plans and the work begins, the architect is in charge. If you visit the job and see something that you don't like, don't talk to the contractor or the men on the job, talk to your architect. If you start bypassing the architect and dealing directly with your contractor or, even worse, the men on the job, you'll be in a mess.

You'll have a justifiably mad and unhappy architect on your hands, a confused contractor and a lot of added expenses. If you lack the necessary self-control to keep your mouth shut, don't visit the job when the men are working. Inspect in the evenings or on Sundays. When an architect is supervising a job, any changes from the plans and specifications for the work must be authorized by him and these changes should be confirmed in writing. The original goes to the contractor and a copy to you for your files. A competent architect and contractor are not going to make any changes that will involve increased expense, unless these changes are approved by you.

To sum things up, if we had the money and if we had a complex problem in concept and design, we'd call in an architect to draw up the plans, at least. If we had an old barn and couldn't see how to divide up the space to get the feel we wanted, we'd get an architect. If we needed an addition to an existing house, if we were going to tear out the innards and start fresh, if we wanted to end up with a perfect gem, if we woke up nights covered with cold sweat because we just couldn't see how to make anything out of what we had just bought, if we had a problem that we couldn't solve, then we'd call in an architect.

THE GENERAL CONTRACTOR

This breed comes in all shapes and sizes. A general contractor may be one lone character working out of an office off his kitchen or he may have a huge organization equipped to build an entire housing community.

A general contractor, whether large or small, is equipped to handle an entire project, a new house, a remodeling, or a restoration. Here is the way you work with a contractor. You tell the contractor what you want done and he figures out what it will cost. If you like the price, he goes ahead and does the work. The contractor will handle everything—carpentry, masonry, wiring, plumbing, heating, painting, wallpapering, roofing, the works.

This is a pretty good arrangement when there is a great deal to be done that involves many different trades—for example, carpentry, plumbing, and wiring. It is an especially good arrangement if you have an architect draw up the plans so that the contractor has something definite to work from. Some of the larger contractors have their own designers or architects and they are a helpful resource in pulling ideas and plans together. The contractor himself will often have suggestions as to what should be done in the area of design and these should not be discounted just because the contractor has had no formal design training. On the other hand, it has been our experience that, by and large, the ideas offered by a contractor are sound but not very exciting. Contractors put more emphasis on soundness of construction than on esthetics and they tend to be more conventional than revolutionary in their approach. They prefer traditional houses as opposed to modern because that is what they generally know the best. Anything that looks too new or complex, they're apt to shy away from, even though it might be the best and least expensive solution to your problem. This is understandable, because once a contractor begins to work on an innovative project, the job is going to require a good deal more supervision than when the men are working on a design and with materials with which they are familiar.

A bid from a general contractor will be higher than if you get individual bids from the various subcontractors involved. By subcontractors we mean the independent outfits that specialize in plumbing, heating, wiring, and so on.

Usually the general contractor will have his own carpenters and perhaps painters, but will use subcontractors for plumbing, heating, wiring, masonry, and other specialties. His bid is higher because you are paying for his supervision and coordination of the various subcontractors, and this requires considerable skill. Subcontractors are probably the most independent group in the entire world and it takes a general contractor to keep them in hand. He can do this because he usually uses the same subcontractors on all his work, and if they don't show up on the day they are supposed to show, or if they don't do the job according to his instructions, he will stop using them and turn to more reliable subcontractors. A private individual doesn't have this power over the subcontractors because for all they know or care this is probably the only job you'll ever give them, and if you don't like the way things are done, so what? Just as the architect has certain powers over the general contractor because of future jobs, so the general contractor has power over the subcontractors. It all may sound a little strange if you are in some line of work where there isn't quite this much independence but that's the way it is in the construction field.

LOCATING A GENERAL CONTRACTOR

It is a little easier to find a general contractor than an architect simply because there are more contractors than architects, and they can advertise and promote themselves, while an A.I.A. architect is supposed to shun publicity. But finding a good general contractor who will get the work done in a relatively short time is something else again. Contractors have much in common with writers; each is often more interested in lining up more new work than in doing the work already commissioned. Almost any contractor will drop everything to rush over and make a bid on a new job. If the bid is accepted, you may never see him again that year. He's off getting more work. This is probably a slight exaggeration, but only slight.

If you are a new boy in town and looking for a good general contractor you might start off at the office of the lender who holds your mortgage. Small-town banks usually keep pretty close tabs on what's going on in the world of contractors and while they might not wish to tell you which ones are no good, they will tell you which ones are good. Your real estate broker may also have a few names to give you and you might also check with the attorney who handled the closing, if he is a local resident. Check also with friends you may know in the area, acquaintances, or neighbors. People usually like to recommend good contractors in the way they like to recommend good doctors, dentists, or hairdressers. If everything works out fine, they can take some of the credit. If it goes sour, it was probably your fault.

What you want to find out about a contractor is how reliable he is and what sort of work he and his men do. Some general contractors are extremely reliable but the workmanship is sloppy, and some have very skilled workers but are about as reliable as the weather forecasts. There is, for example, the phantom contractor. He'll start on a job and then fade away. One day you just won't be able to find him. Call his office and he's out somewhere. Call his home and he hasn't come in. Call late at night and he still isn't there. Call early in the morning, six o'clock early, and you've just missed him. Some contractors can't stand the telephone. You won't get near this type so don't bother to leave your name or number because he has never returned a call in his life and doesn't plan to start doing it now.

One afternoon some years back, we were having a cup of coffee with a contractor in his kitchen. We were there at five or so in the afternoon because we had just dumped two small prefabricated houses in the middle of a rather heavily traveled road, and on a hill at that. This little incident occurred right after World War II. We had decided to enlarge a cabin we had built in the woods some years before. Lumber was hard to come by at this time and we had the happy notion of buying a couple of prefabricated cabins that we had seen on display in a New York department store and tacking them onto our cabin as a temporary expansion program. We ordered the cabins and almost forgot about them until one afternoon the railroad office called to say that the cabins had arrived and we'd have to pick them up immediately because the boxcar they were in had to go on to some other point. We did some fast telephoning, finally borrowed a truck from a friend, and off we went. The truck was an interesting truck because, not only was it very old and very slow, but there was something very wrong with the ignition wires. Every once in a while the engine would just die and you had to jiggle two wires quickly to bring it back to life. This truck also happened to be a dump truck.

We managed to get it down to the railroad yard and were able to talk some of the men there into helping us load the cabin panels into the truck.

Off we went and things were going pretty well until we started up that long winding hill. We were crawling along at about a foot a minute when a great honking arose behind us and we saw that right in back of us was a young lady in a red convertible who was in an obvious hurry, and wanted us to pull over so she could pass or have us move along a bit faster than we were doing. We couldn't pull over, so we decided that maybe we could pick up a few more feet per second if we shifted into another gear. Just as we started to shift, the engine cut out. We jiggled the wires, the engine came on just as we had moved into another gear. The truck gave a mighty lurch forward, the dump dumped, and the assortment of house panels ended up directly in front of the red convertible. Somehow the young lady managed to swing out and avoid running into them and somehow she managed to swing past us without hitting an oncoming car. She also managed to give us a pretty withering look as she drove past. Anyway, she probably will never honk at a truck again.

Do you know what passing motorists say to you if you are sitting on a pile of house panels in the middle of a road? They say, "Hey, Mac, you dropped something." Our only hope was that eventually a state trooper would come along and arrest us for obstructing traffic and take us to a nice quiet police station so that someone else would have to figure out what to do with all those panels, but when a state trooper did come along all he said was, "Hey, Mac, you dropped something" and went on his way. After what seemed a long, long time, the contractor we mentioned earlier came along in a truck with some of his men and after a few "Hey, Mac, you dropped something"s helped me load the panels on his truck and mine and get them to where they were going, and that is why I was in his kitchen that afternoon having coffee.

While we were having coffee the phone rang constantly and the contractor's wife naturally answered it. "No, he's not home yet. I'm not sure when he is expected. I think he said he had to go to New Haven to pick up something for a job. Yes, I'll have him call you as soon as he gets back."

A minute later another call. "What, he *isn't* at your place? Are you sure? He said this morning he'd be at your place all day. The very last thing he said this morning was that if I needed him he'd be at your place all day because he knew how anxious you were to get the roof finished. Well, I just don't know where he can be. Perhaps I'd better call the police. Something terrible may have happened. Good-bye."

Two minutes later, "Oh, Mr. Smith. Yes, he hasn't left the country but he's not home right now. He did say that if you called again to tell you that he'd be at your place the first thing in the morning, around seven thirty. Oh yes, the whole crew will be there I'm sure, because Ed was here a minute ago and he was off to load the truck so it would be ready the first thing in the morning."

And so it went. Of course, all contractors are not phantoms and many are hard to get in touch with simply because they go around from job to job inspecting the work and keeping things moving along. And a good contractor usually starts off pretty early in the morning and he works until pretty late at night. On one job, I found that if I called the contractor at his office at 7:00 A.M. I could reach him. After 7:30 he was off and unreachable the rest of the day and evening unless I wanted to call him at his home around midnight.

The best way to find out just how reliable a contractor is about sticking with the job until it is finished is to talk with people who have used him. Ask them frankly if he is the type who gets the job done, or the type that lets it drag on all summer. The same approach can be used to get a reading on workmanship, although it has been our experience that many home owners prefer not to be critical of workmanship because they feel it might put their house in a dubious light if they went around telling anyone who asked that the roof wasn't much good or the floors were poorly installed or that the woodwork was a mess.

You want to get a firm bid from your contractor. If he can't give you a firm bid, then you had better forget him, because to go into a major renovation project without knowing how much it is going to cost is just plain crazy. And home owners always think that things are going to cost far less than they actually do. If Mr. X thinks an addition to his house will cost about $5,000, you can be pretty certain that the actual cost will probably be nearer to $10,000. And it is always best to get two or more contractors to bid on a job. That doesn't mean, however, that you should automatically accept the lowest bid. Consider the reputation of the contractor, his reliability, how soon he can start on the project, when he believes he can have it completed, and also his personality. If you have an extensive job to do and you are the one who will be dealing with the contractor, then you need to have someone with whom you feel you can work. And also someone who will work with you to get what you want rather than what he wants.

A bid, of course, isn't going to mean a thing unless it is solidly based on detailed plans and working drawings, plus specifications that indicate brand, color, and design of the various materials going into the job. For example, you might wish to have plumbing fixtures of a certain brand and color or a particular brand and pattern of tile on the floors. If you use an architect for the design portion of the job, he will furnish the plans and the specifications. If you don't have an architect or a designer, you ought to do this job yourself. Try to put down on paper everything you want done before you get involved with a contractor. You can then go over the job with the contractor, and if he is competent he will make notes of any items that you have not covered. Eventually he'll come back with a bid that will be based on his interpretation of your discussion and plans. His description of the work to be done should be highly detailed. For example, if you are installing a new bathroom the contractor's description might read as follows:

Item 23. New bathroom as indicated on plans. Frame walls, insulate all walls, cover, and tape with wallboard. Install white ceramic tile around tub. Fixtures are to be Brand X, white, model numbers x12, x13, x19. Install electric baseboard unit. Install window as indicated on plan, medicine cabinet over lavatory, brand W, model 52856. Install light fixtures as indicated on plan. Walls to be papered, trim to be painted with primer and two coats of alkyd paint, color to be selected by owner. Cost: $1,873.98.

Now while this is a lot better than just saying "Install bathroom, $1,873.98," it isn't perfect, because we don't mention the brand of ceramic tile and there can be slight variations in shades in different brands. We don't indicate the style and brand of wall accessories to use and we don't say what sort of lighting fixtures are to be used and we don't know if we are talking about a $7.98 medicine cabinet or one for $35.00.

If the contractor's bid is going to mean anything, it should be based on everything that is to be done, with an exact description of the kind of materials and products that are to be used.

A good contractor will be of great help, but it is ultimately your responsibility to cover every detail with him and see that all this is included in the bid.

Once the contractor submits a bid, go over it with him to clear up any items that seem a bit vague or have been omitted. You can also eliminate certain items if you are getting in over your head financially.

After you have made up your mind as to which contractor to use, you sign an agreement with him based on the detailed specifications of the work included in the bid, and he and his boys go to work. He will usually indicate a completion date in this agreement but don't get the idea that you can start legal action if he isn't finished on the day he says he will be. In the contracting business there are so many acts of man and God that can keep a project from being completed on time that no one to my knowledge has ever even tried to use the courts to move a contractor along.

We divide general contractors into two groups, little operators and big operators. If you decided to go with a little operator he'll probably be on the job a good deal of the time, working right along with his help. This has certain advantages for you, especially if you did not do what we said you should do and draw up detailed plans and specifications but are instead playing things by ear. If the contractor is on the job every day you can often make changes that won't be too costly if made before too much time and material have gone into the job. If you thought you'd like something, but now decide you don't, this can be eliminated or modified. If you want something extra added, your contractor can give you a price right then and there, and if you agree, the extra can be added. Be sure, though, and this is extremely important, that the price is written down on both your list and his and that you both initial the change and agreed price. A clear, written stipulation can save considerable unhappiness later on when the final bill is totaled.

With a little operator the whole operation is perhaps not as business-like as with the big operator but it is a lot more personal. A big operator, of course, is all business and very efficient. The work will probably go faster under his direction because he can throw a number of men on the job if you apply enough pressure. It will also probably go faster because the big operator has to work on a tight schedule and he wants to get his men in and out so that they can be moved onto other jobs. With the big operator, you have to be careful about changing your mind or improvising. If you visit the job and see something that you want changed, go to the boss contractor to have the changes made. The men on the job are working for him, not you, and if you start giving directions, there will be no end of trouble and all the trouble will cost you money. The same holds true, of course, with the little operator; talk about changes with him, not his men.

If there is a job foreman on the project and the contractor has told you that the foreman can authorize changes, watch out. The foreman will have the changes made, but he won't be in a position to tell you the cost, and perhaps if you knew the cost you might change your mind again and go along as planned. Changes that involve work already completed are very expensive because you will pay for the original work, you will pay to have it removed, and pay again for the new work. This can add up to a great deal of labor. And modifications of the original estimate have a way of mounting up. Such and such may only cost $49 and something else $75, but do this a few times and you've gotten rid of $500, scarcely knowing where it went.

When we recently wanted to add a small second-story deck with a garage and terrace underneath to the rear of our house, we got in touch with a nice young contractor, told him our wants, and he came back with a bid of about $3,500 for the job. This was too much. We gave up the idea of a garage and cut down the size of the deck. After a few other changes we got a new bid of $1,845, which was much better. We decided to go ahead with the project, but before the job was too far along we happened to see a terrace with attractive bluestone blocks that were definitely superior to the concrete slab we had planned to use. So we changed from concrete to bluestone, with an additional charge of $450 for the stone. We added another flight of outdoor stairs and we did a few other little things such as putting up a wood screen rather than the masonry blocks planned, and pretty soon we got the final bill, which came to $2,889.20. And none of the changes we made involved tearing out work already completed.

Try not to change your mind once you have decided on the amount of money you can put into the project. If you do, be sure that you know in advance what the changes are going to cost and get this in writing from your contractor.

It is important, too, that whether you are dealing with a small contractor, a big contractor, or an architect, there should be just one official spokesman in the family. It becomes extremely confusing if one day the husband is in charge, and the next day his wife gives the orders. Let that member of the household who can devote the most time to the project be the one who deals with the architect or contractor. Naturally you talk the job over together and decide what has to be done, but do this in private, not on the job. It can put an architect or a contractor in a difficult position if a husband and wife start to squabble in their presence about something involving the job.

Before you sign an agreement with a contractor find out the manner in which the payments are to be made, if this has not been made clear in the letter of agreement. On small jobs the contractor may request full payment as soon as the work has been completed. On larger projects, involving several thousand dollars, he may specify that the payment be broken down and certain sums sent to him as the work progresses. This is a good arrangement that is usually acceptable to your lender, if you have a construction mortgage.

Where the payments are staggered, the contractor sends you a statement after a certain amount of work has been done, requesting partial payment. You notify your lender who verifies that the work has been done. The lender then sends you the money and you send it along to your contractor. The final payment is not made until the job has been finished and you are satisfied that it fulfills the terms of the agreement with the contractor.

If you are using a construction mortgage to pay for the work entirely, you should have a contractor who can afford to advance the necessary money for labor and materials, so that these partial payments are spread out over decent intervals and are for sizable amounts. Lenders don't like to bother having to go out constantly to inspect a job and then advance small amounts. They prefer to write larger checks at fewer intervals but only if the amount of work justifies the money involved. You won't have this concern with big contractors, but some of the small ones do get short of funds and start coming to you for enough money to pay the help for the past week or enough to buy some materials because at the moment their credit is not in very good shape.

The last time we worked with a big operator we had a construction mortgage for about $10,000. The first partial payment was for $3,000 and the next, a couple of months later, was for $3,000. The final payment was supposed to be $4,000, but because we had added a few items here and there it came to $6,000. On the deck and bluestone terrace we didn't pay a cent until the job was done and then we paid the full amount. On another job, we worked with a very small operator who needed money almost every week. It's fine if you have enough in your checking account to cover these small weekly payments until enough work has been done so you can get money from your lender, but if you are a little short yourself, it can mean trouble for you, as well as your contractor. He may disappear from time to time to pick up some quick money on a few small jobs to keep himself going.

Occasionally a small contractor who doesn't have much working capital may request a payment in advance, before any work is done. A lender won't advance money to you for work that hasn't been done and you had better follow his example and refuse to do it yourself. The contractor may be having financial problems and may need the money to pay for labor and materials used on another job, or he may need it for his own personal use. The other hitch in paying for work not done is that the contractor might be a little slow in getting started or let the work drag on and on. He can stall you and stall you and you don't have much option, because he already has the money and you can't get someone else in to do the work unless you want to give up that partial payment. A request for payment in advance also may indicate a bad credit picture where the contractor has to pay cash in advance for all his materials and can't get short-term loans from a bank to pay his labor.

PAYMENT TO THE CONTRACTOR

When you get your final bill from a contractor, go over it carefully since even modest renovation will involve many separate items. Also, as the work progressed some changes are sure to have occurred that will make a difference between the amount of the original estimate and the final bill.

Insist on an itemized bill in which each area of work is described. If you have a written agreement with your contractor, and you certainly should, get this out along with any other correspondence from him, for you will need it all in going over his bill.

First check over the bill to see that each item charged has been completed to your satisfaction. This should be done on the job. If there are any loose ends or anything not completed or properly done, get hold of the contractor at once and have these matters straightened out to your satisfaction before you make payment.

If changes have been made, you will either be charged for extra work and materials, or, you should get a deduction or credit for work not undertaken. Check any changes, plus or minus against the original bid or against any correspondence you may have had with the contractor.

Suppose, for example, that the original bid on installing a bathroom included putting in a new window, but you changed your mind and decided to get along with the existing window. The final bill on the bathroom should be for the amount of the original bid less the cost of the proposed window and labor to install it. Even if this change was put in writing, the contractor may have put it aside or neglected to pass it along to whoever made out your bill. Unless you check the bill carefully you might pay for a window that was never installed. Perhaps painting was called for, and you decided to wallpaper instead. Here, you will have paid more for the wallpaper and probably extra for the labor to hang it but you should get a credit for the paint, which was not used.

It is going to take a good deal of time to check over the bill along with inspecting all the work on a renovation job but such checking is worth it many times over.

It's much easier to have something fixed that wasn't properly done or not completed, before you've paid the bill than after the contractor has said good-bye to your job and is totally involved with another.

Perhaps we have been lucky but in all the years that we have spent working with houses, we have never run into a dishonest contractor, carpenter, plumber, mason, painter, or electrician. Some have been a bit shiftless and a few drank a little more than was good for them or the work they were doing for us. Some were rather neurotic and talked constantly about their problems. Many have been poor at addition and have made mistakes in their bills, but not always in their own favor. There have been those who were harder and faster workers than others and some more skilled at their trade than others, but none has been dishonest. By and large they have shown no more and no less inclination to take advantage of us than some of our business associates.

If you are working with local people you shouldn't have to worry about dishonesty, any more than you worry about dishonesty on the part of your local grocery store or the corner service station.

There are, of course, some out and out crooks in the home improvement field. You have probably read about them in newspapers or magazines. These characters don't really have any home base. They drift about the country and after making a killing in one community move onto the next before anyone can catch up with them.

You have to be pretty naive to become involved with this sort of home-improvement fraud. For example, one approach used by the heating-improvement crook is to knock at your door and offer to inspect your heating system. He takes the furnace apart and when he has all the pieces on the floor he tells you that some of the parts have to be replaced. By the time he has finished, you have had to pay him to take the thing apart, replace parts that didn't need replacing, and then pay to have him put the thing back together. Allowing a complete stranger to take your heating system apart is a fairly foolish thing to do.

Sometimes a complete stranger will knock at your door and say he represents a roofing concern and that his company would like to put a new roof on your house for free as a demonstration for other home owners in the area. You get the roofing job free, but would you please sign this document that gives the roofing outfit the right to point with pride to the roof on your house? Would you sign that paper without reading it? And if you did read it, wouldn't you be able to note that what you were signing was a contract to purchase a new roof? And would you believe that anyone would give you a new roof for free?

We once spent a day with a salesman of aluminum siding who had at one time worked for one of these swindling home-improvement outfits. He recalled the "good old times" and some of the tricks used to get the most out of anyone who responded to a bait advertisement. The advertisement offered something at a very low price but once a possible buyer had bitten, a salesman called on him to persuade him to buy something much more expensive and for more than he would normally pay through a reputable dealer. Our acquaintance told us how this worked with an advertisement for low-cost storm windows and doors. When the salesman called on the home owner who had responded to the advertisement, he would try to move him away from the low-cost units onto the more expensive kind. If the home owner insisted on the window that was advertised, the salesman would say, "Fine, and with each window or door we will give you absolutely free a carton of steel wool." The home owner would ask, "Why the steel wool?" and the reply would be that with unfinished aluminum a discoloration occurs after a few weeks and must be removed with steel wool. For some reason this little idea worked in most cases and the home owner would end up with the more expensive type of storm window and door.

You can spot these home-improvement swindlers rather easily without even bothering to call the Better Business Bureau. They make house-to-house calls, they are from out of town, and if they have a local office it is usually a desk and a telephone and not much else. Most of them handle such matters as exterior siding, storm windows and doors, roofing, termite control, heating systems, and driveways.

Many of them, by the way, will have financing arrangements made through nationally known organizations. Don't let your knowledge of the outfit that does the financing give you a feeling of security. All the financers care about is getting their money, and if the roof that costs twice as much as it should starts to leak, they couldn't care less.

BE YOUR OWN CONTRACTOR

Serving as your own contractor is tricky and requires enormous time and patience. It can, however, save you a good deal of money because you eliminate the need for a general contractor. It is you who will co-ordinate the job and the schedules and deal with the workmen. But you must be prepared to stick with the job and really give it the time required. It will take time to get hold of the various subcontractors or "trades," as they are often called in the building field, and to supervise and coordinate their work. And it will take time in the completion of the project because you probably can't enforce as tight a work schedule on your crew as a general contractor can, for reasons that have already been covered.

But being your own contractor can be great fun and a rewarding experience. You'll get a feel of the work that you just can't get when you use an architect or a general contractor. You'll become familiar with the plumbing system, the heating system, the wiring, the insulation, trim, and everything else that is going into your house. You'll become familiar with such terms as "Romex," "BX," "studding," "sheetrock," "soil pipe," "shim," and many other things you've probably never heard of. You will see, because you will spend a good deal of time on the job, how this thing that you recently purchased begins to take shape, and that's fun. But it does require patience, time, and tact.

Your first job is to line up a crew of subcontractors, and the number of different ones you need will depend on the extent of the work. You may need only a carpenter and an electrician or you may also need a plumber, mason, painter, and sheetrock man. You'll have to do some asking around to find the most reliable ones, and then you call them in to get bids on the work. Plumbers, electricians, and heating subcontractors can usually give you a pretty firm bid on a renovation project because they can determine quite easily how much time and material are involved. A carpenter, on the other hand, doesn't always know what he is getting into in an old house; he may prefer not to make a firm bid but rather to operate on a "time-plus-materials" basis. This, believe it or not, means exactly what it says. The carpenter charges you so much an hour for his and his helpers' labor, plus the materials involved. We still prefer to get a firm bid on any work other than the most minor carpentry jobs, but if the carpenter has a good reputation and if this is the only way he will work, you may have to go along. The large contractor can give you a firm bid covering carpentry work because his volume of business is such that if he drops a few dollars of profit on your job, he'll probably pick up the loss on the next one. The lone carpenter doesn't have this volume and so he has to play a slightly different game.

Do take the trouble to find out how good your carpenter is before you get involved in a "time-plus-materials" arrangement. If he is a slowpoke, you aren't going to do well on the deal. If he's a demon for work, you are going to come out ahead. We know one carpenter who works only on a time-plus-materials basis, and he is a whiz. The job just rushes along when he's doing the work himself. This man became so busy after a while that he hired a helper, and while the helper was good, he was slow and it would take him almost twice the time that it took his boss to do a job. So if you are going to use a time-plus-materials basis for your carpentry, get someone who is not only good but fast. You can find out about this paragon only by asking people.

It should be obvious that if you have someone working on time-plus-materials you don't waste his time and your money in idle conversation. He may be able to afford to sit back and yatter with you about this and that but he can do this because you are paying him the same amount for listening to you as he gets for working for you, so keep him working and forget the conversation.

And keep your friends away from anyone on time-plus, because just as sure as you're born, they'll engage him in a lengthy discussion about the price of nails and pretty soon an hour of your money has gone down the drain.

One of the trickiest areas in being your own contractor is coordinating the operation. This means knowing when the carpentry work is going to be far enough along so that the plumber or electrician can come in, and when they will be out of the way so that the carpenter can get back and finish his work. A good way of handling this is to select your carpenter first and let him suggest whom you might get for the plumbing, wiring, and so on. If the men in the various trades know each other and have worked together in the past, they'll often do a good job of coordinating the work themselves and your involvement will be minimal. If the men like each other this arrangement can work out very well indeed. We know of cases where a plumber has come over on a Sunday afternoon to finish off his part of the work so that his friend the carpenter could go to work on the job first thing Monday morning. The carpenter is usually the one best suited to help you pick your little team, because in most cases his work continues right through the operation. He has to do the rough framing before the electrician or plumber can do much of anything and he'll be back to complete his end of the work after they have finished. The carpenter is on stage almost constantly, whereas the others are bit players, albeit important ones.

Even if you have put together a team that works smoothly, you are still the one in charge and if there is a hang-up because something has not been clearly spelled out, it is your responsibility to clarify matters as soon as possible. It would be ideal if you could be on hand to inspect the work every day or two and are able to get over on short notice if a tie-up occurs. But much depends on the team, how complete and detailed the plans are, and how complex the job.

When you do visit the job, make your visits brief and to the point. If your subcontractors have given you a firm bid, they know that the quicker they get finished, the sooner they can take on another job. If you engage them in long conversations you are wasting their time and their money and they won't appreciate it one bit. If they are working on time-plus-materials you should know by now that you should not talk too much. Say your piece and then get out of their way. But don't be afraid to speak up if you see something being done that wasn't called for or that you don't like. And be prepared to make quick decisions. Once the job gets under way, the time has passed for "I'd like to talk this over with my husband when he gets back from his business trip" or "I'll ask my wife if she can drop over day after tomorrow or the first of next week. She knows more about this than I do."

As we suggested earlier, decide which one of you is running the show. Let that one deal with the subcontractors and let the other partner remain silent.

Financing the job when you are acting as your own contractor may become somewhat complicated. Some of your subcontractors, such as the plumber and electrician, may be well enough established and have big enough shops so that they won't require payment until their work is completed. They are also in and out of the job pretty fast, and this makes a difference.

Some of the people doing the work, however, may have to be paid at frequent intervals. A carpenter, for example, who works independently may need money each week to buy materials and for his own needs. If you are paying all, or a good part, of the renovation costs out of your own funds, and you have sufficient funds, this may not be a problem. If you have a construction mortgage, you can make these payments out of your own funds and get the money back when the amount involved is sufficient to justify inspection by the lender, who will then make a partial or full payment to you. But if you don't have sufficient funds to meet these frequent demands, you may have to take out a short-term personal loan to tide you over until the lender comes through with some of that construction-mortgage money.

In many sections of the country it is not easy to find people to do construction or renovation work. A shortage of skilled and semiskilled labor in the construction field makes it hard even for contractors to get and hold good men. And there are certain times of year when it is even more difficult to get someone to start on a job and stay with it. Spring is a bad time to find help because there is such a heavy demand. Everyone wants something done to his place in the spring, and many contractors are also trying to finish jobs that began in the fall and were held up by winter weather. Summer is not much better. The best time to find people to work on your OB Dream House is in the winter, and this goes for contractors as well as individual workmen. During the winter months, in all but warm climates, new construction goes in fits and starts according to the weather. For a contractor this means that in each month his crew will be idle for a certain number of days unless he has some inside work, such as a nice renovation job, where the boys can be out of the cold and snow and still keep busy. The same thing holds true for the independent operator. A carpenter, come cold weather, may be far more interested in working on the inside of your house than in working outdoors to frame a new one. If you have trouble getting someone interested in working on your property during the summer, try them again when the leaves are off the trees and there is a bite to the wind.

People involved in construction are a rather independent lot. In nice warm weather they may not show up for work because they'd like to get in a little golf or some fishing. In our area the opening of the trout and shad seasons in the spring and the hunting season in the fall brings construction to a temporary halt.

Summer, of course, is the ideal time to get "professional amateurs." Once school is out you may find many fine college and high-school students interested in making a few dollars over the summer, and if you get hold of a good one, you are really in luck. Many young teachers like to pick up extra money and get in some good exercise as well. Some of these young people are highly skilled. We had a young college man who did a great deal of painting for us and he was a delight. He arrived promptly every morning and worked away until 4:30 P.M. sharp. He was not only conscientious, neat, and cheerful but charged less than a professional painter. If you are looking for this type of help, see if you can put a note on the high-school bulletin board before school closes for the summer, or check with any colleges in the area. Run some advertisements in the local paper in the spring. You want to get someone lined up before someone else grabs him.

DO ALL OR MOST OF IT YOURSELF

Doing all or most of the work yourself is certainly the least expensive way to renovate an OB House. It takes the most time and it takes a great deal of effort, but if you are short of money it is perhaps the only way to handle the project. Sometimes even if you have money you may have to do part of the work yourself because you can't get anyone else to do it. Like the little red hen, if you want the ear of corn planted you may have to plant it yourself.

Some lenders are not too keen on going along with a construction loan if you plan to do the work yourself because they have had too many examples of jobs like this that dragged along forever and did not turn out very well. But if you can convince your lenders that their investment is safe and sound and that you are a capable and knowledgeable fellow, you're on your way. This book has been written with the view that many will decide to do at least a certain amount of the work themselves, so it contains a good deal of basic "how to" material.

Our idea of the perfect arrangement for renovating an OB House would be to get our own rough plans worked up first, then take them to a good architect to get his thinking and to have more professional plans and specifications drawn. We'd like to have a general contractor handle the heavy part of the work, such as major structural changes, plumbing, and heating. For the finish work we'd like to work with our own carpenter and painter so that we could supervise every detail firsthand. Then we'd leave for ourselves all the work that we like to do best—a certain amount of digging because we find digging relaxing; putting up interior wood paneling because it goes up quickly and produces an instant and dramatic effect; and painting large spaces such as inside and outside walls, leaving the intricate painting problems to professionals or friends who enjoy this sort of delicate work.

12 How Much Work Can You Do Yourself?

If you have to, if you want to, if the local building codes aren't too restrictive, and if you have the time, you can do all the work yourself. Many amateurs, including our forefathers, have built their own houses. Immediately after the end of World War II, hordes of ex-GIs were working like overstimulated beavers building nests for themselves and their families. We were living at that time in an area that was alive with amateur builders, writers, engineers, advertising men, insurance salesmen, and so on. On Saturday mornings the local hardware store and lumberyard looked like a miniature Fort Benning with the customers in ex-military clothes of every description, picking up supplies for a busy weekend of work. In those days one went to a cocktail party in the hope that one would run into someone who was good at electric wiring or had finally figured out the easy way to install ducts for a heating system. They had all built their houses from scratch, starting by digging a trench for the foundations themselves.

Few of us want to go quite this far, and you, indeed, don't have to, for you will have a structure already. A certain amount of work will

156

still be required, and a good deal of this work you can do yourself without having to acquire specialized skills of the sort required for plumbing and heating installation. Working on your own house can be a highly satisfying experience. It is good to work with your hands and to use muscles that you may have forgotten you have. It's fun to acquire new skills and if you have been blessed with a fairly good sense of coordination you might as well put these gifts to use, because they probably won't be much good to you in the hereafter. And never lose sight of the money you save by doing something yourself. It costs a good deal of money to hire even unskilled labor and the more work you do yourself, the more money you will have to put into other improvements.

Even if you don't have any skill with a hammer or saw, you can certainly tear out and cart away structural and other materials that are not needed. With most OB Houses there is a good deal of ripping out to do before the new work can be started. Old plaster and lath, wallboard from walls and ceilings, unnecessary interior partitions, worn-out flooring or floor coverings, and even old roofing may need tearing out. You can yank out old bathroom fixtures, old cabinets, and everything else under the sun that has to go. And doing just this sort of work is going to save you money. Renovation work is so much more expensive than new construction because the old has to be removed before the new can be installed. The carpenter gets the same amount of money an hour for tearing out old wallboard as he gets to do cabinetwork. If you do all the rough stuff yourself, you will have saved a good many hundreds of dollars even if you don't lift another finger on the job.

If there are trenches to be dug for water lines, sewer pipes, or footings, this, too, is something you might do yourself. We once ran out and grabbed a shovel out of the hands of a plumber and started to dig like mad when we realized that his time was costing us $10 an hour, and, in our book, that is too much to pay a ditchdigger. Digging a ditch may not be the most creative work in the world, but if you are in good health it is fine exercise and can save you a bundle of money.

If you have hired your own carpenter you might wish to work along with him as an unpaid helper. It will save him time, and you money, if there are two willing hands to hold a board that he wants to cut, fetch materials as he needs them, hold one end of a heavy piece of lumber while he nails it in place, and so on. You can learn a tremendous amount about carpentry by working with and observing a carpenter as he goes about the job. Eventually, you'll probably have the chance to put some of these skills to work yourself. If you do make this sort of arrangement with a carpenter, or anyone else working around the place, keep your conversation to a minimum. Long heart-to-heart chats take time, and, as we constantly remind you, time costs you money.

Painting is something else that almost anyone can do. The paints available today for interior and exterior work are virtually foolproof and you can certainly save some money here. You'll find out all about this in the chapter on "Painting and Finishing."

You can remove old paint and finishes yourself. There may be a good deal of this work to do on an OB House and it will have to be done before the new finish can be applied. You may not be able to strip a door as fast as a professional painter but you can do it for a lot less money. We asked a painter who was working on our place how long it would take him to strip a door and he estimated about half a day. At $5 an hour this came to about $20. We did the doors ourself. It took us a full day to do one door but we saved $20 on each door we did. This work is covered in "Removing Paint and Finishes."

Wallpapering is another job you can handle. You can get it pre-pasted or use a prepared paste. Ceilings, of course, are rather tricky but walls are not bad, and this is nice clean work for either men or women.

With a bit of practice you can replace panes of glass in windows and this is a skill worth having because window panes get broken from time to time. Check this out in the chapter entitled "Windows."

Insulating walls, ceilings, and floors is something else you can handle if the wall, ceiling, or floor framing is exposed. As we mentioned in the chapter on "Insulating," if the framework is not exposed, the insulation will have to be blown into the wall, and this must be done by a professional with the proper equipment.

Applying a new roof of asphalt or wood shingles is not too difficult, if the roof is not complicated and if you are dealing with a one-story structure. If it is a tricky roof with many different planes and valleys, or if there is a good distance from the roof to the ground, you might be better off to leave this job to a professional.

You can also reshingle exterior walls, and if you have a helper, you can put up clapboard or board-and-batten siding. Wood shingles are ideal when you're working alone because they are so easy to handle. We once saw an OB House being reshingled by an assortment of people and it turned out that most of them didn't even know the people who owned the house. They just happened along, saw someone putting up shingles, and decided that it looked like fun. They asked if they could help and the owner, being a kind and generous man, allowed them to do a little of the work.

So far we have limited the jobs you can do yourself to those that don't require extensive tools or only rather primary skills. If you can use a hammer and saw and measure accurately, there are a vast number of jobs you can handle.

You can do much or all of the rough framing for interior partitions, ceilings and can also frame the openings for doors and windows. By the way, if you plan to do this sort of work we suggest that you use the metal framing anchors. You can get these at your lumber yard and they come in shapes to cover just about every type of joint you are likely to encounter. They produce an extremely strong joint and eliminate the chance of using too few or too many nails. At the end of this chapter you will find illustrations covering the most common framing situations.

Installing and taping gypsum wallboard is another job that can be handled by the amateur. You will need someone to help you put the large sheets into place and hold them there until they are nailed to the framework. The standard 4-by-8-foot sheet of half-inch gypsum wallboard is pretty heavy, and difficult for even a professional to handle by himself. Applying the tape to the joints and filling in over the nailheads with the cement does not require strength, just patience and attention to detail. It is something a woman can do just as well as and often better than a man.

Any amateur should be able to install sub-flooring himself, and many types of finish flooring also lend themselves to nonprofessional installation. Hardwood flooring and resilient floor tile all can be installed by amateurs. Covering a floor with sheet material is best left to the professionals.

We recently visited a renovation job, a very good one, where all the cabinet work had been done by the owner. It was very fine work and he had never done anything like this before, but he gave it a try, decided it was his dish of tea and away he went. Certainly if you have a profession or a hobby that requires precision and close attention to detail, you have the proper background for cabinetwork. If you decide to go ahead and do it yourself, it would be worth investing in a table saw.

Repairing existing masonry and installing new are almost sure to be needed around the place. Pouring concrete footings and foundations may be jobs that you do not wish to tackle or should not tackle yourself, but small projects such as footings for posts, and walks, along with repairs, are jobs you can handle.

Electric wiring is a job you probably would be better off not to undertake yourself, although the actual installation of the wiring and the making of most of the connections does not require any great skill. The same is true of putting in the wires in new work or where framework is exposed. Here only drilling the necessary holes and securing the wire cables in place is required. Connecting the ends of the wires to outlets and fixtures is much like connecting the wires from a lamp to the plug.

The trick in electric wiring is planning the system. Special knowledge and training are required to determine how many circuits are required, which fixtures and outlets are going on which circuit, and how the wiring for the switches is going to be arranged. The complexity of the work is increased by the fact that the electrical layout will vary with each house. Planning the system should be done by a licensed electrician, and most areas have a local code requiring that all electrical wiring installation be done by a licensed electrician.

Installing the plumbing system is something else that you should avoid. The fresh-water portion isn't so bad, once you learn how to make a tight joint and know what fittings to use, because there is pressure in these lines to force the water through them. The waste and drainage system is quite different. Here you depend on gravity to carry the water through the lines, and unless the lines are given the proper downward pitch along their entire length, the system isn't going to work. Installing plumbing also requires special tools and skills and here, too, local codes may prohibit anyone other than a licensed plumber from installing a system.

When we were young we lived near the late Hendrick Willem van Loon, the historian and writer. Mr. van Loon had a story about a conversation he had with a plumber who was doing some work for him. Mr. van Loon was watching the plumber work and said something to the effect that plumbing was rather exacting and difficult work. The plumber picked this up and went on at some length about the hardships of being a plumber. "Now it's different with a carpenter," he said. "If a carpenter cuts a board the wrong width he can usually plane it down to size so it fits. If the boards don't meet snug, he can fill the crack with putty or cover it with paint. Carpenters don't have to do a lot of their work laying on their stomachs and they don't ever burn their hands or faces with hot lead. Jesus Christ was a very smart man. He was a carpenter!"

But then again, we were chatting with an artist who had just fixed up a little farmhouse himself. We complimented him on the fine workmanship of the plumbing system and he told us that the entire system had been installed by a business executive who happened to be spending the summer in the area and whose hobby was plumbing. He was simply delighted to find a house that required a complete plumbing system; he sent home for his tools and came over every day to work until the system was finished.

▶ *Recommended Schedule for Nailing the Framing and Sheathing of a Well-Constructed Wood-Frame House*

Joining	Nailing Method	Nails		
		Number	Size	Placement
Header to joist	End-nail	3	16d	
Joist to sill or girder	Toenail	2–3	10d or 8d	
Header and stringer joist to sill	Toenail		10d	16 inches on center
Bridging to joist	Toenail each end	2	8d	
Ledger strip to beam, 2 inches thick		3	16d	At each joist
Sub-floor, boards:				
1 by 6 inches and smaller		2	8d	To each joist
1 by 8 inches		3	8d	To each joist
Sub-floor, plywood:				
At edges			8d	6 inches on center
At intermediate joists			8d	8 inches on center
Sub-floor (2 by 6 inches, T&G) to joist or girder	*Blind-nail* (casing) and face-nail.	2	16d	
Soleplate to stud, horizontal assembly	End-nail	2	16d	At each stud
Top plate to stud	End-nail	2	16d	
Stud to soleplate	Toenail	4	8d	
Soleplate to joist or blocking	*Face-nail*		16d	16 inches on center
Doubled studs	Face-nail, stagger		10d	16 inches on center
End stud of intersecting wall to exterior wall stud	Face-nail		16d	16 inches on center
Upper top plate to lower top plate	Face-nail		16d	16 inches on center
Upper top plate, laps and intersections	Face-nail	2	16d	
Continuous header, 2 pieces, each edge			12d	12 inches on center
Ceiling joist to top wall plates	Toenail	3	8d	
Ceiling joist laps at partition	Face-nail	4	16d	
Rafter to top plate	Toenail	2	8d	
Rafter to ceiling joist	Face-nail	5	10d	
Rafter to valley or hip rafter	Toenail	3	10d	
Ridge board to rafter	End-nail	3	10d	
Rafter to rafter through ridge board	Toenail	4	8d	
	Edge-nail	1	10d	
Collar beam to rafter:				
2-inch member	Face-nail	2	12d	
1-inch member	Face-nail	3	8d	
1-inch diagonal let-in brace to each stud and plate (4 nails at top)		2	8d	

Joining	Nailing Method	Nails		
		Number	Size	Placement
Built-up corner studs:				
Studs to blocking	Face-nail	2	10d	Each side
Intersecting stud to corner studs	Face-nail		16d	12 inches on center
Built-up girders and beams, 3 or more members	Face-nail		20d	32 inches on center, each side
Wall sheathing:				
1 by 8 inches or less, horizontal	Face-nail	2	8d	At each stud
1 by 6 inches or greater, diagonal	Face-nail	3	8d	At each stud
Wall sheathing, vertically applied plywood:				
⅜ inch and less thick	Face-nail		6d	6-inch edge
½ inch and over thick	Face-nail		8d	12-inch intermediate
Wall sheathing, vertically applied fiberboard:				
½ inch thick	Face-nail			1½-inch roofing nail
²⁵⁄₃₂ inch thick	Face-nail			1¾-inch roofing nail
Roof sheathing, boards, 4-, 6-, 8-inch width	Face-nail	2	8d	At each rafter
Roof sheathing plywood:				
⅜ inch and less thick	Face-nail		6d	6-inch edge and 12-inch intermediate
½ inch and over thick	Face-nail		8d	

THE FRAMING PORTFOLIO

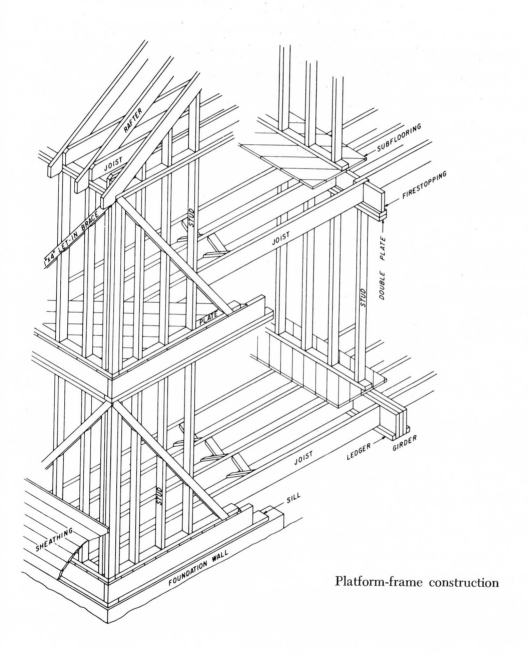

Platform-frame construction

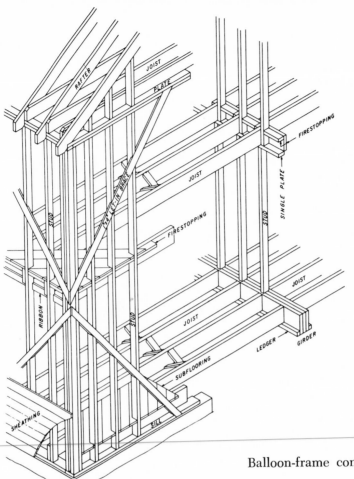

Balloon-frame construction

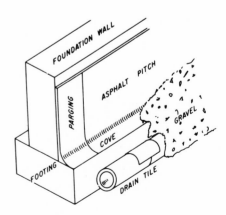

Continuous foundation
wall and footing

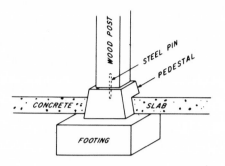

Support for basement
or cellar post

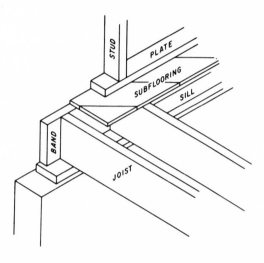

First-floor framing at exterior wall—
platform-frame construction

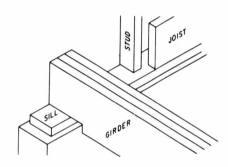

First-floor framing at
girder and exterior wall—
balloon-frame construction

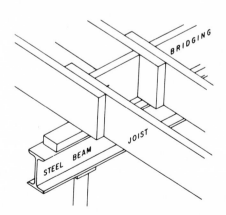

Joists resting on steel beam

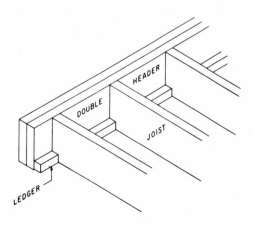

Framing of tail joists
to header on ledger strip

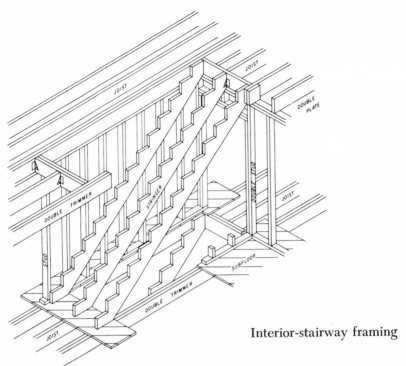

Interior-stairway framing

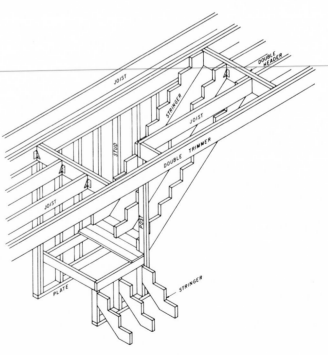

Framing for stairway with a landing

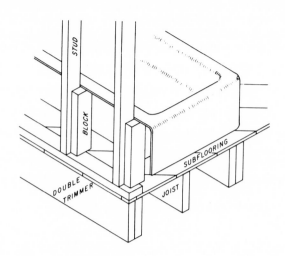

Support of bathtub
against wall framing

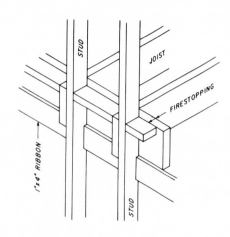

Second-floor framing
over bearing partition—
balloon-frame construction

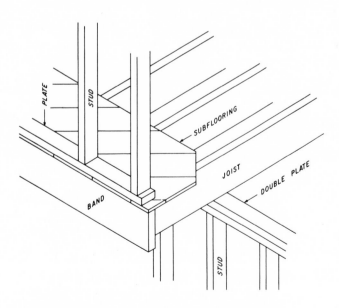

Overhang of exterior wall at second floor
with joists at right angles to wall below

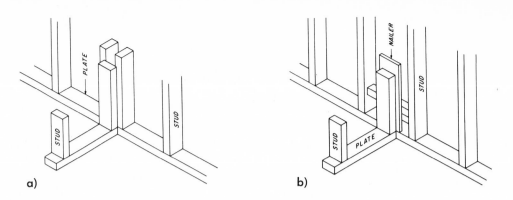

a) b)

Assembly of studs where partition meets wall

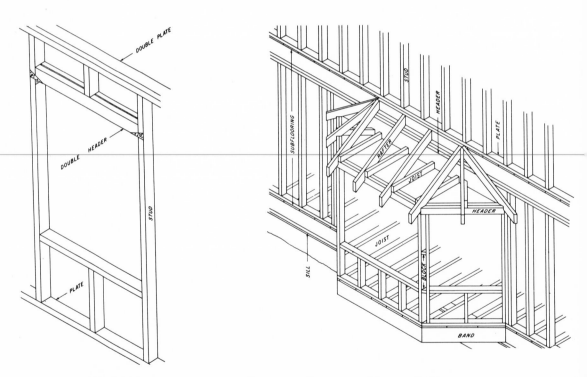

Framing around exterior-wall
opening with header
supported by framing anchors

Framing of bay window

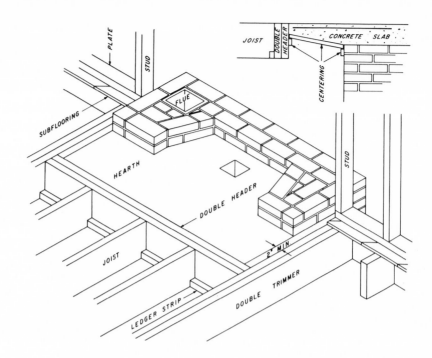

Floor-framing
around fireplace

Hearth centering
detail

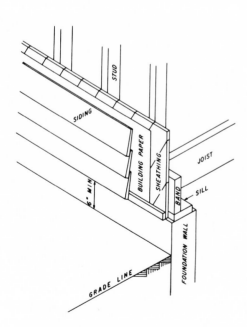

Clearance between
exterior siding and ground

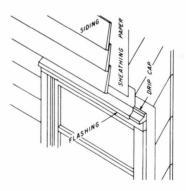

Application of bevel siding
over wood sheathing

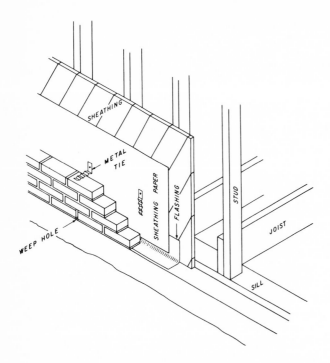

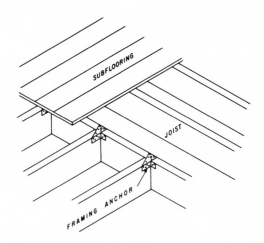

Application of masonry veneer
over sheathing and wood framing

Alternate joint detail

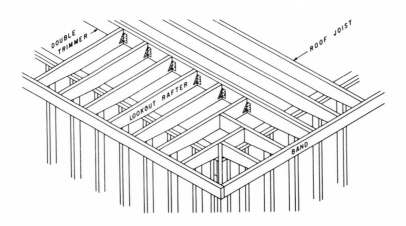

Corner framing for flat roofs

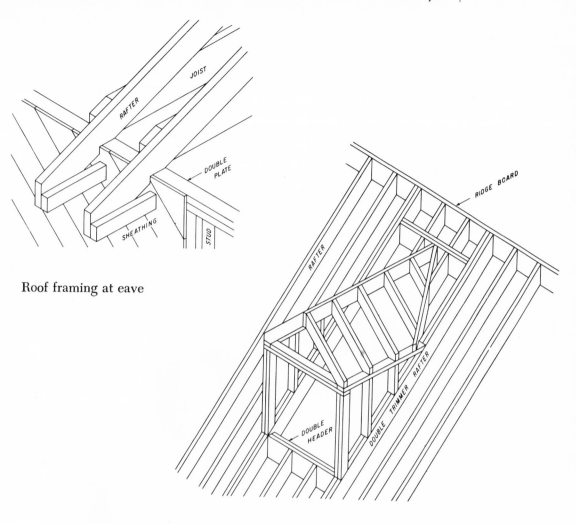

Roof framing at eave

Method of framing gable dormer

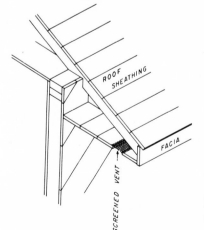

Method for installing
ventilation in roof overhang

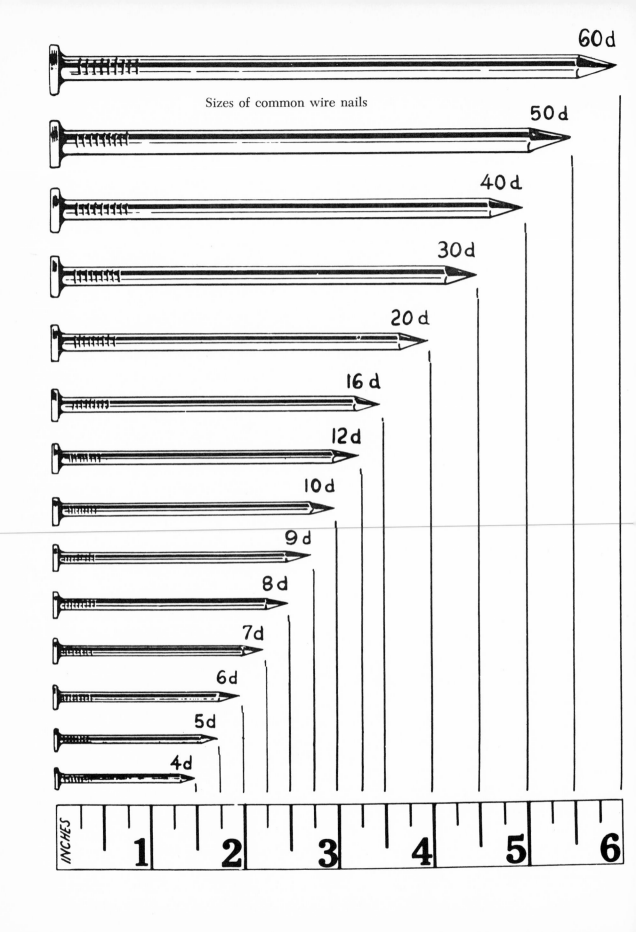

Sizes of common wire nails

How Long Does It Take? **13**

"How long does it take to renovate an Offbeat Dream House?" A good question.

As you read over the case histories of families who have renovated OB Houses you will note the wide range in time required to complete these renovations. Some houses were renovated in three or four months; some required years and they still have work to be done on them. You don't have to be experienced in the construction field to know that regardless of its size and condition, no house is going to take years to remodel or renovate if a crew of men is working on it five days a week. When you read or hear of long-term renovation projects, you can be sure that the work was done in stages. After a certain amount of work was done there was a lapse of time, and then another area of the house was tackled. A renovation project is often handled in this way if the family is in no great rush to complete the job or has not decided exactly what it wants. Then, too, a renovation job must often be handled in this manner when there is a limited budget. Time must be allowed between stages of work in order to allow the financial well to fill up.

Naturally enough, the time required for a renovation job depends also on how the work is done. If you commission an architect to draw up the plans and supervise the work, the job can go rapidly even with a very complex and extensive project. By the way, if you are going to utilize the services of an architect the time to start looking for the right one is directly after you've found a piece of property that is of interest to you. We might go a step further and say that the time to look for an architect is when you first decide that you might want to buy an OB House.

If you decide to do all or most of the work yourself, renovation can take months or years, depending on how fast you work and how much time you can devote to the project. The Goodspeeds, for example, whose renovation project is described among the case histories later in this book, have been working on their place for almost 20 years and, because they enjoy this sort of work, look forward to the projects they will tackle in the years to come. But most of us, even if we plan to do some of the work ourselves, are usually in a rush to complete the project and consequently are interested in how to do this.

You should understand that the time-consuming aspect of a renovation job is not so much the actual work itself, assuming that it is done by professionals, but getting to the point where the work can begin. And the work can't begin until you know what you want done, until you have selected a contractor, until the contractor has been able to fit your job into his schedule, and until all the materials are available to do the job. These are the items that take time to coordinate and these are the factors that can make a renovation job drag on unless you get started on them as early in the game as you can.

If you want a renovation project to move right along, here is your basic timetable:

1. Decide what you want to do with the place and make some rough drawings of what you have in mind
2. As soon as you've done this, select a contractor
3. Finish off the final plans and specifications and give these to the contractor
4. Work begins

Using this timetable, it would be possible for the actual work to start on the day after you take title to the property. This could mean a saving of one or two months as opposed to doing nothing at all until you have actually taken title.

Let's discuss the timetable in more detail:

ROUGH PLANS AND IDEAS

You must have some idea of what you plan to do with the property before it is worth your while to talk seriously to a contractor. You don't have to be specific on every detail at this stage of the game, but you should be able to give him an idea of the extent of the project. If you have an agreement with the present owner of the property so that you have access to it, you can start working on your plans as soon as your offer to buy has been accepted. You and your architect, if you are using one, need to spend enough time in the house so that you can begin to plan. You want to draw a plan of what you have and then rough in what you want to do in the way of renovation work. We have said earlier that where a tricky and complex renovation job is involved, with many choices as to the direction to take, we'd prefer to live in the place for a time before making a final decision. But if you are in a hurry to get going and the project isn't too complex in regard to planning, a few long visits to the structure should be enough to work out the rough plans.

LINING UP A CONTRACTOR

Just as soon as you have an idea of the amount and type of work that will be required, go over the project with contractors. Start getting the names of qualified contractors in your area as quickly as you can so that by the time you have rough plans you'll know of people to call in. You will be interested not only in the cost estimate on the job and the general reputation of the contractor but also the time when he can begin the work. It would be ideal to find a contractor who could start work on the day after you take title, but this can happen only if you start on your plans and selection of the contractor well in advance of closing.

COMPLETING PLANS AND SPECIFICATIONS

If you have been pushing yourself to complete the steps just described, you should have some time intervening after you have found a contractor and before the closing. Use this time to finish your plans and to draw up specifications of the materials you wish to use on the job. Once these have been completed, discuss them with your contractor. After he has gone over this material, he can give you a firm bid on the job and you can sign a letter of agreement with him specifying the amount of money involved and the day he will start work. But don't let it go at that. If there are still some weeks before the work is to begin, keep in touch with the contractor. Call him once a week just to let him know you're on the ball. Keep him posted and tell him you're looking forward to seeing him and his crew on the job on the day specified in the letter of agreement.

If you are planning to function as your own general contractor, then as soon as you have your rough plans, start lining up the various subcontractors you will need—carpenters, plumbers, masons, painters, and electricians.

Even if you are not in a desperate rush or cannot get your plans set too far in advance, begin checking out contractors as soon as you have some idea of the amount of work involved. Few good contractors can start work the day following a telephone call announcing that their bid has been accepted. Contractors schedule jobs many months in advance and trying to get one to begin work on a few days' notice is as realistic as expecting a doctor to see you at the time for which your appointment was made, or driving into a garage and expecting your car to be serviced then and there. The earlier you get your project on a contractor's schedule, the better.

If you want to begin a renovation job in the spring or summer, make arrangements during the preceding winter. Call a contractor on the first of May and ask him when he can start on a job for you and he'll start talking about Thanksgiving or the week between Christmas and New Year's. In most sections of the country, spring, summer, and fall are extremely busy times for contractors. Things do slow down in winter but working during the winter can create some other time-consuming delays. After the ground freezes, certain kinds of work such as digging trenches for foundations or water pipes comes to a stop. This work can, of course, be done when the ground is frozen but most contractors dislike getting involved in it because of the cost. Therefore, if you have a project that involves work of this nature and it isn't done before the ground freezes, you'll have to sit around twiddling your thumbs and praying for a January thaw or an early spring.

Delays in obtaining materials can also cause a slowdown of construction work. The distribution of building materials is not always equal to that of a nationally advertised breakfast food or a new and improved toothpaste. This is especially true of the more specialized building products such as custom-made spiral staircase materials. A considerable amount of time as well as money can be wasted on a job while waiting for an essential item to arrive. And we have found that somehow when a vital item is required and must be shipped from a distant point, a railroad or trucking strike is in process or the item becomes lost in transit.

To avoid delays to the extent possible, discuss with your contractor early in the game—as soon as you have your final plans and specifications put together—the materials and equipment needed for your job. Have him check on the availability of all items that he knows are not commonly stocked by local lumberyards and building-supply houses. Any item not locally available should be ordered at once so that when needed it will be on hand and not half a continent away.

You will find it helpful to set up a timetable for these preliminaries. Assuming that you want to get going with the job in a hurry and that you have one month from the time you agree to buy until you take legal title, here is how you might work out a timetable.

First Week.   Start pulling your rough plans together. Get the names of contractors and find out which ones are in a position to take on a project in the immediate future. Do not waste time with someone who can't handle your job for six months or so. By the end of this week you should have the names of several contractors who are distinct possibilities.

Second Week. Finish your rough plans and make appointments with the various contractors you have selected to discuss the plans and the project in general. Do this early in the week so that by the end of that same week you can obtain estimates from each contractor on the cost of the job.

Third Week. Select the contractor you plan to use. Get the final plans completed along with specifications and give them to the contractor so that you can discuss them with him in detail. Ask the contractor to have a firm bid based on final plans and specifications in your hands by the end of the week or the first of following week.

Fourth Week. Go over the bid with contractor and, if it is satisfactory, get it in writing along with a commitment from him as to the day work will start.

As you can see, the job of getting off to a fast start is up to you. If you don't get your plans set, if you don't get around to calling contractors, if you don't push contractors to submit their estimates, matters can drag along for weeks and even months. On the other hand, if you set deadlines for yourself, live up to your deadlines, and push the others to meet the deadlines you set for them, you may quite easily find that the day after you take title to the property the work on your Offbeat Dream House can begin.

Off to Work 14

Part of the pleasure in fixing up a house is doing some of the work yourself. Of course, there are many who have renovated houses without lifting a hammer and have found the entire project most satisfying. Still, to my mind, having someone do all the work for you just can't be the same as if you had done some of it yourself, because putting your own labor into the job makes it very much your baby. So for those of you who expect to get out there and do some work, here is a quick refresher course in the gentle art of manual labor.

WEAR SUITABLE CLOTHING

Let's start off by getting the right sort of clothing. We want something comfortable, something that will be easy to work in and also something that affords protection. You can do a good many jobs like painting, sanding, or putting panes of glass in a window, wearing sneakers, tight-fitting Levis and a bright-colored sports shirt or blouse, but this is not the ideal costume to wear if you are ripping out a partition, putting in a new one, hauling stone or block, or working with paint removers. Years ago in our bachelor days, a friend and I were putting on a roof and a young lady came around one day to help us

181

along. We were installing black asphalt shingles and she was wearing white tennis shorts and if you wear white tennis shorts and sit on black asphalt shingles on a hot day for long enough, you only look chic from the front.

You should have a pair of good shoes, and the best kind are those made for workmen. They have thick soles with a nonslip design, a reinforced toe so that you can drop something pretty heavy on them before it really hurts, and they come high enough to protect the ankle. If you wear these with a pair of heavy socks, your feet will be quite happy and there will be less chance of a turned ankle, a nail coming through the sole, or a bruised foot.

Next come pants, and you want to avoid anything tight-fitting, because this restricts movement. Pants made for workmen are cut much fuller in the legs, thigh, and bottom than those made for drones. Granted, the ones made for workmen are not as becoming as the tight-fitting variety, especially for girls, but they are comfortable, do not restrict movement, and are durable.

We personally prefer long trousers for any heavy work, regardless of the temperature. Shorts are fine for light stuff but for heavy work where you may have to get down on your knees or handle materials that could give you a nasty scratch, long trousers are best.

Shirts, too, should have long sleeves to provide protection when required. They should be cut loose enough to be comfortable, but not so loose that they get in the way. Workmen's blue shirts are ideal.

You will want a pair of work gloves, a couple of pairs, in fact. For heavy work get a pair of leather gauntlets. These will protect your wrists as well as your hands. For light work such as painting and sanding, cotton work gloves are fine. Unless you don't mind a lot of little cuts and scratches, wear gloves as much as possible if you are not too experienced in handling tools and materials. A piece of coarse steel wool can give you a nasty little cut, or a handsaw may jump out of the cut and scratch your wrist. You should also have a cap to wear when you are doing work that involves dust, such as removing old plaster. And if you're sensitive to dust, wear a mask.

WATCH OUT FOR YOUR HEALTH

Get a tetanus shot or, if you have had one, a booster. They don't hurt and should you step on a rusty nail or get cut on a piece of metal you won't have to rush about trying to find a doctor to give you an anti-tetanus shot. You should also buy a little first-aid kit and keep this handy on the job—nothing too complicated but enough to take care of minor cuts and burns. Get a pair of safety goggles and wear them when it seems sensible.

If you haven't been doing much physical work lately, break yourself in gradually. Don't try to use all your muscles the first day. Take it very slowly at the beginning. Don't do heavy work for hour on hour. Do a little heavy stuff and then switch to lighter work. When you start feeling tired, stop work. There is much more chance of getting hurt when you are tired, and work you do then often has to be redone the following day because you just didn't do it correctly. After you have been working for a few days you will be surprised at how quickly your muscles tone up and how many hours you can work before feeling tired.

Men in construction work, and they should know, have their own special routine. They get to work quite early in the morning, seven or eight o'clock. They work until noon, have a light lunch, and then work until around four o'clock. You will probably find that your most productive period is in the morning, so try to get started early. Have a good breakfast and a light lunch. Drink plenty of liquids, especially in hot weather and when you are doing hard physical work. Taking a salt tablet if you perspire a lot is not a bad idea. Be extremely careful about taking liquor when working. A beer at lunch probably won't hurt, but two beers will make you a little slow and careless and sleepy. Don't drink hard liquor if you expect to go back to work, and do not ever serve it to friends who may come over to give you a hand. Having a group of friends come over and bringing out a pitcher of cold martinis may be an attractive way to entertain but it is not the way to get a job done and one of these friends might also get hurt, so keep the martinis out of sight until quitting time.

If you have a workman on the job, don't serve him beer or liquor until he has finished for the day. Most good workmen won't touch even beer while they are on the job because they know it slows them up.

A WARNING ABOUT FRIENDS

Once you get started on an Offbeat Dream House project, some of your friends will be dying to visit for a day or a weekend to give you a hand. This is fine, but often they are more trouble than they are worth when it comes to giving you any real help. If you have to spend an entire weekend supervising your friends on the job, you may not get too much done yourself. Even worse is spending the time hunting up jobs that you think they can handle. It might be best to wait until you have the kind of work that you feel your friends could manage, painting, for example. And before you get involved with friends working on your place, check with your insurance agent to be certain that if they should get hurt, you, and they, will be covered.

WHAT TOOLS WILL YOU NEED?

The number and type of tools you'll need will depend on how much you plan to do and the kind of work involved. One thing you should not do is rush off and buy every tool that catches your eye. Tools are expensive and few things are as expensive as a tool that you don't need. Some men collect tools the same way some women collect cookbooks. It may be all right for women to act this way but a man is supposed to be a reasonable animal and should not buy something he can't use. (My wife said "Hah!" when she read that.)

A good approach to tools is to buy some that are new, some that are used or second hand, and rent others. ("How about something blue?" my wife asked.) Buy those tools new that involve cutting edges or accuracy. This would include planes, chisels, saws, and squares. Rough tools such as sledgehammers, picks, crowbars, wrecking bars, that can't be easily harmed and are only used occasionally, can often be picked up secondhand at considerable saving. Specialized equipment that is used only once and for a relatively short time, power saws and heavy-duty sanders, for example, can be rented by the day or week.

CARPENTRY TOOLS

You will probably need some tools for ripping out old work, some for rough carpentry, and some for the finish carpentry work. If you have to get yourself these tools, here is what you will need:

1. A claw hammer. They come in different weights, so pick the heaviest one that seems comfortable to you. If the hammer is too heavy you'll tire easily, but if it's too light you'll have trouble driving in heavy nails.
2. A carpenter's hatchet is a useful tool to have. It is both hatchet and hammer and good for rough work.
3. You will want a set of screwdrivers to handle different-sized screws.
4. You will need at least one saw, a crosscut saw for cutting boards across the grain. If a board is to be cut lengthwise, a ripsaw is best but you can get along with a crosscut.
5. You will definitely need a plane. A block plane is the little fellow and is good for a great many jobs.
6. If you have items to shave down, such as doors, better get a big 14-inch jack plane.
7. A brace and bit will be needed for making large holes.
8. A push-pull drill will be necessary for small holes.
9. A ⅜-inch electric drill is good for making holes in wood as well as in masonry and metal.
10. You should also get a star drill for making holes in masonry.
11. A chisel is needed for making cuts in wood that can't be made with a saw or plane. Get a heavy-duty type with a 1-inch blade. Pick up other sizes as required.
12. As far as measuring tools go, get a 96-inch steel tape. You might as well buy two because they have a habit of getting misplaced.
13. For marking cuts in large boards, you need a framing square.

14. A combination square will be needed for marking cuts in small stock—that is, stock under 12 inches wide.

15. You will also need a level, which is used to determine if a piece of material is absolutely horizontal or vertical.

16. A putty knife.

17. A pair of pliers.

18. A nail set.

19. A hacksaw for cutting metal.

20. If considerable demolition work must be done you will need a wrecking bar;

21. a pull and pry bar;

22. perhaps a crowbar;

23. and perhaps a sledgehammer.

24. You will need a couple of sawhorses to hold material for cutting. You can waste a great amount of time trying to cut material if you don't have an adequate setup on which to rest the materials. You can buy sawhorses or make them yourself out of 2-by-4s, and metal fittings that are made for this purpose and sold at hardware and lumber yards.

25. Be sure to include in your list a stepladder.

26. You may need a 20-foot extension ladder if you are going to be working on outside walls.

POWER TOOLS

If you plan to do a lot of the heavy framing, such as walls and floors, where you are going to have to have numerous cuts in heavy stock, you should consider buying or renting a portable power saw. It will save you a great deal of time and will produce straighter cuts than if done by hand. You can get a good 7-inch portable saw for about $35, and it can be used on all the rough carpentry. If you plan to do the trim and cabinetwork yourself, then you should rent or buy a tilting-arbor or radial-arm saw, for these will provide the highly accurate cuts required for this sort of work. These units cost from about $100 up.

Along with the ⅜-inch drill, these saws are the two power tools that you should seriously consider buying at this stage of the game. The stores are filled with wonderful power equipment—sanders, paint sprayers, planes, and drill presses—but they are rather specialized and you are usually better off to rent them as they are needed.

MISCELLANEOUS TOOLS

For masonry work you will want a mason's trowel. You'll need a wheelbarrow, a steel one, for mixing mortar, but this can also be used for a variety of work during and after the renovation project. You will also need a hoe and a shovel for mixing mortar and concrete.

You should have some kind of box in which to keep hand tools. It need not be fancy, but tools do need a home if they are not going to become misplaced. You'll save yourself considerable time and frustration if you get into the habit of replacing a tool in the box as soon as you have finished using it. Watch a good carpenter at work and you'll notice that he never has to run around like a chicken with its head cut off, searching among boards and debris for a tool. He has automatically put the tool in its place so that it is ready for him the next time. The tool box should be arranged in such a way that saws, chisels, and other tools with cutting edges can be set so that the cutting edge won't come into contact with metal and become dulled.

Now that you have the proper clothes and the tools, you need just one more item before you start work and that is self-discipline. When an amateur becomes involved in a building project, there is a strong desire to rush ahead and do those things that will produce the most immediate and dramatic results. When we were on our first building project, we were in such a hurry to get a structure framed and roofed that we didn't take time to bother with adequate foundations. We just had four house jacks at each corner; then the time came to put in decent foundations, and believe me, it's a lot easier to put in foundations before a structure is built than afterward. If there is a grand design in construction, part of it is based on discipline. You do the most essential things first, you work from bottom to top, and you don't add the window boxes and geraniums until you have put in the footings.

We know of one man who bought an OB House and spent the entire summer and fall digging out an old pond so that he would have a place where he could ice-skate in the winter. His wife thought that it was more important to get indoor plumbing and she finally left him. Another couple we know got a fixation on killing poison ivy that was on a fence about 300 feet from their house. There was nothing wrong with this endeavor except that half the windows in the house were missing and while our friends were chasing the poison ivy a pair of bats started a colony in their attic.

► *Special Money-Saving Tips*

You can save about $250 on framing and applying sub-flooring to an area 20 by 20 feet if you do the job yourself.

You can save more than $100 on construction of a flight of wooden outdoor steps by doing the construction work yourself.

You can save more than $500 on framing, sheathing, and roofing a one-car garage by doing it yourself.

Time-Savers 15

Weekend renovators are always up against the problem of not having enough time. There are just so many hours on a weekend or a vacation and there is always so much to do that the one thing you can't afford is frittering away even a few hours. Careful planning and the use of time-saving materials and tools will help you to get the most out of your limited time.

SAVE TIME BY PLANNING AHEAD

You can avoid wasting time by planning ahead, so that when you are ready to go to work, you have all the materials and tools you will need for the projects involved. Watch a good carpenter on a job and you will see that a little before quitting time he stops to figure out what he will need in the way of materials and equipment for the next day's work. He checks over his supplies on the job to be sure that he has enough nails of the right size, enough lumber of a certain size, and if additional materials are required, he will list these and pick them up on his way to the job in the morning. You will seldom find a good carpenter or any other experienced craftsman who has to leave a job to pick up something that he needs, or is unable to continue because he

189

lacks a certain material or tool. Use this same approach yourself. Knock off work early enough on Sunday afternoon, before you are too tired, and figure out what you are going to do over the next weekend. Analyze each project and make a list of the materials and other equipment you will need so that you can order them to be delivered before Saturday or pick them up Friday afternoon. Don't waste time on Saturday rushing around in crowded lumber yards and hardware stores picking up items that should have been on the job Saturday morning when you were ready to start.

It takes a little practice before you can see quickly what you will need for a particular project. In the beginning, you are just going to have to spend the time analyzing the job step by step, but by so doing you will save time in the long run. Suppose, for example, you have planned to hang a door the following weekend. You need a door of the correct size and you need the right lock set and hinges of the right size. You may also need a jack plane to bring the door down to the correct width and height. You may even need a saw if the door is considerably larger than the opening. You will need one or more special-sized drills so that the lock and latch can be installed. You will, of course, need a screw driver and you will want to check over all the hardware to be sure that all the proper screws are included. If you don't have all these parts, you won't be able to hang the door and get the job finished.

On any renovation job some frustrating surprises are bound to occur because there was no way to plan for them in advance. You might have to disconnect a length of pipe and find that it can't be budged with the pipe wrench that you so thoughtfully had on hand for this very purpose. What you may need is a hacksaw and that may be the one thing you can't lay your hands on. There is just no way of knowing about such time-wasting delays in advance, but you can keep them down to a minimum by trying to anticipate your needs to the degree possible.

The weather can also interfere with carefully laid plans. Plan a weekend's work with the idea that you may not be able to work outside, but have an alternate project for indoors, with the required materials and equipment. It can be extremely frustrating if you had your heart set on opening the roof to install a skylight but must putter around for a couple of days because it happened to rain and you didn't have the materials for an inside project.

You can waste much precious time in trying to do by yourself a task that really requires two people. We once framed part of a roof alone and we figured it took us just about five times longer to put one rafter in place than it did when we had someone helping us. You do not often need a really skilled helper. What you need is someone to hold the other end of a board while you are getting it into place for nailing, or someone to help you position a sheet of gypsum wallboard and hold it there until you can get some nails in. Sometimes all you need is another pair of hands to hold one end of a measuring tape.

When you plan a project, analyze what is going to be done, then decide whether it can be done a lot faster if you have someone to help. If you can't get a helper, then hold off doing the job until one is available. Trying to do everything alone not only can waste time but may bring poor results.

Planning your projects must also take into account the time lapse necessary between certain phases of the work. This is particularly true of painting and decorating. If you want to paint a room but holes in the plaster must be patched first, the patch has to dry before you can begin to paint. If you install gypsum wallboard and tape the joints, you have to wait for the first coat of cement at the joints to dry before you can sand them and apply the next coat of cement. To get the maximum use from your time, you need to have other projects on which you can move ahead until you are able to return to the original one.

It will also save you time if you plan a day's work so that you do the exacting work in the early part of the day when you are fresh and alert. After five or six hours of hard work, most of us grow a bit weary and weariness can make us careless. You should not do fine cabinetwork or anything else that requires maximum concentration and skill when you are fatigued. Do the tricky work in the morning and use the late afternoon for rough stuff where a few minor mistakes won't be a disaster.

ORGANIZE YOUR MATERIALS AND TOOLS

Make sure that your materials and tools are well organized. Materials should be stored where they are readily available and where you can easily see what you have and do not have. Lumber should be set aside according to size and length. Nails are better stored in boxes with the tops open so that you can see at a glance what you have. Rummaging through bags of nails wastes time and doesn't give a quick reading on what you have and the quantity.

Tools require even better organization than materials. A good craftsman not only learns that it is quicker to replace a tool where it can be easily reached than to toss it aside and have to hunt for it later, but also discovers that tossing tools aside is a good way to damage them. This kind of treatment will dull the cutting edges of saws and chisels.

Dull cutting tools not only make it difficult to do good work but they are time-wasters. With reasonable care, a cutting tool of good quality stays sharp for a long time. Eventually, of course, it will become dull. When a cutting tool starts to work with difficulty, get it sharpened at once. Most hardware stores will sharpen tools such as saws, chisels, plane blades, and drills, or they can tell you where this work can be done.

TIME-SAVING TOOLS

Power tools, of course, are great time-savers. Which ones to buy or rent depends on the job at hand and some of them have been discussed in the chapter "Off to Work."

Certainly when a large amount of lumber must be cut, a power saw is the ideal tool to have. A portable saw is good for rough work and a tilting-arbor saw can be used for both rough and finish work.

An electric drill is good for boring holes through wood, metal, and masonry; an attachment makes it possible to use this same tool for inserting wood screws. If a job requires many wood screws, this attachment is certainly going to save time as well as work. We remember watching two carpenters set off one morning to attach a plate made of 2-by-10 stock to the side of a house that was more than 40 feet in length. They tacked the pieces of 2-by-10 in place with a few nails and then used a heavy-duty drill to make holes about every 2 feet. Next, they put another attachment on the drill and used this to install large-diameter screws that were about ½ inch in diameter and about 6 inches in length. With the drill, this job took just a few minutes, but if they had to put those screws in by hand with a wrench it would probably have taken them all morning.

Heavy-duty sanders, gasoline or electric chain saws for cutting heavy beams and clearing out trees, routers for cutting grooves and mortises in wood, and all the other specialized power tools are tremendous time-savers. They probably won't be used enough to justify buying them, but they are certainly worth renting.

MAKE USE OF SPECIAL PRODUCTS

Many special products can be used to save time.

Metal framing plates are excellent for fastening in place the lumber used for walls and interior partitions, ceilings, and roofs. These plates also eliminate the need for some of the tricky cuts required when the lumber is to be joined together only with nails. They also eliminate a problem that so often faces the amateur, which is how many nails are required to make the joint strong. Often too many nails are used, thus producing a weak joint rather than a strong one. The metal plates have predrilled holes for the nails so you can't use too many.

Fast-drying latex paints are available for both inside and outside work. These paints dry in an hour or so, enabling you to apply two or even three coats to a surface in a single day. If you work fast you can do an entire room in a day and have it ready for use that same evening. These paints can also be applied over a damp surface.

Bare wood must have a primer before it can be painted, and an ordinary primer takes about a day to dry There are, however, fast-drying primers that will dry in about 40 minutes, so that you can prime and then apply a finish coat of paint to a surface in the same day.

Plaster of paris is an excellent material for filling holes in plaster because it dries in a very short time. This rapid drying can be a disadvantage if a large area must be repaired because the material dries so quickly that you hardly have time to apply the plaster. For small holes, it can't be beaten, however.

Fast-drying fillers are also available for use over nailheads in wood. These are ready for sanding and painting a few hours after they have been applied.

One way to fasten a piece of wood or other material to a masonry surface is to drill a hole in the masonry and then use an anchor bolt to secure the material. A much faster approach is to use something called a *stud driver*. You can get a type that will drive a special stud right through the material and into the masonry. If you have a great many wood strips to fasten to a masonry wall, this tool is worth having.

You'll find a variety of time-saving materials at your local hardware and paint store. With some, the time they actually save does not justify the cost, but many are excellent and allow you to get a lot more done than otherwise—and for a relatively small additional charge.

What to Do First 16

Your first goal in renovating your Offbeat Dream House is to make the place livable. This is essential if you plan to do much of the work yourself, because you don't want to waste time driving back and forth between the job and wherever it is that you eat and sleep. It is also rather foolish to pay money to a local inn or motel when you already have a place of your own. If you live and eat at your own place you will be able to start work early in the morning, knock off when you get tired, rest for a time, and then go back to work. Then, too, as we've mentioned earlier, by spending abundant time there you will be able to get the feel of the new place and determine how well your original plans will work. No doubt you will make some changes for the better, because you have had time to study the plans in relation to the structure.

It is not too difficult or expensive to make a house, even a rather run-down house, comfortable if it has the basic essentials—water, light, and some form of heat. You may need some paper window shades for privacy, some cots to sleep on, and a few cooking utensils.

If you have a structure that lacks all improvements, you should first try to get electricity. It isn't necessary to have the entire place wired. In fact you wouldn't want to do that job at this time anyway. What you should get is a *construction service entrance* consisting of an electric

195

meter, a fuse box, and a box containing some outlets. With this you will have a source of power for lights, power tools, a refrigerator, and other needed appliances. Call your local electric company, which can arrange to put this construction service entrance in for you.

Until such time as you get electricity you can operate with kerosene or gasoline lamps. Much of the equipment made for outdoor camping is ideal for solving some of the living problems you will face until your place is fixed up.

Water is essential, so your next move is to get a water supply. If there is a source of water but it is not run to the house, get a pump and a line installed so that you have a cold-water faucet inside the house. Until such time as you have your plans set and know exactly where the bathroom is going to be placed, this arrangement will have to do. You can use a chemical toilet and heat hot water on an electric hot plate. This arrangement is primitive, but you can live with it.

If warmth is required, electric heaters and warm clothing are the best solution for a short-term haul. A kerosene space heater is also good, and worth the money if you expect that it will be some weeks or months before central heating is installed.

RECHECK YOUR PLANS

Once you can live in your new home and are able to spend time there, keep going over your plans. If you have empty space, such as a warehouse or barn, draw out the partitions with chalk on the floor to give yourself a better idea of how the plan will look when it is transformed into walls and doors. Try to avoid doing any construction or demolition work until you are satisfied, completely satisfied, that the plans are the best that can be devised to suit your needs.

MAKE IT WEATHERTIGHT

You should make certain that the roof does not leak—or if it does, repair the leaks or put on a new roof. If you don't plan to make any changes in the roof, such as adding dormers or a skylight, and if it is in poor condition, this might be the best time to reroof. If you do plan changes that will affect the roof, patch it if possible and put off reroofing until the structural changes have been made.

Replace broken or missing panes of glass in windows that are in good condition and that you plan to retain. If the sash is eventually going to be replaced, tack a piece of cardboard or thin plywood over the opening to keep out the wind and the rain. Inspect the exterior siding and renail any loose pieces. Many outbuildings have a single layer of siding and often cracks between the boards are wide enough to let the wind and weather through. You can make these walls weathertight by covering them on the outside with heavy-duty plastic sheeting. This material is sold at lumber yards and can be applied with staples to woodwork.

CLEARING OUT

Your next move might well be to get rid of whatever junk may be in and around the place. Unless you are certain about your plans, don't do any ripping out at this point. Just remove the loose materials, old furniture, and useless lumber and boards. Start at the basement or basement crawl space and work up to the attic. You don't want trash underfoot, for it will just get in the way. Locate someone in the area with a truck to haul the collection away to a dump area. If you have a considerable renovation job on your hands you will have a large quantity of waste to be hauled away from time to time. This waste is a fire hazard, so don't let too much of it accumulate.

FOUNDATIONS

Do not put money and work into a place unless you are sure that the foundations are solid. If the foundations are continuous and made of poured concrete, masonry block, or stone (even if it is laid up without mortar), then you can assume that there isn't much, if any, work required here. You may wish at some point to make the dry stone wall watertight by filling in the joints between the stone with mortar and then applying a coat over the entire surface, but this can usually wait until other matters more pressing have been attended to. There is always the chance, however, that the foundations have settled unevenly so that the structure resting on them is not level. You can determine this by placing a ball—any ball, including a tennis ball, will do—in the middle of the floor and noting the direction in which it rolls and how fast. If it rushes over to one corner of the room or area, that corner is low, very low. In this event it would be wise to call in a contractor and have him jack the structure up to make it level.

If the structure rests on posts, either of wood or masonry, it is desirable to put in a solid foundation of masonry block, and it is essential to do this if the house is to be heated in winter. As explained earlier, some farm buildings have no foundations but are built on wooden mud sills that rest directly on the ground or on a few stones. These should be replaced with masonry foundations and this job is certainly one for a contractor because it involves jacking up the structure so that the mud sills can be removed and adequate foundations installed.

At the same time you are inspecting and determining what work must be done on the foundations, inspect the beams and joists that support the first floor. Make any necessary changes that are required here to give you a solid and level first floor. This subject is covered in detail in the chapter on "Floors and Flooring."

If you are going to have a contractor come in to do work on the foundations and if the first floor needs additional support, you might as well let him do both these jobs for you. It will be easier and less expensive in the long run if the two jobs are done at the same time.

CLEARING OUT THE INTERIOR

As soon as you are completely satisfied with your plans, you can go ahead and rip out those walls and partitions that will not be required. Tearing out can be fun; it is a good way to get rid of hostilities, but remember that you are a house renovator and not a house wrecker. Remove only that which you are sure you don't need and be careful—you do not want to damage work that is to remain. It is easy to get so carried away ripping out a partition that a piece of lumber crashes through a window that you had planned to save. So take it easy. Also remember that if you remove materials carefully you may be able to use them for some other purpose and thereby save yourself money.

If you have an empty barn, there may not be too much of anything to rip out. An old home is quite another matter, and you may find that you'll have several truckloads of stuff that has to come out.

Before you start this work it is a good idea to cover the floors with building paper. If the floors are good, this covering will protect them, but even if the floors are eventually to be covered with a finish flooring, the paper will make it easier to clean up. You can buy this inexpensive building paper at a lumberyard and tack it down with staples or masking tape.

Try to remove items in the largest pieces that you can handle. If you are ripping old wallboard off a wall, try to take it down a sheet at a time. If you break it up into little bits it will take many trips to carry it to the truck, whereas it will take only one trip if it is in a solid sheet.

REMOVING INTERIOR WALL AND CEILING COVERINGS

You will want to remove interior wall and ceiling coverings when a partition is to be removed or when the material is not sound or if you wish to use something else in its place. The most common types of covering you'll find are wallboard, which comes in 4-by-8-foot sheets, and plaster. Wallboard is fastened to the framework with nails, and these you can remove with a claw hammer. In many older houses you may find that wallboard has been applied over old plaster; in this case, after the wallboard is out of the way, the plaster and lath should go too.

Plaster and Lath. Where wall and ceiling plaster is in extremely poor condition, it will have to be removed. Many plaster surfaces, as discussed in *Restoring Plaster Walls and Ceilings* in the chapter on "Interior Walls and Ceilings," can be saved, but if the plaster has pulled away from the lath, it is beyond hope. You can tell if this is the case by pushing against the plaster with your hand. If it moves, it is no longer attached to the lath. If there are many large areas where the plaster has fallen out, if the plaster feels very damp, or if you wish to remove the partition, the plaster and the lath will have to go.

The first step in this operation is to remove the trim from around windows and doors and between walls and floor and walls and ceiling. If the trim is worth saving, do this carefully so as not to damage the wood any more than is absolutely necessary. Trim is fastened with finishing or casing nails and these have small heads. Use a pull and pry bar to ease the wood gently away from the surface. Work along the entire length of the wood, moving it a little bit at a time. The nails probably won't come out. Instead the wood will be pulled away from the nails and after the trim has been removed the nails can be removed with a claw hammer. If the nails don't pull through the wood easily, put a block of scrap wood on the trim and tap it back into place. The nailheads will pop beyond the surface, where they can be pulled with the claw hammer. Protect the wood from being dented by the hammer with a piece of scrap wood placed between the hammer head and trim. If you wish to save the trim, store it where it will be out of your way.

Now for the plaster and lath. Removing them is dirty work. Wear a cap, heavy gloves, and long sleeves. It is wise to wear goggles, also, especially if you have to do a ceiling. If dust bothers you, wear a mask. You should have on hand a number of empty cartons in which you can put the plaster. Tossing it out the window is fast but then you will have to spend time picking it up and tossing it into the truck so it can be hauled away.

Do the ceiling first. Use a wrecking bar or pry bar to make a hole in the plaster, slip the tool under the plaster as far as it can go, then give a pull, and duck. Some plaster will be in such poor condition that you don't need any tools to remove it except your hands. Once the ceiling is done, do the walls. A great deal of dust is involved in this job. Open windows and close off the door to the area so that the dust won't spread over the rest of the place. Pile the old plaster into the cartons and take it out of the room.

In most old houses the plaster is applied to wood lath, and old wood lath isn't good for much except kindling wood and garden stakes. You may be able to rip it off with your hands but if it won't respond, use the wrecking bar. After you get a good many pieces of lath down, put them together, tie them up, and take them outside. Lath has a nasty habit of getting tangled up and if you wait until you have a whole room full you'll spend hours trying to get the stuff in some sort of order to haul away.

Removing Partitions.   You have learned from the chapter "What Is It and What Does It Do?" that there are two types of partitions—load-bearing and non-load-bearing. If you are going to remove a partition, you must know which type it is because if this partition is ripped out, some other means of support for the ceiling above must be provided. Non-load-bearing partitions are those that run in the same direction as the ceiling joists. You can determine this from above, in the attic or attic crawl space, or because you have exposed the ceiling joists. Even if there is an attic floor you can find which way the joists run because they will run at right angles to the direction of the flooring. If there is any doubt in your mind as to the direction of the joists, have a carpenter or contractor handle this end of the job for you.

Barns, farm buildings, warehouses, and garages, are often so constructed that they contain no load-bearing partitions at all. Sometimes there are just partial walls that are open at the top; these can be removed with ease.

A word of warning here about partitions. They may have something inside that does not meet the eye. It may be a water pipe, heating line, or electric cable. Wiring is not a great problem but you will definitely want to *turn off the power* and have this line disconnected before you start work so that you won't get a shock. Water and heating lines are something else again, and in an old house it is not always possible to determine where they run until you open a partition or a wall. Usually they can be moved but it is going to cost money.

The framework of a partition is not difficult to remove. The vertical pieces (the studding) are nailed to a plate at the top and bottom. Nails are usually "toe-nailed," that is, driven in at an angle. You can pull them out with a wrecking bar in most cases. If you don't have any use for the studs you can often set one end free of the stud by giving it a few good raps with a heavy hammer and then prying it loose.

THE NEW WORK

Once you have cleared the structure of all the items to be eliminated, the work of reconstruction begins. First the framing is done and that means the framing for rooms, halls, closets, and such. Once the framing is in place, the rough wiring can be installed. This involves the cables and the outlet boxes that will serve for ceiling and wall fixtures, as well as the ordinary wall outlets. If the planning for electric wiring has been done carefully, the electrician can do almost all his work at this time. He can complete everything except installation of the metal or plastic plates that go on over outlets and switches, and any fixtures that are required. These few minor items will have to wait until the walls and ceilings are finished and decorated. You can do all or most of these little installation jobs yourself.

With all the framing up, the plumber can also get to work and do the "roughing in" for the bathroom and kitchen. This consists of installing the fresh-water and waste lines and bringing them to the point where they will be connected to the various fixtures. The bathtub is usually put into place at this time because it is much easier to get a tub into place before finished walls and a door frame are installed. The other fixtures will wait until walls and floors are finished.

If you have been getting along without a bathroom, you don't have to wait to complete work on the entire house before putting one in. What you should do is to finish off the bathroom right away. Get the bathroom walls covered with gypsum wallboard or whatever materials you plan to use, and the same for the ceiling. Install the finish floor for the bathroom—probably tile, linoleum, or vinyl. Hang the bathroom door. At this time you don't even have to bother covering both sides of the walls that frame the bathroom, just the sides that face the room. If you do this, your plumber can install the toilet and lavatory and you're in business.

The plumbing for a kitchen is not so easy to rush unless you are going to install a ready-made cabinet sink. If you are going to use one of these units rather than a custom-built cabinet sink, the walls in back of the sink area can be completed and the sink can be installed and connected to the fresh-water and waste lines.

The major portion of the heating system also goes in at this time. Here again the heating contractor may not be able to complete all the work until more of the other work has been completed, but he can manage to arrange things so that you can have some heat immediately.

Until the plumbing, heating, and especially the wiring have been done, not much can be accomplished inside in the way of installing wall covering and flooring. This might be a good time to do some other essentials, such as replacing broken window panes, stripping paint off doors where required, and applying new siding. You should make sure that all windows and doors are in good condition before you get into any finish work. It is easy to remove and work on these units when there are no decorated walls and woodwork, but if you wait to fool with them until everything else is finished you may have a lot of touching up to do.

When the basic wiring, heating, and plumbing have been completed, outside walls and ceiling should be insulated if the framework for these elements is exposed. See the chapter on "Insulation." After this has been done, the interior wall coverings are applied. See the section on *Interior Wall Materials* in the chapter on "Interior Walls and Ceilings." Make certain that whoever applies these leaves the necessary openings where there are electric outlets and plumbing lines. Time after time we have seen it happen that wallboard or plaster is applied right over outlet boxes and capped pipes, and this means a lot of time spent tapping around to find the location of these things in back of the wall material, and then cutting out an area so they will be exposed.

The finish floor goes down next and should be immediately covered with building paper because you don't want to have it scratched or spattered with paint. Once it is in place the remainder of the bathroom fixtures can go into place along with the kitchen fixtures. Your heating man can come back to finish up his work.

The final carpentry work consists of trim around doors, windows, and base molding. Once the trim is in place, the holes above the nail heads will have to be filled with spackle and the wood given a light sanding. Knots should be given a coat of orange shellac so that they will not bleed through the finish paint.

You are almost finished now. There is, however, still some painting to do. Take each room one at a time. Do the ceiling first, then the walls, and finally the woodwork. If you are using wallpaper as well as paint, do the painting before you hang the paper.

Once the ceiling and walls are decorated, the ceiling light fixtures can be connected into place and the plates installed for outlets and electric switches.

When you are certain that a room is completely finished, strip off the building paper from the floor and that's that.

Of course, you may still have a good deal of work to do on the outside of the house. It may need painting, and you may find it necessary to strip off the old paint before you apply the new. It may be that you wish to apply new exterior siding, build a deck, porch, or terrace. You will want to attend to these things as quickly as possible, but they should be done after you have completed the inside of the house and not before.

Materials 17

If you are going to use a contractor on the renovation project you probably don't have to be too concerned as to where he gets his materials. You do, of course, want to be certain that if you have specified a certain brand of window, for example, he gets this brand and not the brand that happens to be carried by his favorite lumberyard.

If you are going to do a lot of the work yourself, however, then you will have to become very much involved with all of the many different materials that go into the project, where you get them, and how to order them. The vast majority of these materials are going to come from a lumberyard. Actually they are really building supply houses, for most of them carry materials other than lumber.

LUMBER YARDS

The chances are that there will be several lumberyards in your general area. Before you settle on one it is wise to visit them all and see which one is best for you. If possible, you want a yard that can supply you with all your basic requirements. These include lumber, windows, doors, insulation, wallboard, roofing materials, nails, cement, sand, gravel, masonry block, and just about everything else you will require,

205

with the possible exception of paint, wallpaper, and small items of hardware that you can pick up at a paint or hardware store. A great many of the materials you get from the yard will have to be delivered by truck —they can't even fit into a large station wagon—so you can save time if you are able to place an order with one outfit for all the materials you will require for a period of time.

You also want a lumberyard where the people are helpful. You will need their help in estimating the amount of material you will need for a particular job. If the clerks are good, they will also help you to get everything you need for the proper installation of materials. If, for example, you want enough wallboard to cover a wall 8 by 24 feet, a good clerk will not only give you enough wallboard to do the job but will also see that you have enough of the right type and size of nail, will inquire if you have tape and joint cement, sandpaper, and the right tool for applying the cement.

Don't make your visits to yards early in the morning, because that's the time when they are rushed, filling the orders for contractors and carpenters who need materials for that day or are putting in their orders for future deliveries. Wait until around 9 o'clock before you go visiting. This is also a good rule to follow after you have selected a particular lumberyard. Don't come in around 7:30 A.M. and expect a clerk to sit down with you and explain how you should install flashing around the chimney. Wait until the rush hour is over. Introduce yourself to the boss of the yard and tell him what you are planning to do and that you need all the help you can get. If he says something to the effect that if he isn't around to help you, "Speak to Marty over there," you've probably got something good going for you. If you are acting as your own contractor, tell him that and tell him you'd like a contractor's discount on your purchases. This should be 10 per cent or possibly more.

Once you find a yard where you feel you will be happy, establish credit so that you will be able to call in or drop off an order and it can be delivered to your job even if you don't happen to be around at that particular time. This kind of arrangement is important for weekend builders because many yards don't deliver on Saturday. In fact, a good many yards only stay open until noon on Saturday. If you need materials for the coming weekend, order them early in the week so that they are certain to be there when you are ready to go to work Saturday morning.

You will save yourself time and frustration if you don't underestimate your requirements when you order materials. One of the great faults with most amateur builders is that they don't order enough and are always running out of some essential item on Saturday night or Sunday. This sort of shortage can waste money if you happen to have someone around whom you are paying, and there isn't much for him to do. So get away from that old habit of buying a pound of nails, a quart of paint, and half a dozen wood screws. If you've got a lot of heavy framing to do, you may need a keg of nails. And when you order lumber, always figure on adding 20 per cent for waste. You may not waste that much but if you add this amount to your order the chances are that you will have enough to complete that particular project.

Until you get to be a semi-pro, and can figure very accurately, that 20-per-cent waste figure is a good one to use on just about everything.

It has taken us a long time to get away from the habit of always ordering the minimum amount of everything. But since we have broken the habit, we haven't run out of anything.

BASIC MATERIALS

Before you order from a lumberyard, you need some idea of what you need and what it is called. Start first with *dimension lumber*. This is the lumber used for framing walls, floors, and roof. It is a structural lumber and comes in many sizes, but the majority is roughly 2 inches thick. There are 2 by 2s and 2 by 3s and 2 by 4s. These measurements are all in inches. The 2 by 3 and 2 by 4 are used primarily for wall studs and are often called *studding*. Material used for floors, sills, leaders, and roof framing, runs from 2 inches by 6 up to the 2 by 12s, in two inch intervals. Also in this group is the 4 by 4, which is used for posts and other rather specialized jobs. Dimension lumber starts at 8 feet in length and runs in 2-foot intervals up to 24 feet. This lumber, along with other single pieces, is given its width and thickness in the rough state before it is run through a planer. A 2 by 4 does not actually measure 2 inches by 4 inches but is actually 1⅝ inches by 3⅝ inches, or thereabouts.

You can save yourself considerable waste with dimension lumber if you select the length that is just right for the job. For example, if you need some 9-foot lengths you would do better to order an 18-foot length that would give you two pieces without any waste, than to order 10-foot lengths and waste a foot on each piece.

BOARDS

When we speak of boards, in most cases, we mean lumber 1 inch thick. Boards range in width from 2 inches up to 12 inches. Some boards have perfectly flat edges, while others have a groove cut into one edge and a tongue formed on the other so that when the boards are set side by side they interlock to produce a strong and also very tight joint. These boards are called *tongue and groove* or *T&G,* and they are used for subflooring, sheathing for roofs and walls, and the better grades for interior paneling and siding. Boards are priced not only according to length and width but also according to the kind of wood and the quality. Boards used for subflooring and sheathing are relatively inexpensive. A perfect piece of pine board that is free of knots and as smooth as glass is a very expensive item. Boards of this quality are used only on cabinetwork that is to be given a stain or clear finish, rather than paint. If a board is to be painted, firm knots are no problem. Before you order boards other than the rough stuff for sheathing, ask to see a sample of what you are getting and get a price. You may find that you can get away with a lower-grade board that will be much less expensive than the board for which you originally asked.

Boards will measure somewhat less than their nominal size, just as was the case with dimension stuff. A 1-by-12-inch board will actually be ¾ of an inch by 11½ inches. If you need a board thicker than ¾ of an inch, then you order something called a *five quarter* (5/4). This measured 1¼ inches before it went through the planer, and will measure just a little over 1 inch in thickness when you get it.

A few lumberyards will still quote you the cost of dimension lumber and boards by the *board foot*. This is a unit of measurement that was used in the lumber business for many years. It is a measurement based on a board 1 by 12 by 12 inches. If you get a price in board feet, ask the clerk to convert it for you into the cost per lineal foot. More and more lumberyards are pricing their lumber in this manner—the cost per lineal foot depending on the size and quality of the material involved.

Lumberyards stock a wide selection of wood molding and this is sold by the foot. They usually have a sample board that shows the range of patterns available.

PLYWOOD

There are two basic types of plywood. One is the construction grade used for sheathing, subfloors, and other structural work. It is made out of Douglas fir. The other is the interior grade made for cabinetwork and wood paneling for walls, and it is made of rather costly woods for attractive appearance of the surface veneer. Construction plywood comes in two types. One type can be used where it will not be exposed to moisture; the other type is made with waterproof adhesive so that it can be exposed to the rain. The standard size sheet of plywood is 4 feet by 8 feet and the standard thickness sizes are ¼, ⅜, ½, and ¾ of an inch, and 1 inch.

NAILS

You are going to need a great many nails of many different types and sizes. The size of most common nails is expressed by the term *penny* and this is expressed as *d*. No one seems to be absolutely certain on how all this got started but one thought is that it had something to do with the number of nails you would get for an English penny, and a penny is expressed as *d*. In any event, if you go into a lumberyard or hardware store to order some nails, you say, "Let me have five pounds of eight-penny nails," and if you are writing out an order you write: "5 lbs—8d nails."

Nails are made of steel, aluminum, and galvanized steel. The common steel nail is good to use on ordinary work where the heads will not be exposed to the weather. Aluminum nails are fine for exterior siding because the heads won't rust. Galvanized nails are often used where maximum strength is required because they have more holding power than steel nails. They, too, are rust resistant.

The common nail starts with the 4d, which is 1½ inches long, and runs up to the 20d nail, which is 4 inches long. For most rough work where you will be working with dimension lumber you use 8d and 16d nails. Then there are a great many nails for specialized work, which you should order when you order the materials. Special nails are available for gypsum wallboard, for asphalt shingles, and for wood shingles, and there are small-headed nails called *finishing*, or *casing*, nails for interior woodwork. Plywood is often applied to floors with a spiral, or grooved, nail to provide great holding power. Whenever you purchase a material, ask the clerk which nail is recommended for use with it. Also find out how many to use and how they should be spaced.

Nails are relatively inexpensive, so be sure to have enough on hand— more than enough, in fact.

The lumberyard can also supply insulation used for walls and ceilings, gypsum board or sheet rock for walls and ceilings, along with the tape and joint cement; doors and window units; roofing materials; and other specialized items. If you need to do some concrete work, you can order the cement here also, as well as sand and gravel. Cement is sold by the bag; sand and gravel by the cubic yard. Bricks and masonry blocks are sold by the unit.

While many lumberyards do carry a certain amount of house hardware along with tools, you may need to line up a hardware store for some of the items you will want. Your lumberyard may not have the type or brand of hardware you wish to use for hinges, lock sets, pulls, and such accessories. If you are looking for something rather special along these lines you may have to visit some of the specialized city shops that carry a wide variety of house hardware. But a local hardware store will be fine for glass for window panes, putty, and other small items that the lumberyard does not stock. Painting requirements are covered in the chapter on "Painting and Finishing."

As mentioned in the chapter on "Planning," a wide range of materials is available, but unfortunately all these materials are seldom, if ever, found under one roof. Before you decide on a particular product or material for the job, you must shop around to find out what is available. Unless you do this, you may find that after something has been installed, something else could have been used that would have done a better job, or done the job in less time or for less money.

USED MATERIALS

There are several good reasons for using old or used materials on certain parts of a restoration job or even in an ordinary remodeling project. The first, of course, is that old materials may harmonize better than new materials with what you have and are trying to achieve. If you are transforming a barn into a dwelling and you want to carry out the barn motif with exposed timbers, then you'll probably want to get your hands on some old timbers. New timbers just would not look right even if they were "distressed," which means that you hack at them with a chisel or hatchet, stain them and even beat them with a chain to give them a worn appearance.

Addison Mizner, who designed and built some of Florida's wonderful Spanish-style mansions during the twenties, was a master at "distressing." After completing a room he would go to work on it to make it look aged. This might involve building a fire out of tar paper in the fireplace with the damper closed so that the walls and ceilings became smoke stained, or taking a sledgehammer to a new, marble fireplace so that when the parts were put back together with plaster the fireplace would look as if it had been through a battle with the Moors. But "distressing" is not the same as something genuinely old and original. If you like the mellow look of old brick and want a fireplace or wall built of it, then you will want to look for old bricks, because new bricks, even the new bricks made to look old, just won't be the same. There is, by the way, such a demand for old-looking bricks that new bricks that were formerly tossed aside because of imperfections, sell for more than the perfect ones.

The other reason for using old or salvaged materials is that they may save you money. Not always, mind you, but often. Where we live, old barn siding is worth its weight in gold, and the same goes for hand-hewn beams. If you have the stuff on your property, it will pay you to use it, but, unless your heart is set on them, to go out and buy old materials would probably be much more costly than using new materials.

On the other hand, if you are doing a fairly major restoration, you may have a good deal of material that you rip out of one area which can be used in another. If you remove a partition you will have quite a few pieces of studs that might be used elsewhere. A little building on our property is filled with materials we salvaged out of the main house and which we will eventually use when we get around to fixing up the little place. There are windows, doors, framing material, plywood, and all sorts of good things that would have gone to the dump if we hadn't been conservation minded.

But you don't have to depend on salvage from your own project for used materials. In most areas you can find a used-building-materials outfit or a salvage yard. You can find amazing things at a salvage yard—old timbers, wood paneling, mantels, stair railings, doors, stained-glass windows, lighting fixtures, marble, and just about everything else that can be hauled out of an old house or building. The ideal way to do this sort of shopping is to borrow a small truck and take along a strong friend so that when you find something you like you can haul it away. Having the stuff delivered can be expensive.

If you plan to work with used or salvaged materials, remember that it will probably take time to put them into shape before it can be used. This can cost money unless you do it yourself. If you are paying a carpenter $5.50 an hour and he spends one entire hour taking the nails out of a piece of 2 by 4, you aren't ahead, even if you have gotten the piece of 2 by 4 for free. On the other hand, if you are not paying anyone to do the work but are doing it yourself, then you do save money—perhaps not much, but some.

Most salvage yards sell their goods pretty much as they find them and it is up to you to pull out the nails, remove the mortar from the old bricks, or strip the paint off the old wood mantel. If the yard does this work for you, the price of the materials is going to increase greatly. By the way, getting the mortar off old bricks is not difficult, but it takes time. Use a cold chisel and hammer and tap away. If there is an old brick building going down in your area, you can usually get the bricks free just for hauling them away.

You can still find some real buys at salvage yards, but they are becoming rare. Architects, interior decorators, and antique dealers have found out about such possibilities and often have the inside track, so that they get a call from the yard the minute something comes in that might be of interest to them. Several years ago we met a sad-looking man who as a little boy used to pick up a few pennies here and there by selling lead that he got from a salvage yard. He got the lead by breaking up Tiffany lamp shades and that memory makes him sad today.

You will find that most workmen don't relish the idea of working with used materials. They like their materials new because that way they are cleaner and easier to handle. And often it takes longer to install an old object than it would a new. A plumber might give you a bid on installing a lavatory; then if you produced some antique fixtures that would take him twice as long to install as new ones, he might not be too happy and would probably tell you he had to have more money for doing the job.

Carpenters don't like used wood because they never know when they will hit a hidden nail with their saw or chisel. A good carpenter likes to have sharp tools and, naturally, doesn't want to take a chance on ruining them.

Whenever materials, old or new, are delivered, try to get them indoors or under some kind of shelter. This is not just to keep them from getting wet. Many people would never consider taking anything that wasn't their property, except building materials. For some reason a piece of 2 by 4 or a sheet of plywood that happens to be on your property might just jump into the car of someone who is driving along the road. If you are a weekend builder who isn't around during the week, you should leave a key with the lumberyard people so that they can put the material inside the house, or arrange for the delivery to be made on Friday so your materials won't sit around all week long tempting people.

Here's a handy shopping list that will help you remember all that you'll need in the way of materials.

► *Building-Materials Shopping List*

1. Dimension Lumber
   A. Size
   B. Quantity
   C. Metal framing anchors
   D. Nails: size and quantity

2. Board
   A. Grade
   B. Thickness and width
   C. Quantity
   D. Nails

3. Trim and molding
   A. Design or shape
   B. Quantity
   C. Nails

4. Plywood
   A. Thickness
   B. Exterior or interior
   C. Grade
   D. Quantity
   E. Nails

5. Hardboard
   A. Thickness
   B. Quantity
   C. Nails

6. Exterior siding
   A. Material
   B. Grade
   C. Quantity
   D. Nails

7. Roofing
   A. Material
   B. Grade
   C. Quantity
   D. Nails
   E. Flashing and shears for cutting it.

8. Insulation
   A. Type
   B. Thickness
   C. Quantity
   D. Staple gun and staples

9. Gypsum wallboard
   A. Thickness
   B. Quantity
   C. Tape
   D. Cement
   E. Outside-corner metal strips
   F. Nails

10. Flooring
    A. Type
    B. Quantity
    C. Underlayment or building paper
    D. Adhesive or nails
11. Windows
    A. Style
    B. Size
    C. Quantity
12. Doors
    A. Style
    B. Size
    C. Hardware
        a. Hinges
        b. Lock set
        c. Screws
13. Ceiling tile
    A. Style or design
    B. Quantity
14. Masonry: quantity
    A. Brick
    B. Block
    C. Cement
    D. Sand
    E. Gravel
15. Paint and finishes
    A. Type
    B. Color
    C. Quantity
    D. Thinner
    E. Brushes or roller

► *Special Money-Saving Tips*

You can often save as much as 10 per cent on materials by purchasing them from cash-and-carry building-supply houses.

If you are acting as your own general contractor and have considerable work to be done, many building-supply houses will give you the same discount they would give a regular contractor—but you must be sure to ask for it.

18 Masonry

You may not know what you have been missing until you try your hand at masonry work, because this activity can be extremely satisfying. And the chances are that you will have plenty of this work to do around an OB Dream House.

Let's start with the basics, and that means *Portland-cement*. Portland-cement is a binding agent. It has little strength by itself but when mixed with sand or with sand and gravel it produces a rocklike substance.

MORTAR

A mixture of cement, sand, and water, mortar is used for laying up brick, stone, and masonry block. It is also used to repair cracks in concrete. A coat of mortar is sometimes applied over an entire surface such as a wall, and this coating is called *stucco*.

You can buy a bag of mortar mix at most hardware stores and lumberyards. The cement and sand are thoroughly mixed and only water needs to be added. Packaged mortar of this kind is fine for small jobs because it is so convenient but it becomes expensive when a considerable amount of mortar is required. To prepare this packaged mortar

216

ready for use, pour a quantity into a metal wheelbarrow and form it into a ring. Pour water slowly into the center of the ring and then mix the materials with a hoe.

When large amounts of mortar are needed, you'll save yourself money by buying the cement and sand and mixing them together yourself. Use one part cement to three parts sand. Put the sand into the wheelbarrow first, then add the cement and mix with a hoe until the color of the mix is even. We measure out the cement and sand by the shovelful. As with the packaged mortar, form the mix into a ring, gently pour in the water, and mix with the hoe.

With either the packaged mortar or the mortar you mix yourself be sure you remember to pour the water in gently so that you don't wash the cement out of the sand. You also don't want to use too much water. Add small quantities and keep mixing with the hoe. What you want to achieve is a good, workable, plastic material.

You have this when you can take a handful of the mortar and form it into a ball that will not crumble apart or lose its shape when you open your hand. If the ball crumbles, you do not have enough water, and if the ball can't hold its shape when you open your hand, you've added too much water. If the mix is too dry, add more water; if it's too wet, you'll have to add a little more cement and sand.

A metal wheelbarrow is a fine container in which to mix mortar because with the packaged mix or the stuff you mix yourself you don't want to make up more than you can use in about 30 minutes. After the water has been added, the chemical action of the cement begins and at the end of 30 minutes the mortar has begun to set. Do not try to make it plastic again by adding water. Toss it out and make up a fresh batch, for once mortar has begun to set, it should not be used.

You can clean the wheelbarrow and tools with water when you're finished for the day.

CONCRETE

A mixture of cement, sand, gravel, and water, concrete is used for such items as footings, foundation walls, walks, and terraces. For most concrete work around the house, you can use a 1-2½-3½ mix. This is 1 part cement, 2½ parts sand, and 3½ parts gravel.

To mix concrete pour out the gravel first and then the sand. Mix these together thoroughly. Then add the cement and mix all ingredients until the color is uniform. Finally, add the water to produce a plastic mixture.

Small amounts of concrete can be mixed in a wheelbarrow or on any flat surface such as a wood platform or concrete floor. You can buy a metal tub that has considerably more capacity than the ordinary wheelbarrow, or you can make your own out of plywood or tongue-and-groove boards.

Mixing concrete by hand when large amounts are required is pretty tough going. You might want to consider renting a small concrete mixer. These are great time-and-work-savers, and even the small ones can turn out a lot of concrete in a day.

For large amounts of concrete that should be poured in one operation, the best approach is to use the already mixed material that is delivered to the site in a truck. This is called *transit-mix concrete* and it costs about $15 a cubic yard. Supply firms usually deliver a minimum amount. The one thing to keep in mind when you order concrete in this form is that there will be a good deal of it, and it must be put in place at once. You should arrange to have someone around to help you when the truck arrives. You should also have one or more wheelbarrows on hand in the event that the truck can't get right up to the job. Make sure that all the forms for the concrete are in place so that there won't be any delays in getting the concrete into them.

ESTIMATING REQUIREMENTS

Concrete requirements should be figured by the cubic yard. Get the length, width, and depth of the proposed job in feet; multiply these together to get the total in cubic feet; divide by twenty-seven to get the number of cubic yards. If you are going to mix the concrete by hand or with a concrete mixer, tell your lumberyard people the number of cubic yards you need and the mix you plan to use. They can figure out how many bags of cement and how many cubic yards of sand and gravel you will need. If you are getting the transit-mix concrete, give them the cubic yards you will require.

We suggest that you give your lumberyard the job of figuring out how much cement, sand, and gravel you need, because estimating these quantities is tricky. You see, if you mix a cubic yard of cement with two cubic yards of sand and three cubic yards of gravel, you don't get six cubic yards of concrete. You get considerably less than this because the fine particles of cement fill in the spaces between the particles of sand, and the cement and sand fill in around the particles of gravel.

FORMS

Concrete needs something to hold it in place until it becomes hard. When it is poured into a hole dug into the ground, the surrounding soil is generally adequate to serve as a form unless it is sand, which won't hold in place. Dig the hole for the concrete so that the sides are as straight as you can make them, and if the ground is very dry, line the opening with building paper so that the dry soil won't absorb the water out of the fresh concrete. If the soil won't hold in place, put something in to hold it—thin plywood, metal, or even heavy cardboard.

Concrete that is poured above the ground will require a form. If you are pouring a slab on the ground for a terrace or walk, all you need in the way of forms are boards along the sides as high as the concrete slab is thick. Lumber 2 inches thick is good for this purpose, and you need a few stakes driven into the ground to hold each board in place. When forms must be higher than this, build them out of ¾-inch plywood or tongue-and-groove boards. Make your form fairly solid, for a mass of concrete will weigh a good many pounds.

POURING CONCRETE

Concrete, as we've noted, should be poured in place as soon as it is mixed. If the depth of the concrete is over 6 inches, don't pour it in all at once. Shovel it into place in layers about 6 inches thick and prod it with the shovel or a hoe, so that it becomes compact. Concrete hardens through a chemical action, and the longer this chemical action continues, the better. After the concrete has been poured, cover the surface with paper or burlap so that the water in the concrete will not evaporate too quickly. Keep fresh concrete covered for several days.

BRICK, BLOCK, AND STONE

If you wish to build a wall out of these materials you will need a footing of poured concrete. The footing goes into a trench dug into the ground and this trench should extend below the level of the local frost line. Any local contractor can tell you the depth of this line in your area. The footing should be about 12 inches thick and at least as wide as the wall is thick. The minimum thickness of a brick or masonry block wall is 8 inches, and 16 inches for a wall of stone.

The common brick measures 8 inches long, 3¾ inches wide, and 2½ inches thick. Each layer of brick is called a *course*. Bricks laid end to end are spoken of as a *stretcher course*. When they are set side by side, the result is called a *header course* and when they are set upright it is called a *soldier course*. The manner in which the various courses are arranged in a wall is called a *bond,* and there are many bonds. Study a few brick walls and you will notice the many variations that are achieved by utilizing different courses. But every solid brick wall should include a certain number of header courses.

Bricks are laid up with mortar, and they should be soaked in water before use. Spray them with a garden hose or soak them in a bucket of water. The mortar joint between the bricks should be about ⅜ of an inch thick, but this can be varied slightly one way or another so that the row of bricks will come out even.

Before you apply the mortar, lay the bricks out along the footing and then make the necessary adjustments so that the mortar joints are more or less even.

All the joints in a brick wall should be packed with mortar. Bricks can be *cut to size* by scoring a line with a cold chisel and then giving them a sharp rap with a hammer.

The standard masonry block is 7⅝ by ⅜ by 15⅝ inches, but you can also get them in a wide variety of sizes and shapes, depending on specific requirements. The standard block has a hollow core. Instead of applying mortar over all surfaces as with bricks, you apply mortar on blocks only along the edges of the block. Blocks do not have to be soaked in water before use. They should be laid up dry. Use the same mortar mix for block as for brick.

Stone is the most difficult of these materials to work with because of the irregular sizes and shapes. Stones are laid up with mortar, and they should be cleaned first because if there is dirt on the surface, you won't get a strong mortar joint. A good rule when working with stone is to lay the stones out where you can easily see them. This will help you to select quickly the one that will fit in a particular spot.

► *Special Money-Saving Tips*

You can save more than $100 on the average house with crawl space by covering the dirt under the crawl space with plastic sheeting rather than with concrete.

You can save $90 in the construction costs of a masonry-block wall consisting of 200 blocks by building it yourself.

You can save more than $50 by repairing mortar joints in existing masonry walls yourself.

You can save $100 by building an average-sized flight of outside concrete steps yourself.

THE MASONRY PORTFOLIO

■ STONE CONSTRUCTION

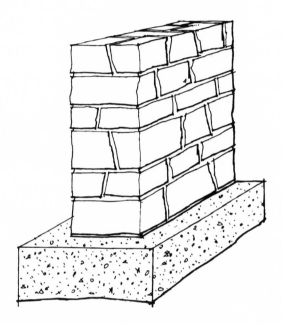

Stone, suitable for construction can sometimes be found on the property and can be purchased from building supply houses by the cubic yard. Any stone structure that is to be laid up with mortar requires a solid footing of either poured concrete or heavy stones set into a trench that is dug to a depth which is below the prevailing frost line. Stone should be washed clean before laying so that the surfaces will be free of dirst, moss, or any foreign matter that would prevent a solid bond between the mortar and the stone. Stone can be broken to size by striking with a small sledgehammer. Examine the stone to determine the direction of the grain and strike along the grain. The strength of a stone wall can be increased by utilizing "bond stone." These are large stones that are placed at varying intervals so that they cover the joints between the stone on the lower course. Width of mortar joints will vary depending on the contour of the stone but they should not be less than 5/8 inch thick. When working with stones spread them out so that you can quickly see which size to use for a particular purpose.

■ MASONRY BLOCK CONSTRUCTION

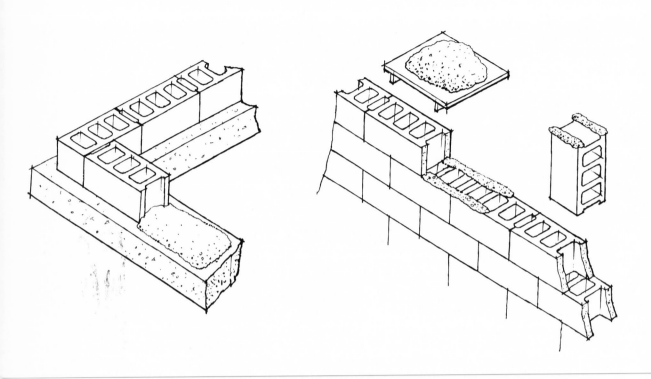

LEFT: Install footing for masonry block and see that it is made level for it will determine the level of the rest of the work. A bed of mortar is applied over the footing and the first course of block set on this. RIGHT: Succeeding courses of block do not require mortar over the entire area of the block. Apply a strip along the side and the ends. Blocks should not be dampened as is the case with brick when laying.

FACING PAGE TOP: Set the block into place and tap down with the trowel. Use a level to insure that each block is level along its length and along its side. Once the block is true, scrape off excess mortar. Each course of block must be staggered so that the horizontal joints of one course do not come directly over those of the course below. BOTTOM: Corners must be built up a few courses ahead of the rest of the wall to insure that the mortar joints between courses will be staggered. Use a level to make sure that the corners are perpendicular.

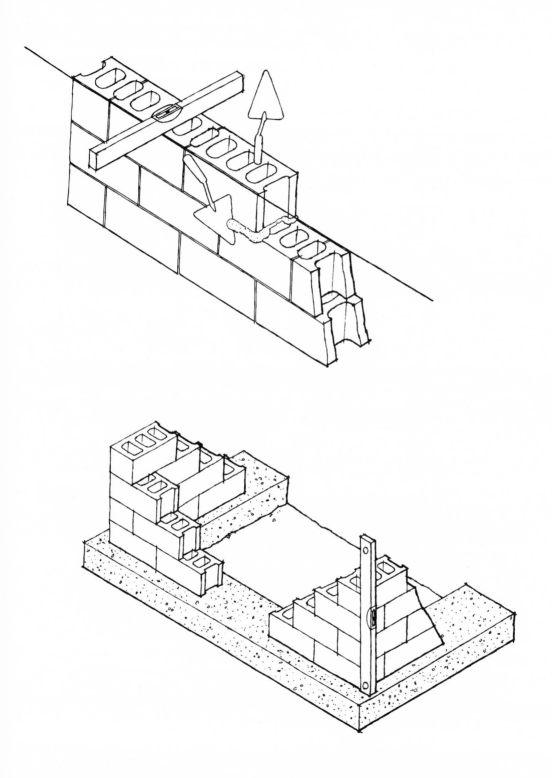

■ BRICK CONSTRUCTION

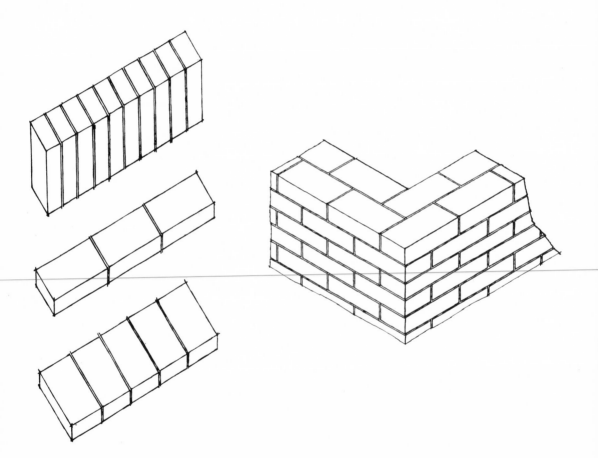

Three courses of brick are (top to bottom) soldier course, stretcher course, and header course. Bricks require a solid footing and foundation and should be wet before they are laid. The minimum thickness for a brick wall is 8 inches, which is equal to the approximate width of two bricks. Mortar joints between courses must be staggered so that they do not fall directly over each other.

Wall Pattern

The manner in which the courses of brick are arranged is called a bond. At left is English bond. There are five stretcher courses and then a header course. The Common bond, at right, has alternating header and stretcher courses.

Floor Pattern

Bricks can be laid in a number of ways for floors, terraces, walks, and patios. Because there is no lateral pressure on bricks used in this manner, the positioning of the joints is not too important.

19 Floors and Flooring

What you do about the floor in a structure depends first of all on what kind of floor you have to start with, and there are a number of possibilities. In many old houses you will find beautiful hardwood floors supported by oversized joists. But then again you might have just the opposite: a weak, sagging floor that consists of a single layer of cheap pine or fir floorboards nailed to undersized joists. You can expect to find the latter type of construction in many summer cabins and cottages. If you have picked up a barn or warehouse, the floor may be of heavy planks or of concrete, or there may be no floor at all—just dirt.

WOOD FLOORS

It is a simple matter to determine if an existing wood floor is solid and more or less level. As suggested earlier, this is a point you should determine while inspecting the house. If you jump on the floor and the windows rattle and the floor bounces, then the floor is not too solid. It may not be ready to fall but a floor in this condition is annoying to live with. Each time it is walked across, furniture will rattle and shake. As also noted earlier, you can check to see how level it is by putting a rubber ball on it and seeing in what direction and at what speed the ball rolls.

REINFORCING WOOD FLOORS

A floor sags or is weak because it isn't getting enough support. The reasons for this lack of support can be many. Sometimes the joists that support the floor have shrunk or sagged a bit. You can tell if this is the case if you can reach the underside of the floor from the basement or crawl space. If you find any space between the top of the joists and the flooring, drive thin, wood wedges—wood shingles are good for this purpose—into this space. Drive them in so that they fit snugly. This will take the "play" out of the floor and stop excessive movement. The same technique can be used to stop squeaks in floors if the squeaks resulted from the fact that the floor boards are riding up and down on the nails that hold them to the joists. This, by the way, is a very common reason for squeaky floors.

Often a floor is weak because the wood girder that is supposed to support the joists is not doing the job. It may be that the girder has shrunk or that it has sagged because there are not enough posts to support it, or because the ends of the posts have sunk into the ground. If the girder has shrunk, drive wood wedges between the top of the girder and the floor joists. If it has sagged, install additional posts or fix the existing ones so that they rest on a solid base. Unless a post rests on a solid concrete floor, it should have a footing or foundation. You can make one easily enough by digging a hole about 1 foot square and 1 foot deep and filling it with concrete. Posts can be of wood but the easiest ones to install are the adjustable metal jack posts. If you prefer to use wood posts, use 4-by-4-inch material.

Fortunately, most of the trouble you are likely to encounter with weak and sagging floors will occur on the first floor, where it is usually possible to reach the underside from the basement or crawl space. When it is not easy to reach the underside of the floor, the job becomes a good deal more complicated as you will see later in this chapter. First floors have many ailments because they usually have to carry heavy loads in the form of furniture, and also because they don't get support from below in the form of partitions. Unless the floor is framed correctly with the right-sized lumber, it will probably act up in one way or another.

In an old house the trouble with the floor is often caused by lack of a girder. This not only makes for a weak floor but one that will very definitely sag in the middle. A girder of the type that should have been installed when the house was built is a job best left to a contractor, but you can use an alternate method that you can probably handle yourself. Prop a long piece of 4 by 4 up under the joists where the sag occurs and then install jack posts about every 8 feet along the length of the girder. In spite of the fact that the girder is not tied into the foundations at each end, it will provide adequate support. Do not try to make the floor level all at once with the jacks on the posts, because this might crack plaster walls and ceilings. Turn the jacks up a fraction of an inch every few days to give the house structure a chance to adjust gradually.

If the floor has not sagged but is so weak that it shakes when you walk across it, the joists can be reinforced. This is done by nailing 2-by-4s to each side of each joist. The ends of these members should be supported by the foundation wall or the sill, and the edges should come flush with the edge of the joist. This method can also be used instead of installing a girder, which might reduce the headroom in the basement more than is desirable. If the joists have sagged, a temporary girder is put in so that the joists can be made level, and after they have been reinforced, the girder is removed.

Many floors sag and are weak not because the builder of the house didn't know what he was doing, but because others, over the years have been careless. Many old-time plumbers apparently had no love or concern for structural carpentry. If they wanted to run a pipe somewhere, they simply took out their saw, or sometimes their ax, and cut away a great chunk of a joist or girder. Sometimes the owner decided he wanted to put in a flight of stairs to the basement or something similar, and cut away a good deal of essential framing. It is obvious that if you need a 2-by-8-inch joist to provide adequate support and someone comes along and cuts away 3 inches of it, you don't have a 2-by-8-inch joist anymore, you have a 2-by-5-inch joist and that just may not be adequate. If you find this sort of condition, you can deal with it by installing posts under any of the members that have been cut away, or reinforcing them with 2-by-4s. The house we now have has suffered so much at the hands of plumbers, steam fitters, electricians, and others, that one area of the basement contains so many posts that the place looks like a forest.

If you are dealing with a very large building, such as a barn or warehouse, and you have a weak floor, the solution may be to install a steel girder, and this, naturally is something to be done by a contractor.

SECOND-FLOOR PROBLEMS

Dealing with a weak or sagging floor when you can't easily get at the underside presents a problem. You can, of course, reach the framework by ripping off the ceiling of the room below. If the ceiling is going to have to be replaced anyway, this is certainly the best approach. If the ceiling is going to remain, then the only way to reach the joists is to take up the floor. Once the flooring is up, you will be able to see what the trouble is all about. It may be that some plumber or heating man years ago cut out some of the joists, or it may be that they cracked because too heavy a load was placed on them at one time or another. Perhaps the joists were too small to begin with. We have found that in most old houses it is the bathroom floor that gives the most trouble and that is because the floor of an old house was never originally designed to carry the heavy plumbing fixtures. The bathroom was installed in a room that was designed as a bedroom or a closet, and the original builder of the house never dreamed that someone would not only put a heavy cast-iron bathtub on the floor but would then fill the tub with water and put someone in the water. You can correct matters by reinforcing the joists with 2-by-4s spiked to each side. If the floor has sagged, you can make it level by nailing thin strips of wood to the top of the joists to produce a level surface. The wood strips will have to be cut in varying thicknesses, and here you need a table saw, or you should have your lumberyard cut them to your specifications.

One other way of dealing with a second- or third-story floor that sags or is weak is to build something under it. The obvious thing would be a partition, but perhaps a storage wall or open bookshelf might fit into your plans for this particular spot. And, of course, you can always install a girder and encase it in wood so that when it is painted to match the ceiling it won't be too conspicuous.

FLOORING

Once you have your floors solid and level you can go on to the next step, which is to analyze what you have in the way of floors and what can be done with them. You can find about every sort of flooring in every sort of condition in an OB House. You may find a double thickness of wood flooring, which is very good, because you can use it just as is or as a base for resilient flooring, such as linoleum, vinyl, or carpeting. Then again, you may have just a single thickness of wood flooring, which isn't quite so good. In more or less standard construction, there is the rough or sub-flooring, which is nailed to the floor joists. It is applied either at right angles or diagonally to the joists. Over the sub-flooring goes a layer of building paper, and over that the finish flooring, which is nailed to the sub-flooring.

If the sub-floor is applied at right angles to the joists, then the finish floor must go at right angles to the subfloor, which will mean that the finish floor runs parallel to the joists. Only the crudest amateur would ever apply the finish flooring in the same direction as the subflooring. If the subfloor was applied diagonally to the joists, then the finish flooring can go either at right angles to the joists or parallel to them. That is why the sub-flooring is often put down diagonally to the joists— it allows the finish flooring to go down in either direction. Clever, isn't it?

Next, go into the basement or crawl space and look up at the exposed flooring between the floor joists. If the boards you see from this vantage point run diagonally to the joists and the flooring in the room abve runs at right angles or parallel to the joists, you have two thicknesses of flooring and you are fine. If the sub-flooring runs at right angles to the joists and the flooring you see in the room above runs parallel to the joists, there are two thicknesses. If the boards on the underside run in the same direction as the boards on the floor in the room above, you've got a single thickness. If you have a finish floor of parquet (small blocks or strips of wood set out in a design), you have two thicknesses, because parquet needs a base of wood or sometimes concrete.

If you have two layers of floor you are in luck, because you can get along with them just as they are or by sanding and refinishing. You may also be fortunate in finding that under old linoleum, and/or paint and grime, you have attractive hardwood or pine floors.

You are apt to find lovely hardwood floors in Victorian houses and in town and row houses. When these houses were built, floors were put down by master craftsmen and the wood used was as fine as the workmanship. If you have a floor like this, it is worth refinishing, even if you have to do it by hand and on your knees. In many older houses, you will find floors made out of pine that refinishes beautifully, but it may be hard to tell this through all the coats of paint that were so often applied to this type of floor. But even if the finish flooring isn't anything to brag about, it will still serve as a good base for resilient flooring or carpeting.

A single thickness of flooring is something else again, but it is not a major disaster. Many people live quite happily in houses with a single layer of flooring. How well you get along with your floor depends on what you have and what you want. If you have a house with a single layer of lovely old pine planks that have been around for years and years, it would certainly be a crime to cover them with hardboard or plywood so you could put down wall-to-wall carpeting. Floors like this are the exception, however, and are found only in houses a hundred or more years old. What you generally find is a floor made out of ordinary wood that may have been stained, painted, or covered with inexpensive linoleum. Our old beachhouse, "The Sandpiper," had upstairs floors made of the cheapest fir that nature could produce. There were nice, wide cracks to collect dust, and the boards were constantly splintering, so that it was worth your life to walk on them barefooted. The solution here was to cover them with hardboard or plywood and then indoor-outdoor carpeting, which is inexpensive, easy to put down, and great where people are walking around in wet swim suits.

If the floors are not too bad and you are working on a limited budget, several coats of deck paint are your best bet. Drive any exposed nail-heads below the surface and fill the holes with plastic wood or wood putty. If the cracks between the boards are wide, fill them with wood putty. A couple of coats of deck paint will hide a multitude of flaws and provide you with quite an attractive floor.

Another solution is to cover the floor with sheets of ⅜-inch hardboard or ⅜-inch plywood and then apply resilient flooring or carpeting over this. Never apply resilient materials or carpeting over a single thickness of flooring. The boards may give a little, and if a floor covering is cemented to them, it will come loose. Rough, bumpy spots or cracks between the boards will show through, and in time, damage the covering. Hardboard and plywood are not expensive, so spend the small amount of extra time and money to make sure that you have a satisfactory surface before applying carpeting or resilient flooring, neither of which is inexpensive.

Before you put down either hard board or plywood, go over the floor and make sure that the boards are secure and don't squeak. If you find a squeak, put in a few additional nails. Spiral or screw-type nails are best for this job because they have much greater holding power than ordinary nails. If there are high spots, plane them down. Low spots can be filled with wood putty or several layers of building paper.

Single floors can, of course, be covered with a new finish wood floor—either hardwood or softwood.

RECONDITIONING WOOD FLOORS

If you have floors that you can live with, it still may be necessary to do some work on them. Sometimes all that is required is a good cleaning to make them bright again. Turpentine or paint thinner is good for this job; avoid using water to clean a floor. Stubborn dirt spots and many areas where the finish has become discolored can be taken care of by rubbing with fine steel wool dampened in turpentine or thinner.

If the finish is in poor condition, if it is worn off in spots or discolored, or if the wood has been scratched or stained, you had better refinish the floor. Before you start this operation, go over the floor and make sure that all nailheads are set below the surface. Nail down any squeaky boards.

There are several ways to remove the old finish and prepare the wood for a new finish. You can do the job with a paint remover and then sand by hand, or you can use a hand scraper. We used a hand scraper just once, with a small floor, and we'll never do it again. The best and most sensible way to do this job is with an electric floor sander.

You can rent a floor sander from a hardware, paint, or tool-rental store. Actually, you need two sanders. One is the big fellow that is used for most of the area and the other is a little fellow called an *edger*. This is used to get close to walls and into corners. But even so, some spots will have to be done by hand with sandpaper or a scraper.

When you rent the two sanders, you will also get the sandpaper for them. The large sander is a belt-type sander, and the small one is a disc, so you will need two types of sandpaper. You should get three grades of each—coarse, medium, and fine. The coarse grade is used to remove the finish from the wood, take out the deep scratches, and any high spots. The medium grade removes the rough surface left by the coarse paper, and the fine paper produces a smooth surface suitable for the finish.

It has been our experience that everyone from whom you rent floor-sanding equipment assumes that refinishing floors is your profession, and that you are, therefore, thoroughly familiar with the equipment. We suggest that before you load the equipment into the back of your car you find out the proper way to attach the paper to the sander, and any other bits of information that the clerk will offer. One thing he should tell you, and this is also usually printed on the sander: "Never allow the sanding drum to touch the floor when the sander is running unless the sander is moving." This is a sound piece of advice because if you let the drum touch the floor when the sander is stationary, it will carve a little depression in the floor in nothing flat. The large drum sander is equipped with a lever, so that the sanding drum can be pulled up off the floor when you want to catch your breath or turn around to sand in the opposite direction. You don't have this problem with the little edger, which has a disc rather than a drum. You just want to hold on tight, because if you let go of the edger while it is running, it will scoot off in all directions.

Both sanders will have a vacuum-cleaner attachment and a bag so that most of the dust they produce will be picked up as you go along. But they won't pick up all the dust, so close off the room where you are working, unless you aren't concerned about dust getting into the rest of the house.

Start off with the large sander, using the coarse paper. First, sand across the grain. All subsequent sanding should be done in the direction of the wood grain—in the same direction as the floor boards run.

It is quite an experience the first time you have the sander running and you lower the drum down to the floor, because the machine tries to run away from you and you have to use considerable effort to hold it back. It will take a little time before you get the hang of things and find just the right speed for moving the machine across the floor so that all the finish is stripped away. If the floor is in poor condition, with many deep scratches or low spots in the wood, you may have to do more than just two go-rounds with the coarse paper—the first across the boards, and all others in the same direction as the boards are laid.

Once you have completed the major portion of the floor with the large sander, do the edges and corners with the edger. Use a hand scraper for any spots that you can't reach.

Now repeat the entire process, using the medium paper. Stay with this until all the roughness made by the coarse paper has been removed.

Before you do the final sanding with the fine sandpaper, figure out a way to keep from soiling that lovely clean wood on which you have worked so hard. Either don't wear shoes for the final sanding operation or slip a pair of old socks over your shoes so you won't leave footprints. Have some building paper on hand for covering the exposed wood until you can get a finish on it. We know of a man who has never completely recovered from the shock of watching a large puppy with muddy paws prance over a floor that the man had just sanded. Before you put the paper down, give the room a good vacuuming to remove all traces of dust. If the floor doesn't require too much work, you should be able to do an average-sized room in a day.

Get a finish on the freshly sanded floor as soon as you possibly can. Many types and brands of finish are available for this work. Probably the most foolproof and easiest to apply are the penetrating sealers. These are water and alcohol proof and can take a lot of wear. They can be applied with a brush and will dry in about eight hours. It is best to use two coats, and the first coat, when hard, should be buffed with steel wool. You can rent a machine for this job.

Don't expect the impossible out of a floor sander. If you happen to have an old barn or warehouse with heavy plank floors, sanding them is not going to transform them into something out of the Hall of Mirrors. If you have heavy planks and want to keep them as a finish floor it might be smart to take them up and haul them to a lumberyard, where they could be run through a planer. This would remove the outside surface and get down to smooth, solid wood. You could also have the yard cut tongues and grooves into the boards, so that when they were reinstalled they would fit tightly together. This is a good approach to use with any old floor made out of wide planks or thick boards, especially if there are wide cracks between the boards, or if they are in very poor surface condition.

CONCRETE

Many structures that might catch your fancy will have a first floor made out of concrete, but if it is a barn or similar structure the floor won't be quite like the concrete floors in houses built in the past few years. Such floors have worked out quite satisfactorily, but these concrete first floors were designed and built for dwellings. The concrete is not poured directly on the ground, but on a thick base of gravel, so that the concrete won't absorb moisture from the earth. The edges of the concrete slab are insulated. Often there are heating coils in the concrete that not only provide heat for the house but also keep the concrete warm in winter. But a concrete floor that was put down for a barn a good many years ago is quite different. It may have been poured directly over the earth, or with just enough gravel under it to provide a solid base. That means it will be cold in winter and may sweat in hot, humid weather. It may become damp from ground moisture during wet weather. And it may be rather rough, uneven, or cracked. How it is going to act in cold weather and in hot, humid weather is something you may be able to find out only by living with it.

If you decide to take a chance with the concrete floor as it stands, you can patch the cracks and, if necessary, apply a thin coat of concrete over the old to produce a level, smooth surface. For a finish you can use a concrete floor enamel or a type of resilient flooring recommended for concrete slabs on ground. We know some people who covered the concrete with clay floor tile, which makes a most attractive floor, but is a little hard and cold underfoot. The same holds true if you cover the floor with stone—it is attractive but not very "giving." Indoor-outdoor carpeting is a good material to consider. It is relatively inexpensive, soft, won't be harmed by moisture, and has some value as insulation.

If you decide that you don't want to live with a concrete floor, you have several options. If the concrete floor is level, you can take short lengths of 2-by-4s—about 3 inches long—and cement them face down into the concrete with an adhesive made for this sort of work. The 2-by-4s should be staggered just a bit so that the ends do not come together but overlap slightly. Set these rows about 16 inches apart and then cover them with wood flooring or sheets of ¾-inch plywood to serve as a base for resilient flooring or carpeting. The air space between the concrete and the wood flooring will act as insulation, preventing the finish flooring from becoming chilled by the concrete, and it will also prevent the flooring from becoming damp.

Another way of handling this matter is to lay planks of 4-inch-thick Styrofoam plastic over the concrete and cover them with sheets of ¾-inch plywood. Over the plywood you can apply wood, resilient flooring, or carpeting.

If there is plenty of headroom, you can build wood floor suspended above the concrete. This would involve the installation of joists set several inches above the concrete and covered with sub-flooring and a finish floor.

► *Special Money-Saving Tips*

You can save more than $50 on each average-sized room by refinishing the existing wood floor rather than replacing it or covering it with a new material.

If a floor needs additional support, you can save $7 by installing an adjustable jack post yourself.

THE FLOORING PORTFOLIO

If floor sags underfoot or squeaks, the cause may be a space between the girder or joists or between post and girder. Either condition can be corrected by driving wood shingles into space as indicated in drawing.

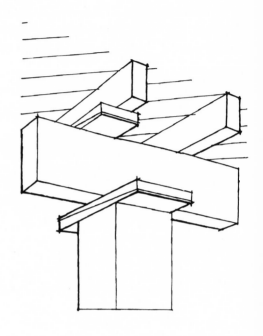

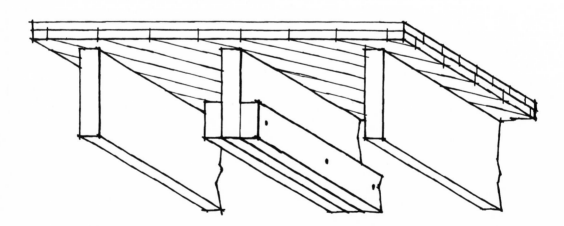

Undersized joists can be reinforced by fastening a length of 2-inch-by-4-inch stock to each side of the joist as shown in drawing. Reinforcing members should extend full length of joist and should be supported at each end by sill or foundation wall.

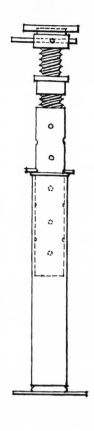

The most convenient post to use for supporting a girder or joist or to level a floor is the adjustable jack post. Combining a metal post with an adjustable jack, such posts cost about $10 each.

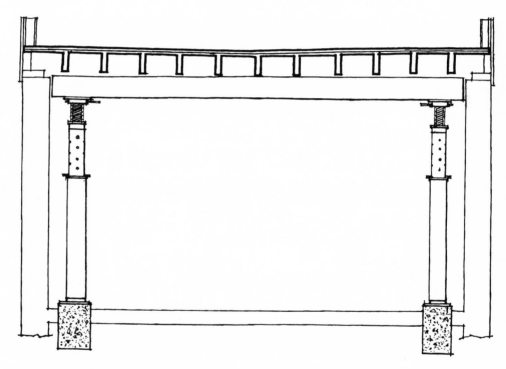

A sagging or weak floor can be fixed by installing a 4-inch-by-4-inch girder that is supported at each end by a post. It is best to provide any post—wood or metal—with a concrete footing, as shown, so that it will not break through the existing concrete floor and sink into the ground.

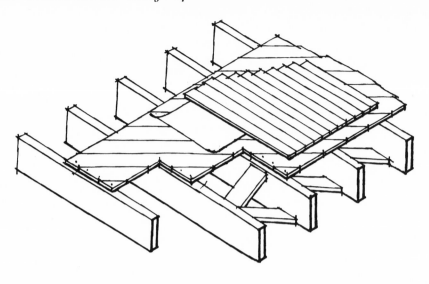

When the sub-flooring is put down diagonal to the joists, finish flooring can be run either parallel or at right angles to the joists.

When sub-flooring is applied at right angles to the joists, the finish flooring must be applied at right angles to it and therefore run parallel to the joists.

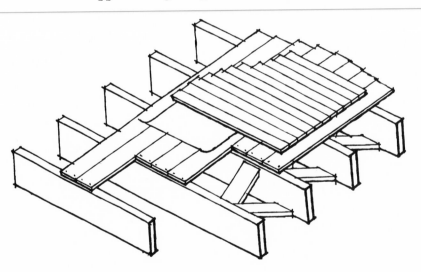

Exterior Walls 20

If you are lucky and the exterior siding of your house is adequate, the exterior surface might be one of the last jobs you have to tackle. On the other hand, if the outside walls are going to require drastic treatment, this should be undertaken at an early stage in the renovation work.

CONVENTIONAL CONSTRUCTION

On the standard wood-framed house the exterior siding is applied over sheathing. The siding may be clapboard, wood shingles, board and batten, or possibly asbestos shingles. If these materials are in fair condition, you may only have to make some minor repairs and repaint, if painting is required. You should certainly try to avoid applying new siding, because this is an expensive operation even if you do the work yourself. Even if you have to strip the old paint off the existing siding, it will involve less work and money than applying new siding.

Loose or missing wood shingles and asbestos shingles would be renailed or replaced. Cracks in clapboard and vertical board-and-batten siding can be filled with wood putty. Use aluminum nails because these will not rust and stain the woodwork after it has been painted.

If you wish to repaint the siding, this job can be done whenever it is convenient, after more pressing work on the renovation project has been completed.

If the exterior surface of the house is made of stucco, this can be repaired if it has cracked or developed holes. Use ordinary Portland-cement mortar. Cut out the cracks and holes along the edges with a cold chisel and a hammer so that the inside of the crack is wider than the outside, dampen the sides, and then pack in the mortar. Stucco can be painted, as can asbestos shingles.

Many older houses were covered with asbestos shingles in order to reduce the cost of painting upkeep. If you don't happen to care for the pattern or texture of asbestos shingles, you might take a few off and see what you find underneath. If the old wood siding is in good condition, you might find it practical to remove the shingles and repaint the original siding.

Another material you run across in old houses and outbuildings is *insulating siding*. This is an asphalt-base material made to resemble brick or stone. It is not particularly attractive, and our advice would be to remove it. If the siding underneath is no good, you can apply new siding over the old. This is not a rush job, however, because the insulating siding, while perhaps unattractive, will probably do an excellent job of keeping out the weather.

UNCONVENTIONAL WOOD CONSTRUCTION

If you are dealing with a barn, an outbuilding or a summer cottage, it may well be that instead of a layer of exterior siding applied over sheathing, you have only the siding. Barns are usually built this way. Many summer cottages have only a single layer of material for the outside walls, and this is often a type of novelty siding made to resemble logs, or a type of horizontal siding with extensive designs cut into the wood.

If you have a barn or an outbuilding with attractive weathered boards, you'll want to save them. The best thing to do is to take them down carefully and set them aside. Next, you should cover the framework of the structure with sheathing. If you are having trouble figuring out how to insulate the walls, you might do well to use rigid insulating sheathing boards. These will not only provide insulation but will also make the wall tight against wind and water.

The original boards can go back in place over the sheathing and you will then have a nice, solid, tight wall with a certain degree of insulation. If you plan to insulate the wall from the inside, you can use ordinary wood sheathing or plywood.

If the original siding on the structure isn't worth leaving exposed, avoid taking it off, because it has value for its structural strength and some value as insulation. If you can't insulate the wall from the outside, or inside, apply the insulating board over the original siding and then apply new siding over this. You'll end up with a pretty tight outside wall. The one drawback to this "overcoating," is that you will have to build out the trim around doors, windows, corners, and along the eaves where there may be trim. This is necessary so that the trim will extend out beyond the siding. It usually involves merely adding a layer or two of boards of the same width as the original ones.

Overcoating can be used on any wood structure where you need added rigidity and tightness and perhaps some added insulation. You don't, of course, have to apply the insulating board. If the walls are already adequately insulated, the new siding can be applied right over the old. Often a layer of building paper applied over the old siding will be all that is needed to provide a suitable base for the new siding. Sometimes, you will have to add nailing strips for the new siding at certain points.

TYPES OF SIDING

If you decide you need new siding, you have quite a range from which to choose. The most popular sidings are wood shingles, wood clapboard, board and batten, asbestos shingles, plastic clapboard, and aluminum clapboard.

If you are going to do the job yourself, your best bet is probably wood shingles. These are very good for a loner because one person can handle the job with ease. You don't need anyone around to help you lift a wood shingle and fit it into place. You can tack up one or you can tack up a hundred, and stop and start whenever you get the urge. As with floor tile, if you ruin one, the loss isn't very great. If you cut a length of clapboard an inch too short you have ruined it and have wasted some money, but if you ruin one shingle, your loss is rather small.

Board and batten you can also probably handle yourself if the outside walls aren't too high. One person can handle a 10-inch length of board without too much difficulty, but if you are working with 16-foot board, you will probably need a helper.

Wood clapboard really requires a helping hand, as do plastic and aluminum siding. Aluminum siding has a baked-on paint finish, and color is an integral part of plastic siding. Neither will peel or crack. These are often installed by companies who specialize in roofing and siding, and some of them will give you a good price on a job. You should check on the reputation of the outfit you are considering, because some of them are not all they crack themselves up to be. Your local Better Business Bureau can give you a reading on them.

You can also use hardboard for siding. It is a dense material that comes in 4-by-8-foot sheets or in the form of clapboard. Plywood is also used for siding, as is asbestos board.

Which material to use depends mainly on your taste and the style of dwelling on which you are working. Large panels of plywood, hardboard, or asbestos board painted various bright colors might not look so great on an old farmhouse, but they might be just right for a barn, chicken coop, or beach house that was being given a contemporary look.

One little thing that you might want to remember if you plan to do any extensive work on the siding is that it may involve working around the area where the electric lines and telephone lines are attached to the house. If you are just painting or removing the old paint before repainting, these won't get in your way, but if you are removing old siding or applying new siding, they will. Your local telephone and power company do not take kindly to anyone tinkering around with their lines, so if these have to be disconnected, call your phone and/or power company and arrange to have them send their own people over. It is best to have them come in the morning to disconnect the lines and return that evening to connect them back to the house.

MASONRY WALLS

By masonry, we mean outside walls made of stone, brick, brick veneer, or masonry block. Walls of these materials are fairly durable but in checking on these you should look first for a large crack running up the wall. This might indicate that the footing or foundation has settled a bit. If it has stopped settling, you need have no real concern. On the other hand, if it is still moving, you may be in for a little trouble. It would be a wise idea if, before you patch the crack, you draw a line at the point where the crack stops, then keep an eye on what happens for the next few months. If the crack continues to grow beyond this point, better call in a masonry contractor and have him check the wall to see where the trouble may be. The condition might easily be corrected with some reinforcing rods or it might require giving the footing a broader base.

Small cracks that run only a few feet are not much to worry about. It is when the crack goes right through a stone, brick, or block, that you know all is not well.

You can paint any form of masonry with a latex or masonry paint. Most of these are designed to seal pores and fine cracks in order to make the wall more watertight. But remember, once masonry has been painted, the paint is there to stay, unless you want to call someone in and have it sandblasted off. You can't remove it by burning or with a scraper or paint remover. If the masonry has already been painted and you don't wish to go to the cost of sandblasting, repaint.

The weakest areas in any masonry wall are the mortar joints. These will crack and the mortar will fall out. When it does, the wall can begin to leak. These joints can be repaired with cement mortar. Clean out the loose and cracked mortar. Use a cold chisel for this job. Dust out the opening, wet it down, and then pack in the mortar. You might find it handy to get a couple of special tools for this job because getting the mortar between the units is not all that easy. There is something called a *flat-brick jointer,* which is handy, and also a *tuck pointing trowel,* which should prove useful. You will find it considerably better to work with these than to try to push the mortar into place with your fingers.

Sometimes damp spots will appear on the inside walls. These indicate the presence of a leak in the masonry wall. To trace the leak, the first place to look is at the mortar joints. If these are faulty, they can allow water to get into the wall and run through until the water shows on the inside surface. Often the leak is not caused by a failure in the masonry wall but because there are open joints between the masonry and the window and door frames. These should be sealed with caulking com pound. Pay particular attention to the top of the frame because if this area is not sealed, water splashing from a clogged roof gutter might be entering the wall and running down inside.

You will find instances, of course, where the wall is at fault, and in that case steps must be taken to waterproof it. It may be that the mortar joints are porous; these can be sealed with a clear masonry-waterproofing compound. Another solution is to paint the outside of the wall with a waterproofing paint that will seal porous masonry blocks or bricks, as well as fine cracks and porous joints. An inferior grade of masonry block can be quite porous, and a good treatment here is to coat the wall on the outside with cement mortar. This produces a stucco finish that may be more attractive than the plain block and will certainly make the wall watertight.

Life is too short to spend any more time than necessary fooling around with exterior walls. Get your walls in proper shape so that you can more or less forget them. Select materials and finishes that please you, but keep in mind that the less upkeep the better.

THE SIDING PORTFOLIO

The amount of exposure for horizontally applied siding, whether shingles or clapboard, should be fixed so that the siding coming directly above a window or door opening will not have to be notched out. Figure above right shows the correct method of application, and Figure below left the incorrect method.

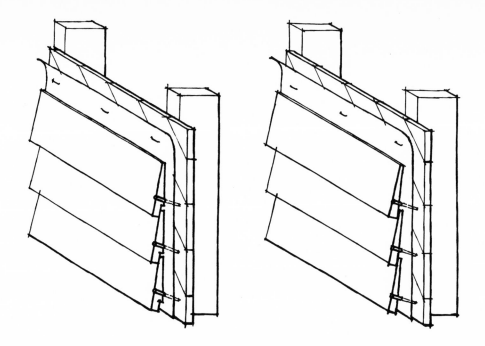

LEFT: Rabbeted bevel siding is secured with a single nail at each stud. The nail should be long enough to penetrate through the sheathing into the studding. Nails should be driven in 1 inch above the thick edge of each piece of siding, as shown. RIGHT: For plain bevel siding, the nails should be driven at or just above the thin edge of the underlying piece of siding.

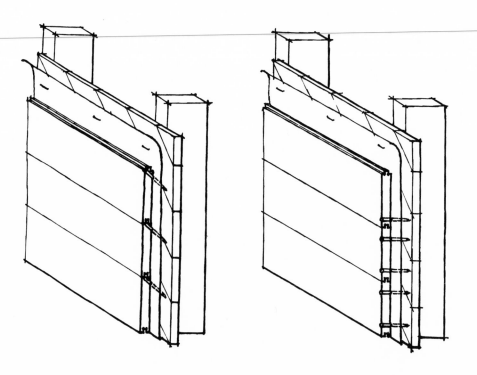

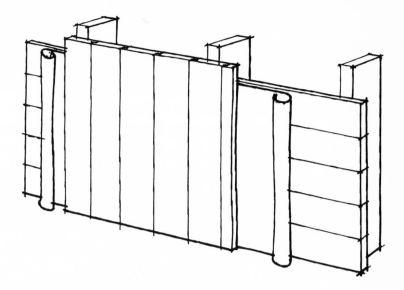

Siding applied vertically requires wood sheathing as a nailing base or horizontal members installed between vertical pieces of studding.

RIGHT: Wood shingles on walls should be spaced about 1/4 inch apart to allow for expansion and to prevent possible buckling. Shingles in each course should be arranged so that joints between shingles do not fall directly over the joists in the course below. FAR RIGHT: Once the amount of exposure for the shingles has been determined, make an exposure gauge out of a piece of wood so that you can easily check the exposure of each course as you work up the walls.

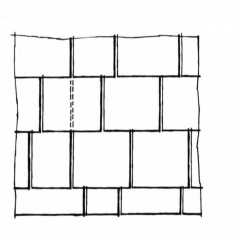

FACING PAGE FAR LEFT BOTTOM: Tongue-and-groove siding can be applied both horizontally and vertically. The best method of application is with blind-nailing, which eliminates the need for countersinking the nailheads and filling over them with putty or filler. Only one nail at each stud is necessary. LEFT BOTTOM: Face-nailing requires that the nailheads be set below the wood surface. On boards 6 inches or less in width, one nail per stud is adequate. For boards 8 inches or wider, use two nails.

Interior Walls and Ceilings   21

The variety of materials used for walls and ceilings in an OB House is infinite. Sometimes you will have perfectly splendid plaster walls and ceilings, and sometimes the plaster will be in such poor condition that it must be removed. You may, on the other hand, find that some of the walls of your house are paneled with lovely woods. Even if they happen to be covered with many coats of paint, the time and effort required to remove the paint are well worth the trouble. In many old houses you may find paneling of rather common wood, and while it may not be worth leaving exposed, it can provide a good base for paint.

If the structure is relatively new or has had some interior work done by the previous owner, the walls and ceilings may be of gypsum wallboard. If the material was properly installed so that the joints between sections are not visible, you can leave the material in place. If the joints are quite visible, if there are cracks between sections, and many exposed nailheads, it might be worth the time and effort to take down the old material and start off fresh.

In many summer cottages and farmhouses the walls and ceilings are covered with a fibrous kind of wallboard with the joints between sections covered with strips of wood. This type of insulating wallboard

253

was popular a good many years ago because it was so inexpensive and could be put up quite easily. It is not very attractive, however, and it can't be papered. If you have it, you would do well to rip it down and install gypsum wallboard.

Other materials you might run across are hardboard and plywood. Both are extremely durable and make a satisfactory base for paint, but the only effective way to conceal the joints between sections is to cover them with wood or metal strips.

If you happen to find a ceiling in your house made out of tin and you don't want it, take it down carefully because it is worth quite a good deal to antique dealers and interior decorators.

If you are in any doubt about the condition of walls and ceilings, we suggest you take down the old surface and apply a new one. This is not a difficult or expensive operation if it is done when other major renovation work is going on. It is, however, a headache to have to replace a wall or ceiling after you have finished the job and find that the existing surfaces are not satisfactory.

GYPSUM WALLBOARD

If you have to remove the existing materials from walls and ceilings because of their condition or if you have to install a new partition or cover an existing framework, the best material to use for the job is gypsum wallboard. This consists of a core of gypsum plaster encased in a heavy paper covering. The standard sheet is 4 by 8 feet, but it is available in longer lengths. The ½-inch-thick sheets are best for residential work.

Gypsum wallboard is used extensively today in both new and old construction, and in many areas has taken the place of plaster. It goes up rapidly and with a minimum of mess. When properly installed, you can't tell a gypsum wallboard surface from one of plaster unless you are an expert and tap on the surface to determine the difference in sound. Because the joints between sections are concealed, a wall or ceiling made of this material can be painted or papered. Gypsum wallboard is sometimes called *sheet rock* or *dry wall.*

The success of a gypsum-wallboard surface depends on how well the material was installed. If the installation is not done skillfully, the joints between sections will show even if the surface has been papered or painted.

Application of Gypsum Wallboard. Sheets of this material come with a recess along the edges. When the sheets are nailed into place, a coat of special cement called *joint cement* is applied to the joint and then a strip of special paper tape is pressed into the cement to act as reinforcing. The surface of the joint is smoothed out with a broad putty knife and allowed to dry. After it is dry, the joint is given a light sanding and another coat of the cement is applied and feathered out at the edges so that there are no vsisible ridges between the joint and the surface of the board. It usually takes several applications of the cement before the joint is perfectly smooth.

Inside corners are reinforced with tape and treated in the same manner as the joints. Outside corners are covered with metal strips.

Special nails are used for fastening the wallboard to the framework. The heads are set so that they dent, but do not break, the paper covering on the boards. It is best to use a hammer with a convex head for this job. The nailheads should be covered with joint cement.

You can figure that it will cost about 17 cents a square foot to have gypsum wallboard installed by a professional. This price includes the material, fastening in place, and taping the joints. You can do the job yourself if you exercise proper care but you will need someone to help you, for the standard-sized sheets are rather heavy and difficult to handle alone. Putting them on a ceiling is a hard job, and we'd leave this to a professional.

Gypsum wallboard makes a satisfactory wall or ceiling for any room in the house. With modern adhesives it is also suitable as a base for ceramic wall tile for a bathroom or kitchen.

OTHER MATERIALS

Prefinished plywood makes an attractive wall material and is not difficult for the amateur to install. Wood paneling of pine, redwood, or cypress boards is handsome, too, and can be done by you if you enjoy working with wood. You don't have to stick to conventional wood or boards for paneling. We have seen walls covered with red cedar shingles, cedar clapboard, and even oak flooring, and the results have been very effective.

While paneling can be applied over an existing wall covering, it is best if you remove the old material so that the paneling can be nailed directly to the wall framework. If you are going to use individual boards, you should install horizontal pieces of framing between the uprights so that the boards can be nailed at other points beside top and bottom. Install horizontal framing pieces about every 3 feet.

Ceiling tile is an excellent treatment for ceilings, and is not difficult to apply. Ceiling tile comes in a variety of shapes, patterns, and colors and not only produces a good ceiling but also helps reduce noise level in a room. Ceiling tile is sometimes called *acoustical tile*. These tiles can be installed over an existing ceiling, if it is solid, or applied to the ceiling joints. Either way, a framework of 1 by 3 inches is first secured in place to provide a suitable nailing-base for the tile.

WALL SURFACES IN MASONRY STRUCTURES

In solid masonry construction of brick, stone, or block you may find that the interior side of the masonry has been handled in a variety of ways. There may, of course, be nothing with the interior masonry exposed, or it may have been coated with paint or plaster. Sometimes the plaster has been applied directly to the masonry, and sometimes lath has been attached to the masonry and the plaster applied over this. You may find that a wood framework has been attached to the masonry and this, in turn, has been covered with plaster or wallboard.

If a masonry wall is attractive, you may wish to leave it exposed or, if it has been covered with plaster or some other material, you may want to rip these off so that the masonry can be exposed. With exposed masonry, two points should be considered: (1) it does not absorb sound and therefore a room with one or two walls or masonry may become a little noisy; and (2) it tends to show condensation. In cold climates a masonry wall that is not too thick may become rather cold on the interior surface and you may get some sweating on the wall during very cold weather when the inside air is warm and humid. Probably the only way to find out if this condition is going to occur is to live with the wall for a winter and see what happens. If the wall does sweat, the condition can be corrected by covering the inside surface with a framework of 2-by-4s and installing gypsum wallboard or some other form of wall surface. In warm climates there is no problem with condensation on inside surfaces of solid masonry walls.

Reconditioning Plaster Walls and Ceilings. If your house has plaster walls and ceilings that are not too far gone, they can be repaired. Holes, even large ones, can be patched, as can cracks along the surface or at the corners. But when plaster has broken away from the lath, you are better off to remove the plaster completely and apply wallboard. You can tell if plaster is no longer attached to the lath because there may be areas where it has bulged out from the wall or ceiling. You can also tell by pressing your hand against it. If the plaster gives when you press on it, it is advisable to get rid of it. We once salvaged plaster walls in this condition by giving them coat after coat of gypsum-wallboard joint cement but we'll never do it again because it took us weeks and weeks and we have no idea of how long this treatment will be effective and when cracks will start to appear.

If the plaster is solid and just needs patching here and there, it is worth the effort to make repairs.

Large holes—holes several inches or even feet in area—are filled with prepared plaster that is mixed with water before it is applied. Remove the old plaster from between the lath and cut back the edges of the surrounding plaster until you reach plaster that is firm. Cut the edges back with a putty knife so that the inside of the edge is deeper than the outside. This will help hold the plaster patch in place. Wet down the edges of the old plaster and then stir up your mixture for the patch. You want to add just enough water to make the plaster easy to work with but not so much that it becomes overly moist and will not stay in place.

Apply the patch several coats at a time. The first coat should be forced into place with the trowel so that it goes in back of the wood lath to form a bulge, which is what holds the plaster to wood lath. If you just coat the plaster over the lath, it won't hold well. Keep applying the plaster until the patch comes to within about ¼ inch of the surface and then let the patch harden for a day. The final coat is applied right over the main patch and should be brought out so that it is even with the surrounding plaster. A length of board can be helpful in achieving this result. Just slide the board back and forth over the patch, allowing the ends to rest on the surrounding plaster.

Small cracks and holes in plaster can be filled with patching plaster or plaster of paris. A painter introduced us to a very fine mix for patching that is made by adding plaster of paris to gypsum-wallboard joint cement. You add just enough of the plaster so that the mixture is workable and then you slap it into place; it produces a very strong patch. A good way of handling long cracks is to give them a coat of joint cement, then cover them with gypsum-wallboard tape and apply a few coats of joint cement over this.

Smoothing Rough-Textured Plaster Walls. You can smooth these out so that they will be suitable for wallpaper by coating them with several thin applications of joint cement.

► *Special Money-Saving Tips*

You can save about $40 on an average-sized room by removing the old wall and ceiling materials yourself.

You can save about $120 on the relocation of each 10-foot-long partition by doing this job yourself.

You can save about $75 on the average-sized room if you can repair the existing surfaces rather than ripping them off and having new material installed.

You can save about $50 on the average-sized room if you install gypsum wallboard on the walls and ceiling yourself.

Insulation 22

Wherever you live and whatever sort of structure you select as the basis for your Offbeat Dream House, you are going to need insulation. If you have a year-round house where the winters are cold, insulation is necessary to make the house more comfortable and to reduce the cost of heating. If the house is to be used only in summer, insulation is needed to keep the house from getting too hot.

The roof or the ceilings of the rooms directly below the roof are the areas most necessary to insulate. Here is where you get the greatest heat gain in summer and the most heat loss in winter. If you want to check this, go into an uninsulated attic about three o'clock on a hot summer afternoon. After that hot sun has been beating down on the roof for a good many hours, the attic can become almost hot enough to bake bread in it. And if the attic floor or the ceiling of the rooms below is not insulated, trying to sleep on a hot night is like trying to sleep under an oven. In winter, just the reverse action takes place. All that nice warm air inside the house that is costing you money to produce flows up through the house and out into the cold. So whatever else you do in the way of insulation, be sure that the upper section of the house is insulated.

259

Next to the roof, the outside walls of the house are the most important area to insulate. It isn't absolutely essential to insulate the walls of a summer house, but all the outside walls of a year-round house in cold areas definitely must be insulated.

If the house is to be heated, and there is an unheated area such as a basement, crawl space, or garage under the first floor, then the underside of the floor should be insulated. If you plan to use electric heat, it is essential that you thoroughly insulate the roof, walls, and floor.

For electric heat the common practice is to use 6-inch-thick insulation for roof or ceilings, 4-inch-thick insulation on the walls and 3-inch-thick material for the floors. Where other forms of heating equipment are to be used or for a summer house, 3-inch-thick insulation is adequate.

While the primary purpose of insulation is to reduce heat loss and heat gain, it can also be used to reduce sound transmission within a house. You might, for example, wish to insulate all the walls of the bathroom so that each time water is drawn, the sound will not be heard in other areas. It might be desirable to insulate a wall between a living room and a bedroom, so that if someone wishes to go to bed, they won't be disturbed. If you have an upstairs or downstairs area that will be used for children or teen-agers, it might be wise to insulate the floor to help control the transmission of sounds.

The basic reason we insulate, of course, is to make the house more comfortable, and an interesting phenomenon is involved with this business of comfort. If you are sitting not too far away from an outside wall that is not insulated, you may feel cold in spite of the fact that the temperature of the air around you is quite high. What is happening is that the cold wall is drawing heat away from your body just as if it were a magnet. You may have experienced this same sensation sitting near the window in a train or plane. In spite of the fact that the air around you is warm, the side of you facing that window is cold—often uncomfortably cold.

TYPES OF INSULATION

Many different types of insulation are available. The most common is that made of glass fibers or mineral wool. The small air cells trapped in the material reduce the passage of heat, and also reduce sound-transmission. This type of insulation comes in several forms. One frequently used form comes in long rolls designed to fit standard-space walls, ceilings, and roof framing. It can be fastened in place between the framing members with staples or nails, or simply pressed into place. This type is also available in standard 4-foot lengths, which are somewhat easier than the rolls for the individual worker to handle alone. Either form is excellent but can only be used on new work or where the existing wall and ceiling coverings have been removed so that the framework is exposed.

Insulation of this sort is not difficult to apply yourself. You should first measure the area to be insulated so that you can give the lumberyard the number of square feet to be covered. The person waiting on you at the yard can figure out the amount of insulation you will need. You should also measure the spacing of the framing so that you can get the correct width.

Get an instruction sheet from your dealer as to the proper method of attaching the insulation, and if you need a stapler, rent or borrow a heavy-duty type from your dealer, along with the necessary amount of staples. You can use nails instead of staples, but staples are much easier to handle and make the work go more quickly. The main trick in applying the insulation is to make accurate measurements when cutting, so that no spaces are left unfilled. If you have to cut the insulation to fit around electric wiring or plumbing, make these cuts as neat as possible, so that there won't be gaps in the coverage.

You will notice on one side of the insulation instructions to "Apply This Vapor Barrier Side Toward the Living Space," or words to this effect. Be sure that you do just this, because it can make quite a difference if you don't. The purpose of the vapor barrier is to keep the moist air inside the house from reaching the insulation. If this should happen, the moist air would condense into a liquid when it came in contact with the cold outside surface of the wall or roof. If the liquid is absorbed by the insulation, it reduces the insulation's effectiveness. Unless latex paint has been used on the exterior of the house, it can also make the paint blister and peel. This water vapor inside the house is a gas and can pass through ordinary paint on inside walls as well as through plaster and gypsum board. The vapor barrier on the insulation is especially treated so that this gas cannot flow through it. *The vapor-barrier side should always face the room or heated side of the area being insulated.* When a floor is insulated, the vapor barrier goes against the flooring.

In some OB Dream Houses you will have to install additional framing to provide a base on which to attach the insulation. For example, a barn or similar structure may not be framed sufficiently to take a standard-width insulation. You will have to add framing. This will serve not only as a base for your insulation but also as a base for the interior-wall materials.

Another common type of insulation is the granular or fill variety that comes in bags and is poured between the framing. This is good to use on something like an attic floor when the framework is exposed, or where you can take up the existing floor without too much effort. It is also good to use for spots that you can't reach with other types of insulation. For example, in the house in which we now live, a water line runs up an outside wall for about 5 feet before it goes into the wall. We built a box around this line and filled the box with granular insulation to prevent the line from freezing.

There is also a reflective type of insulation made of sheets of aluminum. This is installed between the wall and roof framework. In warm weather it reflects heat back to its source, which is outside, and in winter it reflects the heat back into the house. It is tricky stuff to install and is best left to a professional because if it isn't put in just right, it doesn't work.

If the framework of an area to be insulated is not exposed, you have to take another tack. Here you fill the wall cavity with the granular type of insulation. This, too, must be done by a professional, because the insulation has to be blown into the wall cavity. Work of this sort is handled by insulation contractors and you can usually find them listed in the yellow pages of your phone book. They will either remove sections of the siding and sheathing, or drill holes through the outside walls and then blow the insulation into the cavity. They have special equipment for this purpose. They can insulate walls, floors, and just about any area where a cavity can be reached with a hose.

Not every structure will have the wall cavities that make this type of application possible. This particular house of ours does not because it is a plank house. Some structures are built in such fashion that in order to reach all sections of the wall cavity, so many holes would have to be drilled in the wall that it would become like a sieve. What can be done here is to apply insulating boards to the outside walls and cover these with siding. This involves a good deal of labor, but if the siding is to be replaced anyway, the time and effort required to put up the insulating board would be justified. Insulating boards are large, rigid sheets, and they run from ¾ of an inch in thickness to several inches. The very thick types are often used on contemporary houses where the roof or ceiling rafters of a room are to be left exposed.

Plastics such as Styrofoam are also used as insulation and while their cost at the present time is somewhat higher than ordinary insulating materials, they will probably be used more and more, because they are easy to handle, do not absorb water, and have a high degree of insulating value.

THE INSULATION PORTFOLIO

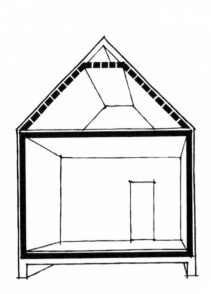 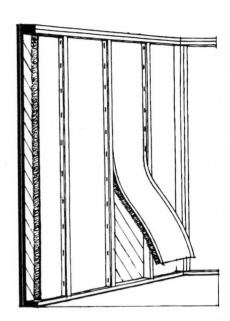

LEFT: Heavy, dark, solid lines indicate area of house requiring insulation to reduce heat loss to a minimum. If attic space is not to be used for living purposes, insulate attic floor as shown by heavy dark line. If attic space is to be used for rooms, now or in the future, insulate as indicated by the heavy broken line.

RIGHT: The standard insulation used on vertical framing is applied by fastening the flange on the side of the insulation to the inside face of the framing with staples. Lengths of insulation should be cut so that there is a tight fit at top and bottom.

FACING PAGE BOTTOM: An existing interior wall can be insulated by applying sheets of insulating board over the old siding and applying new siding over the insulation.

Granular or fill insulation is applied by pouring between the joints. A handmade leveling board helps get the insulation to an even thickness. The paper vapor barrier should be placed between the joists before the insulation is poured into place.

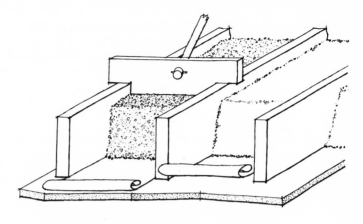

To reduce sound transmission through a wall, stagger the studding as shown and weave insulation between the framing members.

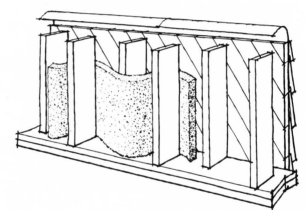

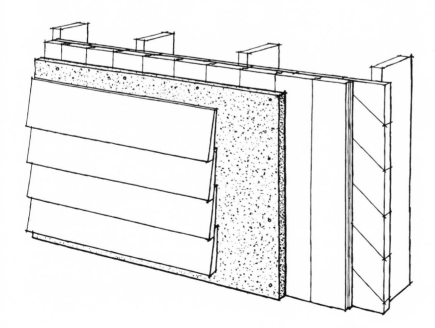

23 Roofs

Once you have a good roof installed, you can forget it. A properly installed roof utilizing roofing materials of good quality should last as long as you occupy a house. Don't, however, assume that the roof you put on will outlast your children and your grandchildren.

If you have purchased a house with a good roof, you can pretty much skip this chapter. You are extremely fortunate.

TYPES OF ROOFING MATERIALS

You can expect to find almost any type of roofing material on an OB house. On a pitched roof, which is the roof from which you can slide off, as opposed to the flat roof, from which you only fall off, you find wood shingles, wood shakes (hand-split shingles with a rough texture), asphalt shingles, asbestos shingles, aluminum sheets, clay tile, slate, and possibly even straw. We have actually run across a few OB structures with thatched roofs. Which brings to mind the fact that they are having a bad time installing thatched roofs in England now because today's straw is not as good as the old-fashioned stuff.

Sometimes you'll find a pitched roof covered with roll roofing, sheets of asphalt roofing paper nailed at the edges. You find quite a lot of this used in outbuildings and on run-down houses where something inexpensive was needed to keep water out.

Some roofs are covered with sheets of corrugated galvanized iron, and in certain sections of the country you will find tin, or terne, roofs. They were popular some years back because they are fire resistant and not easily damaged by high winds. In such roofs the sections of roofing were soldered together. You'll find many of these on farmhouses and farm outbuildings.

In Florida and other tropical or sub-tropical areas you will find something called *Bermuda roof*, which is made with a concrete-base shingle. Clay tile is also popular in these areas.

Flat roofs are usually covered with *built-up roofing*. This consists of several layers of asphalt-roll roofing cemented together with roofing cement. Often the surface will be covered with gravel or mineral granules.

Assuming that the material was properly installed, many roofing materials will last almost indefinitely, and if a leak occurs here and there, it can be repaired. Asbestos shingles, slate shingles, and clay tile can last almost forever. If a few have been damaged or have come loose or fallen out, they can be refastened or replaced without much difficulty. You should have this work done by an expert, however, because walking around on these roofs, if you don't know what you are doing, can do considerable damage. If you have a slate or clay-tile roof, by all means save it if possible, for this kind of installation is not only handsome but durable. It is also expensive to install today.

A tin, or terne, roof is also one that should last for a good many years. They do become rusty, but if the metal is sound, it can be coated with paint or with a roofing compound to give it a fresh look and add a few more years to its life.

The most common roofing materials are wood shingles and asphalt shingles, and these are the ones you are most likely to find on an existing house. These are also the materials that you will probably select if it is necessary to reroof.

While both wood and asphalt shingles will last a good many years, there does come a point where they give out. Wood shingles may become so dry that they curl up at the edges, or the nails that hold them rust away so that the shingles pull loose. Shingles that get a large amount of shade may decay. Asphalt shingles eventually dry out; the mineral granules on the surface wash away and while the roof may still be fairly tight, it is not very attractive. When the shingles are in this condition, a high wind can curl them up so that water can get under them. This is the time for a new roof.

REROOFING

If the existing roof is covered with wood shingles, you can apply new wood shingles or asphalt shingles right over the old ones. You do not have to remove the old shingles. As a matter of fact, aside from the saving you will make in time and money by leaving them in place, they offer some benefit in added insulation. A little preparation work is involved before the new shingles can be applied, but this is nothing compared to the work required to remove the old shingles. If the existing roof is covered with asphalt shingles, you can apply new asphalt shingles over the old, but you should not apply wood shingles over asphalt shingles—the asphalt shingles should be removed. If the old roof happens to be of tin, slate, or tile, these materials must be removed before either wood or asphalt shingles can be applied.

Wood Shingles. The best-quality wood shingles are red cedar and are classified by the Red Cedar Shingle & Handsplit Shake Bureau as No. 1 Blue Label. The next best is the No. 2 Red Label. Wood shingles come in 16-inch, 18-inch, and 24-inch sizes. They are usually applied in their natural state, but if a color is desired, they can be stained before application.

Asphalt Shingles. The points to consider in buying asphalt shingles are the weight, color, and texture. Asphalt shingles come in different weights, and the heavier the shingle the longer it will last. The standard shingle is the 235-pound shingle; that means that the number of shingles required to cover a square—a space 10 feet by 10 feet—will weigh 235 pounds. Weights range up to 380 pounds. The heavier the shingle the less apt it is to be damaged by wind. Many shingles today, however, come with a self-sealer, so that after they have been applied, they cement themselves together to produce an excellent wind-and-water-resistant surface. Asphalt shingles come in a wide range of color. The color is produced by the mineral granules applied to the exposed portion of the shingle. Color is a matter of choice, but a white or light-colored roof is going to reflect heat away from the house in summer while a black or dark roof will absorb it. Asphalt shingles also come in many different textures and, here again, which one to use is a matter of taste.

Roofing can be applied by the same contractor who may be doing other work on the house. There are also firms that specialize in roofing and siding. What about doing the job yourself? Well, if you are talking about asphalt or wood shingles, the answer can be "yes." It depends, of course, on how complicated the roof is. If it's a simple roof, you'll have few, if any, problems. If it is a roof with many hips and valleys, an amateur will not find it easy.

Whether or not you do the reroofing yourself also depends on the amount of roof to be covered and the height of the roof. As we get older, height seems to bother us more, or perhaps we just don't fall as easily as we did when we were younger. Not so long ago we could fall 15 feet and land on all fours like a cat without giving it much thought. After a little more aging, we cut this down to 10 feet. This was just about the distance from the eaves to the ground on the last house we reroofed. While we weren't deliberately trying to test whether this was too much of a fall, we did fall, and it was. Experienced roofers don't seem to have any trouble with heights. We once wrote a news story on how a professional applies a roof and we ended up one day on one of the highest and steepest roofs we ever hope to be on. The roofer was old enough to be our father, but he dance around up there without a care in the world. We just hung to the chimney, and he finally had to help us down to the ladder that was resting against the eaves.

We would say that if the roof is not so high that you could take a serious fall from it, and if you observe normal safety precautions, you can handle a modest-sized roof yourself. The safety precautions involve wearing shoes that won't slip—rubber soles are fine for this work—and using a toe board so you won't slide (this is just a length of 2 by 4 spiked into the roof or held in place with metal brackets. As the work progresses, you move this board up the roof. It not only makes work easier because you have something to support your weight, but if you start to slip, you have something to grab.

Detailed instructions for applying wood shingles can be obtained by writing to the Red Cedar Shingle & Handsplit Shake Bureau, 5510 White Building, Seattle, Washington 98101. If you want information on the proper application of asphalt shingles, write to the Asphalt Roofing Manufacturers Association, 757 Third Avenue, New York, New York 10017.

These are the only two types of roofing material that we would advise the amateur to install. Asbestos shingles, tile, and slate should be left to the professionals.

ROOF REPAIRS

Sometimes a roof may leak because of a single minor flaw that can be repaired.

A wood shingle may pull loose as the result of improper nailing; you need only push it back into place and nail it down with a couple of shingle nails. As the nailheads will be exposed, give them a dab of roofing cement. If a shingle is curled badly, split it up the center, put a piece of roofing paper under it, and then nail the two portions down and coat the nailheads with roofing cement.

Often wood shingles are not applied to a solid deck. Instead, you will find individual boards nailed to the rafters with considerable space between each board in order to insure good circulation of air on the underside of the shingles. This manner of shingling is often found on houses in warm climates. But you will also find this type of application on roofs in cold areas. You can often see little flecks of light coming through the roof if you look up at the underside. Don't worry about these unless there are signs that water is coming through. Usually these small openings seal themselves the minute the wood becomes moist and swells, but even if they don't, if water hasn't leaked through them so far, it probably won't until the entire roof fails.

High winds sometimes lift up the exposed ends of asphalt shingles. These can be pushed back in place and held down with a spot of roofing cement applied to the underside of the exposed portion of the shingle. Leaks in asphalt shingles caused by someone accidentally putting a hole through them can be fixed by sealing the opening with roofing cement.

Many leaks in roofs are not the fault of the roofing but of the flashing —the metal used to make a watertight joint where the roof joins the chimney—or at the valleys where flashing is used between two roof planes. Most of these problems can be solved by sealing the joint with roofing cement, or filling any hole or rust spot in the flashing with roofing cement.

THE ROOFING PORTFOLIO

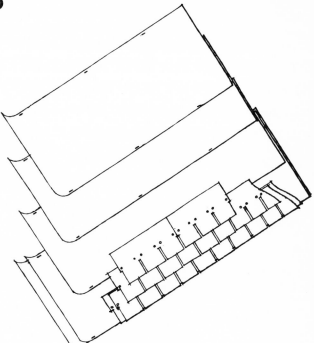

The correct method of applying asphalt shingles on a new roof. Roof sheathing is first covered with asphalt building paper. Two courses of shingles are applied at eaves. Shingles must be staggered so that slots between tabs do not fall over the ones below. Each shingle is fastened with six nails as shown.

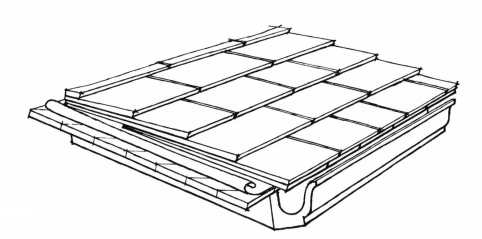

Wood shingles, like asphalt shingles, are doubled at eaves and extend slightly beyond edge of roof.

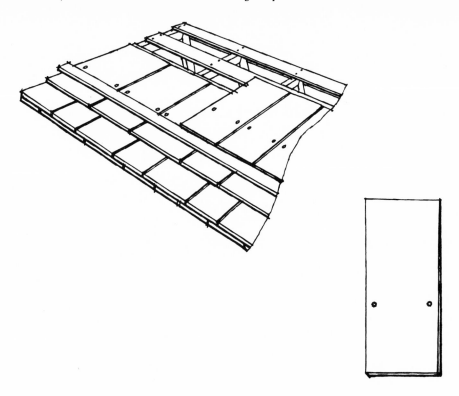

LEFT: An easy way to make sure that a row of wood shingles will be perfectly straight is to tack a straight strip of wood to the roof, as shown, to serve as a guide. When a course of shingles has been applied, remove the guide and position it for the next course.

RIGHT: Wood shingles should be secured with two nails placed as shown. The heads of the nails should be covered by the shingle above.

FACING PAGE TOP: Flashing is used to make a watertight joint where roof joins the chimney. Flashing runs under the roofing and is carried up along the side of the masonry. The ends are bent over and set into the mortar joints.

FACING PAGE BOTTOM: Detail showing the counterflashing that is placed over the roofing after roofing is in place over the regular flashing. Flashing set into chimney masonry can be secured with mortar, or lead plugs, and sealed with caulking compound.

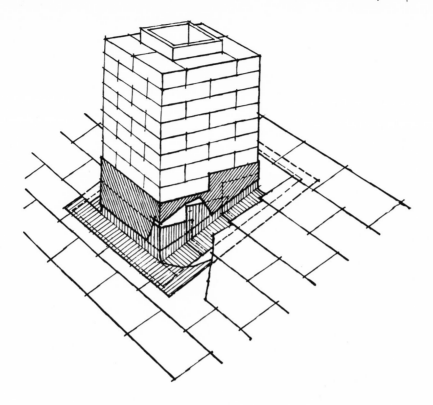

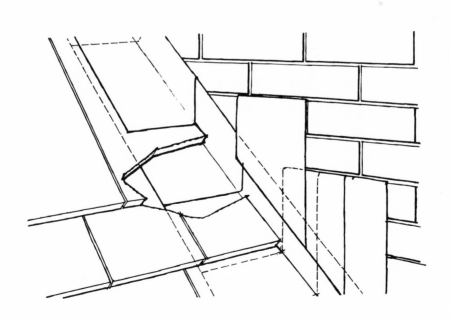

24 Windows

There are two basic types of windows: those that can be opened and those that can't. The first group is *movable,* and the second group is *fixed.* Let's first discuss the movable window.

The portion of a window unit that contains the glass and moves is called the *sash.* The panes of glass in a window sash are often called *lights.* The number and size of lights in a sash will vary according to style. When you order a sash, you not only want to specify the width and height but also the size and number of lights.

The little strips of wood or metal that separate the lights are called *muntins.* When two or more window units are placed side by side, the vertical piece that separates them is called a *mullion.* The opening that is framed in the wall to accommodate a window unit is called the *rough opening* and this must be custom made to accommodate the particular window unit to be installed.

Most windows used today are factory made and come in stock sizes. The range of styles and sizes is wide, and you can find out what is available by asking your architect, contractor, or lumberyard or by writing to the various manufacturers of window units. You can have window units made to order, but these are expensive and we suggest that you use the stock items wherever possible.

276

Windows for use in residential work are made of wood or aluminum. If you live in a warm climate, either type will be satisfactory. If you live in a cold climate, stick to wood units because in cold weather you can get a good deal of condensation on a metal unit. Metal is a good conductor of cold as well as heat, and the inside surface of a metal window frame will become extremely cold if the outside temperature is low. Wood is not as good a conductor as metal, and therefore the inside of a wood frame won't become so cold.

Probably the best window unit made today is one of wood encased in plastic. The plastic coating protects the wood from the elements and eliminates the need for painting, while the wood under it provides the necessary degree of insulation. Wooden windows of good quality are treated during construction with wood preservatives to stabilize the wood so that it does not expand and contract as the result of changes in moisture content, and also to eliminate the chance of decay.

The best type of aluminum window comes with a baked-enamel finish. Aluminum does not rust but it does become discolored, and the discoloration is especially severe where it is used around salt water. The enamel coating protects the metal and also makes the units more attractive.

SCREENS AND STORM SASHES

Most good-quality stock windows come with screens and storm sashes. These usually have aluminum frames to make them easy to handle. Screens are needed in almost all areas to keep out insects, and storm sashes are required in all but very warm areas to reduce heat loss, as well as to reduce the formation of condensation on window glass in cold weather. If you need screens and storm sashes for existing windows, you can get aluminum combination units and these will cost about $20 per standard window. They are exceedingly practical.

With some windows, the need for a separate storm sash is eliminated by the use of double, or insulating glass, in place of ordinary glass. This consists of two layers of glass with an air space between them. The layers are sealed together at the edges so that air is trapped between the two glass surfaces. The dead air between the glass acts as insulation and prevents the inner glass from becoming cold. In heated houses, this type of glass should be used on sliding glass doors as well as on large fixed or picture windows that are either impossible or difficult to equip with a storm sash.

TYPES OF WINDOWS

Windows come in several styles and some are better for certain conditions than others.

Double-Hung Units. Probably the most familiar window, is the one in which the lower sash slides up and the upper sash slides down. The sash is held in the desired position by ropes, weights, and pulleys, or, in the more modern type of unit, by a friction device or springs. This is a good all-purpose unit, but it has one disadvantage, and that is you have to get right up close to it and use two hands to open and close the sash. This can be an inconvenience if an object such as a kitchen work counter or a living-room sofa is located in front of the window.

Casement. The casement window is the one with the sash that swings on hinges in the same way that a door does. You will find many homemade casement units in barns, outbuildings, and similar structures because if there was an old sash around, it was a simple matter to make a rough opening and frame and set the sash in place with a couple of hinges. A hook-and-eye device was used to keep the sash closed, and a longer hook was used to keep it open. Modern factory-made casement windows are something else. They are usually tightly fitted, so that when they are closed, air doesn't come in around the edges of the sash. The sash is opened and closed with a metal adjuster with a crank, which will hold the sash in any desired position. Because they can be operated with one hand, casement windows are good for spots over the kitchen sink and work counters or for any other area where the window is difficult to reach. They also provide 100-per-cent ventilation when open.

Awning Windows.   Awning windows are similar in construction to the casement type, except that the sash is hinged at the top so that it swings up to perform like an awning. These windows are often used under or alongside a large fixed window to provide ventilation, and are also good to install high on a wall in a room where wall space is limited or where you may want more privacy than is provided by windows set at the standard height on the wall. They can be left open even during heavy rains.

A variation of the awning window is called a *hopper window*, which is hinged at the bottom.

Bay Windows and Bow Windows.   These are units that extend beyond the wall of a house. They provide additional floor space.

Sliding Windows.   The sliding window is one in which the sash moves from the right or left. Sliding windows are often used in place of a large fixed window because they can be opened for ventilation.

All the window styles just described come in a wide range of sizes. If you are going to need new windows in your house, you should obtain a listing of the available sizes and styles and use this as your guide in deciding which type of unit and what size are best suited for a particular purpose.

RECONDITIONING EXISTING WINDOWS

New windows are not inexpensive, so if the condition of the existing ones is not too bad, and you wish to save money, you'll recondition as many as you can. But if you do have the money and the windows are not in great condition or not suitable for your purposes, we suggest that you get new ones.

Let's assume that there isn't enough money available to replace the existing windows and that you have decided to go to work on them. We will start off with the double-hung window because, in a way, that is the most difficult to handle.

First, remove the sash from the frame. This is necessary if the sash is stuck, if the sash cords are broken, or if you just want to get the sash out so that you can work on it and the frame separately. From the room side, remove one or both of the little strips of wood that hold the sash in place and are attached to the side of the frame. These are held in place by screws or finishing nails. Sometimes it is only necessary to remove one; sometimes both have to come off. Once this has been done, the lower sash can be pulled out of the frame. If it is connected to a sash cord, slip the knot in the cord out of the side of the sash.

To remove the upper sash, remove one or both of the wood strips that separate the lower and upper sash. These, too, are held in place with finishing nails or screws. With the strips of wood removed, the upper sash can be pulled out of the frame. You can't remove either sash from the outside—the work must be done inside because of the way the window frame is made.

When you have finished work on a sash and are putting it back into the frame, check the movement to be sure that it slides easily. If it does not, sand the edges lightly with sandpaper. If you find that a sash cord has been broken, you will have to replace it. To do this, get the sash weight out of the inside of the frame. There is a little wood or metal door on the inside of the frame at the base near the window sill. You will probably have to hunt to find it. Remove the screw or nail that holds it in place and you can reach inside and get the sash weight. Take off the old cord from the weight and feed a new one over the pully and down until you can pull it out and tie it to the sash weight. Put the weight back and replace the pocket cover. To fasten the cord to the sash, hold the sash in position, pull the cord until the weight is hanging free just a fraction of an inch from the bottom, then tie a knot in the cord at the point where it is to be connected to the sash.

A casement sash is a good deal easier to remove than a double-hung one. All you have to do here is to remove the screws from the hinges. If the unit has an adjuster, remove the screws that hold this to the sash.

As soon as the sash or sashes have been removed, you can get a good look at the condition of the frame. You may find that some of the painted areas, especially the sill, are in poor condition. Strip off the old paint and clean out the joints between wood members with a putty knife or any other tool that seems to do the trick. These joints that are exposed to the weather are rather critical, because if they are not tight, water will get into the frame and even through it to the inside wall. Fill the cracks with plastic wood, wood putty, or white-lead paste thinned with turpentine so it can be worked into the fine cracks. Next the wood should be given a prime coat of paint. When this is dry the areas that are exposed to the weather should be given a coat or two of exterior paint. The other parts can wait until you do the inside painting in the room.

If the frame happens to be of metal, wire brush it to remove loose paint and rust. Touch up rust spots with a metal primer and inspect to see that the joint between the metal frame and the wood frame is sealed tight with caulking compound. If it isn't, seal it.

The Sash. If a sash needs work, put it on a bench where you can work on it in comfort. It may be that the outside painted surface is in poor condition, the paint having peeled or cracked. Strip it off with a paint remover. If the putty around the glass is in good condition, avoid leaving the remover on it for any length of time because it may soften the putty. If the putty is in poor condition, badly cracked, or falling out in places, it will have to be removed, so the paint remover won't hurt it anyway. If any of the lights are broken or missing, the putty around these openings must be removed. Sometimes it can be removed with a putty knife, but if that doesn't do the trick, soften it up with a paint remover. Be careful when you use a putty knife, because if the knife slips, you may crack the glass.

With the putty out of the way, you will see that the glass is held in place with little triangular pieces of metal driven into the wood. These are called *points*. The points should be removed, and if the glass is unbroken, it should be taken out and put aside. Clean the opening in the sash with steel wool and then give it a coat of paint. If you have stripped all the paint off the sash, paint the entire sash. If new panes are needed, you can get them cut to size at most hardware stores. Measure the opening to determine the size of the pane you need but deduct about ¹⁄₁₆ to ⅛ of an inch from each dimension to allow for irregularities in the opening or in the glass.

To install a piece of glass, first apply a thin bed of putty or glazing compound to the part of the sash against which the glass rests. This should be about ¹⁄₁₆ of an inch thick. Put the glass in place and press down gently so that it makes continuous contact with the putty on all four sides.

With the glass in place, secure it there with the points. Use two points on each side of a piece of glass measuring about 8 by 13 inches. For larger-sized panes, use additional points. Points are pushed into place with a screwdriver. The next step is to apply a continuous strip of putty around the outdoor edges of the glass. The strip is made by rolling a gob of putty or compound between your palms until you have a long, thick strip. Press this around the joint between glass and sash. Take a putty knife and smooth off the putty or compound so that you produce a smooth, sloping joint on all sides. If you will take a look at some outside windows, you can easily see how this type of joint is most effective in keeping rain and moisture away from the wood.

It will take a little practice before you can do this quickly and come out with a nice, smooth joint. Be careful not to make the strip of putty too wide or you will be able to see it on the glass from the inside. Either white-lead putty or glazing compound can be used for this job. Glazing compound is somewhat easier to use but either will do. After a day or so, a coat of paint should be applied.

It is best not to paint the sides of the sash that move up and down because this may cause them to stick or become difficult to work. A coat of linseed oil or a sealer can be used in place of paint.

Metal Windows. The glass in a metal window is held in place by strips of metal and these, in turn, are secured to the sash by metal screws or clips. Once the metal strip has been removed, the broken glass can be removed. Clean off all traces of the compound used to seal the glass in the frame. Use glazing compound on a metal sash and be sure that it is applied in such a fashion that the glass does not come into direct contact with the metal. If it does, unequal expansion and contraction between the metal and the glass might crack the glass.

► *Special Money-Saving Tips*

It can cost you about $1 plus materials to have someone replace the average-sized pane of window glass. If you have 20 panes that need replacing, you can do this job yourself and save $20.

Assuming that you are using a standard, stock unit, a new window sash will cost about $5. You can save more than $100 in the average house if you repair the existing window-sash units rather than replacing them.

You can save more than $20 on each window unit that must be replaced, if you obtain a unit that will fit into the existing opening—rather than changing the size of the opening.

25 Plumbing

For a nation that takes as much pride as we Americans do in our indoor plumbing, it is amazing how little most of us know about it. Of course, there is no reason why we should all be experts on the subject, but if your renovation job is going to require the installation of a plumbing system or changes in the existing one, you should learn something about it.

THE PLUMBER

Let's start off with the plumber because it is important to know how he operates.

He is usually a licensed plumber. This means that a unit of local government has issued him a license permitting him to install and make major changes in a plumbing system on the basis of his training, knowledge, and experience. Even in many very small communities you will find that plumbing installations must be done by a licensed plumber. This is not true in every community, but you will find it so in most. The stipulation is obviously reasonable because plumbing can affect the health of the family, and you certainly don't want some unqualified nitwit getting your pipes mixed up. However, the fact that a plumber

284

must have a license also means that those licensed by a community have something of a monopoly going for them. A plumber from one area may not be able to work in the adjoining area unless he has a license issued by that area.

The plumber is also often a dealer in plumbing fixtures and plumbing equipment. He sells the materials as well as installing them. In other words, if you want to install a bathtub, you don't usually go to a building-supply house and buy one and then get a plumber to install it for you. In most cases you go to the plumber or plumbing contractor, and he sells you the fixture and also installs it. The plumber thus makes his money not just from the installation work, but also from the markup on the equipment that he gets as a retailer.

A plumber frequently handles one brand of equipment, which makes him, in effect, a franchised dealer. This means that if you pick out a local plumber who handles Brand X fixtures, Brand X fixtures are what you will get, unless you can convince the plumber to pick up another brand that you may have selected. This can be done, but you will usually run into a lot of grumbling. You might be better off to decide on the brand of fixtures you wish to use, then track down the plumber who handles this brand. More will be said about this subject later in this chapter, under the heading of *Fixtures*.

Only the very large general contracting firms have their own plumbing crews. Most contractors use subcontractors for plumbing work. When it is time for the plumbing to be installed, the contractor calls in the plumber, who does his job and gets out. Unless you have specific plans and specifications on how this work is to be done, the plumber will do it his way. Of course, if you are dealing with the plumber directly, you can go over the job with him in advance so that it will be done in the way that you wish.

The installation of the basic plumbing system, meaning the pipes for fresh water and drainage, is a rather exact science. The system either works or leaks. You either get water when you open a faucet or you don't get water.

Some plumbers may be more expensive than others, some are more tidy than others, and some are easier to work with than others. But, by and large, you don't have to be concerned about the quality of work-manship. What you do want to concern yourself with is getting the fixtures and other elements that you want.

PLUMBING

A plumbing system consists of two distinct parts. There is the fresh-water system—cold and hot water—and then there is the drainage, or waste, system. Let's discuss the fresh-water system.

The Fresh-Water System. If you don't have city water, a good place to start work is with the pump. If you have an existing pump, ascertain the brand and who can service it locally. If the brand is an obscure one and you can't find a plumber who can service it for you, consider buy-ing a new pump. It may seem a waste of money to buy a new one when you have an existing pump that is working, but remember that if some-thing should go wrong with it, you may not have water for a good many days or even weeks. We once had to replace a pump because it went out of order, and the nearest source of spare parts was just about a thousand miles away. It is best to get a pump through a local source, so you can be sure that you will get good service when you need it. If you are starting from scratch, your plumber will install the pump and will naturally use the brand that he carries.

A pump requires a water-storage tank. The tank can sweat during warm, humid weather, so see to it that you do not place the tank in an area you might eventually want to use for living purposes. Be sure also that the tank pump and tank are placed in an area where they will not freeze.

With city water, of course, you don't require a pump or tank unless you happen to be at the end of the line, where the pressure in the city lines is so low that you don't get a sufficient flow of water in the upper areas of the house. In this event, it may be a good idea to install a small pump and tank just to give a little boost to the water pressure.

The fresh-water distribution system is connected into the water-storage tank or into the line that runs from the city water main into the house. Since World War II copper tubing has been used for the fresh-water system. This is far superior to the galvanized-iron pipe used before this time, because it does not rust. The smooth interior of the copper tubing allows for a greater flow of water in a pipe with a smaller diameter. In new work, a plumber will use copper tubing. If you are adding to the existing plumbing system, or making alterations, it would be very wise to have all the galvanized-iron pipe replaced with copper tubing.

If you can possibly afford to do so, make this replacement because you can never be sure how long it will be before the old galvanized pipes start to leak or become so clogged with rust that the flow of water is reduced to a trickle. A plumbing system is only as strong as its weakest piece of pipe or fitting, and even if the system is 99.99-per-cent perfect, that other 1 per cent can put the entire system out of business. We know of one case where a buyer acquired an old house in which all the inside pipes had recently been replaced with copper tubing. After a few months, there was no water. It was then discovered that the underground pipe to the well had not been replaced. This pipe was galvanized iron and had become so clogged with rust that the pump couldn't pull water through it. All that lovely copper tubing inside the house wasn't worth anything until the underground line had been replaced. Either heavy-duty copper tubing or plastic should be used for underground lines.

We heard an interesting little story about clogged underground pipes from a Mr. Swain, who used to help us cut and saw trees. His story had to do with a farmer who owned land on both sides of a main highway. A spring on one side of the highway was connected to a water trough for the livestock on the other side of the road. The spring and water trough were connected by 300 feet of 2-inch underground pipe through which the water flowed by gravity, the spring being just a bit higher than the water trough. One day the flow of water stopped because the pipe had become clogged with mud from the spring. The farmer called in various people, and all told him the same story. It would cost about $500 to put in a new line, they said, because it was impossible to clear the existing one.

While the farmer was mulling over his problem, a stranger appeared and allowed he had heard about the situation and could clear the line for $150. The farmer said in effect, "You're crazy, man, the line can't be cleared, the mud is packed in there as solid as concrete." The stranger said he would clear the line for $150 and he'd clear it in a couple of hours at that. The farmer told him to go ahead and try if he hadn't anything better to do.

The stranger headed up to the spring and disappeared into the little shed over the spring. A few minutes later he came back, went over to the watering trough, sat down, lighted his pipe and seemed rather pleased with life. The farmer couldn't figure out what was going on, so he went over and sat down next to the stranger. They sat and talked for about an hour, then the stranger got up, looked at the end of the pipe in the watering trough, and said, "Should be any minute now."

Sure enough, in a few moments a little trickle of dirty water came out of the pipe. The flow grew and grew until suddenly a big gob of mud popped out. The stranger grabbed at the mud and pulled out a crayfish. Taking a wooden matchbox from his pocket he carefully placed the crayfish in it and put the matchbox back in his pocket. By that time a good strong flow of water was gushing from the pipe and the water was beginning to run clear. The farmer was happy and ran to the house to get the money for the stranger.

You see, a crayfish gets about by moving his tail down and up in a sort of scooping motion. This means that he must always go backward. The stranger put him into the pipe backward, so the crayfish, not wishing to remain in the pipe, had to push his way through its entire length. That meant he had to dig right through the mud. We have no reason to believe that this story is not true.

In any event, don't just check and replace pipes inside the house. Making sure that the underground pipes are in good shape is quite as essential.

Make sure, too, that the fresh-water system is designed so that it can easily be drained from one or two central points. This is important if the house is going to be used only in warm weather in any area where freezing occurs. If you have a well-designed system, you can easily drain it yourself. You won't have to worry about getting a plumber to drain it and then turn it back on in the spring. Even in a year-round house, there may be times when you may wish to drain the system for the winter. Most plumbers will install a good system for draining, but some may need a reminder.

If you want faucets outside the house, be sure to point out the desired locations to the plumber. You won't pay too much extra for additional faucets; or sill cocks, as they are called, or for other extras, such as a line run to a spot where you might later on wish to have a washing machine, or for an outside shower, if this work is done when the main plumbing job is underway. If, however, you call in a plumber to do these little jobs after the rest of the work has been completed, the installation can be expensive.

With this in mind, if you have future plans for an additional bathroom, it would be wise to have the *roughing in* done while the other work is in progress. By roughing in, we mean bringing the fresh and waste lines to the area where the bathroom is to be and capping, or sealing them. When you get around to adding the bathroom, the heavy rough work will have been done, and all that will be needed is to remove the caps from the lines and then connect the fixtures to the lines already in place.

After the fresh-water lines are installed, inspect the system to make sure that everything you asked for has been done. Plumbers sometimes forget. Also check any exposed lines to make sure that they have been properly secured to the house framework. If they can be easily moved because of inadequate supports, you may get a banging in the lines when a faucet is closed. This vibration in the lines is not only annoying, but if it goes on long enough can open up a joint in the line so that you will have a leak. Putting in the metal brackets that secure the pipes is often left to the plumber's helper, and he will sometimes use just as few as he can get away with.

Hot Water. An essential element of the fresh-water system is an adequate supply of hot water. If you have a boiler used for the central-heating system, you can use this as a source of hot water, but we have never found this arrangement too satisfactory. Water is usually used at a faster rate than it can be heated and with the heating system described the hot water often runs out when you take a long shower.

We have found that an independent hot-water heater is a far more satisfactory method of getting an adequate amount of hot water at the desired temperature than depending on the central-heating system. The independent hot-water heater consists of a storage tank and a means of heating the water. Gas, electricity, or oil can be used for heating. We have used all three methods and have been happy with all. If you use gas for heating and for cooking, you may find that as far as operating costs go, gas is your best bet for heating water. If you use bottled gas for cooking, you can get a hot-water heater that runs on that. If you cook and/or heat with electricity, an electric hot-water heater could well be the most economical way of obtaining hot water, because, as is the case with gas, the more you use, the lower the cost per unit.

You will find that most utility concerns have special rates that apply as consumption increases. If you use oil as a heating fuel, an oil heater might be your best bet.

Today you don't have to buy a hot-water heater. You can rent one by the month from your local gas or electric company, or from your fuel oil dealer. This is a really great idea because with a rental unit you don't have to worry about a thing. If the heater goes on the blink, whoever you rented it from comes over to service it; if they can't fix it in a hurry, they yank it out and put in a new one, and the servicing or replacement doesn't add to the regular monthly charge. Right now, we have an oil hot-water heater that costs us $2 a month plus the oil we use, which isn't that much. The fuel-oil company installed the heater free—it took a man the best part of a day to do the job—and all we had to do was to agree that we would use it for twelve months. If, at the end of that time, we were dissatisfied with the arrangement, the company would remove it and reconnect the old system, which consisted of a coil in the boiler. Electric and gas concerns offer the same plan. They'll put the equipment in for you and do all the worrying. Some electric companies will even install free the heavy-duty service entrance required for an electric hot-water heater, just so that they can install one of their heaters.

The matter of a chimney may have some influence on which system you select. With gas or oil, you need a chimney to the outside but not with electricity. Often the system can be connected into an existing chimney, but if not, one will either have to be built or you will have to change to electricity.

There is no reason in the world today why you can't expect the same abundance of hot water in your house—even if it's a vacation house way off in no place—that you get in a good hotel or well-managed city apartment building.

All three types of heaters are good. Select the one that gives you the best deal, with the lowest operating costs.

The Drainage System. This is the half of the plumbing system that removes the waste and carries it out of the house to the sewer line or septic tank. Up until a few years ago the main portion of the drainage system was made of cast-iron pipe. Today, in most areas, the system is made with copper pipe, which is easier to work with than cast iron and takes up less room because it has a smaller outside diameter. In some sections of the country, plastic pipe can be used if the local code permits.

The drainage system becomes an important factor in determining where a bathroom can be installed in an existing house. It is usually possible to bring fresh water to any section of the house without much trouble because the copper tubing can easily be threaded through walls and floors. Drainage pipes, however, are much larger in diameter than fresh-water lines and must have a constant downward slope. As the amount of space between the floor and the ceiling below is limited, it can mean that a second-floor bathroom could only be installed a certain number of feet away from the existing lines. The drainage system must be also vented to the outdoors, to prevent a partial vacuum in the system from occurring. This is accomplished by running an extension up through the roof of the house to the drain system.

If you are willing to spend the money, you can have a bathroom installed any place you might wish, but if you want to save as much money as you can, go over the house with your plumber or contractor and let him point out the areas where a bathroom can be put for the least amount of money.

PLUMBING FIXTURES

Bathroom Fixtures. Most people don't know much about plumbing fixtures except that they come in a good many different colors. The result of this ignorance is that you generally get told by someone else what you should have, rather than telling someone else what you want. Part of the trouble is the manner in which most plumbing fixtures are sold—as we mentioned earlier, they are merchandised through the local plumber, who often handles only one particular brand. Often he has no display area where you can inspect the fixtures at first hand. Instead, the selection is usually made from a catalogue, and while many catalogues are excellent, they don't always tell you everything you should know before you buy.

Bathroom fixtures represent a rather large investment. A bathtub will run around $200 plus installation costs. A modest lavatory will run from $50 to $100, and a water closet will run from about $100 to more than $200. These items are going to be around for quite a long time. You don't usually replace bathroom fixtures after a few years simply because you have become disenchanted with the color, so when you select bathroom fixtures, select them with care.

You can find out about the variety of plumbing fixtures available by writing to the various manufacturers and asking them to send you their catalogues and literature. Most of these concerns advertise in the various home service magazines. You can also check your local yellow pages for listings under "Plumbing Contractors." Many plumbing contractors will name in their advertisements the brands of equipment they handle, and you can visit them and pick up a catalogue. If you live in or near a metropolitan center, you can visit the showrooms maintained by the various manufacturers and inspect their products at first hand. Become plumbing-fixture conscious. When you visit a friend's house, take a good look at the fixtures and if they appeal to you, find out who makes them.

You should know that there is a considerable difference in price between white fixtures and colored ones. For example: the price of a particular lavatory in white is $53, but the same fixture in color will cost $80. This price difference can be an important consideration if you are working on a tight budget. You will also find a considerable range in price on the fittings required for a lavatory or bathtub. The standard fittings will run a good many dollars less than the deluxe types and while the deluxe may look a lot more attractive, the standard will do just as good a job of turning the water on and off and opening and closing the drain.

Lavatories. These are sometimes called "wash basins," but if you want to be professional, you should call them what they're called in the trade—lavatories. They come in many shapes and sizes. One type is hung on the wall and requires no legs for support. The absence of legs makes it a little easier to clean the floor underneath. Legs are required for support on the larger units, although some smaller units also have legs.

One of the points to check on a lavatory is the size and depth of the bowl. If you want something to use for washing garments, you should get a unit with a sizable bowl. If the unit is going to be used only for washing hands and brushing teeth, you don't need a very large or deep bowl. The width of the ledge around the bowl is also important, for this is where toilet articles can be set. If you have a very narrow ledge, you won't be able to set much on it, and what you do set there has a good chance of getting knocked onto the floor. The location of the water spout is also important. The spout should project far enough out over the bowl so that you can get your hands under it. If the outlet through which the water flows is set too close to the bowl, you can't even fill a glass of water under it. Some lavatories come equipped with a hose-and-spray attachment similar to those found on kitchen sinks, and these are handy for washing hair.

It is also possible to get built-in lavatories as well as the free-standing types. These units are set into a counter, which can be surfaced with tile or rigid plastic. The built-in counter is put together by the carpenter on the job, and then the plumbing unit is set into it.

Water Closets. This particular fixture goes under many different names. Sometimes it is referred to as the "toilet," the "john," the "biffy," or some other euphemism, but in the trade it is called a *water closet* It comes in several basic designs. The most economical is the so-called "washdown," but we don't recommend it except where economy is of paramount importance. This unit has a round bowl. The inside surfaces soil rather easily, so it requires a considerable amount of cleaning. The passageway that carries away the waste is narrow compared to that in other units, which means there is a good deal of noise when the bowl is flushed. The passageway can also become clogged more easily than one with a larger opening.

The water closets of better quality utilize a siphon-jet action to remove the waste from the bowl. The bowl will thus require less cleaning because it won't be as easily soiled. The bowl is elongated rather than almost round, as is the case with the washdown unit. This type of bowl is a desirable feature, especially for large individuals.

The better water closets are also virtually noiseless, which is especially desirable in a guest lavatory close to the living area of the house. Also available are units that remove odors from the bowl by drawing them into the drainage system. Wall-hung units that make for easier cleaning can be had, as can tanks with insulated interiors that will not sweat in warm weather or when the moisture content of the air in the bathroom is high. The sweating can also be eliminated by running a hot-water line into the tank so that the water in the tank is warm rather than cold.

Bathtubs. These come in a variety of shapes, and some are a good deal more comfortable than others. The standard length for a tub is 5 feet, and they run in depth from 14 inches to 16 inches. If you want a tub in which a large person can really soak, you should get the 16-inch tub. Most bathtubs made today have nonslip bottoms and their manufacturers have made a real effort to design a unit that will be comfortable to soak in. Whether a particular shape will be comfortable for you is something else again. When and if we buy our next bathtub, we are going to try it for size before we make a purchase. People are always testing beds before they buy them, so why not kick off your shoes and stretch out in a bathtub to see how it works for you?

Modern bathtubs come with all sorts of special fittings, and many of them are very fine. Some have built-in grab rails so that you can easily lower yourself into the tub and pull yourself up. Some have units that pull out of the wall to hold grooming equipment or a book. Some offer two shower heads at different heights—"His" and "Hers"—and some come with a flexible hose and spray so that you can shower comfortably regardless of your height.

Corner bathtubs that measure 48 inches by 48 inches are also available and, where space is a factor, they work out very well.

The Kitchen Sink.   This is another fixture that you buy from your plumber, so check on these when you are looking into bathroom fixtures. There are a whale of a lot of different sizes and designs in sinks, and we would not attempt to say which one is best because this is such a matter of personal choice. Just be sure that you look over the entire range to see which one seems best for you.

Most plumbing fixtures are made of steel or cast iron with a finish of baked enamel or vitreous china. The vitreous china units are generally more expensive, but desirable because they do not chip. Plastic fixtures are also available, and you can expect to see more and more of these. We have not had any personal experience with plastic units, but from all we have heard, they seem to work out well. There are also companies that make complete plastic bathrooms that come as complete units with the fixtures built right into the floor and walls. A unit of this type can be set in place, the pipes and wires connected into the house system, and it is ready to go. Such an installation affords a tremendous saving in time, and is ideal for new construction. Whether or not this sort of unit would work into your renovation plan is hard to say, but it might be worth investigating.

You should specify to your plumber not only the brand, style, and color of fixtures and the style of fittings that go with them but, in the absence of detailed plans, the location of the fixtures in the bathroom. If the bathroom is new and there is plenty of space, the three fixtures can be arranged in one of several ways. If you do not tell the plumber where you wish the various fixtures to go, he will put them where he thinks best. Usually a plumber will arrange fixtures in the way that is most economical from the standpoint of labor, but this arrangement may not be ideal for your needs. You might be happier to spend a few extra dollars in labor to get an arrangement better suited to your needs. Some plumbers love to put bathtubs under windows; unless you like this arrangement (it's not very good for several reasons), tell your plumber not to do so.

WELLS

We have left the subject of wells until the end of this chapter because it may be of interest to only a few readers. Everyone will probably need plumbing fixtures, but we hope that only a few will need a well.

There are, as we mentioned earlier, two kinds of wells. There is the shallow "dug" well and the deep, or drilled, well. A dug well is far less expensive than a drilled well, but it is only practical where there is a good supply of water near the surface. If you are looking for a really dependable water supply, you should have a drilled well.

A drilled well goes down many feet to tap water sources that flow far below the surface. There is no way of telling in advance where you should drill or how far you must drill before you hit an adequate supply of water. You may have heard tales about divining rods and people who use "dowsers" to pick out just the right spot to drill for a well, but don't put too much stock in this. If anyone could determine that easily just where to drill to hit a good supply of water in the least time, he would become a very rich man. Putting in a drilled well is really pretty much a matter of chance. The last one we put in went down to 156 feet before we found water. Up the ridge from us, a well came in at 68 feet, and one below us came in at 103 feet, so you see you can't tell. Just hope you'll be lucky.

Well-drillers charge by the foot, and the going price today is about $5.50 per foot. There will also be an additional charge for the iron casing that must be put down to bedrock, and this can vary considerably. You want to pray that the drill will hit rock fairly close to the surface of the ground and then that it will hit water rather soon after. In any event, drilling a well is going to cost money, and you would certainly be wise to set aside at least $1,100 for this operation. You can hope that this will not only cover the cost of the well, but also the pump and the line from the well to the house—but don't bet on it.

You might check with several well-drillers to see if you can get a break in price. Because it takes a good deal of time and effort to bring the rig into an area and set it up, some drillers will give you a price break if they happen to be doing another job in your general area.

After a well hits water, the water should be tested not only for purity, but to find out how hard it is and what sort of minerals it might contain. Your county agent is usually available for this testing, and independent laboratories also do such tests. If the water is extremely hard, you may wish to install a water softener, and if it contains a high percentage of minerals (such as iron), you might need a filter to remove them.

► *Special Money-Saving Tips*

You can save as much as $75 per bathroom on fixtures if you use white fixtures rather than colored ones.

On the installation of a bathroom and kitchen, it is possible to save more than $100 if bathroom and kitchen are placed back to back or close enough together so that they can utilize the same central plumbing core of fresh-water and waste lines.

If the lavatory and water closet must be removed and then replaced so that flooring or walls can be applied in the area, you can save $45 by doing this yourself.

You can save $50 to $100 by digging trenches for fresh-water and waste lines yourself.

26 Heating

There are relatively few sections of the United States where it is possible to live comfortably all year round in a house that has no heat. Even a summer house, unless it is in the very warm areas of the nation, can use some heat on days when the weather is damp and cool. In a summer place you can get along with a fireplace and perhaps an electric or oil space heater, but for year-round dwellings or those that are used for weekends throughout the year you need central heating.

If you are going to put in central heating, or if the existing plant must be replaced, you should know something about what is available. Heating systems are of two basic types—one in which heat is generated by electricity, and the other in which it is generated by combustion of oil or gas.

ELECTRIC HEAT

Heating by electricity is relatively new but is becoming popular because it is simple to install, does not require a chimney, a furnace, or a boiler, and is highly flexible. For example, with electric heat you can use baseboard units along the walls, or you can have a system where the heating coils are imbedded in the ceiling or the walls. If you prefer, each room can be provided with its own heater blower. This is done in summer-vacation houses where you might want heat only in certain rooms at certain times of the day. Any type of electric heat can be installed in such a way that a thermostat is located in each room to regulate the temperature. Compared with the cost of installing other systems, installation of electric heat is relatively inexpensive. The major consideration is the cost of operation. How much it costs will depend not only on the local electric rates, but on the construction of the house and its location.

Rates are not the same all over the country, and some utility companies have a more favorable rate for electric heat than others. Thus your decision about using electric heat should, in part at least, be based on the electric rates in your area. This is, of course, assuming that you want to keep your heating costs to a minimum. If money is of no concern then there is no reason to worry about a little thing like an electric rate.

Another important factor to consider regarding the use of electric heat, is the construction of the house. From the standpoint of heating economy, electric heat is most efficient when it is installed in a house that is tight, extremely well insulated, and supplied with insulating glass or storm windows. And naturally, any heat is going to cost less in a compact house than in a sprawling barnlike structure.

We seriously considered putting electric heat in our present house. The winters are on the cold side, but the electric rate is favorable, the house is rather compact, and areas that are not used in winter can easily be closed off. The hitch was that the outside walls are not insulated and can't very well be insulated because there is no wall cavity into which to put the insulation. The outside walls are made of big planks— 3 by 8, 3 by 10, and 3 by 12 inches—set vertically and running from basement to attic. The siding is nailed to one side and the lath to the other and there is no room for any insulation. With this handicap, the cost of electric-heat operation would be pretty high, so we dropped the idea, and decided to live with our whispering, whimpering, and wheezing steam system.

Needless to say, if you live in an area where winters are long and cold, the operation of an electric system, or any other kind of system, is going to be more costly than if you live where the winters are short and mild.

If you wish to find out about using electric heat in your house, call in an electric-heating contractor or your local utility company. The contractor or an engineer from the utility company will come over to check out the house and determine about how much heating it will cost, based on what you have now and what you can do to cut heat loss to a minimum. Then you or your general contractor must decide whether all this is feasible. Can the house be adequately insulated? Can all windows and glass areas be provided with storm sashes or double glazing? And can all this work be done within your budget? If it can't be done within your budget, you can either go ahead with the electric heat anyway and figure it is going to cost more to operate than otherwise, or—if the cost is too high—go to some other form of heat.

Some people worry about using electric heat because they are afraid of being left in the cold for a long period if a power failure occurs. Every type of modern heating system depends on electricity in one form or another, so when the power goes off you are going to be cold, regardless of what you have. Of course, if your system is an antique, if you have a hand-fired coal or wood furnace or boilers, then you don't have to worry about a power failure—just your back and arms.

FUEL-OPERATED HEATING SYSTEMS

Heating units that burn either gas or oil give excellent heat and if the system is kept in good condition are clean, odorless, and safe. Which fuel to use depends largely on where you live. If you live in a town or city where there is a gas line, your obvious choice is gas. If you live where there is no gas, your choice is oil. Gas is desirable because if it is connected into your house from a main it is always available. With oil, you will need a storage tank—either a 275-gallon tank in the basement, or a 550-tank or larger set underground. If you use oil and live close to a supplier, the smaller tank is adequate, but if you live way off in the sticks and have bad winters, the large-capacity tank will help eliminate the chance of your running out of oil if the delivery truck can't make it up your road.

By the way, if you live in an area without gas mains, you can still use bottled or propane gas for cooking and for hot water, but bottled gas is seldom used for heating purposes, because of the high cost.

With either gas or oil you'll need a chimney, and if you don't have one or the one you have is used for the fireplace, you'll need either a new chimney or separate flue for the heating system. These do not have to be of masonry. Most local building codes permit metal prefabricated chimneys, which cost far less than masonry ones and can often be installed in a matter of hours. You will still want to make the house as well insulated and tight as you can. Heat loss is going to cost you money whether you use oil, gas, or electricity. The difference is that electricity might cost more than gas or oil.

As gas and oil burners, along with the furnace or boiler in which they are installed, contain moving parts, a certain amount of service is required to keep the equipment in good condition. The concerns that supply you with fuel usually have some sort of service arrangement whereby they will inspect and adjust the equipment at regular intervals. Oil and gas can be used with either the furnace used for forced-warm-air heat or the boiler used for circulating-hot-water heat.

FORCED-WARM-AIR HEAT

A forced-warm-air system consists of a furnace in which air is heated. The heated air is distributed to the various rooms and parts of the house by means of ducts and comes up through registers installed in the floor or at the base of the walls. Modern registers are compact and quite inconspicuous. The furnace has a blower to force the air through the ducts and also a filter to remove dust and dirt from the air. A well-installed forced-warm-air system is quiet, clean, and free from cold or hot drafts. If you wish, you can connect a cooling element to the system so that in summer it will provide the house with central air conditioning.

Certain types of warm-air furnaces can be placed just about anywhere in the house that seems convenient and will handle the unit. If you have no basement but there is crawl space, the furnace can be hung under the house; it can also be placed in the attic or in a first-floor utility room. This system is highly responsive, which makes it especially good for a weekend house. You can leave the thermostat set at 60 degrees; move it up to 70 degrees when you arrive for the weekend and almost immediately the heat will begin to come up through the registers. In a very few minutes the room temperature is up to 70 degrees and you can take off your coat and be comfortable.

The one problem with installing a forced-warm-air system in remodeling is that it may be difficult to get the ducts into place. The problem does not occur in new house construction because the ducts are installed shortly after the framing is in. If you are working in a shell, or if you have gutted the house, you won't have any problem either, but if the walls and ceilings are left as they are, it becomes difficult to get the ducts in and keep them out of sight. Sometimes they are run up along the corner of a room and then boxed in. Sometimes the walls and ceiling are cut away so the ducts can be installed and are then patched afterwards. And sometimes the ducts are left as they are for all to see. We once visited a delightful modern house where the round composition ducts were exposed as architectural detail. We also remember a big renovated barn where the first-floor ceiling framework was exposed and the metal ducts, painted various bright colors, ran across it in all different directions; it was extremely attractive.

If you decide on forced warm air, you want to be careful about the firm you select to do the installation work. You want a system that is well designed so that you don't find one area getting too much heat and another not enough. When warm-air systems first became popular, the only people who seemed qualified to install them were people who did sheet-metal work, because the system required a good bit of this type of work. It is one thing to know how to handle sheet metal, and it is another thing to know how to design a heating system that will provide comfortable heat. There are still some firms putting in forced-warm-air heating systems that should stick to sheet-metal work. When you install forced-warm-air heat, you need a concern that has trained designers who can custom design a system to fit your house. You may have to ask a number of people before you find an outfit that seems qualified, but it is worth the effort.

CIRCULATING-HOT-WATER HEAT

A circulating-hot-water heating system consists of a boiler to heat the water and a pump that circulates the water through the pipes and through radiators or convectors that are installed throughout the house. In some installations, coils are set in a concrete floor slab or in the ceiling. The unit can be fired by oil or by gas and makes a fine heating system. Modern radiators, convectors, and baseboard units used for this kind of installation are highly compact. Convectors can be recessed into the walls so that they require little floor space, and the same holds true for the baseboard units. The circulating-hot-water system provides quiet and even heat. It is not quite as responsive as the forced-warm-air system because it takes longer for the heated water to go through the pipes and heat up the radiators or convectors, but this is no great problem. It is often an easier system to install in an existing house because the copper pipes can usually be threaded up through walls and across ceilings with a minimum amount of trouble.

The modern boiler, too, is beautifully compact and can be equipped with such attachments as an automatic feed that adds water automatically when required, or a low-water cut-off that will stop the burner if, for one reason or another, the water level in the boiler is too low for safe operation. These systems are installed by plumbing and heating contractors.

Before any heating system is installed, be sure to go over the house or the plans with the heating contractor in regard to the placement of the various heat outlets in the rooms. Unless you are using some sort of panel heating where the heat comes from electric or hot water coils imbedded in the walls, ceiling, or floor of the room, there will be heating units in various areas of the house. If you are using forced warm air, these units will be registers placed in the floor or at the base of walls. If you are using circulating hot water, the units will be either radiators, convectors, or baseboard units. Baseboard units are also used with electric heat.

It is the usual practice to place these heating units near outside walls and under windows as these are the coldest spots in a room. It sometimes turns out that a register or something else related to the heating unit is placed in the very spot where you planned to have the living-room sofa or the dining-room table. If you go over the house or the plans of the house with the heating contractor and tell him how you wish to furnish and use each room, he will be able to plan his system with your specific requirements in mind. If you don't take the time to do this, the heating contractor will install the system in the way he thinks best—but best only from his point of view.

With a heating system that requires a furnace or a boiler be sure to discuss the location of this unit with the contractor. If you don't, he may locate it in the spot that you planned eventually to use as a family room or laundry.

OTHER MEANS OF HEATING

Not everyone will need a central heating system. In a summer vacation place, about all you need is enough heat to take the chill away, and a fireplace will do this job nicely. The least expensive fireplace is a free-standing metal type with prefabricated metal chimney. This unit does not have to be placed against a wall—it can be placed in the middle of a room if you wish. It gives off considerable heat and can be installed in a matter of hours.

A masonry fireplace, unless you elect to build it yourself, is expensive, and even when done by a professional takes quite a long time to complete. If you are going to put in a masonry fireplace with the idea of using it for heat as well as the pleasure of a cheerful fire blazing away, you should consider using one of the circulating-hot-air units. This is a metal fireplace with an air chamber around those portions where the fire burns. The fire heats the air in this chamber, which then circulates out into the room through registers. These units can be encased in masonry, and except for the inside, which is metal instead of firebrick, appear to be just like any other masonry fireplace. They give much more heat than the conventional fireplace, however. In fact, if you run a fire in one of them for a whole day it can heat several rooms of a house.

We have a rather interesting condition with one of these circulating-air fireplaces in the house in which we live now. When it was installed, which was before our time, someone decided to run ducts from it to provide heat to an unfinished area upstairs. During the course of our renovation work, we turned the area into a closet, not realizing that the duct was there. We were not doing this work ourselves, and the closet was finished and the register painted to match the inside of the closet before we got out to the job to inspect it. The first time we had a good fire going for a few hours, we thought the closet was on fire because it was so hot. The carpenter had neglected to inform us about the duct and had not closed it off. We are in the process now of moving the register and the duct, so that all that heat can go into a hall where it is needed and not into a closet where it can only please the moths.

In addition to the fireplaces just described, there are also small, oil-fired floor furnaces that can be hung under the floor. These can have a central register set into the floor or ducts can be installed to carry heat to other rooms on the same floor. You will need a chimney with these but it can be a prefabricated metal type. Various kinds of electric heaters are also available; some are free-standing and others are attached to the wall. And we should not forget wood stoves, which are still used in certain parts of the country to provide heat for the entire winter. And pretty good heat, at that.

All in all there are many ways of heating your house. Which system you use will depend on what you can afford, what you want, what sort of house you have, and the purpose for which you are going to use the house.

► *Special Money-Saving Tips*

You can often save several hundred dollars on a new heating system if you take advantage of some of the deals offered by local electric, gas, and fuel-oil-delivery concerns. They will often provide certain equipment and labor at greatly reduced prices in order to get you as a customer.

You can save more than $100 on a new heating system by utilizing the same chimney for the furnace or boiler as required for the fireplace.

Electric Wiring 27

If you are going to put new electrical wiring into your Offbeat Dream House or if you plan to make changes or additions to the existing system, you would be wise to try to anticipate as many of your needs as possible over the next few years and have a really good job of wiring done while you're about it. Planning for adequate wiring is not all that easy to figure out, however, because while the electrical industry keeps telling us to be sure that we have adequate wiring, more and more appliances that require electricity are being invented. What we really need is a sort of "instant outlet" that we could just slap on the wall as a source of electricity, without having to worry about wires. Perhaps this will come, but at present each outlet has to have a wire running someplace and where it runs and how it gets there is the first topic we are going to discuss here.

HOUSE WIRING

The wiring in the house begins with an item called *service entrance*. This is the point at which the wires from the utility company come into the house. There will be a meter, inside or outside the house, to measure the amount of electricity consumed and there will be a main switch, so that all the power to the house can be turned off if necessary. From this switch, the electricity is carried to the distribution point, which is the fuse box, or circuit breaker. It is at this point that the wires from various parts of the house are connected.

The electrical system of the house is divided into a number of circuits. There are lighting circuits that supply power for ordinary needs such as electric lights, radios, clocks, and TV sets. Then there are the appliance circuits; these utilize heavier wires so that they can handle a heavier flow of electricity. Appliance circuits are used in the kitchen, dining area, utility room, and other areas of the house where there may be equipment requiring a considerable amount of power. All electric heating appliances such as toasters, skillets, irons, or waffle irons draw a great deal of power.

Finally, there are the *special circuits,* which go to just one piece of equipment. A special circuit will go, for example, to an electric range, or to an electric clothes dryer, or to an oil burner.

Each circuit in the system is protected by a fuse or, in the more modern installations, by a circuit breaker. These devices insure that if an overload or a short circuit occurs in the system, power to the circuit will be cut off until the cause of trouble has been located and remedied. If the electricity were not cut off, the wires could become so hot that they could start a fire. A fuse performs this function by means of a little piece of metal inside it, which melts when the wires start to warm up. A circuit breaker is more convenient, because each circuit is controlled by its own switch, and the switch automatically jumps from "On" to "Off" when there is trouble. When the trouble in the circuit has been corrected, you just move the switch back to "On." When a fuse blows, you have to replace it with a new one, although certain fuses are available that are really six in one and don't have to be replaced until all six elements have blown.

The amount of electricity available is dependent on the size of the service entrance. Not so many years ago, a service entrance with a capacity of 30 amperes was considered adequate for the average house.

This figure jumped a few years ago to 100 amperes, and now the rule in most quality construction is to put in a 200-ampere service entrance. A 30-ampere service entrance provides only 120 volts, which is enough for lights, radio, television, and a few of the small appliances, but isn't good for much of the heavy electrical equipment. It can't operate an electric range, electric hot-water heater, or most standard air-conditioning units. The 100- and 200-ampere service provides 120/240 volts (120 as well as 240 volts where the greater amount is required), which is sufficient to take care of just about any equipment you will be using. A 30-ampere service may be adequate for a summer cabin where electrical requirements are minimal but not for a year round dwelling.

THE ELECTRICIAN

In most communities, the installation of wiring must be done by a licensed electrician. He may be an individual working on his own, or he may work for an electrical contractor. He will plan the system, install the wiring, and furnish the fixtures, unless you furnish your own.

Electrical work, like plumbing, is a rather exact science. It works or it doesn't work, and you soon find out which it does. We once had a house wired, and when the job was done, we happened to notice a wall switch where we were certain we had asked for an outlet. We flicked the switch to "On" and we were right. The circuit breaker kicked off, because the wiring had been installed for an outlet, not a switch. As soon as the switch was thrown there was a short circuit, and the circuit breaker cut off the flow of electricity. These little mistakes in wiring don't happen often, but we mention this incident to help make the point—either the system works or it doesn't work. Any licensed electrician can install a perfectly good system, and if there are a few minor errors, they'll show up when the system is checked out. In selecting an electrician for your job, take into consideration his bid as compared to other bids for the work, his general reputation (will he show up when you want him or is he the kind you can't really depend on?), and his general interest in working with you to plan the best system.

PLANNING THE ELECTRICAL SYSTEM

Before an electrician can give you a bid he must know the amount of work involved. Before discussing the job with him you should first list for him your requirements.

Start this list off with any heavy-duty electrical equipment you plan to install, for the amount of heavy-duty equipment needed will determine the capacity of service that must be installed. Heavy-duty electrical equipment would include an electric range, electric hot-water heater, and electric central heating.

Next, determine the number and location of outlets, switches, and fixtures required throughout the house. The best way of working this out is to have a floor plan of each room and mark the location of these units on the plan. You will be able to determine the best location for outlets if you sketch in the location and approximate size of the major pieces of furniture that are to go into the room. If you do this, outlets can be located to suit the requirements of the room and you will avoid having to use many long lamp cords or extension cords to connect table lamps to outlets. You should, of course, have enough outlets in each room to allow a degree of flexibility so that you can at some future date do a little rearranging of furniture. If you want a ceiling fixture, a wall fixture, or a floor outlet, indicate the location on the plan and make a note as to which item will be installed.

Kitchens require many outlets. If you plan to install an electric range, its location should be included on the plan. Also note other equipment that may require its own wiring, such as a dishwasher, garbage disposal unit in the sink, and clothes washer. You will also need outlets to handle small electrical appliances, because these call for heavier wiring than is required for most of the other circuits in the house. Note on your list where these outlets are to go and for what purpose they will be used. If you plan to have one or more room air conditioners, decide which windows they are to go into so that a heavy-duty line can be run to these areas.

The location and type of wall switch should also be put down on the plan. If a room is to have a ceiling or wall fixture, then it should have a wall switch so that the fixture can be turned on or off from a point near the door or doors. If a room is not to have a ceiling or wall fixture, then one or more of the outlets should be connected to a wall switch so that a light in the room can be turned on and off from the door. This will eliminate having to stumble around in a dark room looking for the switch on a table lamp.

A fixture or an outlet can be controlled by two switches at different locations. Such an arrangement is excellent for hall fixtures and fixtures at the head of a stairway. Actually, it is a good arrangement for any room having two doors, so that you can turn on a light as you enter and turn it off as you leave by the other door. Switches used for this arrangement are called *three-way switches* and they require additional wiring. If you want some of these, indicate their location on the plan and also note that they will be three-way switches. Draw a line to show the two switches that will work together.

Don't forget the outside of the house. You might wish a fixture near the front and back doors, and you may want one or more outside outlets. Put these on your plan.

Once you've got your electrical needs on paper, and have shown it to your electrician, he can come in, go over the job, and give you a fairly firm idea of what the job will cost. You should go over the house with him and discuss all your requirements quite carefully. It may be that in the interest of saving money, the location of some of the outlets should be moved or eliminated. This need not occur in new construction or when the interior wall and ceilings have been removed so that the framework is exposed, but it can make a difference when the wall and ceiling framework is concealed. It might be a costly proposition to install wiring in certain areas, so it's up to you to decide whether it's worth the money to do so, or whether you would prefer to eliminate that particular outlet or fixture.

If the house has existing wiring, you should have the electrician inspect it and ascertain the condition. The existing wiring may be so inadequate or so old that the insulation is crumbling; in this case the electrician will recommend that it be replaced. Better go along with his suggestion, because it will cost much less to have this work done while he is doing the rest of the job than to have to call him back at a later date to patch things up. If the interior of the house has been gutted so that the framework is exposed, installing a new wiring is not much of a job. When the wall and ceiling framework is concealed, fishing new wires through them is time consuming. It can be an expensive operation, but it may be necessary.

Before the electrical work begins, you should go over the plan once again with your electrician to make sure that your wishes are clear to him. If you are working with a general contractor, ask him to have his electrician or electrical subcontractor come to the house so that you can go over the plan with him.

A good electrician may have suggestions regarding the system, and you should listen to him. You don't have to accept his suggestions, of course, unless they fit your needs.

ELECTRICAL FIXTURES

Your electrician or electrical subcontractor can furnish ceiling and wall fixtures, but it has been our experience that what they have available is rather commonplace. As a matter of fact, really good lighting fixtures are hard to come by. By good, we mean as far as design goes. The fixtures that your electrician can supply are perfectly sound functionally, but if you want really unusual fixtures, you will have to hunt them up for yourself. Excellent contemporary units are available at specialized lighting-fixture shops, or you may pick up some interesting old ones at building-salvage yards. Antique stores handle lighting fixtures and sometimes you can find handsome ones at a good price, but generally these run fairly high in cost. Good reproductions of old fixtures are available at special shops and department stores. It's a good idea to buy your fixtures and have them on hand when the electrician is doing the wiring so that he can install them. Fixtures require all sorts of special little fittings so that they can be connected to the outlet box. A good electrician will have a supply of these fittings in his truck or at his shop and can do the installation properly and in very little time.

While the electrical work is being done, it is a good time to have the the telephone wires installed. Check with your local telephone company or your electrician on this. Your electrician can install the metal conduits that may be required, and then the telephone company has only to fish the wires through them and connect the telephone. If you are going to need a roof antenna for television, a cable from the antenna can be carried inside the house to the point where the set is to be located.

In work where the framework of the structure is exposed, the installation of the wiring should be done before any of the wall and ceiling material for any area of the house goes on. Where walls and ceilings remain in place, the wiring should be done before any finishing work is done.

► *Special Money-Saving Tips*

Attractive and well-made ceiling and wall fixtures will cost from about $25 up to more than $100. You can save $100 or more on a typical installation by picking up used fixtures and renewing them. Salvage yards, antiques shops, and used-home-furnishings stores are a source for these fixtures.

28 Paints and Finishes

"Paint I think is lovely stuff and if I ever had enough, I would go around and sing, while I painted everything." We can't remember who wrote this little rhyme that appeared many years ago in a lovely little book for children, but we have remembered the rhyme for a good many decades. It is an appropriate beginning for this particular chapter.

Most of you will find that painting is one of the most satisfying jobs you will do in transforming your OB House into an OB Dream House. In fact, painting is always rather satisfying work for the amateur because the results are fast and dramatic.

When you spend hour after hour on a job and have little to show for your efforts you can become depressed. You can become extremely depressed when your friends come around and don't see that you've made any improvement from the time of their last visit. But painting is not like this at all. When something has been painted, everyone can see that it has been painted, and you can do a large amount of painting in the time it takes you to hang a door, repair a broken sash cord, or some similar job where the result does not seem to equal the time and effort you had to put into it.

Most people also take to painting because here is an area where the careful amateur can do almost as good a job and sometimes even better

314

than the professional. This is not the case with some of the other work that may have to be done around the house. The amateur mason usually turns out work that looks as if it had been done by an amateur, and even carpentry won't always turn out quite as well for you as when it is done by a professional, but painting is different. If you follow the directions and are careful, your very first painting job can turn out beautifully. It may take you considerably longer than it would the professional but the end result can be just as good.

Paint, by the way, is a finish that contains a pigment designed to produce an opaque coating. It hides or conceals the material over which it is applied. There are also natural finishes that contain no pigments and therefore produce a transparent coating. You use these when you want the natural color and grain of the wood to show. Shellac, varnish, and sealers are used for natural finishes.

PAINT STORES

One of the most important requirements for successful painting is a good paint store. Even if you have to drive 20 to 30 miles to get to one, it is well worth the effort. You want a firm with a full line of paints and allied products, and you want one where the clerks know the painting business and will be able to give you sound advice and suggestions. A good paint store is like money in the bank.

Find a store that does custom blending so that you can get the exact color and shade you want. Most good paint stores are equipped to provide this tremendously helpful service. You can go through hundreds of different samples until you find the one you want and then in a matter of minutes the paint is blended to match the sample. Don't change your mind after the paint has been mixed for you though, because you can't return the containers of custom-mixed paints. Somewhere in our basement we have several gallons of custom-mixed blue interior paint worth about $14. We had a change of heart and decided to paint the walls white and the trim blue instead of the other way around, but unfortunately the change of heart occurred after the paint had been mixed.

If you have a good paint store and a smart clerk you can be pretty unknowledgeable about paint and still obtain good results. You do have to know what it is you want to paint, where it is, and how big it is. Some paints are made for interior work and some are made for outside work on surfaces that will be exposed to the weather.

Some paints are made for interior walls and some are made for interior woodwork and furniture. Some paints are made for metal and some are made for concrete. Special paints are designed for wood decks and outside porch floors where they will be exposed to both wear and weather, and special paints are made for roofs. In short, paints and finishes are made for just about every type of building material and situation you might encounter, and often there is only one kind of paint or finish for a particular purpose. Therefore, the first information to give the clerk is the type or kind of material that is to be painted, and its location. He must also know the condition of the surface. If you are talking about an interior wall it makes a difference if the wall is new or has been previously painted. If it is a new wall it will require a coat of wall primer or sealer, but this won't be required on a previously painted wall. If you are repainting a wall with the same color as the original, you can probably get along with one coat, but if you are changing colors, you will probably need two coats. So the clerk needs to know this. He also must know the area to be covered. If it is a wall, measure the width and length in feet, multiply these together and come up with the total area in square feet. If you need enough paint for trim on ten windows, tell him you have ten windows and he can figure out how much paint you will need.

Here is a little list of the information you should give to the clerk:

1. Type of material to be painted
2. Location and use
3. Present condition: painted, unpainted
4. Area or number of units

If there is any doubt about the exact amount of paint required and you are using a standard color, play safe and order more than enough. You can always return the unopened containers of standard colors. If you are using custom-mixed paints, which can't be returned, figure your requirements as accurately as possible and get an extra quart rather than an extra gallon.

For most general work around the house you will probably use either a latex or alkyd paint. These are available for both exterior and interior work. Both of these paints are excellent. The alkyds have almost no "painty" odor and can be thinned, when required, with an odorless thinner rather than turpentine. You can clean brushes and equipment used with this paint with a paint thinner or turpentine. Alkyds can be applied with a brush or roller. Latex is a water-base paint, which means you clean up with plain water. It is a fast-drying finish and will often dry in less than an hour after application by brush or roller.

Besides paints, your paint store can supply you with brushes, rollers, and other equipment for painting. Rollers are excellent for large surfaces such as walls and floors, but you will still need to do some work with a brush to reach those areas that the roller cannot. Brushes come in a wide range of sizes and prices. There is no doubt that in the long run it pays to buy good brushes if you are willing to take proper care of them. This means cleaning them thoroughly after use. If you are the forgetful sort who might run off and neglect to clean your brushes after use, then you should buy the less-expensive kind, so that if they are ruined it won't be a great loss.

Besides brushes you will also need other basic painting equipment such as sandpaper, steel wool, prepared spackle, a stepladder, drop cloths—canvas or plastic—for protecting floors and furniture, and thinners. You may also find that many of the little gadgets at a paint store will catch your fancy. There are brushes with disposable bristles made out of foam plastic, there are little devices to help you paint windows and trim, strainers for removing the skin that sometimes appears on the surface of paint that has been left in a container, and many more.

SURFACE PREPARATION

The people who work with computers have a little saying, "GIGO" (garbage in, garbage out), which means that the quality of the material a computer turns out is dependent on the quality of the material fed into it. If you feed it garbage, you'll get garbage out of it. This general idea also applies to painting and finishing. How well the new paint or finish turns out depends on the condition of the surface. If you put fresh paint over a rough surface, the fresh paint is going to dry rough. If you slap fresh paint over old paint that is peeling, the fresh paint is going to peel right along with the old. If you put paint over a surface that is covered with cracks or full of nail holes, the cracks and nail holes are going to come through. If you paint over a dirty surface, the dirt is going to discolor the fresh paint. Success in painting depends a great deal on proper preparation and attention to detail. The craftsmen who used to apply the finish on fine coachwork used to work in the nude, so that there would be no chance of any dust or lint from their clothes getting onto the freshly applied varnish. And after each coat of varnish was dry they would smooth it off, not with sandpaper or steel wool but with powdered pumice stone or rottenstone and linseed oil. You don't have to go quite this far, but you should make certain that the surface is ready for the paint.

You will find on the label of the paint container directions for surface preparation as well as for application. Read the directions before you start work. Read all the directions—even the fine print and *believe* what the man says. If the paint manufacturer says not to apply the paint to bare wood, don't apply it to bare wood. If he says don't thin, don't thin. If he says use such and such a type of primer, use such and such a type of primer. We have not always been a very good direction reader. Like so many others, we felt that directions should be read only after the event, when something went wrong. But we are much better about this now. The event that changed our way of painting life involved some masonry we were painting with a latex paint. After a time, we took a breather and having nothing else to read we read the directions on the label. The label said that if you dampened the masonry with a hose before starting to paint, the paint would go on far more easily than over a dry surface. We tried it and he was right. So read the directions and do as you're told.

INTERIOR PAINTING

The first thing to do in painting a room, whether you are repainting or starting from scratch with new walls and woodwork, is to get out of your way anything that you don't want painted. Move the furniture out of the room and if you can't get rid of the heavy pieces, push them into the center and cover them with a drop cloth. Remove the plates from light switches and wall outlets, unless they are to be painted with the walls. Disconnect ceiling and wall fixtures so that the metal portions are separated from the surfaces to be painted. You don't have to disconnect the wires. Remove as much of the hardware from doors and windows as you can, unless they are to be painted. Cover the floor with building paper and seal it at the ends and at joints with masking tape. Now you have an area in which you can work with the least amount of inconvenience.

PAINTING—NEW WORK

If you are painting new walls and new woodwork, you will need, besides the required amount of paint for the walls and ceiling, sufficient primer for the woodwork, semigloss enamel for the woodwork, prepared spackle, medium-grade sandpaper, and medium-grade steel wool.

Your first step is to fill in the nail holes as well as any cracks in the woodwork. Use the prepared spackle for this job. It is easy to apply and dries very quickly. The best tool with which to apply the spackle is your own thumb. Fill the holes right up to the surface and remove any excess spackle from around the general area. This job takes quite a little time, because in the average-sized room there will be many nail holes. As soon as the spackle is hard, and it takes only an hour or less to harden, smooth off all the woodwork with sandpaper or steel wool. If there are any knots in the wood, coat these with orange shellac, so that they won't bleed through the paint. Once you have done the sanding operation, dust the woodwork thoroughly and give it a coat of primer. Use the type of primer recommended for use with the trim paint you plan to use. When the primer is dry, sand all surfaces again very lightly, just enough to remove any rough spots in the prime coat. This is as far as you have to go with the woodwork at this time. You do not apply the finish trim paint until the ceiling and walls have been painted.

The next move is to prepare the new ceilings and walls. If they are made of gypsum wallboard, the cement over the nailheads and at the joints may require a light sanding to take down any ridges. The amount of work involved at this point depends on how well the wallboard was installed. Sometimes the installation was done so well that all you have to do is give the wallboard a lick and a promise with the sandpaper. But if the installation was not done carefully, you may find that a good deal of sanding is required before you get perfectly smooth joints. This sanding operation can create quite a bit of dust, so keep the doors to the room closed.

Once the sanding has been finished, give the room a good going over with a vacuum cleaner. Be sure to catch the dust on top of doors and windows, and in corners. A considerable amount will have accumulated at the top of baseboards. Vacuum from the top down and do the floor last. You don't want any of that dust to get blown onto fresh paint. Remember GIGO.

The proper way to paint a room is to do the ceiling first and then the walls. When the walls are finished, do the windows and the doors and the trim around them. Paint the baseboard last.

For the ceilings you can use a standard wall paint or you can use a special ceiling finish that has a fine sand added so that it produces a very slight texture when dry. You may prefer this finish to one that dries with a perfectly smooth surface. It does not show dirt easily, which is a great advantage because ceilings are not much fun to paint, and if you don't have to do the job again for the next five or ten years you are ahead of the game. Textured paint is applied with a brush. Ordinary wall paints can be applied to the ceiling with either a brush or roller. You can get an extension rod for a roller so that you can paint the ceiling without having to get on a stepladder. This appliance can also be used to paint the upper portions of walls. You will, of course, have to do some work from a stepladder, using a brush to treat those spots that you couldn't reach with the roller.

To avoid making a mess, work on ceilings with a relatively dry brush or roller. In other words, don't get too much paint on either one because it will run down the handle and down your arm and will either get all over you or the floor. If you don't have good natural light in the room, put some lamps about so that there won't be any areas in shadow that you might miss.

The walls come next and these are pretty easy to do except where the wall joins the ceiling or where it joins the woodwork. You need a brush to handle these spots and you might find that one of the little metal guides that your paint store sells is handy to keep paint away from areas where it is not supposed to go.

One of the great things about modern paints, is that if you see that you have missed a spot—these aberrations are called "holidays"—you can touch them up while the paint is still wet. In fact, you can even touch them up after the paint is dry. When the patch has dried, you'll never be able to find it.

You will probably need two coats of paint on the walls, as well as on the ceilings, unless you use the textured ceiling paint, in which case one coat will be sufficient.

The next item on the list is the woodwork. Here you need to exercise considerable care not to get the trim paint on the walls. Use a small brush with a chisel tip and one of the little metal guides designed for this purpose, unless you happen to have a very steady hand. If the walls have just been painted, don't try to use masking tape on them, because when you strip off the tape, some of the paint may come along with it. Woodwork will require two coats of paint.

PAINTING—OLD WORK

Painting a new room is in one respect easier than old work, because you know the condition of the surfaces with which you are dealing.

With old work you aren't always sure what the exact conditions are, so you have to spend considerable time in surface preparation.

Let's start off with the woodwork. If the old paint on these surfaces is in poor condition, cracked, or peeling, it should be removed. If the woodwork has been coated with varnish and you wish to paint it, and the varnish is in good condition, a light sanding is all you need and you can paint right over the varnish. If, however, the varnish is cracked, it should be removed before paint or fresh varnish is applied. Directions for removing paint and varnish are given in the chapter on "Removing Paint and Finishes." If the paint is in good condition, just wash it down with Spic and Span and water, sand any rough spots, and repaint.

RENOVATING WALLS AND CEILINGS

If surfaces are painted, wash them down with the same Spic and Span and water solution used for the woodwork. In many old houses you will find that the ceilings and sometimes even the walls were painted with *calcimine*, a water paint once widely used because it was inexpensive, easy to apply, and came in a wide range of colors. It does not, however, make a good base for any fresh paint—even calcimine. Before you can paint over it, the calcimine must be removed; this is done with warm water and sponges. If you do have a calcimined surface, get rid of the calcimine before you apply fresh paint. If the paint does not come off with water, then you have an oil paint, and this is a fine base for any sort of finish you wish to apply over it.

When it comes to old wallpaper, the best policy is to remove it before you apply either new wallpaper or paint. If wallpaper has been up only a few years and is in good condition, you can paint or paper over it without much risk. With old wallpaper you never can tell whether the weight of new paper or even paint might pull it off the walls. You can't be sure that the dyes in the paper won't run and discolor the fresh paint. Old wallpaper was often applied with an overlap joint at the seams rather than a butt joint, and no matter how much you sand these joints, they will show through paint or fresh paper. If you want to play safe, take off the old paper.

HOW TO REMOVE WALLPAPER

The best and easiest way to remove old paper is with a wallpaper steamer, which you can rent at paint, hardware, and tool-rental stores. This unit consists of a tank, which is filled with water. The water is heated by electricity or propane gas, a hose is connected to the tank, and at the other end of the hose is the gadget that lets the steam out. You apply the steam to the paper and when the paste has been softened, you strip the paper off in vertical sheets with the aid of a broad putty knife.

This work goes rapidly with a steamer, and practically no mess other than the stripped-off paper is involved. If you can't obtain a steamer, you can do the job with water to which you add prepared wallpaper remover sold at paint and hardware stores. The remover helps the water cut through the paper to soften up the paste. Apply the solution with a brush or sponge. Strip the paper off in vertical sections, working from top to bottom, and apply additional solution if the paper shows resistance. Be careful not to damage the plaster with the putty knife. When plaster is wet you can scratch or gouge it quite easily.

In some cases you will find that the wallpaper has been painted over or has been coated with varnish. Go over the surface with coarse sandpaper to cut through the paint or varnish so that the steam or wallpaper remover can reach it. If you don't, the job will take hours and hours.

It is not advisable to remove wallpaper when it has been applied to a gypsum-wallboard surface that was not coated with a varnish size before the paper was applied. The problem here is that if you remove the wallpaper, the paper covering on the wallboard may come along with it. About the only way to confirm the existence of this situation is to do a little testing in an inconspicuous corner. Wet down a small area of the paper and remove it. If you find that the paper lining of the gypsum board tears off with the wallpaper, then you know that the gypsum wallboard was not sized before the paper was applied. We ran into this condition in one room of a house where, for some reason, someone had installed a new wall of gypsum wallboard and had then papered it. The wallpaper had an overlap joint and the dyes were water soluble. We sanded the joints down as much as possible, then coated the entire wall with several thin coats of gypsum-board joint cement. This eventually produced a good surface for either paint or paper.

You may find that before a wall or ceiling is ready for paint you must do a good deal of work in filling holes and cracks. Large holes are covered in the section above dealing with "Reconditioning Walls." Small holes and cracks are easy to handle. Use your putty knife, or anything with a sharp edge, to undercut the plaster surrounding the crack or holes so that the inside of the opening is wider than the outside. This produces a key that helps hold the patch in place. You don't need to do this for tiny holes left by nails or picture hooks. These, along with cracks, can be filled with patching plaster, which you can get at a paint or hardware store. You must mix it according to directions and apply it with a putty knife. Dampen the plaster around the opening, so that it won't draw the water out of the patching plaster and cause it to dry too quickly. Many professional painters prefer to use plaster of paris for patching, because it dries in a matter of minutes but, for this very reason, we have found it tricky to use except for small holes and cracks.

Once plaster of paris has been mixed with water it begins to set immediately and if you have a large crack to fill you may find that the stuff in the container you used for mixing is hard before you are halfway through the crack. The prepared patching plaster sets more slowly and gives you time to work.

Areas on a painted wall where the paint has chipped can be filled in with spackling compound or joint cement.

After a wall or ceiling has been patched and the patches are hard, sand them smooth.

Once this work has been completed, prime the patches with the same paint you plan to use on the rest of the surface, and when these patches are dry, start your painting operation.

If you plan to paper a wall rather than paint it, you go through the same steps in the preparation of the surface that you would for painting, but with one additional step. That is to coat the surface with a size. For plaster you can use a prepared glue size. For gypsum wallboard you use a varnish size. Prepared wallpaper pastes are available at paint and hardware stores along with the size. If you are going to paper a bathroom or kitchen where the air often has a high moisture content, be sure to use a water-resistant paste and don't let anyone tell you that an ordinary paste will do just as well in these locations—it won't. Your wallpaper dealer can supply you with the very complete instructions for hanging wallpaper that have been prepared by the Wallpaper Council. Prepasted papers come with their own instructions for application.

NATURAL FINISHES

You may not, of course, wish to paint all the woodwork in your house. If the wood is attractive and if it fits in with your general decorating approach, you may wish to leave the wood in its natural state. It does, however, require some sort of protective coating so that it will not absorb dirt and will not discolor from the sun. There are all sorts of finishes you can use for this purpose. An excellent finish is provided by a thin coat of white shellac that is coated with wax when dry. Varnish can also be used but it produces a slightly yellow shade. Wood sealers come in a wide variety, some clear and some containing pigments that will change the color of the wood slightly but still allow the grain to show. You can also stain the wood with a prepared stain, then apply a clear sealer to it. You must remember, however, that just because you stain a piece of pine with a cherry stain, you are not going to end up with cherry wood. The pine will have a color rather like that of cherry wood, but it will still be pine. If it is cheap pine, it will look like cheap pine, colored to imitate cherry.

A good paint store will have a sample board showing the various stains and pigmented wood sealers. However, if you really want to know how the finish is going to work out on your job, try a small amount on the wood you plan to use. There can be quite a range in color, depending on the type of wood to which it is applied.

EXTERIOR PAINTING

Whether or not you elect to paint the exterior yourself will depend on how much ambition you have, the state of your funds, and how big a house you have. Painting the outside of even a small house takes a sizable amount of time, and if your house is a huge monster it will take weeks and will probably require extensive scaffolding. Nevertheless, many people have painted their own houses, so if you have to do it, it can be done.

Probably the most time-consuming work in painting an OB House is the preparation of the surface, because in many OB houses the old paint will be in poor condition. It may, for example, suffer from a condition known as *alligatoring*, which means that the surface is covered with deep cracks that might run through all the coats right down to the wood. If you want a smooth paint job, all this old stuff will have to come off. Peeling paint is also a common problem. In an old house or other structure, it can only mean that moisture has reached the wood in back of the paint or that the paint was applied to a damp or dirty surface. In most cases, however, moisture is the cause. Rain may be getting into the wood through cracks around windows and doors, or at the cornice. Peeling also often occurs as the result of condensation of water vapor from inside the house. What happens here is that in cold weather the warm, moist inside air flows through the wall, and condenses when it hits the cold sheathing or siding. This new liquid condensation is then drawn through the wood by the heat of the sun. The water wants to get out and it takes the paint film off the wood in the process. You will often find this condition limited to the kitchen and bathroom areas of the house, where there is a high moisture content in the air, especially during cold weather. The paint that is peeling should be removed; if an entire wall is peeling, all the paint should come off.

A good many problems with exterior peeling can now be avoided by using a latex paint on the outside wall. This paint will allow the moisture vapor from the inside to flow out through the paint film without damage to the paint. The latex paint and the special primer for it must be applied to bare wood; it won't work if you apply it over ordinary paint.

Instructions for removing paint from outside walls are given in "Removing Paint and Finishes."

Checking is another paint condition you may run across, is somewhat similar to alligatoring, but here the cracks are only on the surface coat of paint. You don't have to remove all the paint to correct this situation. Use a scraper or coarse sandpaper to smooth out the finish, and it will take the new paint off with no trouble.

By the way, you don't have to be quite as fussy with outside painting as you do with interior work. If there are rough spots here and there, they will not be a problem as long as the old paint is secure when you apply the new.

Often with outside paint you will run into a condition known as *chalking*. Here, when you run your finger or hand across the paint, the pigments come off on your skin as a sort of chalk. This is a perfectly normal condition and you don't need to worry about it.

Among the other little chores that must be attended to before you paint the outside of a structure, you must make sure that all the joints between the siding and the window and door frames are sealed tight. Caulking compound is the best sealer to use here. If the joints are extremely wide—½ an inch or so, you can save both time and caulking compound by first filling the joints with oakum, a material used for caulking boats. You may not always be able to find oakum at a paint, hardware, or marine-supply store but search diligently for it—it's a great saver of time and effort.

Any exposed nailheads in the siding should be set below the wood surface and the holes filled with spackling compound or putty. If nails are missing, replace them with aluminum nails that won't rust.

While painting the exterior you should also clean out the gutters and check them for leaks. If you don't do this, the overflow from them might stain your freshly painted walls. Leaks in metal and wood gutters can usually be fixed by coating the inside of the gutter with roofing cement, cementing a strip of roofing paper into this, and then giving the paper another coat of the cement.

When you paint the outside of a house, you start at the top and work down. Do the walls first. When they are dry, do the trim around the doors and windows. You will find that it is usually easier to remove the window sashes from second-story windows and work on them on the ground than to try to do this from a ladder.

Exterior paints can be applied with a brush or roller. For wood shingles and other rough-textured materials, a roller with a long nap is the best. Special rollers are made for painting clapboard and beveled siding.

You can, if you wish, paint exterior walls of masonry, such as brick, stone, masonry block, stucco, or asbestos shingles. Many exterior paints can be used on either wood or masonry. Latex paints, for example, work equally well on both materials. Use a roller with a long nap or an old or inexpensive paint brush for masonry. The rough surface of masonry will quickly wear down the bristles of a brush, and you don't want to ruin a good new brush by using it on this material.

Exterior woodwork can also be given a natural or clear finish. The best types of finish to use here are the penetrating sealers, which come clear or pigmented. They require a minimum amount of surface preparation and when they begin to fade or discolor after a period of time, you simply wipe the surface clean and slap on another coat. They can't alligator, peel, or act up in any way. Don't use varnish on exterior woodwork unless you want to create unnecessary work for yourself. After a year or so the varnish—even spar or marine varnish—will start to deteriorate, and when this happens it has to be stripped off before the fresh varnish can be applied. Those portions that get the most weather and sun will go first, and this gives the surface a very uneven appearance.

GENERAL NOTES ON PAINTING

Mixing. Most paint and hardware stores have mechanical agitators that do a thorough job of mixing paints if they are to be used immediately. If, when you open the container you find that the pigments have settled to the bottom, pour the liquid at the top into a clean container, then take a paint paddle and mix the material at the bottom until it has an even, creamy consistency. Start pouring the liquid back into the original container, stirring as you pour. When the original container is full, pour the entire contents back into the second container. This is called *boxing*. Repeat the procedure several times before using the paint.

Latex paints, varnish, and some enamels should not be boxed because this gets air bubbles in the liquid. Stir these materials gently with a paddle.

Paint Storage. When you want to store a partially full container of paint for future use, clean the paint off the rim so that the lid will fit tightly. Some people like to turn the container upside down so that there will be no chance of air reaching the paint. When air does get into it, a skin forms on the surface and this has to be removed before the paint can be used again. If the skin breaks up when you try to remove it, the paint will have to be strained through a piece of cheesecloth, a paint strainer, or wire screening to remove the little lumps, and this is a messy job. If you do not plan to use a partially full container of paint for some time, pour it into a smaller container with a tight fitting lid. We save all sorts of old jars with screw caps for this purpose. It is a good idea to keep a small amount of leftover paint on hand for touch-up jobs. Just be sure to mark on the container where the paint was used—in which room or area—for fast identification.

Latex paint should never be stored where it might freeze, for this will ruin it.

Paint Brushes. Brushes and rollers used with latex paints can be cleaned in water to which a small arount of household detergent has been added. We never bother with the detergent, however, because we usually clean our brushes outside with a garden hose. Brushes used with alkyd and oil paints should be cleaned with turpentine or a paint thinner. Remove as much of the paint from the brush or roller as you can by working it out over old newspapers, then soak it in the thinner. If you are going to use a brush in the next day or so, you can save time by not cleaning it. Suspend it in a container of thinner so that the bristles are completely covered, but don't allow the bristles to rest on the bottom of the container because this might put a dent in them that may be impossible to remove. Sometimes you can wrap the bristles of a brush in aluminum foil or transparent plastic wrap and they will keep pliable for several days without having to be cleaned.

Brushes that have been used in paint should never be used for shellac, varnish, or any clear finish, because no matter how well the brushes may have been cleaned, some of the pigment will remain and will discolor the clear finish. Keep a set of brushes just for work with clear finishes. By the way, brushes used for varnish are cleaned with turpentine or paint thinner. Brushes used for shellac are cleaned with denatured alcohol.

It is virtually impossible to remove all the paint from a roller, so you should always use a fresh one when starting with a paint of a different color. When you buy a roller, get several replacements for it so that they will be available when you need them.

TYPES OF PAINT

There is probably a special paint available for any paint or finishing job about the house. In addition to the types mentioned before there are paints designed for metal roofs, for aluminum, for concrete floors, for appliances in the kitchen, and even for ranges where the temperature may reach above 400 degrees. There are paints designed for bathroom tile, for things that children might wish to chew on, for canvas awnings, and for the inside of swimming and garden pools. As we said earlier in this chapter, if you have a good paint store and if you tell the people who wait on you there what you have to paint or refinish and what it is made of, they can come up with the right paint for the job—most of the time.

Removing Paint and Finishes 29

It would be surprising indeed if you find an OB House where you will not have to remove a certain amount of old paint, varnish, and other finishes from wood. If the finish is cracked, peeling, or chipped, you can occasionally get by just stripping off the outer layers until you get down to those that are in good condition, but this is risky. It is better to take the paint off right down to the bare wood. Only then can you be certain that the fresh paint you apply is going to adhere properly and dry smoothly.

You will also have to remove paint if you want a natural finish on wood. In the case of interior woodwork or paneling, you will often find that the wood under all those layers of old paint is quite beautiful, and should be given a transparent finish to allow the grain and color of the wood to show. Varnished woodwork, too, takes on a very dark tone after many coats of varnish over the years. Stripping off the old varnish will bring the wood back to its natural state.

It is a good deal easier to remove a finish from something if you can put it on a bench or table where you can work in comfort. In stripping a door, for example, if you take it down and work on it when it is in a horizontal position, you will find the work going much faster than if you try to work on it without taking it down. The same holds true for window sashes and cabinet doors. Even with interior trim, you will find it easier in the long run, to remove the trim, strip it, and then replace it, rather than trying to do this work with the trim in place. You will see the advantage to this method if you ever try to strip paint off a baseboard. There is just no way to do it with any degree of comfort and ease while you're practically standing on your head or squatting on the floor.

METHODS OF REMOVING PAINT FINISHES

You can remove paint in several ways. You can soften the paint with heat, so that it can be scraped away. You can soften the paint with a paint and varnish remover, so that it can be scraped or brushed away, or you can scrape it off with a paint scraper. And on some jobs, such as floors, you use a power sander. We have had to strip away just about every inch of paint in our present house—inside and out—and we use all methods. We have found that certain paints respond better to heat, than to a solvent, and then there are those where the opposite is true. Some paints come off easily with a hand scraper, and some that you just can't seem to budge with a scraper do respond either to heat or a solvent. We switch back and forth, trying one and then another method until we hit the right one. For some jobs, of course, only one method is possible. On a stair railing, for example, only a solvent should be used. You can't remove a finish from turnings and moldings with a scraper.

On most jobs you will be dealing with many coats of paint, and regardless of the method you use you will find it easier to strip off one coat at a time. We have seldom found that we can strip off all coats in one operation.

Besides the basic tools for removing paint, you will need a lot of coarse and medium-grade steel wool, sandpaper, a putty knife with a broad blade as well as one with a 1-inch blade, and plenty of old rags. Also have a metal container on hand to hold the debris.

HOW TO APPLY HEAT WHEN REMOVING PAINT

You can use either a gasoline blow torch, a propane-gas scraper, or an electric unit when you remove paint with heat. We have found the propane-gas and the electric units much more convenient than the gasoline blow torch, and considerably safer to handle. Propane-gas and electric paint removers come with built-in scrapers. The propane-gas unit costs about $8 and the electric units run to about $12. A gasoline blow torch costs about $15.

The trick in using heat to remove paint is to apply enough heat to soften the paint so that it can be scraped off easily with a putty knife or with the scraper that is part of the unit. This takes a little practice so don't be discouraged if at first you don't seem to be making much progress. You don't want to *burn* the paint off; you merely want to soften it. If you allow the heat to remain in one spot too long you are going to scorch the wood, and that means you'll have to sand out the discoloration. On the other hand, if you don't get the paint hot enough, it isn't going to come off easily. It would be wise to get in a little practice on a piece of scrap or waste wood so that you get the feel of things before you start working in earnest. Needless to say, the paint must be scraped off while it is hot and it won't stay hot for long once the heat has been removed. You have only a few short seconds to get at it before it cools and hardens. So just work on one small area at a time.

A propane-gas scraper is especially handy because it doesn't require an electric cord, and can therefore be used anyplace. The great drawback of using this device, however, is that you are working with an open flame, creating a fire hazard. Never use a gasoline blow torch or propane-gas scraper on clapboard or bevel exterior siding. The flame can lick up under one of the boards and start a fire in the wall cavity. You won't necessarily know about this until you've got a full-sized fire on your hands. We heard of a case not too long ago where a painter had been using a blow torch to remove paint from a clapboard house.

He went home for lunch and when he came back not much of the house remained.

Using a flame on any type of exterior siding is risky, so play safe and use an electric scraper, paint remover, or hand scraper.

We don't like to use a flame type of scraper indoors for the same reason—fire. It's easy to forget what you are doing for just a second and allow the flame to hit an inflammable object. We use flame only outdoors, where we don't have the fire hazard. We set up a bench big enough to handle a standard door so that we can work without having to worry about starting a fire. Even an electric scraper can generate enough heat to set fire to an accumulation of paint that might catch under the scraper. If you are using one of these indoors, it is wise to have a fire extinguisher handy. Just in case.

With any of these methods there is always a chance of scorching the wood; it is therefore best not to use them if the wood is to be given a natural finish. For this same reason, don't use flame on furniture. A scorch stain is no great problem, however, if the wood is to be painted.

Once you have removed most of the old paint with a flame, you will still have to catch some odds and ends, either with a hand scraper or with steel wool or sandpaper. It is virtually impossible to remove paint from delicate molding with flame and a scraper. You have to get into these areas by hand with the aid of a paint remover.

PAINT REMOVERS

The most practical type of remover is the paste type. It is available at paint and hardware stores. A paint remover softens the paint through chemical action. Paint remover is pretty strong stuff and you should handle it with care. If you get it on your skin it will burn—not badly perhaps, but you will be uncomfortable. Wear rubber gloves and long sleeves when using it. Be careful not to splatter any on your face or in your eyes. If you do get any on yourself, wash it off at once with water.

We do a great deal of work with paint removers, most of it on our paint-removing bench outside. The weather becomes pretty hot sometimes and we like to work without a shirt. The result is that from time to time we get the stuff on our arms and chest. We keep a garden hose handy, so we can flush the stuff off in a hurry. You get pretty wet this way, so if you can stand wearing a shirt with long sleeves, you're better off. Avoid using a paint remover in the bright sun because it doesn't work as effectively. Too much sun speeds up the evaporation of the remover and gives it less time to work on the paint. When you use a remover outside, try to remain in the shade.

Pour a quantity of remover into a clean container and apply it freely over the surface with an old, but clean, paint brush. If you don't have an old brush to spare, buy an inexpensive one and use it just for this purpose. Spread the remover over the surface in one thick coat. Don't brush it back and forth, just spread it on once and then wait for the remover to take action. It usually takes about a half hour for the remover to do its job. Test the way things are going by using a putty knife to see how easily the paint comes off.

When the paint appears to be fairly soft, go to work and strip it off. The manufacturers of many paint removers make the claim that the softened paint can be removed with water, but we have never had any luck with using water. We use coarse steel wool, a broad putty knife, and sometimes even a paint scraper.

If you are working on a surface that has been given many coats of paint, you will not be able to take all this paint off in one operation. You will probably have to make several applications of the remover, stripping off each coat a layer or two at a time. And you won't be able to get at every last scrap of paint with the remover. You'll still have to do a little work with steel wool or sandpaper.

After the paint has been removed, the wood should be wiped down with a paint thinner such as turpentine or benzine to neutralize the remover.

A paint remover can be used anywhere, but because removers contain solvents, you'll want to work with them where there is adequate ventilation in order not to breathe the concentrated fumes of powerful chemicals which can be hazardous to the health. Do not use paint removers near an open flame because many of the solvents are inflammable. Because the action of the solvent begins to work immediately, be careful not to get the remover on any painted surface where you do not wish to remove the paint. If woodwork is to be stripped and it can't be removed from the house, strip it before any other painting or refinishing is completed.

Paint removers are not inexpensive. They cost about $4 or $5 a gallon, and are therefore seldom used to strip exterior walls. Even on small jobs you can use a large quantity of remover. We used a gallon and a half just on a stair rail, but it had many, many coats of varnish.

Some types of paint respond extremely well to a hand paint scraper. The best hand scraper that we have found has four different blades in a single head. Some are for coarse work and others for fine work, and you can switch as they become dulled. Wear gloves when you work with a scraper or you may get a few skinned knuckles.

Sometimes you find paint that is so loose that it almost falls off at a touch. Often in such cases all you need to do is to work the paint over with a wire brush. A wire brush is also useful if you are working with heat or a paint remover. It can get into spots that you can't easily reach with a putty knife or a scraper.

You can remove a thin coat of paint with coarse sandpaper but sandpaper is not much good when a number of thick coats are involved. Portable electric-belt sanders can be used to strip off thick accumulations of paint but they are tricky—there's always the chance they'll remove too much wood along with the paint. Use a sander to remove a finish on floors only; this method of removing a finish is discussed in the chapter on "Floors."

Among the miscellaneous paint-removing equipment you may need is an old toothbrush for applying paint remover in corners and molding, some nails of varying sizes for removing the softened paint from out-of-the-way spots, and, as was mentioned earlier, an abundance of coarse and medium steel wool, sandpaper, and old rags.

No matter what system you use, removing paint is going to create quite a mess, so for this reason, too, do as much of the work outdoors as possible.

HOW TO REMOVE PAINT IN VARIOUS PARTS OF THE HOUSE

Doors.   Take doors down and work on them outside. The hinges on many doors have a loose pin that connects the two hinge-plates together, and you can drive this pin up from the bottom to separate the two plates. This is considerably easier than removing the hinges. If the pin won't move, remove the screws from the hinge plate attached to the door. In either case, remove the bottom hinge first, put a wedge under the door to hold it upright and in position, and then remove the hinge. Remove all hardware—knobs, plates, and latch—from the door. If the door is going to be repainted, get the old paint off down to the wood but don't worry about traces of paint in the wood grain; they won't cause any problem. If you want to give the door a natural finish, however, then every last trace of paint must be eradicated, and some sanding may be required to get it out of the grain. Flush doors can be stripped with heat, but a panel door will require some work with a paint remover because of the molding around the panels. After all the finish has been removed, if the door is to be repainted, give it a prime coat of paint before you rehang it.

Windows.   As with doors, the best way to handle a window sash is to take it out of the frame and work at it on a bench. You will find directions for removing a window sash in the chapter covering windows. In handling the sash, be careful not to crack any of the glass.

A paste remover is the best thing to use on a window sash, because heat might cause the glass to crack. If the paint is to be removed from the putty around the glass, don't let the remover remain there any longer than is necessary to soften the paint because the remover will also soften the putty.

Interior Woodwork.   The trim around doors and windows can usually be treated with a paint remover, scraper, or electric scraper. If the trim is plain, the scrapers may work beautifully, but if it has an abundance of tricky carving, you'll have to use a paint remover and coarse steel wool. Baseboards are extremely difficult to handle because of the awkward position you have to assume while working on them. If at all possible, take the baseboards off and do them on a bench; you'll save time in the long run. We have a neighbor who did this with all the trim in a room he was doing over. His house has highly ornate interior woodwork and it would have taken forever to strip the paint off with the woodwork in place. If you are going to have to replace the entire wall surface in a room, you will have to remove the trim anyway.

Wood Paneling.   You can use either heat or a paste remover here on wood paneling. If a considerable quantity of wood needs to be stripped, you might consider taking it down and hauling it over to a lumberyard that has a planer. The boards can be run through the planer, which will not only strip off the old paint but leave a nice smooth surface. This procedure would be quicker and easier in the end, and you might find that it didn't cost much more than the cost of the paint remover that would be required.

Interior Walls and Ceilings.   You seldom, if ever, find it necessary to strip all the old paint from interior walls and ceilings. A broad putty knife can be used to remove any loose or blistered paint and these areas can then be patched with spackle or gypsum-board joint cement to bring them level with the surrounding surface. If the old paint is cracked, a thin coat or two of joint cement can be applied over the entire wall to smooth it out.

Exterior Siding.   Here you are dealing with many square feet, so the work can best be handled by an electric paint scraper. You should plan to do this job when you have plenty of time, because you will not only have to remove the old paint but also apply the new. The amount of work involved here would certainly justify renting some scaffolding from a lumberyard, paint store, or tool-rental outfit. You don't have to be quite as thorough with exterior siding as you do with interior work.

Just make sure that you strip off most of the old paint so that you have a solid base.

Masonry.   What happens if you own a wonderful old brick place and find that under those coats of paint there are the beautiful salmon-pink bricks that they just don't make anymore? The only solution here is get someone over to sandblast. The same holds true of all other forms of masonry. You can remove the loose material with a steel brush or very coarse sandpaper so that a surface is available to take paint, but you can't remove all the old paint yourself.

30 Environment

Not all the work involved with an OB Dream House is going to be on the house itself. The grounds around the house may require quite a little of your attention. You may find undergrowth and brush to remove, trees to cut down or prune, drainage problems to solve, retaining walls to build, before you get the grounds into shape. Unless you need a change of pace now and then, most of these outdoor projects should be set aside until the house itself is in order. Fixing a leaky roof should be given a higher priority than taking down an old tree in the back yard. But sooner or later, you will get involved in outdoor work.

Your general approach to the land around your house should be to make the most of what you have, rather than spending a great deal of time and money rearranging items that took nature a good many years to put together. You certainly don't want to do what so many developers do—"scarify" the land by taking everything out with a bulldozer and then starting from scratch. Try to work with what you have in the way of land contours and vegetation, not only to save money but because what you probably have to start with is real and what you will end up with if you fool around too much will be something artificial. This, of course, is a matter of personal opinion, but that's the way I feel about it.

340

DESTROYING UNDERBRUSH

The best way to get rid of a large quantity of underbrush and trash vegetation is to spray it with a brush killer. This works excellently on such items as sumac, poison ivy, poison oak, Virginia creeper, and honeysuckle. You need a good-sized spray container for this job, and you can buy one with a 3-gallon capacity for about $15. Mix the weed killer with water and then spray it on the leaves. Weed killer is pretty strong stuff, so read the directions on the container carefully and don't use the equipment you use with weed killer for any other spraying operation, especially with vegetables. No matter how carefully you clean this equipment after use, some of the poison seems to remain inside and this can cause trouble. A sad man down the way from us killed off many of his roses because he used the same spray equipment to kill off insects on the roses as he had used the year before to destroy poison ivy.

These weed killers should not be used where the underbrush is mixed in with trees and shrubs that you wish to save. But where they can be used, brush killers are extremely effective because they not only kill off the growing weed or tree but get into the root structure and prevent regrowth. We had a healthy stand of sumac that we cut down one spring. By midsummer it had all grown back again. Then we gave it a treatment with brush killer and that did the trick; the sumac has never come back.

Where you can't use a spray you'll have to tackle the brush or undergrowth with a pair of clippers, a brush hook, or an ax.

REMOVING TREES

Removing a few unwanted trees presents no great problem. You can cut them down with an ax. If you have a great many trees to remove, buy or rent a chain saw, or get someone with a chain saw to do the job for you. If there is a good local market for fireplace wood, you might make a deal with the man who owns the chain saw, to reduce the cost of taking out the trees. We once worked out a deal when we had a great many trees to remove; we gave the wood to the man who cut them down and he deducted a proportionate amount from his bill. It is, strangely enough, often easier to sell fireplace wood than it is to give it away.

Cutting the trees down and then to fireplace length is not much of a job with a gasoline or electric chain saw. A chain saw is more dangerous than any other type of power saw, however, because it is heavier and therefore more difficult to handle. Take the time, before you start using the saw, to clear a good, safe working place. Get rid of dead branches on the ground along with underbrush that might trip you. Find a level spot to stand on, where you won't slip on wet leaves or grass.

If you have a place in the woods, or one that is surrounded by many trees, you should seriously consider removing quite a few trees. Certainly you should take some out in the immediate vicinity of the house. There is a strong tendency among many people, especially if they come from the city, to avoid cutting down a tree at any cost. Tree cutting, they feel, is a sacrilege. However, too many trees near the house are not good for the house. The trees give off a considerable amount of moisture, which can make a place damp; they reduce circulation of air around the house; and they can also be a fire hazard. In addition, when too many trees are too close together they don't get a chance to develop properly. If you have a large wooded lot, you ask your county agent or a representative of the state forestry service to visit your property and tell you which trees to remove and which ones to save.

PRUNING TREES

Dead branches or branches that interfere with utility lines and other vital service equipment should be removed. The correct way to do this is to make a cut on the underside of the branch or limb about two feet from the trunk. When the limb begins to sag so that the saw binds, take the saw out and make a cut from above, about two inches from the undercut. The limb or branch will soon fall, leaving a stump about two feet long. Cut the stump off as close to the trunk as you can without damaging the trunk with the saw. Brace the limb during the last few minutes of the cutting so that it will not fall and tear some of the bark off the tree. If the limb is too heavy to hold, use a rope tied to a branch higher up to give it support. Once the limb is out of the way, coat the exposed wood on the trunk with asphalt cement or one of the prepared tree dressings.

Clearing out a large amount of underbrush and trees is going to leave you with a sizable pile of trash. The method of disposal is to burn it, but many communities no longer allow this, not only because of the fire hazard but also because such fires add to the general air-pollution problem. You might check to see if trash burning is allowed in your community and whether your local fire department will come over to supervise the operation. Many fire departments do this sort of work because it reduces the risk factor and gives the boys a chance to use all their nice fancy fire-fighting equipment. They especially love to supervise burning down an old structure that isn't worth salvaging.

STUMP REMOVAL

When a tree is cut down a stump always remains, and getting rid of this stump can sometimes be a problem. If the stump is not in your way, cut it off close to the ground and cover it with earth. In a few years it will rot away. If the stump must be removed, the process can be done by hand, but this is a miserable job if you are dealing with a good-sized stump. It entails digging a fairly large hole around the stump and then cutting through the roots with an ax so the stump can be pulled out. The best way to get rid of large stumps is to have someone come in and pull them out with a heavy truck or bulldozer. If you plan to use this method, let the stump extend three or four feet above the ground so that there will be something to hitch a chain or cable to, or for a bulldozer to push against.

REMOVING BOULDERS

Years ago we heard that you could break up large boulders by building a fire around them to get them hot and then pouring cold water over them. The theory here is that the sudden contraction cracks the boulder, but the technique has never worked for us. The best way to deal with a large boulder is to leave it alone. If this isn't possible, try cracking it with a heavy sledgehammer. If that approach doesn't work, blast the boulder apart. You will need an expert to do this job for you. We have fooled around with dynamite only once and that was when we were eleven years old and didn't know any better. But an expert can break up a boulder close to the house without much trouble. As a matter of fact, we once watched a real craftsman break up a large boulder right under a house. The basement was being enlarged, and the boulder got in the way, so the man doing the job cracked the boulder apart and he scarcely rattled a dish in the house. He was elderly and almost blind and needed someone to lead him around, but he used his hands to see how the grain of the boulder ran and where the holes should be drilled for the charges. It was quite a thing to see.

BUILDING A BOULDER

We were brought up in New England, where the one thing in plentiful supply is boulders and rocks, but just because New England has such an abundance doesn't mean that all sections of the country have the same.

If you happen to need a sizable rock or boulder for your landscaping plan, you can make one rather easily. All you need are a few pieces of board, some chicken wire, and some cement mortar. Use gray Portland cement for the cement mortar unless you want a light-colored rock, in which case use plain cement.

Build a crude framework out of the lumber and then drape the chicken wire over it and shape the wire to form the sort of boulder you want. Now just slap the mortar over the chicken wire. Put on a cotton work glove and apply the mortar by hand; smear the mortar about so that you get the desired shape and texture. The mortar should be about an inch thick, but you can make it as thick as you need to get the shape you want.

HOW TO BUILD A RETAINING WALL

You will need a retaining wall if you wish to make a level area out of a slope or to hold an earth embankment in place. You can build retaining walls out of stone, masonry block, poured concrete, or even old railroad ties if you can obtain them locally.

Stones are fine for a retaining wall if you have enough available and they are the right size. Ideally, for this purpose, you want rather large stones. If you can lift and carry it, the stone is about right. If you can run with it, it's too light. You need large stones for this job because they will be laid up without mortar and consequently it will be the mass that will give the wall its strength.

Use small stones to fill in around the large ones. Arrange each stone so that they interlock to provide strength. You don't use mortar on a retaining wall of stone because if you have a solid wall, water in back of it will exert enough pressure to either push the wall over or crack it. Without mortar between the stones, water in back of the wall can drain off through the cracks. The wall should be at least 16 inches wide. Dig a trench several feet deep and put the largest stones in it to serve as a foundation for the wall. If you have some nice big ones, ease them in with a crowbar.

A retaining wall can be built with masonry block, but this material is not ideal for the purpose. A masonry-block wall will not withstand much lateral pressure unless it is heavily reinforced. For reinforcement you will need a poured-concrete footing with metal rods set in that extend to the height of the wall. The blocks are laid up so that these rods run through the cavity in the block and these cavities are filled with mortar. It is also wise to use metal reinforcing strips along the horizontal joints. All in all, the labor involved is just too much for what you get.

Poured concrete makes a fine retaining wall, especially if it is reinforced, but unless you do the job yourself, the cost is high.

Railroad ties, if you can obtain them cheaply enough and if you have someone to work with you, are ideal for retaining walls. You can't, however, just pile them up one on top of another and expect them to hold. They should be held together with a few ½-inch metal rods; and about every 8 feet you want to set one at right angles to tie the wall into the soil in back of it.

DRAINAGE

Low spots in the ground adjacent to the house can usually be filled in with earth so that they do not collect and hold water. If the land around the house presents a serious drainage problem, you may have to regrade. Get a bulldozer to move the earth about and then add filling where required.

Installing some kind of drainage system is another solution. Sometimes all you need is a *dry ditch;* here you simply dig a ditch along the area where water collects. The ditch should be about a foot wide and a few feet deep, with a slight downward pitch so that water flowing into it will flow away from the house. Fill the ditch with some stones 4 or 5 inches in diameter, and that's it.

A more complicated system involves setting perforated drainage pipe a few inches below the surface of the ground and connecting it to a *dry well.* A dry well is just a big hole in the ground. You can make it any size you want but one that is 4 feet in diameter and 6 feet deep is suitable for the purpose. Line the sides with stone or masonry block laid up without mortar and bring in the drainage lines at the top. Cover the top with a reinforced-concrete cover. A dry well is also a fine way to handle the discharge from roof gutters and downspouts. Connect the bottom of the downspout to lengths of drainage pipe that run to the dry well. Be sure that they have a downward pitch toward the well.

If the road or driveway to your property is on a grade, ditches should be dug on each side to take care of large quantities of water. Be sure to do this if the road or drive is of earth or gravel, because if the drainage isn't good, a heavy rain can wash the road away. The ditches need only be about 1 or 2 feet wide and a few feet deep. You can toss in a few small rocks to keep the soil from falling in. While you're at it, you might make sure that the road or drive has a slight crown—that is, that the middle is somewhat higher than the sides. Water falling on the crown will run to the sides and into the ditches rather than right down the road. A road scraper can do this job for you, but if you can't find or afford to get one, create the crown by hand with shovel, hoe, and rake. It's good exercise.

CREATING A TERRACE OR PATIO

If you want a first-class terrace you can build it by making an excavation about 16 inches deep, with a base of gravel about 8 inches thick. Over this you pour a 4-inch concrete slab and over that you put a 1-inch bed of mortar. Lay flagstone or bricks in the mortar bed and fill the joints between the stones or bricks with mortar. This is a lot easier said than done.

The easiest way to do the job produces a terrace that is almost as good as the first-class job. Make an excavation about 9 inches deep, pour in about 8 inches of gravel and pack it down. Next, put a 1-inch layer of sand over the gravel and compact it with a lawn roller or by spraying with a fine spray from the garden hose. The stones or brick are laid directly on this sand base without any mortar. Add or subtract sand as required, so that the stones or bricks are level and sit firmly. Leave a space about ¾ of an inch to 1½ inches between the units. After the stones or bricks are in place, sprinkle sand over the surface and sweep it around so that it fills the joints. This method produces a very durable terrace and about the only trouble you will have with it is that the sand between the joints will have to be replaced from time to time, especially after a heavy rain. We have a terrace made in a similar fashion and we did have trouble with the sand. Ants kept making nests in it and heavy rains would wash it out. We licked the problem by mixing up equal parts of gray Portland cement and sand and sweeping this mixture into the joints. We gave it a light wetting with a garden hose after it was in place. The result has been highly satisfactory. You can get rid of the ants, by the way, by pouring carbon tetrachloride over the sand.

Stones and bricks can, of course, be laid directly over the soil but they will not be level.

We once ran into a man who liked to make a special kind of concrete flagstone, which he used all over his property. He collected interesting looking little stones wherever he went, and when he had a good quantity, he would make a flagstone. He used strips of aluminum about 4 inches wide to make his form, which was usually round. This he would set in a smooth surface. Then he would arrange his stones inside the form. Next, he would gently pour in the concrete. When the concrete was hard, he stripped off the form, turned the concrete upside down, and there inbedded on the underside were all the nice little stones.

We also once heard of a man who spent an entire winter making colored concrete bricks in empty milk cartons. He mixed a dry coloring powder into the concrete and then poured this into the carton and let it dry. I never did find out what he did with all the bricks and it really isn't a very practical method of making concrete bricks unless someone in the family drinks a lot of milk.

► *Special Money-Saving Tips*

You can save $100 by laying flagstone or brick yourself for a patio or terrace 24 feet by 24 feet.

You can save more than $150 on a 10-foot-by-20-foot wood deck by framing it yourself.

You can save $20 by taking down one average-sized tree and removing the debris yourself.

THEIR
DREAM HOUSES
CAME TRUE

The Step-by-Step
Case Histories
of 20 Families
and How They Got
the Job Done

The Edward Bonser Family:
A Waterside Garage in Maine . . .

RIGHT: The old garage. It was not much to look at, but it had a beautiful view of the water.

BELOW: The boathouse today, on the site of the garage. Ramp makes it a simple matter to pull boats out of the water and into the lower area for storage. Underside of the second-floor deck is decorated with colorful lobster-pot buoys.

. . . Inspired a Boathouse Home

The Bonser Family:

"It's just perfect for all of us"

MR. AND MRS. Edward Bonser bought a small, rather typical summer cottage at Hills Beach in Biddeford, Maine. The cottage, somewhat back from the water, was in the middle of three lots fronting on an open expanse of bay, with the blue Atlantic just beyond. It was a marvelous spot for fishing, lobstering, and duck-hunting.

With the cottage came a dilapidated garage just at the water's edge. Originally it had been part of the main house, but previous owners had moved it about 50 feet away. For several years the Bonsers and their son used it as a one-car garage and general catch-all. An upstairs portion was used as a playroom and as a dormitory for guest overflow. The second floor offered an especially fine view of the water, and this part of the garage naturally became known as the "Crow's Nest."

Fairly extensive remodeling was done to the cottage at the time of purchase. This included winterizing, adding a wing with a 20-foot living room, and replacing small, view-blocking windows with large expanses of window walls and a picture window in a bedroom overlooking the bay.

The Bonsers next turned their attention to the old garage, which they wanted to convert into a combination boathouse, garage, and apartment. The building turned out to be in such poor condition, however, that they decided it would be easier and probably less expensive to demolish it and start off fresh.

Working with the same architect they had used in remodeling the cottage, plans were drawn for the new construction, using the same simple lines as those of the original garage but with about twice as much space. Construction was slated to begin in the fall because the family didn't "want the place in chaos all summer," to quote Mrs. Bonser. Work on the project was complete by the end of winter.

Now completed, the new boathouse is a tri-functional joy to the whole family. On the waterside, the lower floor stores the two Bonser boats, a canoe and a Boston Whaler, and also provides outdoor living space with a deck above the terrace for shelter. On the street side, there is space for two cars, lawn and garden equipment, and in the middle a stairway to a now deluxe "Crow's Nest" on the second floor. Light, airy, and roomy, this upstairs apartment is designed for easy maintenance and carefree living. Large window expanses on two sides, with sliding glass doors opening onto a sun deck, give a feeling of cruising in a comfortable yacht. An open kitchen and serving bar at the rear of the large living room make the cook or bartender very much a part of whatever is going on. A full bath adjoins the kitchen, and built-in closets offer space for clothes and other storage. Built-in studio beds along the side walls for seating and sleeping add to the feeling of being on a yacht. Mrs. Bonser has used indoor-outdoor carpeting throughout, even on the deck.

A finished attic is reached by a flight of folding stairs that descends to the center of the living room. The attic provides space for sleeping and for storage.

The boathouse apartment was planned as a comfortable and attractive place where the Bonsers and their friends could enjoy outdoor life. The living room looks out over the water—a bay that in summer is covered with small boats—and the Bonsers have their own lobster pots, practically in their front yard.

While the Bonsers have their main home in Connecticut as well as the original cottage on the Biddeford property, they prefer living in the boathouse. It was designed for year-round living because the Bonsers enjoy the fall and winter in Maine almost as much as they do the Maine summer.

The Bonser Family:
How a Boathouse was Planned to Include
Carefree Quarters for Year-Round Living

LEFT: First-floor plan provides space for two-car garage as well as for boats. When boats are in the water, this space can be used as a protected outdoor living area.

RIGHT: Second floor has been made into living quarters. Large living room opens onto deck. Kitchen at rear of living room is open, to give the entire area an open, spacious feeling. Living-room ceiling trapdoor and disappearing stairs lead to third floor, which provides space for additional sleeping quarters.

The Robert Thompson Family:
They Changed an Old Coach House . . .

Here is the structure the Thompsons had at the start of their work.

BELOW: Today the coach house is a charming, extremely spacious home.

. . . into a Williamsburg-Style House

The Thompson Family:
  *"The building inspector suggested
  we level the building and start fresh"*

MR. AND MRS. Robert Thompson purchased a house in Lincolnshire, Illinois, that had been part of an estate. After they had lived in it for a time they became concerned about a widening of a highway. Whoever wrote "Let me live in a house by the side of a road and be a friend of man" didn't know that highways not only grow in length but also in width. Part of the original estate contained some property with a carriage house and a silo, and the Thompsons bought this parcel to give them a little more space. After they had made the purchase they rented the coach house to a church group as a meeting hall. The rear section was used for the village clerk's office and also as a place for voting at election time.

The Thompsons had decided to remodel the coach house and sell it but when the appraiser came along to inspect the property, he suggested selling the house, which would decrease in value as the highway attracted more traffic, and retaining the coach house and the silo. As this suggestion made sense, the Thompsons decided that they would sell the house and remodel the coach house into a home for themselves. They loved the area and the property. There are about 50 old pine trees in the immediate vicinity, and from the present living room the Thompsons have a view of a lovely park.

They found a buyer for their old house and moved out of it in August. The renovation work on the carriage house began the first week in July. For a time the Thompsons had to live with friends and relatives and even in motels, but they had three children then, aged seven, nine, and eleven, and so finally, in desperation, they moved into the "mess" and camped out in their new house while the renovation work was being completed. It is almost impossible to know what it is like to live with three young children in a house that is going through extensive alterations, but it must be an experience that one is not likely to forget.

The renovation work consisted of making the original carriage house into livable quarters and also adding considerable space, including a two-car garage. The Thompsons commissioned an architect, Richard Geudtner, to work up the design of the renovation and addition. As the existing structure was frame, the addition was done in the same manner and the exterior is in the Williamsburg style. One of the problems in planning was the silo, which the Thompsons wished to retain. This sits off the garage wing and will eventually be converted into an office for Mr. Thompson.

Besides having to live in the house with three children while the work was in progress, the Thompsons had a few other problems. The rear section of the foundation was found to be inadequate, and this condition had to be corrected. The Thompsons had some trouble getting approval from the village on certain aspects of the plan, but these matters were finally straightened out. And then there was a building inspector who came over one day and suggested that they level the carriage house and start off fresh. This sort of advice can be disquieting when one is in the midst of a renovation project.

The Thompsons did a good bit of work on the project themselves. Mr. Thompson finished the kitchen cabinets, and they did most of the interior painting and decorating. Like many, they experienced some trouble in getting good help and decided that if the job were to be done right, they would have to do it themselves. The entire renovation project took only four months.

Now that the work is out of the way, the Thompsons are very happy with their new house on their old piece of land.

The Thompson Family:
How They Added Space to the Existing Structure

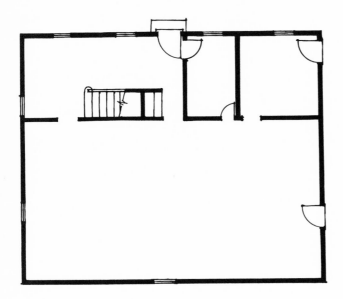

First-floor plan before renovation. The large area had been used by a church group as a meeting room. The smaller area had served as office of the village clerk.

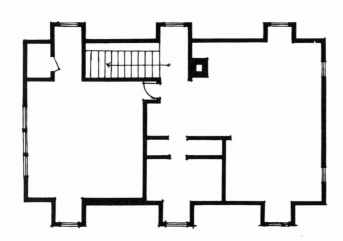

Second floor consisted of only two large unfinished areas and storage space.

Existing space on the first floor was used for the living room, kitchen, utility room, bathroom, and foyer opening off the front entry. The first-floor addition provided space for large family room, two-car garage, and large utility room.

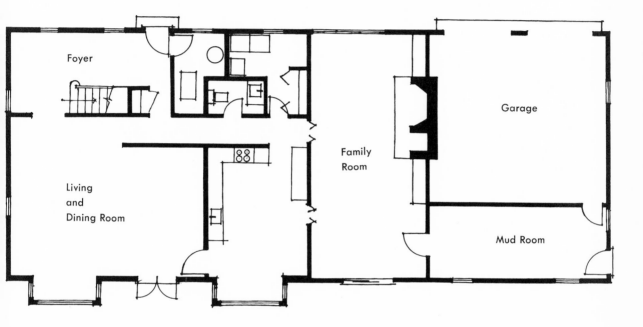

The second floor has two large bedrooms at each end of the hall. Flanking the master bedroom are a dressing room and bath that are also available to the adjoining bedrooms when required. A second bathroom serves the two remaining bedrooms.

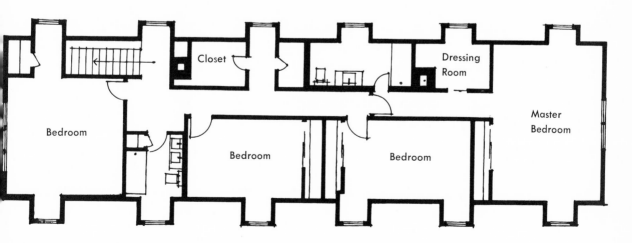

The Sebastian Family:
180-Year-Old
Pioneer Way Station . . .

The original building with the lean-to bathroom that was added by the Sebastians.

. . . Becomes a Gracious Home

After remodeling and additions. The original house is at right, connected to addition. Exteriors were framed with timbers, and stucco applied as exterior siding. New entrance is at left beyond tree.

The Sebastian Family:

"We camped out the first summer"

THERE IS a site on the highest ridge overlooking the Meramee River in Missouri, which, according to neighborhood legend, was once used by the Indians for a lookout point. This seems an extremely reasonable legend and worth believing.

At some point, around 180 years ago, someone built something on this site. Exactly what the purpose of this structure was is difficult to say. The outside walls were made of wood and the inside walls were of handmade brick laid up with clay mud. Eventually this building became one of the way stations for wagon trains moving out beyond the Mississippi to the West and it served this purpose for many years. After the last wagon train had rolled off, the travelers' station became a barn and eventually even the horses went away and the barn just sat there quietly in the wood. It was part of a piece of property that had changed hands only twice since the area was settled.

In the spring of 1963 Otfried and Gertrude Sebastian, newly married, were out looking for a house of their own. They had grown up in the same town in Germany. Gertrude had come to St. Louis to visit her brother. Otfried soon followed her and they were married. The Sebastians were looking for a house in a beautiful setting that they could afford and they were willing to take on a project that required work on their part. When they came across the strange old structure overlooking the Meramee River, they fell in love with it and the beautiful site.

362

They had difficulty in talking the owner into selling them the structure along with four acres. The property had been turned into a bird sanctuary and the owner did not want anything done that would disturb the natural woods. Eventually the Sebastians convinced him that they would leave the woods exactly as they were and only make improvements on the structure. Finally they were able to buy the property.

The building didn't have much going for it except that it was very old and had a lovely location. It had no water, heat, or electricity. The roof was beyond repair. Inside there was not much except the walls of hand-made brick. The first floor contained one big room and one little room, there was a second-floor loft, and that was it.

The Sebastians moved into the place in the summer. This was camping out and rather primitive camping out at that. They slept in the loft. "It was summer and we both love to camp anyway, and so it was fun," Mrs. Sebastian told us and we believe her. But while it may have been fun, the first order of business was to install plumbing and get a bathroom. The little lean-to on the side of the building that shows in the "before" picture was the first thing the Sebastians built—it was a bathroom.

The first phase of the renovation was to make the existing structure as comfortable as possible within the limited amount of space it contained. The large room was made into a living room and the small room in back was turned into a kitchen. The loft continued to serve as the bedroom area. A new roof of cedar shakes was installed, and Mr. Sebastion picked up 15 old doors for $1.50 a piece, which, after he had stripped off the old paint, he used for interior paneling.

Once they had made the basic house comfortable to live in, the Sebastians moved ahead with phase two—adding more space. This started out to be a rather modest project but then Mr. Sebastian was able to pick up a large quantity of old timbers and planks from a wooden bridge that had once spanned the Mississippi River and had been torn down. It was hard to resist using all this lovely wood for something, so the modest expansion project grew into a rather large undertaking.

The Sebastians added a new entrance hall, living room, dining room, and kitchen. They also put in an indoor garden room and a gallery connecting the new addition to the original structure. The former living room was converted into an office and the old kitchen became a guest bedroom. The loft continued to be used as a bedroom area.

They used the lumber from the bridge for framing the additions and also for trim. The new additions have the flavor of a German country chalet but seem to be at home among the woods and hills of Missouri.

The Sebastians did most of the work on the place themselves with the exception of the plumbing, wiring, heating, and plastering. They also used some outside help on some of the other projects, such as framing the additions with the heavy timbers from the bridge.

It took about a year to complete the renovation and the additions. When Mr. Sebastian was not working in his capacity as a landscape designer, he was working on the place or drawing up plans for the projects still to be tackled. Eventually the place was completed. And after they had lived in it for a short time, they sold it.

They got about four times as much for their renovation as they had paid originally. Naturally, they sold it so that they could buy another place and naturally, the new place was also an OB Dream House. This time it happened to be an old run-down farmhouse on about 150 acres of land—a handy amount of land to have if you are in the landscape business.

This old farmhouse is a real beauty. When the Sebastians bought it, it had nothing, no plumbing, no wiring, no heat. They took possession in the late spring so that they could camp out and work on the place during the summer months. This time instead of sleeping in a loft they slept in the barn on the hay. A good deal of work is still to be done on this place but Mrs. Sebastian is terribly excited about it and the way it will look when it is all finished.

One of the aspects of this story that we especially like is that it proves our point that camping out may be the way to get going on fixing up an OB House that you have bought. This is an especially important point to consider if you are planning to do a lot of the work yourself.

This story also confirms our point that if you take over an OB House—no matter what it is—and do something to it, you are pretty sure of being able to sell it, when and if you want to, for a rather good price.

In spite of the fact that the Sebastians obviously put money as well as a great deal of their time and effort into their first project, they came out rather well on the transaction.

There is another interesting aspect to the saga of the Sebastians and that is that it follows the same pattern found with many people who renovate OB Houses. Once the project is completed, they often sell it and move on to a new renovating project. Time after time we have run across people who have taken on an OB House, have worked like horses day and night until it was completed, and when it was finally completed, have sold it to buy another OB house. It would be one thing if these people were doing this just to make money—as a sound investment —but this is not necessarily the primary reason for their action. As long as they are involved in the place, as long as they are working on it, you probably couldn't buy it for love or money. Once the job is finished, however, and they should be enjoying the fruits of their labor, they grow restless and want to tackle another project.

At the very beginning of this book we mentioned that taking on an OB House was a challenge. There are obviously many people who find this challenge so appealing that they barely allow themselves time to catch their breath after finishing one job before they look around for another.

It's good to know that there are so many people like this, for if there were not, many houses and buildings that exist today as comfortable homes would have disappeared from the American scene.

The Sebastian Family:
How the Sebastians Added Space

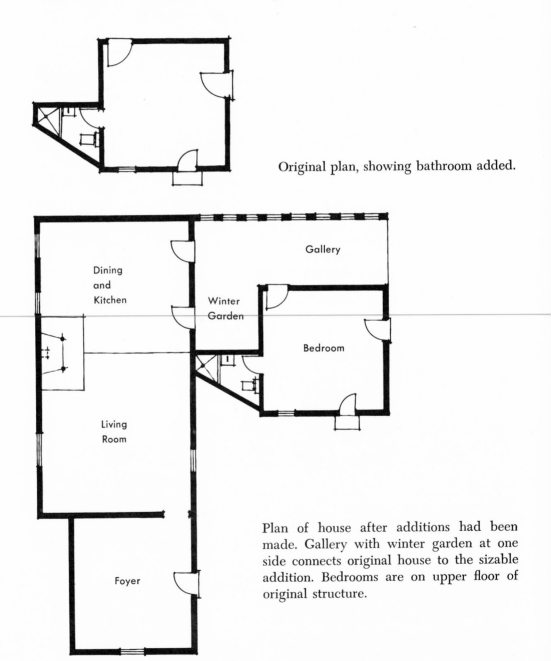

Original plan, showing bathroom added.

Gallery

Dining
and
Kitchen

Winter
Garden

Bedroom

Living
Room

Foyer

Plan of house after additions had been made. Gallery with winter garden at one side connects original house to the sizable addition. Bedrooms are on upper floor of original structure.

Rear view of house showing the unusual rock garden, punctuated with tree stumps. At left is stable, containing space for horses, storage, and sauna bath.

View across part of living room to dining room shows how the heavy bridge timbers were used for both beams and door trim. Stairway leads to a small balcony. Window there could become door to future bedroom and bath over dining room.

The Cobb Family: How a
Federalist Country Town House . . .

Front view of the house at the time it was bought by the Cobbs.

BELOW: Cobb house after major renovation work had been completed. Old paint was removed from front of the house and siding painted white. Clapboard was installed over tongue-and-groove siding at gable end, and shutters were painted yellow. Future plans include installation of period fan light in gable and replacing shingles on side with clapboard.

. . . Was Given a Complete Overhaul

Rear view of house shows the old massive masonry-block garage that obstructed view from first floor.

BELOW: Wood deck and stairs leading to a flagstone terrace replaced the masonry garage. Shingles on side walls will be replaced with clapboard, and shutters added.

The Cobb Family:

*"We were looking for an old barn
but fell in love with this place"*

OUR PRESENT house did not begin its existence as an OB Dream
House. Far from it. Back in 1840 or 1850 when it was built, the house
was a rather formal Federal-style dwelling, surrounded by formal gar-
dens and landscaping. You can find traces in the house and about the
grounds of what it must have been like. The house is situated not too
far from a small village, and the land runs down to a broad river. During
the course of years, different owners did, or did not, do things to the
house, so that eventually the interior became a hodgepodge of rooms
and the outside fell into general disrepair. The man from whom we
bought the place had begun a major restoration job, then decided to
build a new house instead. There were many times during the course
of our restoration work when we considered doing the same. This was
a real problem house.

Actually we were not looking for an OB House when we ran across
this place. Our original idea was to pick up a piece of land near the
water and erect a compact, easily maintained contemporary house, or,
if that didn't work out, we planned to find an old barn and remodel it.
But one day a broker showed us our present house. The next morning
we made an offer that was accepted and we were off.

At the time we made our offer, the house was in rather bad shape.
The paint on two of the exterior walls was so far gone that it scarcely
existed except as a problem for repainting. At the rear of the house was

370

a large, partially complete concrete-masonry-block garage and workshop with a flat roof.

The interior of the house consisted of a living room off the front entry, in fair condition. Behind it was a somewhat smaller room that had been partially restored. Behind this was another room with a fireplace, which the previous owner had made into a living area; behind this was the kitchen area, which was incomplete, lacking floor, cabinets, and other finishing touches. Off to one side of the unfinished kitchen area was a partially finished half bath.

Upstairs the front bedroom was stripped down to the lath. It had only a rough sub-floor and lacked one door—even the frame for the door did not exist. A second bedroom was almost finished except for the floor. There was a very narrow hall and, in the rear, a large unfinished area with a fine view of the river. There was a full bathroom upstairs and this was complete—the only complete room in the house.

The paint on most of the existing interior woodwork was in poor shape. The windows, with few exceptions, needed many new panes of glass and putty. It was a fine house that had been allowed to become an OB House.

Its main attraction was the location, with its splendid view of the river. We fell in love with it, made our offer, and once the offer was accepted, set to work trying to figure out what to do with the place and how much it all would cost.

We made our first mistake in allowing the closing to be set too soon, which didn't really give us enough time for properly planning use of the existing space. We worked out some very rough ideas and called in a contractor to give us an estimate. His estimate came to about $20,000, an amount far more than we wanted to spend on restoring the place. It was also further than our lender was willing to go with a construction mortgage. We worked with our contractor and our lender and finally arrived at a $10,000 figure, which was half of what we needed, but the best we could get.

We went ahead with the closing and then moved right in so that we could pull our final plans together. Again we did not give ourselves enough time for the work involved in making final plans. Our lender was anxious to get the place in livable shape and he was pushing us just a bit. We were in a hurry to make the place livable, so we rushed matters too, and this was unfortunate.

In any event, we decided to concentrate our efforts and money on the rear of the house—both downstairs and upstairs—where there was the view of about 350 feet of rolling lawn extending down to the river. Downstairs we decided to remove a partition to make one large room out of the two existing rear rooms. We installed very wide sliding glass doors along the rear wall, so that the entire section looked out on the river. We installed a kitchen area off to one side, where formerly there had been a dining area. We call this section of the house "the River Room," and it is a delight. The open kitchen allows whoever is cooking to take part in the conversation, yet at the same time there is the feeling that the kitchen is separate from the rest of the room.

Upstairs, we decided to make the large rear room into a master-bedroom suite with bathroom and closets. These two operations were going to take the $10,000 plus a little more. We took title to the house in September, and in November work began on these two areas. This work was not completed until March.

One of the major reasons this work took so much time was that we were not on hand and available for consultation when problems arose; the men had to stop work until the contractor reached us and got our approval of the proposed solution. In any restoration job all sorts of problems arise that cannot be anticipated in advance, and unless you have an architect on the job who can make these decisions for you, there is wasted time and money, plus a certain amount of confusion. If you are going to handle a restoration project yourself, try to be on hand, if possible, and inspect the work each evening, or at least every other day.

The first major problem we ran into was installing the sliding glass doors. This house has plank construction, so there is no wall studding and no wall cavity. The rear wall of the house had to be reframed to accommodate the thickness of the sliding glass unit. As this work was not included in the estimate, we had to pay extra for it. Next, the electrician found that a good deal of the old wiring was in bad shape and had to be replaced. We were hit with an extra charge for this work. And so it went.

By March, the River Room was complete and even painted, and the upstairs bedroom and bath were complete, but not decorated. Originally, we had planned to put a bubble skylight in the upstairs bathroom, as this was an inside bath with no windows. We later changed our plan here because we felt that the skylight protruding from the roof would not be in keeping with the style of the house. We put in an exhaust fan for ventilation and it works quite well, but the bath is really not as pleasant as it would have been had we gone ahead with a skylight that could be opened.

For all this work we had used a general contractor who handled everything—carpentry, plumbing, wiring, painting. This is certainly the simplest way to operate, but because a contractor has considerable overhead, it is not the least expensive way to do a renovation job.

Because we needed to pinch pennies to complete the work that remained, we switched to working with someone who did work on a time-plus-materials basis. We had worked before with Bill and his sidekick, Jack, and they were both excellent workers, not only on carpentry, but on just about everything. Unfortunately, they could only work for us on weekends, so the job went rather slowly. We lived that summer amid great mess and confusion, and it's no fun.

Bill and Jack removed the lath from the front bedroom, insulated the ceiling, built closets, and applied the gypsum wallboard. They also installed doors, woodwork, and replaced windows. We had them widen the upstairs hall, complete the second bedroom, install pine-plank flooring, and complete all the carpentry work upstairs. Bill had developed an interesting method of putting down a pine-plank floor. He would take ordinary 1-by-12-inch boards and cut a groove along each edge. Then he would cut a strip of plywood that fit into these grooves. When the boards were put down side by side, they were held together by a strip of wood known as a *spline,* so that there would be little chance of warping and the edges rising up. We used this type of flooring for all the upstairs rooms except the master bedroom, where we had already used pre-finished hardwood.

The fact that Bill and Jack could do everything made them invaluable. If they removed a partition and wiring then had to be repositioned, they could do it. When we decided to replace the vinyl flooring in the bathroom, they removed the plumbing fixtures, put down the vinyl and replaced the fixtures.

They started work around April and were finished upstairs by the early part of July. I remember this because I spent the 4th of July painting the front bedroom, and that 4th of July was a very hot, humid day. We had used a professional painter to do the master bedroom but we were not too happy with him. One day he just didn't show up, and we never saw him again, which was no great loss.

A tremendous amount of painting was needed, both upstairs and downstairs, and with a few exceptions all the old paint on the woodwork had to be removed. It was at this point that Roger came on the scene. A college man interested in making some money during the summer, Roger worked on the place during the week, and I worked on it over the weekends. Roger was just great. He was cheerful, came when he said he would come, and worked like a beaver. Before he had to go back to college, all the old paint had been stripped away with the exception of that on the main stair rail, and everything had been painted except the front living room.

The front living room turned out to be more of a problem than we expected. The ceiling had previously been covered with canvas, and this Bill replaced with gypsum wallboard. The walls were papered and we assumed that they were fairly sound, but when I removed the paper we found out they were not all that sound. It took the month of September for me to get those walls in shape so that we could paint the room. But by the middle of October, 13 months after we had taken title to the house, the inside was in fair shape.

We still had one major problem to solve and that was what to do about the large masonry-block structure at the rear of the house. This was a problem, not only because it was unattractive but because it was so deep that it obstructed our view of the river. To make matters worse, I had decided to rip part of it down, then got on to something else, so that now its appearance was even worse than before. To allow the roof of the building to serve as a suitable deck meant that it would have to be dropped 8 inches to clear the sill of the sliding glass doors. We decided to cut half the building off so that it would only be as wide as a one-car garage, and let it go at that. We got an estimate on doing this work, and it was way, way too high. So we thought some more.

One day my wife said she had the solution, and she had. We ripped the whole thing down but left enough of the masonry-block walls on either side to enclose a large terrace, which we covered with bluestone. We built a small deck off the River Room, large enough to sit on but not so wide that it obstructs our view of the river. We finished the deck in the spring after less than a month's work and were able to enjoy it all during the summer.

We still have a little way to go on the house. Two of the exterior walls are covered with painted shingles, and we'd like to replace these with clapboard, which is more in keeping with the style of the house. I still have 12 pairs of wood shutters to strip and paint for the windows. We will have to build a garage, and there is some insulating work to do in the attic. But, by and large, the place is about finished. Our renovation took exactly two years.

An item that we can't include in the total cost of the house, plus the renovation work, is the time we ourselves put into it. Since March of 1968 I have spent, with few exceptions, every weekend working on the house. I enjoy most of this work, so it might be considered a pleasure or hobby. If I didn't enjoy working with old houses I might be out playing golf, building ship models, or reconditioning old automobiles. It is difficult therefore to determine where recreation stops and work begins.

We made mistakes. Some were not so much mistakes as things we did not do because we were working on a budget and passed over certain items in favor of others. Most of the real mistakes we made occurred because we were not able to take sufficient time to consider, reconsider, then consider again some of the decisions we had to make. We now wish, for example, that we had removed some walls downstairs to open up almost the entire area, rather than having three separate rooms. We had planned to do this, but because one of the walls was a bearing wall, the budget said "no." We know now that this might not have cost more in the long run than we eventually paid to put these several rooms into shape.

Another mistake, but one we couldn't avoid, was not being on the job more frequently. We were working in the city and were not even able to get out every weekend. Consequently, things were done, or not done, that we would not have let pass had we been available every day or so.

It would have been desirable if, at the very beginning of the renovation, we had done all ripping out at one time, not only to get this messy operation out of the way, but also to expose any problems that might have been encountered later on. Renovating a house one room at a time is not the ideal arrangement. It is better to do the whole thing as a unit. But, again, this was a budgeting matter.

We made a minor mistake in having a desk and cabinets built into an alcove. This ended up costing a lot of money, and the result was not satisfactory enough to justify the expense. We would have done better to buy free-standing units, which would have cost less and could be moved if we decided to sell or wanted to use this space for some other purpose.

One thing we did that is worth passing on concerns the tile in the original bathroom. The walls were covered with a brown tile that we didn't like, but it was going to cost too much to rip the tiles out and replace them. We painted them with an epoxy paint and we were pleased with the result. This, by the way, is the only paint that you should use on tile if it is going to be exposed to moisture. It is difficult stuff to work with because you have to mix the paint with the hardener just before application and get it all on in one operation, but the results are extremely satisfactory. The epoxy paint has been on for more than a year and a half and is in good shape even around the bathtub, where it takes a beating from the shower. The only place where it did not hold was in the soap dishes, and we suspect that they still contained a film of soap when the paint was applied.

All in all, though, we love the place and definitely feel that all the time, effort, and money were more than worthwhile.

The Cobb Family:
The Main Problem Was How Best
to Use the Existing Space

Plan at left shows first floor before remodeling. Plan at right shows how space was rearranged. Major changes included removing partition to make one large room at rear of house, and moving kitchen from rear, where it obstructed view, to area formerly used as dining area. Sliding glass doors were installed along rear wall, opening onto deck and river view.

Plan of original second floor is shown at left. Right plan shows how master bedroom, bath, and closets were placed in large unfinished area. Hall width was increased by taking space from middle bedroom; large closet was added in front bedroom.

Existing fireplace was made of heavy, dark granite blocks that could not easily be replaced or remodeled.

To make granite fireplace less obtrusive, it was painted off white to match color of walls. Mantel was made from butcher's block. Floor in "river room" is slate-gray vinyl tile in brick pattern.

Photograph shows built-in dining area that was removed.

Dining area was converted into open kitchen in "river room." Existing kitchen area was at rear of house.

With kitchen moved to side, rear of living room was opened up with sliding glass doors that provide access to deck and maximum view. Grass-cloth vinyl shades control Western sun in afternoon.

Large rear upstairs room was unfinished at time of purchase.

Unfinished room is now master bedroom. River view was obtained by opening wall with large sliding glass window unit. Vinyl window shades control afternoon sun as they do on first floor. Dressing-room-bath addition makes this area a complete private suite.

The M. G. Miska Family:

Antebellum Farmhouse . . .

The house in 1951 before it was remodeled. With the house came 137 acres, a 17-acre lake, and numerous outbuildings.

BELOW: The house as it looks today. Carport is at right of main structure, and wing at left contains the kitchen and "rock room." The Miskas did a great deal of work on the place themselves.

. . . Modernized With Imagination, Planning, and Hard Labor

The Miska Family:

*"When we got the estimate for finishing off
the 'rock room,' the whole family went back
to work with renewed enthusiasm"*

Iɴ 1951 Dr. and Mrs. M. G. Miska and their two children were living
in an apartment in Chapel Hill, North Carolina. The Miskas felt, however, that apartment living did not suit their way of life, so they bought
137 acres of property. Their land had on it a 17-acre lake, with marvelous fishing—especially bass; a main house (unoccupied); several
tumbledown tenant houses that had originally been slave quarters; and
even more tumbledown outbuildings, including a smoke house and a
woodshed, none of which were worth saving.

The big house was about 60 years old, had 10 small rooms, no central
heating or modern plumbing, and electrical wiring that consisted of
one bare bulb hanging down from the center of each ceiling. The inside
walls were not plastered; most were covered with narrow wooden
boards. The upstairs rooms had been used at some point for curing
tobacco, and the wood was darkly stained, as were the windows, which
had to be cleaned with acid to remove the tobacco residue. The house
had only one closet, 1 foot deep, 3 feet wide, and about 5 feet high.
A one-story porch ran across the front and one side of the house, and
a lean-to sort of porch projected off the back.

Behind the house were an enormous brier of blackberry vines, a neighborhood dump, and, because of the sandy soil, a bog so deep that a man could stand in it and not be seen over the top.

Analyzing the situation, along with their budget, the Miskas decided that one of the tenant houses could be made livable without much investment as long as they were willing to "camp out" there while they worked on the main house. The children thought this part of the project a lark and have fond memories of the months they lived there, even though the only refinements of the house other than electricity were cold running water, and an outhouse built by Dr. Miska in the wild-plum orchard. The Miskas added windows and doors to the little house because most of the old ones were not reparable. A fireplace and an oil heater provided heat.

The Miskas' first investment when they began work on the main house was a secondhand truck with a box on the back for hauling, which they got for $175; an old drag with spikes on it for heavy raking, which cost $5; a new tractor; and a plow with a bush-and-bog disc.

They trucked in 163 loads of fill to cover up the bog and level the land around the house. With the disc and the drag, plus much hand labor, they finally cleared out the blackberry bushes next to the house and the scrub trees that covered the yard. They also removed 14 loads of old tin cans and other trash.

Until this initial clearing and cleaning up was done, the Miskas took no pictures as they never wanted to be reminded of how totally dismal the house had looked.

The remodeling has progressed in four main stages, covering four years. Here is what has been done:

1952

Rewiring. Put in septic tank. Put in small bathroom upstairs.

Put in gas heaters, but found daily living still centered about the fireplaces.

Took out wall between kitchen and larder, which had a shed roof sloping to about 5½ feet in back. Eliminated half of back porch and closed in for back entry. Took out door and two small windows from front of house that faced into sitting area of kitchen. Moved extremely old mantel from tenant (slave) house to kitchen-sitting-area fireplace.

Bricked over top of hearth, which had been cement. Also took old wood stove out of kitchen and put in electric range. Built walk-in closet between children's bedrooms and added closet in master bedroom.

Put gypsum wallboard on downstairs walls and painted.

1956

Added half bath off master bedroom. Put wallboard on upstairs walls, and in kitchen wing which had been the larder.

Took out wall that had made a small room between kitchen-sitting area and living room. Living room contained five doors—removed two outside doors and a small "cubbyhole" window strangely inset high in the wall to the right of the living-room fireplace.

Had floors sanded and discovered them to be a rare Southern pine. Added French doors at front in living room, and a single window next to the existing one so that they now appear as two pairs of windows. Refinished fireplace wall in living room, adding Douglas fir siding to minimize overhang necessitated by strange placement of old window, which was covered.

1957

Enclosed rest of back porch for pantry. Added half bath downstairs. Put storage closets across entire fireplace wall in den. All woodwork, including louvered closet doors, painted gold; walls a Williamsburg red.

Began work on "rock room" addition. This was originally to have been just a hobby room—the family has many hobbies. However, as time went on, they decided to make this a real family room that now also serves as a formal dining room. Here, the faithful old truck came into service again. First it was used to haul up the ancient 12-inch-square beams from the old tobacco barn the Miskas had torn down. Incidentally, all the lovely old beams in the house are this size. Then the Miskas started hauling the rocks from which the walls and handsome fireplace are built. First, they cleared all the rocks possible from their own land. Then they took their neighbors up on offers of rock and cleared it from their fields also. The Miska children remember these expeditions with special enjoyment, as they loved it. Every spare minute for two summers, the family hauled rocks.

The floor is bluestone, quarried in North Carolina; laying it was one of the few parts of building this room that the Miskas had done by outside help. At one point during the building, when the room was about 85 per cent completed, Dr. Miska became so tired of the project that he called in a contractor to give him an estimate for finishing it. When the estimate turned out to be $6,000, the value of the family's labor jumped so high that discouragement vanished—they all went back to work and finished it themselves, for the most part. The room was finished in 1960.

An item of special interest in this room is the fireplace crane, which came from an old log cabin on Mrs. Miska's family farm, where her ancestors had settled in the mid-1700s. Another rare piece is the German carousel horse, almost 200 years old.

The finishing of the room merited a family reunion for which guests descended from all points of the compass. An ancient apple-butter kettle of cast iron, set over an open fire in the back yard, bubbled all day with a feast of genuine Brunswick stew.

1966

The fourth stage of remodeling began when guests arrived one night at the back door and son George jumped up from the kitchen table to greet them, hitting his head on the ceiling so hard he was almost knocked out. The time had come to raise the roof. This rear portion of the kitchen area, which had been the larder, now became the main kitchen. A bay window was added at the back with a built-in window seat; a round table now sits here for family dining. The Miskas replaced the tin roof on this room and reshingled the remainder of the roofing. Mini-brick was laid on the pantry floor.

Insulated house and put in hot water heat. Carport added. Put shutters on outside windows at front of house. Also replaced upstairs window so badly shrunken with the addition of central heating that snow actually blew in along the sides in winter. Opened attic for storage. Covered ceiling board in living room with plaster board and painted. Added brick terrace in back and removed stoop.

During the years since the last remodeling, Dr. Miska had stripped off the old front and side porches, which were rotting. However, so much wind came from the front of the house that the Miskas decided to construct a new, two-story front porch for added weather protection; they used columns as the roof support. The porch floor was paved with brick at this time, also.

The upstairs bath has been modernized, and a portion of the hallway to the bath has been used to build a dressing room.

To add a library in the back of the living room, the Miskas removed the old staircase that had been located there and replaced it with a circular staircase going up from the den. Shelves were built around this "new" end of the room. The walls themselves were not changed.

During each stage of remodeling the Miskas ran into difficulty in working with the original wood of the house. It was green oak, they discovered, which, as it dried and shrank, tightened around each nail and became so hard that an electric saw would not penetrate it. One carpenter bent two crowbars trying to remove old nails. However, the reverse side of the coin is that for the same reasons, the house is extremely sturdy—a quality that first attracted the Miskas to it.

Most of the old windows and doors in the house are one hundred fifty to two hundred years old. The original builder apparently used second-hand parts wherever possible.

A white rail fence encloses the property at the back and along the drive. Mrs. Miska had her heart set on traditional white balls to top the fence posts. A lumberyard told her these would cost $12 each, a price that was out of the question since a huge number was needed. The solution was typical of the Miskas' ingenuity—they bought children's hollow rubber balls, filled them with cement, then cemented them in place on top of the fence posts and painted them white.

The Miska Family:
They Added Space and Also Changed the Existing Space

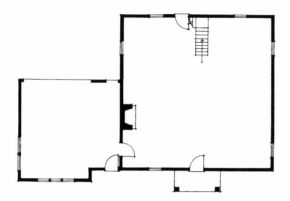

Original layout of first floor.

First floor after it had been renovated. Major change besides addition of "rock room" and carport was reworking of kitchen area to produce kitchen and kitchen-sitting room.

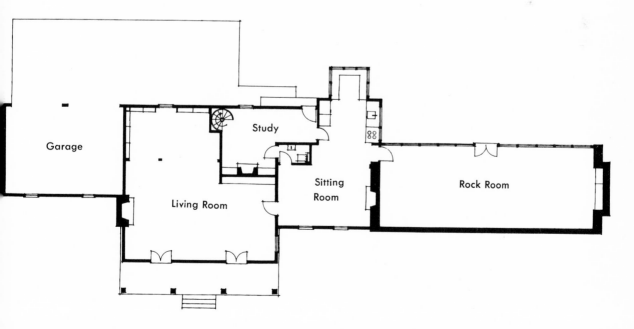

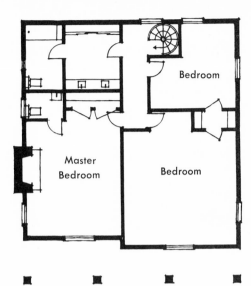

LEFT: Original plan of second floor. RIGHT: Renovated second floor. A hall was eliminated and turned into dressing room that connects with bathroom. Half bath was installed in master bedroom, and closets were added.

The "rock room" from just in front of entrance to kitchen. Old, exposed beams came from tobacco barn torn down on property. All rocks for walls and fireplace were hauled by the Miskas from their own or nearby farms.

Sitting area of kitchen. Mantel was taken from old house on property. Door partially hidden by chair goes to "rock room." Sitting area was originally the main kitchen. Beam in ceiling, at left, shows where larder once joined main house. Old well, located to left of present dishwasher, had to be capped when room was made part of main house.

Bay window added in 1966 remodeling has built-in seat; seat lid is hinged for storage.

The Jack McArdle Family:
A Nondescript Garage . . .

Nondescript garage before remodeling. Although structure appears to be attached to main house, it was actually far enough away to permit the building of a small bedroom for apartment.

. . . Becomes an Income-Producing Apartment

Living room opens onto wood deck that overlooks tidal salt marsh. Glass panels above sliding insulated glass doors add light and feeling of spaciousness. Addition of entry way enhances appearance of unit and provides room for coat closet in hall and completely private access to living quarters.

The McArdle Family:
>*"Because it was our first venture*
>*we decided to get professional help"*

Tнis is a story about a nondescript little frame garage that became an attractive, income-producing apartment, but it is best to start at the beginning of the story, and that concerns the main house on the same property.

The property that Alma and Jack McArdle bought ten years ago had little to recommend it except its location, but location can be an important consideration as to the value and desirability of a piece of property. For anyone, including the McArdles, this piece of property was almost ideal. It was located just a few minutes drive from the center of an attractive little village in Connecticut. It was close to shops and stores, the library, the post office, and schools, and at the back of the property was a view across ten acres of salt meadow with a tidal river. Large sections of the salt meadow had been deeded to a land trust so there was no possibility that it would ever be drained and made suitable for development. A view of Long Island Sound could be seen from the upstairs windows of the house.

The original OB House, two rooms, was an old farmer's cottage that was about 150 years old. Over the years additions had been made. A room here, a room there. Standing in ugly isolation was a two-story garage that had been designed and built to shelter a flivver. Only the top half of the structure was suitable as a garage, while the lower por-

394

tion, set into the ground, was used to store garden tools and miscellaneous junk. This unhappy structure bore no affinity to the house and the immediate solution short of tearing it down was to put a high hedge between the garage and the house.

For several years the McArdles mulled over the possibility of remodeling the garage into some sort of income-producing unit. As is true in most areas, the community in which they lived offered a good market for attractive rental units. The McArdles drew up a good many plans on their own, which included utilizing the lower or downstairs area of the garage as part of the projected living unit. Finally they decided that as they had never before engaged in such a venture and since they had a problem structure, it would be best to call in an architect to plan the job. They selected John Martin, A.I.A., of Middletown, Connecticut, because they had seen some of his work and liked his clean approach and design.

Mr. Martin immediately discarded the idea of using the lower part of the structure as living space because it was set below grade and would be damp and uncomfortable. True, corrective measures could be taken to make it usable but these would be expensive; with a limited budget it would not make sense to do them if some less expensive way could be found to gain the necessary extra space. It turned out that it would be less expensive to add space to the upper portion of the building. The additions consisted of a small entry hall, a coat closet, a window, and a bedroom, which connected the garage to the main house. From the front the entire remodeled garage now appears to be simply a wing of the main house.

The garage was gutted, reframed, and insulated, and walls and ceilings were covered with gypsum wallboard. The living room is 14 feet square and the ceiling goes right up to the peak of the roof. The rear wall of the living room contains a large expanse of glass to make the room appear larger than it actually is and to bring in light. The living room contains a free-standing metal fireplace with a copper hood that was custom made and picked up secondhand. The rear of the living room opens onto a small wood deck with redwood baffles to provide privacy between the two outside areas.

A full bathroom and complete kitchen, along with the bedroom, complete the living area. The basement floor contains a separate heating system for the apartment and provides storage space.

The McArdles used a general contractor to handle the entire renovation job, and the cost came to about $8,700.

All in all this was an extremely effortless renovation project once the design problem had been solved and the plans drawn. About the only difficulty the McArdles experienced was that the bathroom floor tiles were not properly installed and water from the shower was able to get under them; the floor eventually had to be relaid.

As soon as the apartment was complete, the McArdles had no difficulty in renting it. There was a healthy demand for rentals, the place was most attractive, and the price reasonable. All these factors made it possible for the McArdles to be rather selective about their tenants. This is an important consideration because in spite of the fact that Mr. Martin did all that was possible to obtain the maximum amount of privacy between the two dwellings, they are extremely close together. Therefore, the relationship between tenant and landlord must be a rather happy one. If you are an absentee landlord or if your rental unit is far away from your own house, you don't have to be too choosy about the person or people to whom you rent, but if your tenant virtually shares your back yard with you, it's nice to have someone with whom you can get along.

Despite the fact that they had some knowledge of design, the McArdles feel that they were wise to have an architect help them with their first remodeling venture. As a matter of fact, just recently they made some changes in the main house and had an architect work on the plans for this operation. Fortunately for them, they live in an area where there are a good many fine architects, many of whom find small remodeling and renovation projects fun and therefore take them on. Unfortunately, this situation does not exist everywhere and it is often difficult to get a good architect interested in a small or even not so small renovation job.

The McArdles were also wise to use a general contractor to handle the entire job. Both McArdles are busy people and therefore did not have the time necessary to supervise every step of the work, as would have been necessary if they had been their own general contractor. Even if they had been in a position to handle this end, the job would have taken a great deal longer to complete. And with rental units, the longer the job takes, the more money you lose because you rent the property.

Mrs. McArdle mentions another point that is worth passing on and that has to do with the quality of the materials used on the job. The McArdles did not cut corners on the quality of the materials used but neither did they use the most luxurious fixtures and equipment available. When you are renovating for the purpose of renting, there is a fine line to draw in relation to the matter of quality. If you use poor stuff, it will show, and if it doesn't show at first, sooner or later it will get out of order or fail to perform as required. On the other hand, if you go first class all the way and put in the very best of everything, you may have to ask a lot more than the going price of apartments to get a return on your investment. You may have to ask so much, in fact, that you just can't rent the place at all.

The McArdle Family:
How the McArdles Added Living Space
Without Using the Lower Level of the Old Garage

ABOVE: Plan showing addition of bedroom and entry hall. Bathroom and small kitchen were fitted into existing space. From the front, entire apartment appears to be simply another wing of house.

LEFT: View from living room toward salt marsh. Redwood baffles on either side of deck give privacy for entertaining and sunning. Hood and chimney of metal fireplace is seen at right.

Fred Schurecht: An Old Horse Barn . . .

It was just an ordinary old horse barn that had seen better days.

. . . Turns into an Exciting,
Livable House

The original barn has now become an exciting, comfortable, contemporary house. Existing walls were faced with stone, and a large shed dormer was installed in the room. Sliding glass doors in the dormer open onto a balcony and provide light for the second level of the house.

Fred Schurecht:

"Old barns are great fun projects"

THE SIGN nailed on the weathered siding, "3 Acres Barn For Sale" probably did not attract the attention of everyone who passed by, but it did catch the eye of a Fred Schurecht, an architect. He was impressed by the size and the design of the barn and decided that it would be a worthwhile investment to buy the property, remodel the barn into a striking house, and sell it. So he bought the property and went to work on it.

Regarding barns, Mr. Schurecht says: "Barns are simple structures. They're not a problem. It's really just a question of maintaining the character of the original building. Doing over a simple building like a barn is a lot easier than working on an old house because there is very little to remove. You start with a shell. Old barns are great fun projects —they don't have the problems normally associated with remodeling an old house. On this project that was no major problem other than cleaning out the manure."

The height of this barn was such that Mr. Schurecht was able to provide three levels for the interior. On the first, or ground, level he put the garage and a large recreation room. The second level contains the living room, dining room, country kitchen (really two rooms, because one portion is a true living area with armchairs and a television set), and a master bedroom and bath. On the third floor are additional bedrooms and a bath.

400

The original exterior wood siding was covered with fieldstone, but some of the wood on the upper portions remains exposed. Along the front, the roof was opened up so that a large shed dormer could be installed. The dormer opens onto a balcony that runs along the front of the house. The roof and the gable ends were covered with cedar shakes. Large glass areas were installed to provide light to the interior.

Mr. Schurecht likes to use fine old materials when he can find them and where they will produce the results he wishes to achieve. The entry doors were taken from an old Chicago mansion that was being demolished; some of the other doors were also taken from old structures. Mr. Schurecht found a lovely old wrought-iron railing and used this on the stairs that run from the ground floor to the third floor. He used many old shutters on the interior of the house because they give "such control and play of light."

A smaller barn, situated near the road, was dismantled during the remodeling, and the siding from this was used for the walls of the living room. The living room has a cathedral ceiling and most of the ceilings throughout the house are beamed, in keeping with the basic style of the structure. Slate was used extensively for floors throughout the house, but the living-room floor is made of random planks of dark-stained walnut. The massive fieldstone chimney and fireplace extend up through the house.

After nine months Mr. Schurecht had finished the remodeling. He then rented the house for a few years and finally sold it to its present owners, Mr. and Mrs. Jerome Robbins. The Robbins have two children.

Mrs. Robbins decorated the house herself. She has many antiques and some extremely modern pieces as well. The house is a study in contrast, French antiques against barn-siding walls in the living room. Mrs. Robbins has always had French antiques and was skeptical about using them in this house but she says they fit in beautifully. The living room as well as the master bedroom is done in the French mood, whereas the recreation room and the kitchen are ultramodern.

Mrs. Robbins has used nature's colors throughout the house because "The house calls for it—the house has so much of the outdoors indoors," she says. She has used beiges, browns, golds, yellows, and soft oranges.

The Robbins are highly enthusiastic over the layout of the house and report that it functions perfectly for their way of life. The arrangement of the second floor, with the living room, dining room, kitchen, and master bedroom and bath, is an extremely convenient one although it does, Mr. Robbins complains, "make the refrigerator just a little too handy." With the children using the third-floor bedrooms, Mr. and Mrs. Robbins feel that they can entertain whenever they wish without fear of disturbing the youngsters.

We will never learn one fascinating piece of information about this project, however, and that is how many people out looking for property saw this old horse barn and said, "What in the world could you do with that old place except use it for horses?"

RIGHT: Fred Schurecht designed the interior to provide three levels. The first level consists of the entry hall, recreation room, utility room, bath, and small bedroom, plus the garage. The second level contains a complete living unit with a master bedroom and bath, large kitchen with a living area, dining room, and living room. The living-room ceiling is formed by the roof. The third floor, with two bedrooms, bath, and a TV room, or study, makes an ideal area for children.

Fred Schurecht:
How the Old Horse Barn Provided
Enough Space for Three Levels

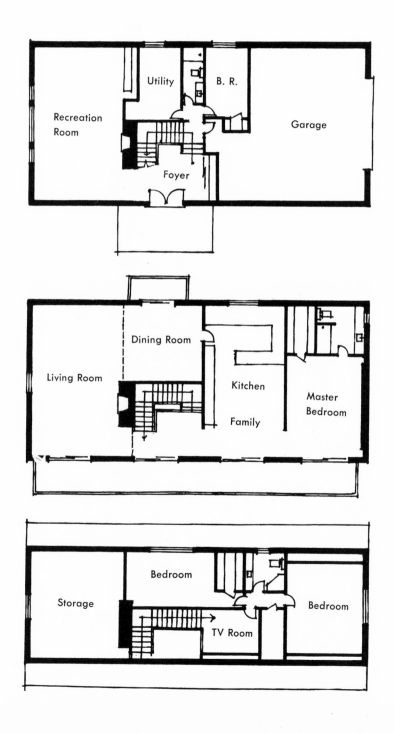

The Goodspeed Family: They
Transformed Part of an Iron Mine . . .

Brick buildings of iron mine as they appeared shortly after the mine closed down at the early part of the century. INSERT: The Goodspeed house as it looked when they began work on it. Roof and floors had been removed for their lumber some years before.

. . . into an Attractive Dwelling

Except for the outside walls, the structure required complete rebuilding. Windows were installed, along with floors and roof. Mr. Goodspeed did much of the work himself. Building at left is Hovis property.

The Goodspeed Family:

"It was the only house I had ever seen
that had real trees growing in it"

AROUND THE TURN of the century, someone established an iron mine in Westchester County, New York, and they did it first class. A complex of brick buildings with walls 18 inches thick was constructed below the mine shaft to process the iron ore, but apparently there wasn't much iron ore at the bottom of the shaft and the operation went bankrupt. Over the years, some of the buildings were torn down, some were partially dismantled for lumber, and some just fell apart. One was used for a time as a barn for cattle and horses, so the property became known as "a barn."

Shortly after the end of World War II, Al Goodspeed and Keith Hovis, who had known each other in Chicago, were looking for a place to buy and renovate and they heard that a certain "barn" was available. They took a look and found the iron-mine complex. The property consisted of about 7 acres of land and two buildings attached by a common wall. One of the buildings was in poor shape; the other was in awful shape, with only walls—no roof. The property was only a short distance from the local village and only a little over an hour by car or train to New York City. Goodspeed and Hovis bought it jointly, and fixed up the better of the two buildings.

A few years after buying the property, Al Goodspeed married and brought his wife, Janna, out to look at what was to become their future home—the unimproved building. "It was the only house I had ever seen that had real trees growing inside it. And it was full of water," Mrs. Goodspeed remembers. But just the same, she was all for the project and so they set off to make it into a house.

Al and Janna moved into the renovated building with Keith Hovis and started to work on the other one. It took them an entire summer of hard work—seven days a week from morning until night—just to make the place livable.

"Al worked from the bottom up," Mrs. Goodspeed says. "He did the floors, then the walls, then the balcony, and finally the roof."

Al Goodspeed did almost all the work on the place himself, with the exception of the wiring and some of the plumbing. While he had never quite done this sort of work before (how many of us have?), he had taken some courses at college in architecture and design, and as a boy had worked summers in a woodworking shop. "You must remember," he says, "that this was right after I had got out of the army and the army makes you rather used to rugged work and a rugged life."

Al and Janna Goodspeed designed the house to fit their very special needs. The lower level consists of studios and workshops. Janna works in ceramics, and her studio is equipped with kilns and other equipment necessary for this art form. Al Goodspeed paints but also works in wood and does design and light residential construction. The lower level is therefore a busy work area.

On the second floor a huge living room runs the length of the house. At the front of this room are three huge glass windows. Al Goodspeed built a fireplace in a deep recess at the far end of the living room but finally ripped it out because "there just wasn't enough space for the fireplace and for people." He built the present one himself a few months ago, "a luxury project—there were other things probably more essential but we love a fireplace."

Toward the rear of the living room is an open kitchen where Mrs. Goodspeed, who likes to cook and to bake delicious bread, can work in her kitchen and still share in the conversation going on in the living room around the fireplace, which is located on the wall opposite the kitchen serving counter. Above the kitchen area is a long balcony with bedrooms and bath. Al Goodspeed built a projection off to the side of the house at this level to provide additional space.

The property contained an abundance—almost an overabundance of old bricks—and these were used for much of the renovation work. Al Goodspeed also picked up a great many secondhand materials. The owner of an adjoining piece of property cut down a large number of sizable trees to improve his view, and Al cut these up into lengths and took the lengths to a saw mill to be cut into planks and boards. This wood was used for flooring, cabinets, and other work throughout the house. The Goodspeeds used these rough-sawn planks for the floor of the living room and then had a floor-sanding party. "The floor sander ran almost continuously for a couple of days. As soon as one person got tired, another would take over."

Needless to say, the Goodspeeds ran into interesting problems with this renovation project. One involved money. Al and Janna couldn't seem to interest anyone in giving them a construction mortgage, so when they needed financing they had to use home-improvement loans. The first of these went to purchase necessary lumber and building materials. The next one was for the plumbing and heating, and the last was for miscellaneous work. Because the house is on a hill, installing a septic tank became something of a challenge. Al Goodspeed found in a Government booklet ("We used a lot of these booklets on this project") a description of how a septic tank could be "hung" on the side of a hill. Eventually he convinced the local building department that this was a workable arrangement and it allowed the tank to be installed.

Another major problem occurred when it came time to put the posts —8 inches by 24 feet long—into place to support the roof. This was solved by Mrs. Goodspeed's father who, as a sculptor, knew how to make a rig that would hoist a heavy object into position.

"The roof was the worst part of the whole project," says Janna. "It was 18 feet off the ground, and every time Al was up there trying to lift the heavy beams into place I was scared to death. But we love the high ceiling. It lets us use an 18-foot high Christmas tree. Last year we had a tree from our own property."

The Goodspeeds had another problem with local bureaucrats when it was decided to divide the property between Mr. Hovis and the Goodspeeds. The zoning regulations called for a minimum distance of 30 feet between two buildings owned by separate individuals and the town fathers couldn't seem to understand at first that the regulation would be difficult to obey in the case of brick structures that shared a common wall. The zoning people finally went in person to the property to take a look at the situation; eventually they granted a variance. The Goodspeeds own their own house with three acres, Mr. Hovis has his house and three acres, and one acre is owned jointly.

The Goodspeeds have three children. All of them grew up in this house and love it as much as do their parents. "One of the things I like best about this place is that it is so flexible," Mrs. Goodspeed says. "We can and do change it to fit our present needs. As the children grow older, we arrange the space differently from the way it was when they were very young. They love it and so do most young people. It is an exciting house.

"It will never be finished," Mrs. Goodspeed comments. "Al and I would be bored to tears if there wasn't always something that had to be done. It helps keep the place alive."

The Goodspeed Family:
They Made a Seemingly
Impossible Structure into a Home

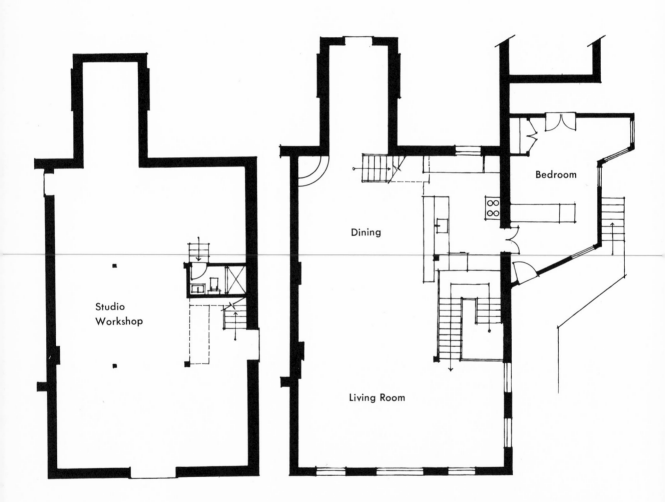

LEFT: Lower level has front entry stairs that go to the second floor, which is living area of house. Al and Janna Goodspeed use lower level for studio and workshop. RIGHT: Second level has kitchen and a wing that was added to provide bedroom on this floor.

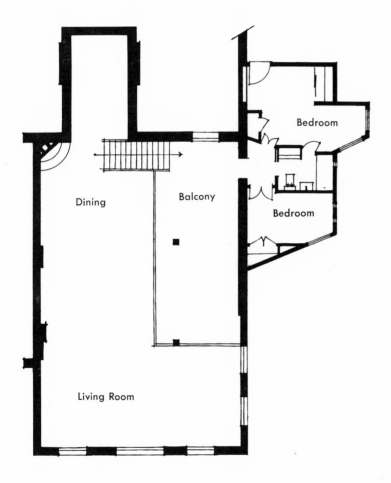

Balcony directly above kitchen provides a sleeping and dressing area; addition beyond it provides space for two bedrooms and bath. Additions were installed by Mr. Goodspeed.

View from front of living room, showing the kitchen area at right and stairs leading up to balcony. Fireplace was built by Mr. Goodspeed.

RIGHT: Exterior of winery as it is today. Windows have been added and enlarged, and roof recovered with wood shingles. Brick chimney and wood-shingle entry way complement beauty of natural stone and walls. Sloping loft has been attractively landscaped over period of years.

The V. O. Chase Family:
A California Winery . . .

The La Questa Winery as it looked in 1949 before Mr. and Mrs. V. O. Chase bought it. Structure was empty except for a partial loft and shelves used for wine storage. Large wooden doors where trucks backed up to load wine opened up into what is now the living room. These doors have been replaced by paneled-glass French doors with natural wood casings.

. . . Is Now a Comfortable Home

The Chase Family:
*"The 18-inch walls make the house
warm in winter, cool in summer"*

Whand Mr. and Mrs. V. O. Chase went out to look for a house, like so many others, they went looking for a house that they could remodel, but also something that would have special charm for them. Eventually they came to an old stone structure that had been built in 1898. It had originally been part of a winery and was the building where the wine was stored. Several frame buildings that were also part of the winery had been torn down some years earlier.

The old wine-storage building had been purchased several times since the winery had ceased operation, but nothing had been done with it. Apparently the 18-inch thickness of the walls had presented problems for the previous owners and they had just given up on remodeling the structure. But the building appeared to be in sound condition and the site was beautiful.

The Chases decided that this piece of property was precisely what they wanted and so they bought it. Mr. Chase, who is an architect, formulated a simple and effective solution to the problem of installing an interior inside the shell of the building. He simply built a frame house within the stone building. The loft and the old shelves used to store the wine were ripped out and replaced by this framework, which was installed in back of the living room and runs from the floor to the roof.

Besides serving as a base for the interior wall coverings, the framework supports the joists for the second floor and also provides added support to the roof. Mr. Chase selected this approach because it seemed the most practical, but he was also concerned over the difficulty of hanging the joists for the second floor from the masonry as well as the resulting lateral pressure on the walls, which might cause them to bulge. With the interior framework, these problems were eliminated. The framework carries all the weight, and the masonry is simply an exterior wall-covering—18 inches thick.

The building lacked both plumbing and heat. The Chases' greatest renovation problem, however, involved adding and enlarging windows and installing doors. The stone walls had originally been laid up with lime mortar, which is not as strong as modern cement mortar. When one stone was removed, it usually meant that a good many others came out along with it. Each time an opening in the walls was made or enlarged, the top of the opening had to be reinforced with 6-inch-by-6-inch angle irons to hold the stones above the opening in place.

In the course of clearing out the property, the Chases made a great find—14 old beams that had once been a part of the frame wine-press building. These fir beams, 3 inches by 14 inches and 33 feet in length, were as dense and as hard as steel. Mr. Chase used them as joists for framing the second floor, and the wood was so tough that even a heavy-duty electric power saw groaned when it bit into the wood.

To avoid the possibility that water might penetrate the old mortar and damage the interior walls and floor, a thick bed of gravel was put down to serve as a base for a new concrete-slab floor. When the concrete slab was poured, it was not brought up to the masonry wall. Instead, a space of several inches was left between the edge of the slab and the masonry. This space was covered by the interior wall material. If water should leak through the masonry wall it will run down the inside surface of the wall and into the gravel base beneath the slab and not damage either the interior wall covering or the flooring applied over the concrete slab.

The interior space on the first floor was divided into a large living room with an 18½-foot ceiling to the roof, a dining room, kitchen, lavatory, and utility room. These rooms were built under the new second level and behind the living room. A fireplace with a brick chimney was built in the living room and the large wooden doors that had facilitated the wine-loading operation in the past were replaced with paneled-glass doors leading outside. A front entry hall was built to provide access to the living room, dining room, and kitchen. A stairway runs from the entry hall to a balcony on the second level, which overlooks the living room. This open balcony is used as a den. Three bedrooms and a bath open off a long hall behind the balcony.

The living room floor consists of wood parquet laid over the concrete slab. Floors in the other rooms on this level are covered with vinyl asbestos. The upstairs rooms have hardwood floors.

Mr. and Mrs. Chase have lived in their renovated wine-storage shed for many years and are still delighted with it. It is perfect for them in every respect and they have found one great advantage to those 18-inch-thick walls: "They make the place delightfully comfortable all year round," Mr. Chase said, "cool in summer and warm in winter."

FACING PAGE TOP: Plan shows how first-floor space was apportioned in the old wine-storage building. Living-room area was left essentially unchanged but included addition of a fireplace and replacing of the old wooden doors. A new entry way was added, providing access to living room and to dining and kitchen areas. An outside entrance to the kitchen is convenient to a downstairs lavatory, and to the utility room, which had been located on the first floor because there was no basement. Stairway running from front entrance goes up to second-level open balcony, bedrooms, and bathroom.

FACING PAGE BOTTOM: Partial second floor utilizes space simply and conveniently. Stairway runs to open balcony, which is used as a den and extends over living room. Bedrooms and bath open off hallway. Hardwood floors were installed on this level, with exception of bathroom floor, which is vinyl tile. Bedrooms have ample closets, and each has windows overlooking the pleasant grounds.

The Chase Family:
Mr. Chase Built a Frame House
within the Stone Building

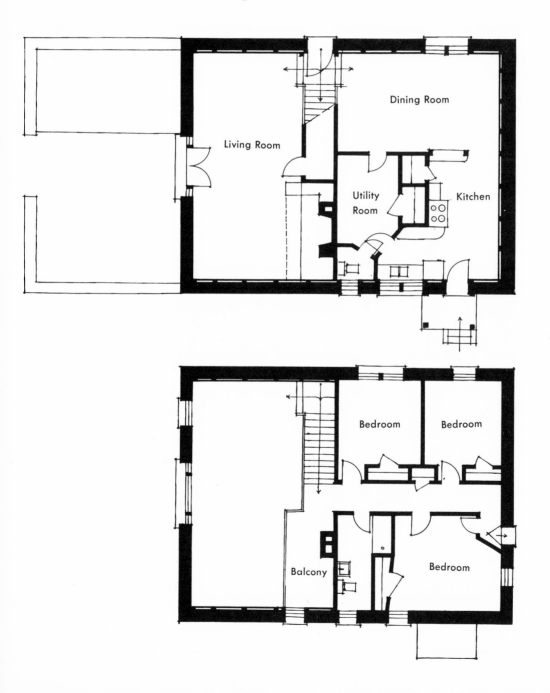

The Ernest Curtin Family:
They Transformed
a Lampshade Factory . . .

The old factory building before it was renovated.

. . . into a Charming Residence

As it looks today. The front entry was placed where the old fire escape had been located. The original factory belltower and hoist at roof peak were retained. Window trim was painted same color as outside walls to make windows appear smaller.

The Curtin Family:

*"We have water, electricity, and a furnace
in the basement. What more do we need?"*

WHEN ORLEAN Stone Curtin and her husband decided to look for a country house, their first idea was to find a barn or an old house that they could remodel. They also wanted an attractive location—a view, preferably of water.

They started their hunt in the office of a real estate broker, plowing through the little cards that described the property available. One of these cards concerned a dilapidated mill or factory, but the broker quickly passed over that one because who would want an old, dilapidated mill?

The Curtins spent the rest of that April day trudging through the houses that seemed interesting. When they had seen nothing that captured their interest, Mrs. Curtin said "What about the mill?" The broker demurred. He was new in the business, and it turned out he wasn't even sure just where the mill was located or how to find it. Mrs. Curtin insisted. After stopping several times to get directions they finally found the mill. It didn't look like much. It was all overgrown with vines, trees, and shrubs, and seemingly in hopeless condition. There didn't even seem to be any way of getting into it. Finally they climbed up a fire escape and crawled in through a window.

The one positive statement that could be made about the interior was that it was vast. The last occupant had been a lampshade manufacturer. The floors were coated with plastic; huge heaters hung down from the ceilings along with naked bulbs in wire baskets. But a view from the window was all Mrs. Curtin needed to see. Below was a mill stream, to the left a river, and beyond a waterfall.

"I'll take it," she told the two bewildered men.

"Are you out of your mind?" was her husband's answer.

"Of course not. We have water, electricity, and a furnace in the basement. What more do we need?"

And so they bought the property. It consisted of the mill, 27 acres that included a lake of about 20 acres, and a small grist mill.

Mrs. Curtin is a well-known professional interior designer who functions professionally under the name of Orlean Stone. She worked with the architect, P. Whitney Webb, in planning the renovation of the mill. The problem they faced was to take this vast amount of space and arrange it so that the interior would remain spacious yet at the same time provide an air of warmth and comfort. This goal they achieved, and the result is a unique and charming house.

Little was done to the exterior. A front door was installed where the fire escape had been located, and the exterior was painted. As the house was originally to be used only as a summer place, the landscaping was planned for easy maintenance—pachysandra, ivy, and perennials.

After the main house had been renovated, Mrs. Curtin turned her attention to the grist mill. The grist mill is now rented as a house.

The Curtins paid a modest amount for the property, which has increased tremendously in value. Perhaps one of the reasons why they were able to get property for such a small amount was, as Mrs. Curtin later learned, that no one in the neighborhood had ever thought of buying it for residential use. They saw it only as a mill or factory and had never even considered turning it into a house. Mrs. Curtin realized, however, that the space, which had overwhelmed so many other people, was an element that could be manipulated to provide exactly what she wanted. This ability to visualize is the key to getting a really outstanding buy in an OB Dream House. If you can see the potential where others can't, you have a distinct advantage. If you can look at an old mill, a garage, or a warehouse and not see them as what they are today but what they can become, you are going to find something that will be perfect for you.

The Curtin Family:
They Wanted to Arrange an Interior
that Would Retain the Feeling of Space
Yet Provide an Air of Warmth and Comfort

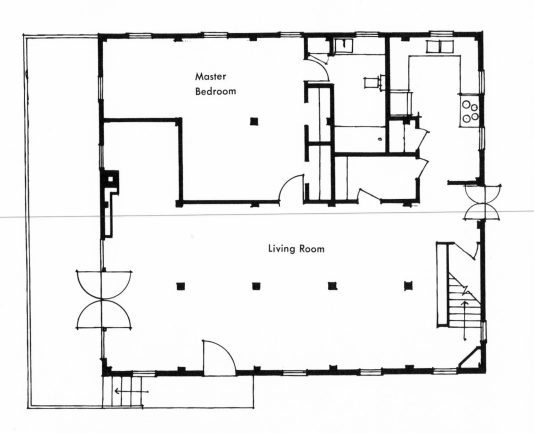

Space on first floor was arranged to provide a larger living room with dining area, adjacent to kitchen. Double doors at opposite end of living room open into terrace overlooking pond. First floor also includes master bedroom and bath, plus good closet and storage space.

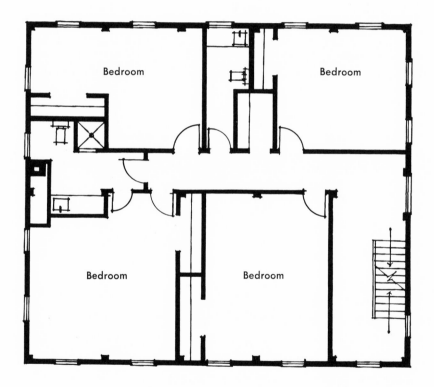

The second floor contained enough space for four bedrooms—three with cross ventilation. Space for a lavatory was made between two bedrooms, and a full bath is at end of the hall.

The Alton O'Neil Family:
A Rooming House . . .

The Alton O'Neil house as it looked when first purchased from Brown University several years ago. The Victorian-vintage, 17-room mansion had been used as a rooming house for many years.

... Comes Back to Life
as a Gracious Home

With porches removed and fire escapes scrapped, the house has regained its former Victorian elegance. Old brick wall that supported porches was cut down and makes an attractive planting area on front and side of dwelling. Part of porch was retained as a portico at front entrance. House was resided with aluminum clapboard.

The O'Neil Family:

"It was really the only piece of property on the market that was in a decent neighborhood"

IT MAY be true that people buy big old houses mainly because they need the sort of space that can only be found in these monsters, but this is not the only reason. Mr. and Mrs. Alton J. O'Neil bought their present house—all 17 rooms and three fireplaces—simply because they needed a place in which to live.

It was necessary for the O'Neils to move from New York to Providence, Rhode Island, at just about the worst time of the year to go house hunting—the period between Thanksgiving and Christmas. Few pieces of property were on the market, and after spending considerable time looking about, the O'Neils finally settled on a house that was just about the only one available in a decent neighborhood. The property was owned by Brown University and consisted of a 17-room main house plus a large carriage house and two town houses attached to each other.

The main house and the two town houses had been converted into rooming houses. Each of the town houses contained 13 rooms. The O'Neils, having recently gone through the successful remodeling of a town house in Brooklyn, saw the potential in the Brown property. They were able to get it at a rather moderate price because it was somewhat run down, and the size of the undertaking had obviously discouraged other interested buyers.

The O'Neils' first step was a rapid fixing up of the third floor of the main building so that they could at least sleep in the house. Until they were able to get the kitchen installed, they had to eat in restaurants.

Having done a renovation job before, Mrs. O'Neil was determined to supervise this one. She knew from experience that if the renovation was going to be a success, she would have to be on hand every minute of every working day.

The major changes on the exterior of the main house were removal of fire escapes that had been installed when the house was converted into a rooming house, and removal of the porches around the first and second floors in order to clean up the exterior appearance and bring in more sunlight. The brick wall around the first-floor porch was cut down to form a planter that runs along the front and side of the house. The exterior siding was in poor condition so the house was re-sided with white aluminum clapboard siding.

Extensive changes were made in the interior. About 15 partitions and partial walls were removed to create better space and to reduce the number of rooms from 17 to 14. Some additional partitions were also installed. A wall in the kitchen had to be removed, and three windows in this area were sealed off to provide space for cabinets. Two fireplaces were also added—one in the dining room and the other in the kitchen.

Most of the existing plaster on the walls and ceilings was in such poor shape that it had to be removed. Mrs. O'Neil estimates that about 80 per cent of the plaster had to be removed, and that is a lot of plaster. Some of it, she feels, might have been saved but she preferred not to take the chance that after the job was completed, some of the plaster surfaces would decide to give up.

The wooden stair rail between first and second floors was replaced with a wrought-iron railing Mrs. O'Neil had picked up from an ancient mansion that was being dismantled.

The first floor now contains a reception room, living room, dining room, kitchen, family room, and powder room. On the second floor is a large master bedroom with a fireplace, bathroom, and dressing room. There are also three other bedrooms on the floor, and one of these has been converted into an office. On the third floor are four more bedrooms and a bathroom.

Mrs. O'Neil did the design work for the renovation project and also acted as her own general contractor. She selected her subcontractors and supervised the entire operation. One of her chief problems, and a common one, was trying to find competent helpers who would come when they said they would come and stick around until the job was finished.

During the course of the renovation work a few happy surprises occurred. When the time came to do the alteration work on the plumbing system, it turned out that the existing pipes were of lead. This was at a time when the price of scrap lead was high and the price of copper tubing relatively low. The money the O'Neils received from the scrap lead helped defray the cost of installing the new copper tubing. A large, solid, copper hot-water tank had to be replaced, and this also brought in quite a few pennies as scrap.

When it came time to tackle the dining room, Mrs. O'Neil discovered that beneath the paint lay lovely solid walnut paneling. It took her about six months, working when time permitted, to strip off some 12 coats of paint and bring the paneling back to its original condition.

In the four years that they have owned the property, Mrs. O'Neil has also renovated the carriage house and the two town houses. The carriage house was turned into an apartment that the O'Neils rent out. The two town houses were converted back into single-family residences, and after these had been rented for a time they were sold to two separate families.

This entire project has been a fairly large operation. It required considerable investment of money and time, but the O'Neils are quite satisfied over the outcome. Their ambitious renovation project of an existing OB House provided them with not only a convenient and attractive home but with the profitable rental and sale of the adjoining property.

FACING PAGE TOP: First-floor plan of house before renovation.

FACING PAGE BOTTOM: Remodeled front entry leads into entrance hall, where stairs go up to second floor. The fireplace was retained in the reception room at right, which leads into spacious family room created by removing two walls and sealing a doorway. New supporting beam was installed after walls were removed and all the heating pipes boxed in. Large bay window overlooks side lawn, and since removal of old porches, room is light and cheerful. Plan shows points at which partitions were removed in kitchen and also resetting of cabinets and appliances.

The O'Neil Family:
Planning Kept Changes to a Minimum

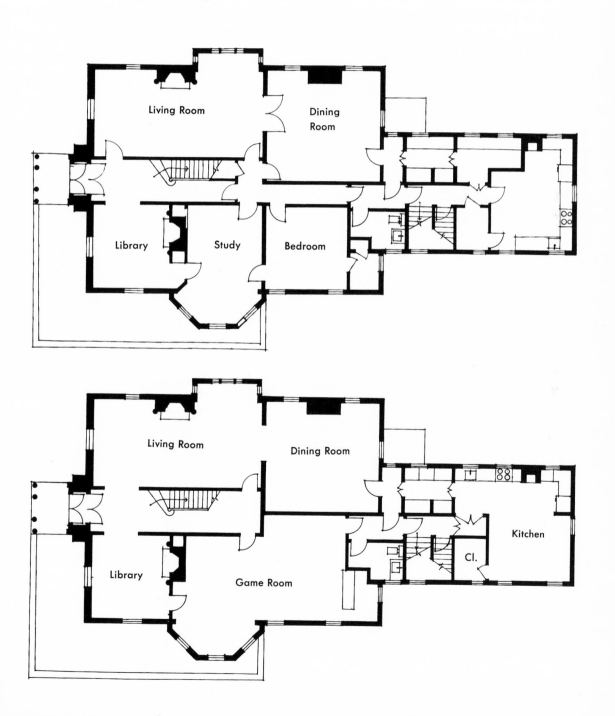

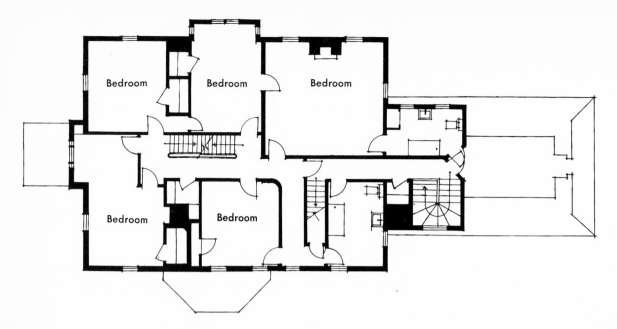

Second-floor plan as it was when the O'Neils purchased house.

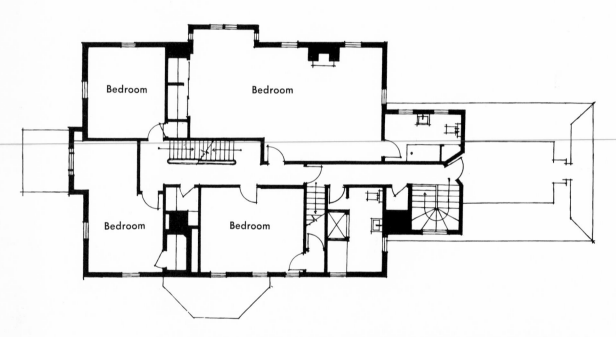

Second-floor plan after extensive alterations. Thirty-five-foot master bedroom was created by removing wall between two bedrooms. Master bath was renovated and storage space added. Door was rehung to swing into bath. Small hall was eliminated and wall removed to enlarge room over bay window. One door was sealed off in this room to create better wall space. Another guest room and bath, plus an office for Mr. O'Neil, complete second floor. Third floor has four large bedrooms and bath.

Mrs. O'Neil in the gold-and-white living room, which was completely re-decorated but underwent no major structural changes. Original fireplace and paneling were retained and repainted. Dining-room paneling, which can be glimpsed through archway, was covered with 12 layers of paint, which Mrs. O'Neil stripped down to the original wood, a rich, mellow walnut. Fireplace of old brick was added in dining room.

Two partitions were removed to enlarge kitchen and provide space for informal dining area. Raised barbecue pit was installed in brick fireplace and new brick-pattern floor covering installed. Windows beside fireplace were blocked so that new cabinets and range could be installed.

FACING PAGE TOP: The "innocuous house" as it looked at the time Mr. Danhausen bought it.

FACING PAGE BOTTOM: A dramatic face lifting. To obtain quiet and privacy from the busy street, windows along the front were filled in with brick. Front entry was moved and a large area of glass was installed over it. At left is the outside spiral staircase that leads to the second floor of the house. This floor is used by Mr. Danhausen as a living room, dining room, and kitchen.

Eldon Danhausen:
A Neglected
Three-Story Row House . . .

. . . Gets a Face-Lift — Inside and Out

433

Eldon Danhausen:

>   *"I tailored the whole environment to my particular needs"*

THIS IS the story of a unique renovation project.

Eldon Danhausen is a well-known sculptor. He wanted a new place in the city of Chicago that would provide him not only with living quarters but also a studio. "This house appealed to me for several reasons," he recalls. "It was an innocuous house, a neglected house—a house that was not built with the beauty with which many of the row houses were constructed. A little ticky-tacky house. I didn't like the idea of desecrating something that was beautiful. It would have broken my heart to strip down a beautiful house, but this was a simple, rectangular shell. Once I removed all the tin coffering that was on the building, I ended up with a simple box . . . simplicity within a cubic space that I was going to use."

Mr. Danhausen also bought this particular house because he believed it to be a practical investment. The property included a front house, or main house, a coach house, and a garden.

The main house is three stories high. The old interior was torn out so that only the shell remained. Then the interior was reconstructed to Mr. Danhausen's exact specifications. As a sculptor, Mr. Danhausen is primarily interested in materials and textures, and all the interior floors and some of the walls were made of poured concrete and terrazzo. In other words, the floor goes right up the walls, and this was one of the areas where Mr. Danhausen had a little trouble in getting his views across to the mason. Some of the other walls are covered with 2-by-10-inch rough-sawn planks that were salvaged when the interior of the house was ripped out.

The exterior of the house was modified at the front to eliminate windows that opened out onto a busy, noisy street and to give a sense of complete privacy. The old brick was painted white.

Mr. Danhausen did not always find it a simple matter, however, to get his ideas translated into action: "One of the problems was getting tradesmen to vary from their usual way of doing things. For instance, asking a stone mason to build a completely round room with floor and walls of concrete aggregate—he felt it was an unbelievable request."

The house contains very little furniture. Some has been sculptured right out of the concrete.

The top floor was remodeled into an apartment that Mr. Danhausen rents. He has two floors for himself and the lower floor, about three feet below ground level, contains the bedrooms and the upper floor is the living area.

The coach house was remodeled to provide space for two studios. Mr. Danhausen uses one and rents the other. He finds it satisfying to have a studio within the general complex, but far enough away so that he can walk to another environment.

When asked how the project has worked out, Mr. Danhausen says, "I wouldn't change anything. In fact, I tailored the whole environment to my particular needs—so much so that it would be extremely difficult to sell the house."

This, of course, is always a problem when you build something or remodel to meet your exact specifications. You must ask yourself whether you would prefer to have a home that isn't quite right for you but that you can always sell in a hurry if you want to, or whether you prefer a house that is just perfect for you in every respect—and take the chance that if you do wish to sell, you can find a buyer with tastes very similar to yours.

Mr. Danhausen has designed and built something that is perfect for him, and the pleasure he gets out of this obviously outweighs his concern over being able to find a ready buyer for the property.

Eldon Danhausen:
The Old Interior Was Torn Out, Then Reconstructed
to the Owner's Exact Specifications

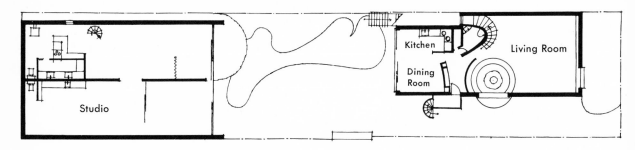

Interior of house was gutted and then rebuilt. Bedrooms are on lower floor, which is set a few feet below street level. Upper floor is rental apartment. Garden separates house from studio at rear.

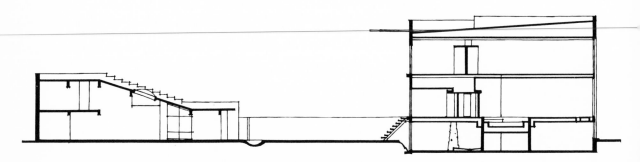

Cross section of house and studio.

FACING PAGE BOTTOM: The mill as it looks today. Siding has been stained with creosote to reduce upkeep and give the place a rustic appearance. New sliding glass doors open into gallery on ground floor.

The Jack Witt Family: An Old Grist Mill . . .

The old grist mill at the time it was purchased by Jack and Nancy Witt.

. . . Now Their Dream House and Studios

The Witt Family:

"I just took a deep breath and looked around
and knew this place was ours"

BOTH Jack and Nancy Witt have lived in cities all their lives, but neither the pace nor the environment of city life really suited them. Both are artists, primarily sculptors, although they also draw, make prints, and work in related art forms.

When they became engaged to be married and started looking for a place to live, their first requirement was ample studio space, and they had high hopes of finding the solution to their needs somewhere out in the country. Consulting a friend who was a real estate broker in the Richmond, Virginia, area, Jack suggested that he find them a sturdy old barn that they could remodel. The broker had no listing of property with a suitable barn, but he did have listed an old grist mill, built around the turn of the century, on 26 acres of rolling farmland near Ashland, Virginia.

The broker drove Nancy and Jack out to see Cross Mill on a cold morning late in the winter of 1966, and it was love at first sight. As Nancy says now: "It's lucky that the weather was cold because this prevented us from seeing the rats and snakes and from noticing the smell of rotting grain that warm weather brought out soon afterward."

Filled with enthusiasm, the Witts thought little about the problem of removing the vast quantities of machinery that filled a good portion of the old mill, or of the fact that the structure had neither heat nor water and only a minimum of electrical wiring. In fact, they were so optimistic that they were sure they could get the mill ready to move into three months later.

The price was right, and artistically the land pleased them with its 8-acre pond, its trees, and rolling fields. The Witts felt that two small tenant houses, pleasantly situated on a hill, were an added bonus and could eventually be converted into guest quarters. They didn't bother to investigate any other property that might have been for sale. This place was perfect with two large high-ceilinged rooms at one end of the mill that were ideal for their separate studios, and the spacious rooms adjoining, which they would turn into living quarters. Not counting the loft, they hade 13,240 square feet of space under the roof!

Once the Witts had taken title to Cross Mill, they returned for a critical inspection of what needed to be done and became slightly appalled at what they had taken on. While the grist-mill machinery was workable, there wasn't exactly a thriving market for it, and any buyer they could find would have to remove it without tearing down the building. Nancy and Jack did finally find a buyer, but he insisted on being given a year's time to remove it. The sale netted enough to pay for about two-thirds of the cost of installing a heating system. The three-months' renovation schedule disappeared entirely when the plumber and heating and electrical contractors arrived to give them a cost estimate on the work involved.

The magnificent amount of space the Witts had so ardently admired at first sight began to hang like the proverbial millstone around their necks. To plaster one room 36 feet by 48 feet (and they had six such rooms) required almost as much labor and materials as to plaster an average-sized house. The same applied to patching and refinishing flooring, painting, and furnishing the house.

At this point the Witts took a second look at the tenant houses. These were not luxurious but they did appear to be habitable, at least by comparison with the mill, and could be fixed up at modest cost. Since both places were small, the Witts joined them with a breezeway and used them as temporary living quarters. The concrete-block additions to the mill were quickly converted to studios, so that each of the Witts could have a place to work. A skylight was added to Nancy's studio, and Jack built himself a foundry in his studio for cast-bronze work and put in welding equipment, which they both needed. They also began cleaning the place up, which was almost a full-time career. The mill had been idle for 18 months, so that mingled with the vast amount of old grain there was plenty of dust and cobwebs.

The renovation work had to be a stop-and-go process involving periods of neglect so that once a certain phase had been completed Nancy and Jack could earn money to pay for the next stage. Essential repairs often had to take precedence over mere beautification. The tin roof, for example, provoked a constant battle with leaks, particularly around the series of vents which had attracted dust and excess flour in the air. The combination of wheat flour and tin, the Witts discovered, forms a corrosive chemical that will eat through the metal roof. Where new damage becomes visible, they patch, and Jack thinks he finally has the problem under control.

To preserve the exterior siding without the huge investment that would have been required for a paint job, the Witts stained it with creosote. This gives the old siding a warm, dappled-brown finish.

They stripped off the old loading platform and its porchlike roof, which extended across a good share of the front of the building. The heavy mill doors were replaced by sliding glass doors set at ground level. The ground level was raised about 4 feet, however, because it had been scooped out to provide easier access for horse-drawn wagons and, later, trucks. The wide walk from the driveway to the front of the house was paved with cobblestones the Witts got from the Richmond urban renewal authorities.

This exterior renovation work proceeded piecemeal along with the interior work. Three local carpenters were retained for the interior work, and both Jack and Nancy worked along with them.

Slowly and by necessity, the Witts evolved a plan of priorities. First the basic expenditures had to be made—for heating and rewiring. In spite of the great mill wheel that can still turn impressively, for several years the only water otherwise available came from a garden hose. The

Witts finally did get the good word that even though some of the land was marshy, a septic tank could be installed.

Long before the water pipes were in, the living and dining rooms began to take shape. While the work progressed, the idea was born to use these two rooms, as soon as they were finished, for a dual purpose— as a gallery for display and for the sale of Nancy's and Jack's art work.

The rough-hewn posts in the ground-floor rooms (kitchen, dining room, and living room) were retained, forming a long gallery hall along the outside wall. Opening from the gallery is the kitchen, located opposite the front door and up three steps. The dining room has been raised to the same level, its floor covered with slate except for a carpeted circular area for the dining-room table. Sides of the raised floor were paneled with old wood from other portions of the mill. From the dining room, a new circular stairway climbs to what will eventually be the hall for the bedrooms. A trap door gives access to stairs leading down to the future family room.

The raised dining room is separated from the main living area by a music room with its grand piano. The old pine floors have been sanded down, filled, and refinished. Behind and above the living room, the old millstones form the focal point of an intimate seating area. Wide plate-glass windows have replaced the small ones that formerly overlooked the pond in the back and the old mill wheel on the side. An iron wheel, not unlike the wheel of a ship, protrudes from the side wall. Open the window to look below, spin the wheel, and the sluice gate opens. Slowly the water fills to the proper level and the old mill wheel begins to turn.

With the living room and dining rooms completed, the second main project became the addition of the bathrooms and kitchen. Since the Witts have sleeping quarters in the little houses on the hill, bedrooms take last priority. The master bedroom will go on the third floor, with the roof raised to permit a window wall that will give the room the feeling of a tree house. The children's rooms and guest rooms will be located above the gallery-living room.

This renovation project is not even at the half-way point in the Witts long-range scheme. The first mile was the hardest—and perhaps the longest—but the rewards are by no means all waiting at the end. They occur daily.

Jack Witt says: "I see people in town so uptight. They're going at such a pace, and they're always worried about something. I can't see living like that. Sometimes I worry, too—when my work isn't going well, or like this morning before we got a lower bid on the water system. Then I walked out the front door, and there was this beautiful frost all over the fields, like silver. And I just took a deep breath and look all around, and knew this place was ours. And I walked down the hill, and by the time I got to the studio, I didn't have a worry in the world."

FACING PAGE: Plans show how the Witts are utilizing the space at their disposal. The ground floor will contain, along with the gallery and studio, the living room, dining area, and kitchen. The second floor will consist primarily of bedrooms and bath; a master-bedroom suite will occupy the third floor. Below ground floor is basement area, which eventually will contain a large game room and additional living room.

The Witt Family:
How the Witts Utilize Their Abundant Space

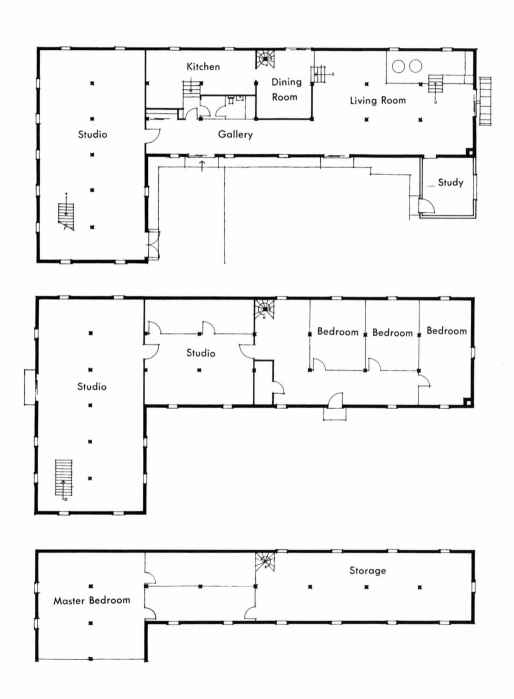

The living room seen from the music room. Wheel in far wall opens sluice gate to bring water to water wheel. Nancy Witt made canvas sofa's sculptured back by stretching canvas on a welded steel frame. At left is housing for the old millstones, which are now used as planters.

Music room, looking toward raised dining room. Table will go in circular carpeted area. Circular stairs lead to hall for future bedrooms.

Front hall, just behind the front door. Coat closet is at right.

The Robert L. Davis Family:
The Evolution of a 22-Room
Victorian Classic . . .

"The Seraph," four-tiered Victorian mansion as it looked when Robert and Helen Davis bought it in 1966. The house, built in the 1860's by well-known New England silversmith Norman Boardman, was in considerable disrepair inside, although quite presentable on the exterior.

... into a Comfortable Home
and Attractive Shop

Eye-catching and dramatic, "The Seraph" as it is today. Siding is painted a rich chocolate brown. Trim and "gingerbread" are white; arched entrance doors, lacquer red. Lamp on post is electrified reproduction of old gas light.

The Davis Family:
"I thought to myself:
'I would like to own this'"

"IN THE SPRING of 1956 I was finishing my second year at the New York School of Interior Design," Robert L. Davis reminisces. "Some friends in Hartford, Connecticut, asked me up for a weekend and we drove from Hartford to the beach at Watch Hill, Rhode Island. On the way, along the Connecticut River, we stopped in East Haddam, where for the first time I saw the great Victorian house built in 1860 by Norman Boardman, a manufacturer of pewter and silver plate during the Civil War period.

"The beautiful house had just been purchased by two women who had converted the front room into an antiques shop. Needless to say, since I am a designer, I hesitated to leave the area before seeing what I could of the inside. Although the 12-foot-high entrance hall was blocked off and I was actually able to get into the two front rooms only, I thought to myself, 'I would like to own this.'"

By January of 1967, Robert Davis and his wife, Helen, did own the Norman Boardman house—all 22 rooms of it—and were working around the clock seven days a week hoping to get the first floor restored by late May or early June.

In 1961, shortly after the Davises were married, Mr. Davis was working in the contract design field and they were living in a small New York City apartment. They had begun to collect antiques, which Mr.

Davis repaired and restored. Mrs. Davis was designing and making her own clothes and was becoming increasingly interested in gourmet cooking and the equipment involved in its preparation. Soon they had projects tucked away all over the apartment—behind the draperies, under the bed—everywhere. The thought occurred to them that they might sell antiques as well as Mrs. Davis's creations. First they just sold to friends and then to friends of friends, and soon they had quite a little operation going.

They moved into larger quarters but these soon became inadequate for their needs. They knew that they had to have a lot more space or forget the entire enterprise. After checking rents in the better locations of New York, they became fairly discouraged about ever finding adequate space in the city that they could afford. They decided that they should try to locate their business outside New York, and for the next two years they spent their vacations checking property in Massachusetts, New Hampshire, and Vermont. They knew pretty much what they wanted—a big Victorian house that would provide ample space for their shops and workrooms and also comfortable living quarters.

Bob Davis had forgotten the town of East Haddam but not the Boardman house. In the spring of 1966 the Davises were driving back to New York from one of their house-hunting trips and happened to pass the house—the house, as Helen Davis says, "that Bob had spoken of so often." To their surprise, the house was up for sale. It was exactly what they wanted. It had plenty of space on the ground floor for shops, and a lower floor that was perfect for storage. There were two upper floors that would make ideal living quarters, and the location was just right—not too far from New York but not too close. They made an offer on the house, and to their joy, it was accepted. They took title to the place in December of that year and moved into it the following January. They set June as the target date for completing enough of the renovation work so that they could open their shops and have living quarters in the house.

When Norman Boardman built his house in 1860, he built it as one would expect a fine silversmith to build—with excellent materials and beautiful workmanship. But over the years the house had been neglected. Now, although it was still as beautiful as ever, it needed a good deal of renovation work—inside and out. It also was filled with debris that had accumulated over the decades. "We were always either going to or coming back from the town dump those first few months," the Davises recall.

The plan of attack was to concentrate on the main floor and get this ready for the shops. One of the rooms was to be for antiques, another for contemporary items, a third for gourmet products, and the fourth for a boutique. The former owners had moved the kitchen from the lower level to the main floor, so the kitchen had to be moved again, this time to the second floor, which was eventually to become the living-dining-kitchen area for the Davises. Three of the main-floor rooms still had the original wallpaper on the walls. All the beautiful ornate plaster ceilings needed extensive repairs, and two, it turned out, had to be replaced. The plaster walls were in poor condition. The floors that were not covered were in a state of disrepair.

It was going to be a real problem to get these four rooms and the large entry hall all finished and decorated by June. To add to the difficulty, the Davises were unable to find a local contractor who could handle the job and get it done on time and in the way that Bob and Helen wanted it done. Finally, Bob approached some construction men he knew in New York City, and they agreed to come out weekends and between jobs to work on the place. There were plenty of extra bedrooms on the second floor so the men slept in the house, and Helen fed them from the makeshift kitchen that had been set up on this floor. Men in one crew worked during the week and returned to their families on Saturday and Sunday, when the weekend crew came out to work. This arrangement went on for about four months, with the work going on seven days a week, always accompanied by the standard amount of noise, dirt, and confusion that is part of any renovation project.

At times the Davises became a little discouraged. The place was so huge, there was so much to be done, and so little time to do it.

In addition to the interior work, all the windows—and there were a great many—had to be removed from their frames and then reset to make them weathertight. The house needed a complete rewiring job, and many of the original lighting fixtures of brass and nickel had to be converted from gas to electricity. No changes were made on the exterior except painting, and repairs of the siding.

The first floor was completed in June, and "The Seraph" opened for business. The Davises were then able to turn their attention to the second floor. This area, consisting originally of four bedrooms and bath was reworked to provide a living room, dining room, sitting room, kitchen, and bath. The first room on this floor to be completed was the kitchen—a large, beautifully designed and decorated kitchen, a joy to Mrs. Davis who for several years had been having to operate with her original makeshift equipment.

The final renovation project was the third floor, which was just getting under way at this writing. It had been the servants' quarters when the house was built. The Davises planned to include in this area the master bedroom, with a fireplace and a 25-foot-high ceiling in the tower of the house; a master bath; a study and workroom for Bob; and a guest room and bath. This floor had no heat other than the fireplace in one room because when the house was built, servants apparently didn't require this luxury in cold weather; the Davises plan to provide the area with electric heat.

Mr. Davis did all the planning that went into this renovation project. Insofar as possible he worked with the existing space, but some walls have been torn down and repositioned and others will be.

The Davises are extremely happy over the results of this project. They have exactly the kind of house they want—a house that contains extremely comfortable living quarters for them and ample space for their business.

The Davis Family:
To Get the Job Done, the Workmen Slept in the Extra Bedrooms and Helen Davis Cooked Their Meals

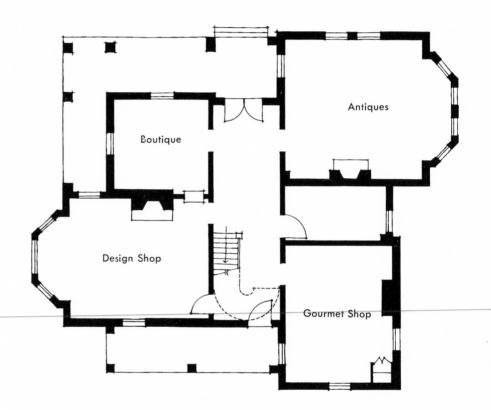

First floor, where shops are now located, was left essentially unchanged except for complete redecorating. Twelve-foot ceilings in all rooms made this a major project in itself. All plaster walls were scraped, spackled, and prepared for new wall coverings. Ceilings that could be saved were repaired and painted; all woodwork was also painted.

FACING PAGE BOTTOM: The original four bedrooms on second floor are now being made into an L-shaped living-dining room, a completely modern kitchen, and a rear sitting room. Two closets were removed from rear bedroom to enlarge kitchen and create access to dining area. In old hall area, two bearing walls are to be removed along with a large closet, to open up living-room-dining-room area completely. The bearing walls will be replaced with a wood girder. Existing bathroom will be remodeled into guest lavatory.

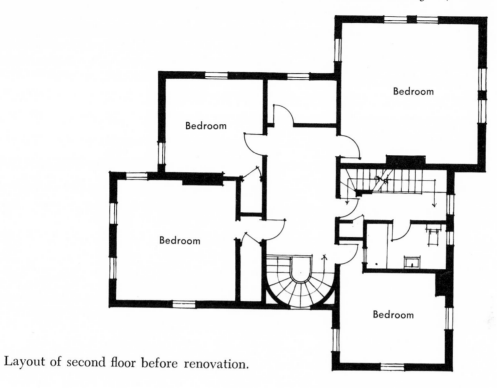

Layout of second floor before renovation.

Third-floor former servants' quarters before renovation.

FACING PAGE BOTTOM: Projected renovation of third floor, which had no plumbing and had been used as attic space for past 50 years. Load-bearing walls in hall will be removed, but replaced with bath area in master-bedroom suite. Present 17-foot ceiling in master bedroom will be opened up to tower area, where beams and joists will be left exposed. Ceiling will then be 25 feet high. Large closet will be built in dressing area; fireplace will be retained in bedroom. Rear bedroom and part of hall are to be converted into complete private guest-room-and-bath suite. Floor in remaining hall area will be raised 10 inches to accommodate plumbing connecting guest bath to main waste line. This part of hall will become atrium-like area with tile floor and indoor garden in center. A single step will be located at each entrance. Rear bedroom over second-floor sitting room will be future study and workroom for Mr. Davis. Fireplace will be blocked here and in guest bedroom. Skylights are planned for study, master bedroom, and atrium. Floor treatment will be of carpeting, wood, and quarry tile.

Close-up of ornate plaster ceiling, which was preserved and repaired to its state of original elegance.

Shops open off main entrance hall. Floor is black-and-white marbled vinyl tile, which gives visual expansion to width of hall. Red indeed-outdoor carpeting runs entire length of hall, starting at front-porch steps. Glass panels at rear are old cranberry glass. Wall coverings are gray silk vinyl up to molding just below top of door frames, then white vinyl to ceiling.

Former living room is now used as antiques room. Walls, which were badly cracked, are now covered with rich, red carpeting, floor to ceiling. Mirror and white marble fireplace were refurbished but left intact. The original brass and nickel lighting fixtures were converted from gas to electricity. Gray floor covering and white woodwork add a crisp touch and enhance Victorian feeling.

The Lee Charlot Family:
They Made a Land-Based Arc . . .

Ark as it was before remodeling. Structure was towed to this site and moored here in the early 1900's. Earlier, it had been a houseboat.

. . . into a Rental Property
and a Retirement House

The ark as it is today. Major changes in the exterior were the addition of large windows and sliding glass doors, extensions on sides and one end, and a bedroom that runs at right angles to the original structure.

The Charlot Family:

"We'll have a retirement home in our own front yard"

BACK BEFORE the turn of the century, the bays and coves around San Francisco were dotted with houseboats known as "arks." In 1906, the year of the great San Francisco earthquake, there were some thirty of these arks in a single cove around Belvedere in Marin County.

Sometime after the fire that resulted from the earthquake, many of these arks were towed to the shore and anchored. In time, foundations were installed so that they became houses for all-year living.

In 1965 Mr. and Mrs. Lee Charlot purchased a house that was built around 1906. It sat on the side of a hill, and below it was one of these arks. The ark had changed hands often and the current owner was about to undertake a major remodeling. In fact, he had completely gutted the structure and had plans for extensive alterations. But the local building department had strict regulations regarding what you could and could not do to an ark and eventually so discouraged the owner that he gave up the project and put the ark on the market.

The Charlots decided to buy the ark for a number of reasons. First, while their house was almost at the edge of the water, they did not have a right of way to the water, but if they owned the ark, they would have legal access to the waterfront. They also looked upon the ark as a good investment, for once it was renovated, it could easily be rented. Second, the Charlots felt that the ark would make them a perfect retirement house. They planned to do a lot of traveling, so they would not need a large place. They could live comfortably in the ark and rent the main house.

When the Charlots took title to the ark, the interior was an empty shell consisting of one large room. Off to one side was a shed that was connected to the main portion of the ark by a breezeway. The ark did have water and sewage lines and also electricity.

Mrs. Charlot and their architect, Donald J. Batchelder, faced the challenge of figuring out how best to utilize the existing space to create comfortable living quarters without having to increase the size of the place. They were forced to work with the existing space because local building regulations prohibited adding space to an ark.

Their solution was to enclose the breezeway and the shed. The result was a comfortable bedroom with enough additional space to allow for a full bath. Next to the bathroom was the kitchen, in the same location as the original one.

Trying to find additional sleeping space was another matter. There just wasn't enough space for another bedroom without chopping the living room down to almost nothing. Mrs. Charlot and Mr. Batchelder finally hit on the idea of creating small extensions in the form of alcoves off each side of the living room. They projected another alcove at the end of the living room for a fireplace. Eventually they persuaded the building department to give them a variance allowing these minor changes in the structure. Each of the alcoves is just wide enough to provide sleeping quarters for one person.

Considerable work had to be done on the foundations because these were in poor shape. This work involved concrete, steel, and wood beams that had to be specially treated so they would not be damaged by the salt water.

The curved ceiling of the original ark was restored, and the exterior walls were covered with wood shingles. Decking was installed along the front portion of the ark that is connected to the boat dock; there is also decking at the rear to provide access to the land. Mrs. Charlot hunted about to find as many materials and fittings as she could that were of the kind used on the original arks. She also saved as much of the original fittings as possible. Additional windows and sliding glass doors were installed to bring in light and provide a view of the busy waterfront.

The final outcome of the renovation project, which took only four months to complete, is exactly what the Charlots hoped it would be. The interior of the ark has much the same feeling as the interior of a ship. There are rough-hewn beams and paneling, and plenty of light finds its way inside. Storage space is abundant but compact—just as you would expect to find on a boat. There are sleeping accommodations for four persons.

At present the Charlots rent the ark to tenants but because the interior was designed to fit their particular requirements, it will make a pleasant retirement house for them when and if they decide to move out of their large place on the hillside.

FACING PAGE TOP: Original ark did not provide sufficient space for adequate year-round living quarters. Previous owner gutted structure but was unable to get building department's permission to renovate it as he wished.

FACING PAGE BOTTOM: Mrs. Charlot and architect Donald J. Batchelder devised a solution acceptable to the building department. Bays, or alcoves, were added to the living room to provide additional sleeping quarters and an area for a fireplace; bedroom wing was formed by enclosing portion of deck.

The Charlot Family:
They Added Space Despite Tough Building Codes

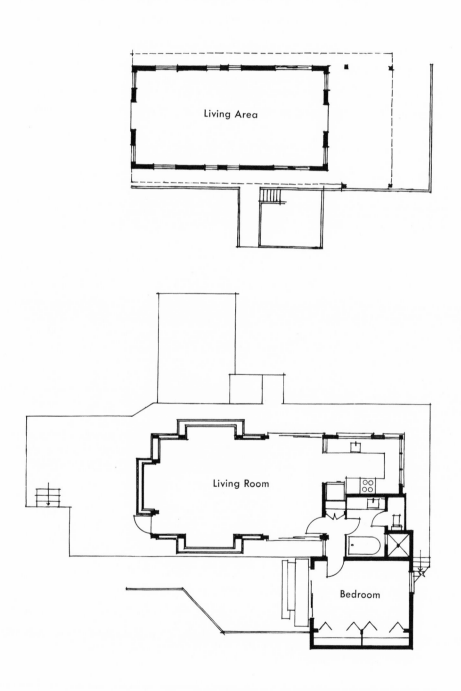

David Ordway: How an Ice House . . .

Group of run-down buildings at the time they were bought by Mr. Ordway. Building at left was made into antiques shop and work rooms. Partially renovated ice house is at center background. Structure at right was in such poor condition that it was demolished.

... *Became an Attractive,*
Functional Dwelling

View of ice house after it had been remodeled by Mr. Ordway. This view shows large window units he installed in the living room to take advantage of the waterfall and the pond.

David Ordway:

"I planned the interior

to make the most of the enchanting site"

W<small>HEN DAVID ORDWAY</small> decided to open an antiques shop in the country, he wanted a location that would provide him not only with space for his shop and work but also with living space. He did considerable hunting about until he found exactly what he wanted in a crumbling Connecticut compound that included an old, abandoned mill, an ice house that had been partially remodeled into a dwelling, and a blacksmith shop. In spite of the run-down condition of these buildings, the foundations and the basic structures were sound. A fourth building on the property was not sound in any way, shape, or form, however, and this had to be torn down.

Mr. Ordway selected the old mill to remodel into his shop and work area. He also renovated the blacksmith shop so that it included a small income-producing apartment and large studio. He chose for his own dwelling the partially renovated ice house with its magnificent location at the edge of a pond and close to a lovely little waterfall.

The original ice house had been put up about 1820 and had good basic lines. About 1900 someone had converted it into a something that somewhat resembled a residence. In 1920 additional work had been done but with little taste. When Mr. Ordway took over, the building was neither an ice house nor a true dwelling. A few windows had been added but not in the right locations to take advantage of the views. Two large shed dormers, one on each side of the roof, had been installed.

The plumbing system was highly primitive, there was little in the way of electrical wiring, and the second floor consisted of only a floor with walls and a roof. All the materials used on the several previous renovation efforts had been the least expensive available at the time, with the result that the building had lost its original character and charm.

One of the previous owners had installed a flight of stairs to the second floor. These had been placed almost precisely in the center of the house, so that it was necessary to plan the new interiors around them or move them. Mr. Ordway decided to leave the stairs alone and work around them.

All existing partitions on the first floor were removed so that an entire new room arrangement could be made. Additional framing was installed and the walls were insulated. The interior space was divided to obtain the maximum benefit from the views of the outside, one being the pond and the other the small waterfall. The living room was placed on one side of the stairs and runs the width of the house. On the other side of the stairs is the large dining room. Existing windows were enlarged and new ones added along with sliding glass doors.

The existing stairs made it difficult to plan the upstairs space, but the solution here was to run a bedroom on each side of the stairs with a bath at one end. Closets were installed under the eaves.

Major structural changes included installation of adequate plumbing, wiring, and heating, and the fireplace in the living room. The stone foundation was in fair shape and required only repairs to the old mortar. New siding was applied along with a new roof.

Mr. Ordway worked out his own design and did a considerable amount of the work on the place himself and with the help of friends. He was lucky enough to find old cabinets from a pharmacy and used these for kitchen cabinets. The kitchen table came from an old drugstore and has seats that swing out. After only a year's work, the unattractive ice house has become an attractive, comfortable place in which to live.

David Ordway:

The Most Intelligent Approach Was to Rip Out
the Existing Partitions and Start off Fresh

Interior of the ice house was torn out and replanned around existing stairs.
LEFT: First floor contains living room, dining room, kitchen, and lavatory.
RIGHT: Second floor contains two large bedrooms with bath at end of hall.

Dining Room

Kitchen

Living Room

Bedroom

Bedroom

The Robert Crozier Family:
They Found the Perfect Barn and . . .

The barn before renovation work began.

. . . Made It into a Conversation Piece

All essential architectural elements of the original barn were retained. The sliding doors at the front were replaced by a fixed window unit and the side door was retained as the front entry.

The Crozier Family:

"Problems—yes. Excitement—yes. Achievement—yes"

Before they bought their barn in Pleasantville, New York, Mr. and Mrs. Robert Crozier were living in a comfortable Colonial house in New Jersey. They had lived in this house for about six years and in that time had done considerable work on it, modernizing the kitchen and redoing the interior. But they were not happy with the schools in the area and Bob Crozier did not relish having to commute each day to New York City by bus. They decided to make a change.

They wanted several acres and an old farmhouse that they could renovate. Their plan was to take a drive every other weekend to look for what they had in mind. When they found an area that appealed to them, they would communicate with real estate brokers and any friends they had in the area, asking them to be on the lookout for a possible buy. One day they discovered Pleasantville and found the area just right for what they wanted. Wonderful big old white frame houses guarded by magnificent ancient trees lined the roads.

The Croziers stopped at the first real estate office they found, but their talk with the broker was not encouraging. Only two houses were available in Pleasantville and neither fitted their requirements. And two acres in the village proper were almost unheard of. It was only after the Croziers had spent most of the day with the broker, looking around Pleasantville that he said, "I have two acres with an old barn on it— would you want to look at it? It has no water, no heat, no electricity."

Their first look was all that the Croziers needed. There were two grassy acres fringed by trees and a small orchard. To one side was a pond surrounded by willows.

The barn seemed structurally sound but dirty and in need of repair. On the ground level it contained four horse stalls with grates and rings and chewed window sills, plus two carriage rooms with concrete floors. The foundation was of stone 18 inches thick.

On the next floor angular beams shot up, forming a square A construction. The interior walls consisted of raw siding on raw 2-inch-by-4-inch framing. There was a small tack room. Bird nests were abundant. On the top floor was the hay loft, reached by a tiny flight of stairs. Also on the top floor were two small rooms—one with a pot-bellied stove. The floors in these small rooms, which had served as quarters for the hired hands, were covered with old linoleum, and the walls were paneled in wood.

Twenty-four feet to the rear of the barn was another building, a two-car garage that was included in the property. This had possibilities as a future studio for Mr. Crozier, who is a commercial artist.

The Croziers were excited about the place. They asked to meet the owner, who lived in a house at the front of the property. They let him know that they wanted an option to buy, but that they knew nothing of the cost to renovate, had little knowledge of how long it would take to sell their present house, and even less about the problems of financing such a project. They gave him a $100 check and a promise to call him within a week to give a definite answer of intent.

Then their worry began. "We knew next to nothing about building costs and only a minimum about construction," Bob Crozier recalls. "We knew even less about financing. We did know that it would take us time to convert and to convert we must have revenue. This revenue had to come from the sale of our present property.

"We then contacted a local architect and asked him to look over the barn and to evaluate its usefulness and construction. We were willing to pay him a nominal fee for this. His services included a 'ball park' figure on building costs. We were pushed for time and asked him to submit recommendations in two weeks.

"In the meanwhile, we had the house in which we were living appraised. Very quickly we knew how much cash we would have to spend. It was going to be very tight.

"The architect came through with his figures—he had contacted a contractor to get even more accurate cost estimates. We were beyond our financial safety point. Our only choice was to reduce the land costs by taking title to less property. We discussed this with the owner, and he agreed to keep a 30-by-100-foot strip, thus reducing our initial investment.

"On this basis, we put our house up for sale and were fortunate enough to find a house rental in Pleasantville that would provide us with a base from which to oversee the building as it progressed. Even though we hired the architect to oversee construction, I felt it was important to keep in close touch with the contractors to help assure some further quality control.

"Everything dovetailed miraculously. We sold our house—at our asking price—to the first person who saw it. We rented the house in Pleasantville, signed the contract with the architect and closed on the barn —all within about ten days.

"Our commitment to the builder was to be contingent upon our getting bank money, which was going to be the toughest nut to crack. Meanwhile, we had two months of summer in which to prepare the barn for a contractor, and we knew that everything we could do would save money.

"So for two months we drove forty miles each weekend to clean up— pile trash, pack junk, and take down inside walls to prepare the raw shell for the builder. While this was being done, the architect worked with us on the plans. Since I'm a designer, it was fairly easy for me to visualize exactly what I wanted. My wife and I talked over every aspect of the plans—we scaled rooms and furniture, discussed traffic flow and conveniences, color and style. All this was passed on to the architect. In the meantime, I went out looking for a bank that would lend us money.

"None would even consider our plan . . . They had every excuse imaginable, but each answer boiled down to no, sorry. I personally went to more than thirty lending institutions within a radius of fifty miles—always the same answer. "A barn . . . a Colonial maybe, but a barn? . . ."

"We finally found a daring banker upstate—in Albany, 150 miles away, who took the risk with us. The owner of the barn also took a second mortgage for the remainder. Once the financing was settled, everything fell more easily into place. Construction began and with a minimum of changes we were in our renovated barn in one year almost to the day. Just in time to celebrate the birth of our third son.

"Problems—yes. Excitement—yes. Achievement—yes. Thirteen years later, we're down to one mortgage. We've since added the studio—our own 300-foot driveway, a two-car garage, a deck, a huge terrace, a bedroom, a bath.

"What did we do ourselves? As I look back, it seems we physically did almost everything! Installed the kitchen cabinets, wood-paneled the living room (from wood we had carefully salvaged), laid tile, built terraces and outdoor steps, helped build a deck, removed the roof from the old garage, added a tool and wood shed, did stone work, planted trees, shrubs, and bushes, built a hearth—to name just a few items.

"Next to having our own family of four sons (three of whom have turned my studio into a rehearsal hall for their drums and guitars), having our own 'barn' has been the *greatest*," Bob Crozier says in summing up. "It is a conversation piece, true. But more than that, it is the ideal home for four sons to grow up in. From the second-floor living room, 30 feet of glass give an unobstructed view of our neighbors' horses a thousand feet away—charging back and forth across their terrain. And we have every reason to believe that we may have between the boys the makings of a Grandpa Moses—who will live with some very pleasant memories of growing up. What could be nicer for any child in times like these?

"Unused barns are getting harder to find—but find one and stick to it. We figure that in another ten years ours will be just as we want it—finished!"

The Crozier Family:
They Got What They Wanted by Talking Over Every Aspect
of Their Plans and Then Talking to the Architect

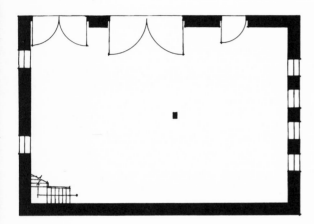

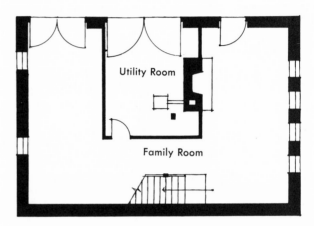

Original basement plan. LEFT: Barn was set into slope so that rear of lower level opens onto the ground. RIGHT: This made it possible to include a utility room and family room on the lower level that opens directly to the outside.

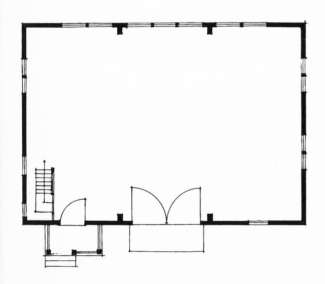

Space on first floor was divided to provide a front entry and hall, living room with fireplace, dining room, kitchen, and lavatory.

Second floor originally consisted of one large and two small rooms. Area was reworked to provide space for a master bedroom and bath, two bedrooms and bath, plus a large upstairs playroom that can be converted into bedrooms.

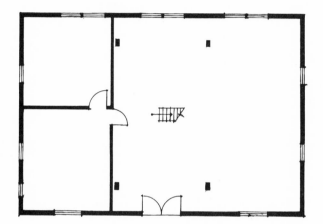

Interior of first floor before renovation work. Sliding doors were replaced by fixed windows and door at right became entry to house.

Finished living room. Heavy framing timbers were left exposed where possible, to retain basic architectural style of barn's interior.

Large room on second floor as work began.

View of second floor showing landing. Stairs in background go to attic.

James Corum:
19th-Century "Railroad" House . . .

The house is believed to be one of the first three built in
Richmond immediately after the Civil War.

... Gets Fresh, Up-to-Date Look

Major exterior changes consisted of stripping off the old porch and "ginger-bread" trim. Most existing windows were replaced and the brick and trim painted.

James Corum:

"In spite of the remodeling headaches,
it's turned into a perfect place for me"

THE HOUSE that James Corum purchased was one of three said to be the first houses built in Richmond, Virginia, after the Civil War. These houses were very similar to row houses, or town houses, except that they were not attached. They are long and narrow, two stories in height, and built of brick. At some point, a previous owner built a frame addition onto the back of the house that Mr. Corum purchased, and this provided space for two rooms, one above the other.

The exterior renovation consisted more of stripping than adding. The old front porch came off along with the gingerbread trim. A single fixed window was added over the stairwell and a glass door was installed on the north side. Most of the other windows were replaced with units containing large panes of glass to allow more light to enter the house. The old brick exterior walls were painted a mellow mustard-gold, and the window trim was painted bronze to match the bronze metal casings.

All the rooms on the first floor were the same size—16 by 16 feet. The living room, which is at the front, was left the original size. Here, Mr. Corum stripped the old Victorian mantel off the fireplace, leaving the exposed brick. Dark random-width hardwood-plank flooring was added to give a formal look to this room. To provide an impression of more space, the wall opposite the fireplace was screened with a full-length mirror.

An archway from the living room opens into a large middle room. This room, now 16 feet by 32 feet, was enlarged by removing the partition between two rooms. On either side of the archway, floor-to-ceiling cabinets, bookshelves, and space for stereo equipment were built. The existing stairway to the second floor, which had run from front to back, was reversed so that it now runs from the back to the front of the house. It was rebuilt out of rough wood. The old plaster on the south wall of the enlarged middle room was removed by sandblasting, and the exposed brick was coated with shellac to give the brick and the mortar a mellow antique effect. Other walls in the room were replastered because the existing plaster was beyond repair. On the north wall, an opening was made for a glass door to the outside walk and terrace.

The ceiling of the large middle room was covered with panels of dark cork. Several wooden crates were also covered with cork to serve as tables. The ceiling fixture, made by Mr. Corum, is a contemporary lantern consisting of a grid of heavy, smoked Plexiglass surrounding 28 clear light bulbs. Instead of a glare of light, the fixture produces a soft, golden glow.

In the kitchen the back wall was removed, and a 16-foot sliding glass was installed; this door opens into a 5-foot-by-8-foot greenhouse that Mr. Corum had built by professionals. The kitchen includes a dining area that is separated from the kitchen proper by a peninsula containing the sink and dishwasher. The old kitchen walls and ceiling had been covered with embossed tin, an unusual wall covering seen in several very old Richmond houses. Jim Corum was extremely disappointed that he was unable to save this material for reuse but in the course of the changes essential to modernize the kitchen, the tin covering was too badly damaged for reuse. Mr. Corum covered the kitchen walls with cedar siding stained dark. The floors in the kitchen and dining area are of brick laid in a herringbone pattern. Counter tops are of yellow plastic laminate, and the dining-room table is topped with the same material in blue.

Upstairs, room partitions were left alone except where the space formerly used by a large closet was added to the small bathroom. The hall floor leading to the master bedroom and bath is covered with natural slate. A 3-foot glass window panel replaces a small window, adding light to what would have been a dark corridor. Because the front room had a fireplace it was selected as the master bedroom. The plaster on the fireplace was removed to expose the brick.

A combination of rough- and smooth-textured materials was used in the bathroom. The outside wall has exposed brick, the opposite wall is covered with mirrors. The west wall is covered with cork, as is the ceiling. The floor is slate, as are the counter tops. The shower stall has a roof that comes to a point in the center and is covered with exterior siding. A skylight was added to the roof.

One of the small bedrooms serves as a dressing room and guest room. The remaining bedroom has become a studio and library.

It took Mr. Corum about five months to complete the renovation of this old house, doing much of the work himself. The result of all his efforts is a charming residence with space tailored to his needs.

FACING PAGE: First- and second-floor plans show how typical "railroad" layout was transformed, with only a few changes, into a light and spacious house.

James Corum:

How a "Railroad" Layout Was Put onto a Contemporary Track

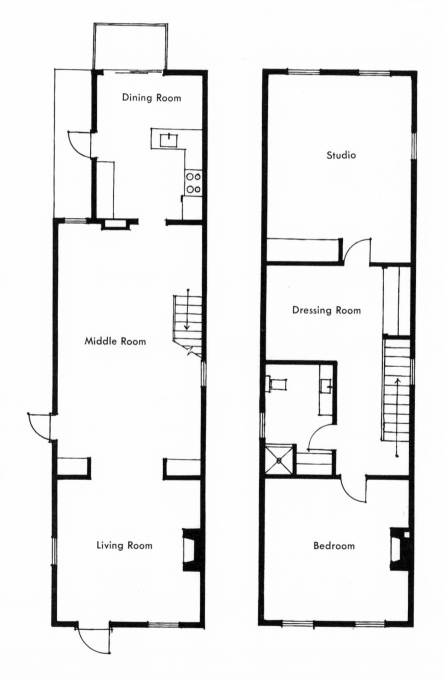

View just beyond the front door in living room, looking through to kitchen at rear of house. Large middle room between living room and kitchen was formed by removing partition between two rooms of equal size. Position of stairs was reversed.

FACING PAGE BOTTOM: Middle room looking toward living room at front of house. Ceiling fixture was designed and built by Mr. Corum.

Kitchen and greenhouse are beyond middle room. Fixed glass panel at left looks onto terrace adjoining kitchen.

The Stanton Family: Converting
a Dark, Heavy Victorian Monster . . .

Snapshot shows appearance of house at the time it was bought by Mr. and Mrs. Stanton.

. . . into a Light and Airy Contemporary House

The exterior was dramatically changed to transform a Newport-style mansion into a contemporary home. Front porch and entry were removed, along with numerous dormers. Pitched roof on wing at left was replaced with flat roof. Skylights were added to bring light into inside area of house. Existing windows were removed or replaced with contemporary units.

Mr. Stanton:

"I just hate to leave it to go to work"

THERE IS no mistake in the makeup of this book. The house shown in the "before" picture at the time that the renovation work began is the same house that is shown in the "after" picture. It has merely changed a good deal for the better.

The original house was built about 1890 in a style we might call "Late Nineteenth-century Newport, Rhode Island." It was a very big place with dark wood shingles on the outside and lots of heavy overhang that kept out the light. Inside and out it was dark, dreary, and conveyed that heavy feeling that one associates with eating too well at a Victorian-era dinner.

But the house was set on a lovely site—a very exciting site on the side of a hill. From this site one looks at the tops of the trees rather than at the trunks or bottoms. The location was obviously the old Lake Michigan shoreline centuries and centuries ago.

Mr. and Mrs. Francis Stanton, plus four children, were attracted to this property not only because of the site but also because of the size and general layout of the house. Mr. Stanton is an architect. Mrs. Stanton is a painter and the daughter of an architect. Both found it easy to visualize what could be done to the house to make it perfect for them.

The basic plan of the house was rather good, so the Stantons left the main shell alone structurally. They literally tore the sides off the house, however, and did pretty much the same thing on the inside. They wanted a house with long, simple lines, and they wanted to give the exterior a vertical rather than a horizontal feeling. They wanted a house with a contemporary feeling rather than something from the late Victorian period.

488

On the exterior they ripped away the overhangs and took away the dormers. They tore off the porches and put in a terrace. They replaced the old windows, added more windows where needed, and installed several sliding glass doors. They also added some skylights to bring more light into the interior. The old wood shingles were removed and replaced with redwood siding applied vertically and stained black.

Major changes on the inside involved removing six of the nine existing fireplaces and removing some of the small rooms on the second floor, once used as servants' quarters, to make space for a large studio for Mrs. Stanton. The old staircase was removed and two circular staircases were installed. An outside staircase, painted powder blue, gives direct access to the studio from the outside and relieves interior traffic.

Under the studio is a huge recreation room—large enough to handle a billiard table plus table tennis. The walls of the recreation room are paneled with pine boards that the Stantons got when the old Winnetka Coal and Lumber Company building was torn down. The pine has weathered beautifully and looks lovely.

The third floor has rooms for the children, baths, and also a laboratory for photography—one of the family's favorite hobbies. "We are a family of projects," Mr. Stanton remarks.

One of the three remaining fireplaces is in the front hall, a welcome note when one comes in from the cold outdoors. The hall floor is concrete with marble chips and is heated by radiant coils. This warm floor attracts the three black cats of the household and they know just where to lie for effect and comfort.

Everyone who was familiar with the original house finds the Stanton's transformation extremely impressive. They can't get over the lightness, the airiness of the house as it now stands.

Asked what made him especially happy about his new house Mr. Stanton said, "Everything. I just hate to leave it to go to work."

It took about two years to complete this renovation project. That is not a long time when you realize how carefully every step of the work was planned to produce just the sort of house that Mr. and Mrs. Stanton wanted.

The Stanton Family:
The Stantons Literally Tore the Sides
off the Place—Inside and Out

Original layout of first floor.

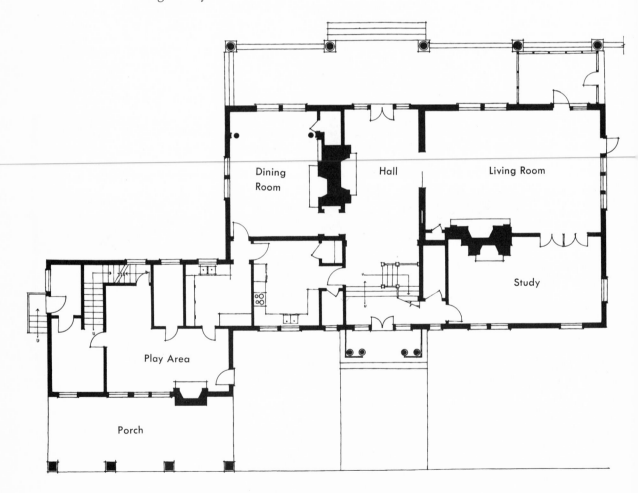

Dining Room

Hall

Living Room

Study

Play Area

Porch

First floor after renovation. Major changes involved removing partitions in wing to make space for large playroom. Existing stairs in this area were removed and replaced with spiral unit. Front entry and kitchen were also reworked.

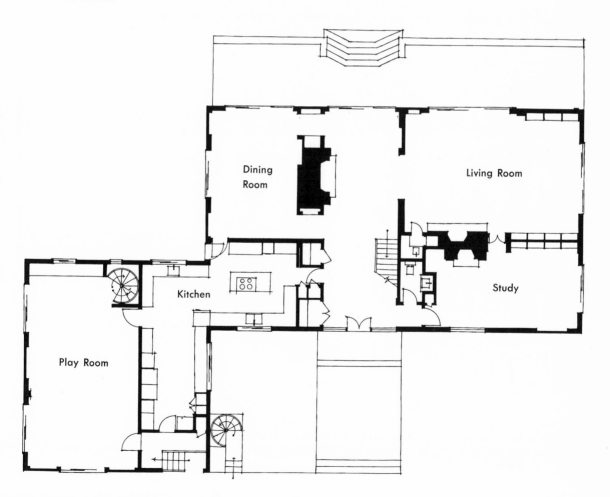

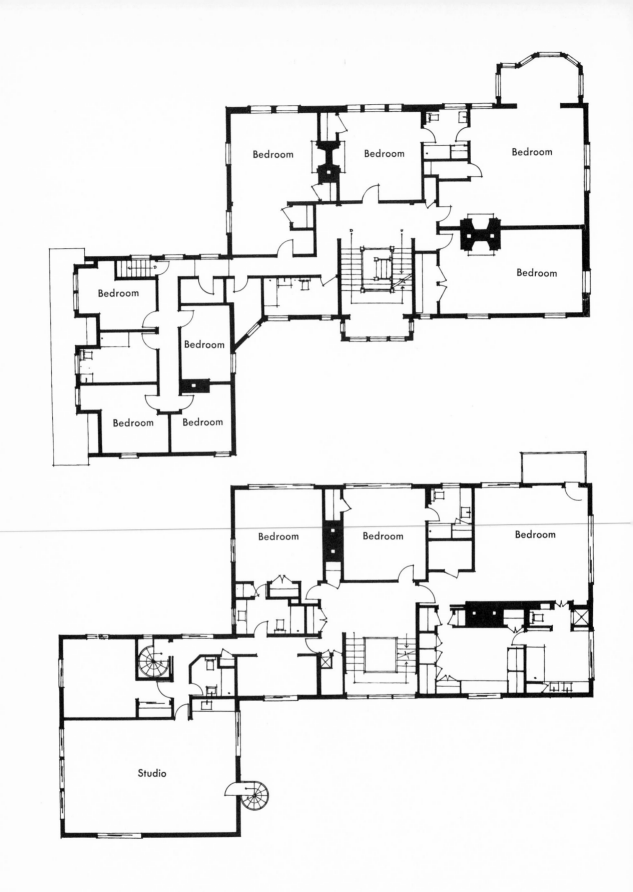

Bedroom

Bedroom

Bedroom

Bedroom

Bedroom

Bedroom

Bedroom

Bedroom

Bedroom

Bedroom

Bedroom

Studio

FACING PAGE TOP: Plan of second floor before renovation.

FACING PAGE BOTTOM: Second floor after renovation. Servants' quarters in wing were eliminated to create area for studio. Studio has outside spiral staircase extending to ground. Old bathroom at front of house was removed and three new bathrooms were added. Fireplaces in bedrooms were closed off, and closets installed.

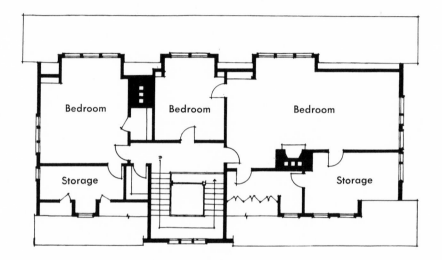

Original plan of third floor.

Relatively little work had to be done in this area. The two existing baths were reworked, fireplaces were closed off, and closets added.

The Lyle Jones Family: They Fell in Love With a Farmhouse...

The house being moved on rollers to the new site by the pond built by Mr. and Mrs. Jones.

494

. . . and Remodeled It into a Permanent Residence

Renovated house on its new site by the pond. Wing at right contains story-and-a-half kitchen-living room with sliding glass doors that open onto terrace.

The Jones Family:

*"First we built the pond, then we
moved the house to the pond"*

In 1963 Mr. and Mrs. Lyle Jones were residing happily in a contemporary house they had built in Chapel Hill, North Carolina. They
decided to invest in some land out in the country, and eventually purchased a sizable parcel. At the time they had no intention of living there,
so they paid little attention to the old farmhouse on the 50 acres they
bought. The house was *T*-shaped, the older part being the stem of the *T*,
with a shed roof covering two rooms downstairs, two loft rooms upstairs,
and a side porch. Apparently, when the original tenants had become
more prosperous, sometime around 1900, they had built on at the front,
in the typical plan of a North Carolina house of that era, four rooms
with a center hall, two rooms upstairs and two downstairs. Later they
had enclosed the front porch and divded the space into a bathroom
and kitchen.

When the Joneses bought the property, they first built a pond in a
natural basin surrounded by trees. This done, they began to wish that
the house could sit at the edge of the pond, as the location was extremely scenic. They got an estimate on moving the old house, first
removing the front porch. The cost was quite reasonable—only about
$1,000—and slowly, with rollers placed underneath and a farm tractor
chained to one end, the old house was moved about 600 feet to a rise at
the edge of the pond. Then Mr. Jones received a grant for a year's study
and the project was abandoned while they left the Chapel Hill area.

When Mr. and Mrs. Jones returned, they were impressed once more
with the loveliness of the site, and the possibility of remodeling the

496

house as a permanent home became more and more appealing. With the help of a good contractor, Mrs. Jones planned a more desirable room arrangement. They decided to remove the second floor in the back wing of the house, lowering the ceiling about 1½ feet to keep it structurally sound and making a combination kitchen-dining room out of the space, which was 15 by 30 feet. The cathedral ceiling would be partially supported by a balcony above the kitchen, which could be used as a child's bedroom. A folding stairway links the kitchen to the balcony.

The four front rooms were each 15 feet square, but the center hall took up considerable space. The Joneses therefore decided to move the old staircase from the front hall to the side of the new room in back and to utilize the stairwell for a bathroom on each floor. The small side porch on the back wing was then enclosed for a half bath and utility room. Each of the original rooms at the front of the house had its own fireplace. When the Joneses decided to put a fireplace in the new room, backing up to the living room fireplace, the contractor advised closing up the bedroom fireplace above, which was done. The others, in the master bedroom downstairs and in the upstairs bedroom, remain operable.

Since the old house had almost no closets, the space on either side of the bedroom fireplaces was enclosed for this purpose. The old stairwell also offered space for a coat closet in the front hall. Bookshelves were built, floor to ceiling, alongside the chimney in the new room.

To take advantage of the view at the back of the house, two pairs of sliding glass doors were placed on that side of the dining room.

To restore the pleasant traditional appearance of the house, a new porch was built in front as an exact replica of the original. To their surprise, the Joneses discovered that a local lumberyard was still turning out posts that duplicated the old roof supports exactly and also matched the old banister posts along the stairway. They kept the old tin roof, which was in good condition, both for its typical appearance, and the pleasant sound it made on a rainy night.

Despite the rather extensive changes in the interior design, the remodeling of the Jones house went smoothly and took only about four months of actual construction time to complete. The Joneses now make the farmhouse their permanent home.

The Jones Family:
They Weren't Stumped by a House
Filled With Little Rooms

Original house contained six rooms, all about 15 feet square. Upstairs loft extends over wing.

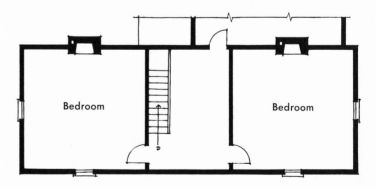

Renovation work consisted of enlarging two front rooms, changing location of stairs, and adding space for downstairs bathroom and laundry. Partition in wing was removed to make a large kitchen-living room. Upstairs landing was reduced in area to provide space for bathroom.

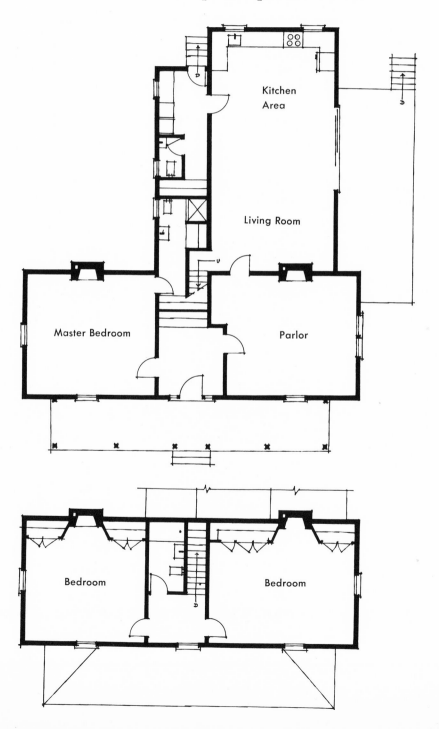

View of living area in wing. Ceiling is story and a half.

Front view of house. Porch was added along with new siding. Original tin roof was retained.

Glossary of Building Terms

Abrasive.   Any material used for sanding, polishing, or grinding. The most common abrasive is sandpaper.

Acoustics.   In building and architecture, the sound properties of a room or structure.

Across the Grain.   At right angles to the direction of the grain in a piece of wood.

Adobe.   A type of brick used extensively in the southwestern United States, usually made of clay that hardens by drying in the sun, as opposed to common brick fired in a kiln.

Air Space.   An empty space between two walls.

Airway.   A space between roof insulation and roof boards for air movement.

Alcove.   An area of a room separated from the main area by partial walls or an arch.

Alteration.   A major or minor structural change in a house or building.

Anchor.   To fasten one object to another.

Anchor Bolts.   Metal bolts used to secure woodwork to masonry.

Apron.   The piece of finished woodwork that fits under the windowsill.

Area.   The total surface of a floor, roof, wall, plot of ground.

Areaway.   An excavation made around the foundation wall to allow light and air to reach the basement when the basement window is placed below the level of the ground.

Armored Cable.   Electric wires encased in a flexible metal covering. Often called BX cable.

Asbestos Board.   A type of building board that comes in sheets and is made of asbestos fibers and Portland cement. It is used for interior and exterior work and is fire and moisture resistant.

Asbestos Shingles.   Shingles similar in construction to asbestos board and used for siding and for roofing. Available in a variety of colors and textures.

Asphalt.   A material used widely in building for such items as waterproof roof coverings of many types, exterior wall coverings, and flooring tile. Most native asphalt is a residue from evaporated petroleum. It is insoluble in water but soluble in gasoline and melts when heated.

Asphalt Shingles.   Waterproof roofing shingles made of felt paper impregnated with asphalt and covered with mineral granules. Available in several weights and patterns and a variety of colors.

Attic.   That portion of a house between the top floor and the roof.

Attic Crawl Space.   Attic space without headroom.

Attic Ventilators.   In houses, screened openings provided to ventilate an attic space. They are located in the soffit area as inlet ventilators and in the gable end or along the ridge as outlet ventilators. They can also consist of power-driven fans used as an exhaust system. See also LOUVER.

Backfill. The replacement of excavated earth into a trench or pier excavation around and against a basement foundadation.

Back Priming. Painting the unexposed side of a piece of lumber before it is installed, to prevent it from absorbing moisture.

Balusters. Vertical posts on a stair railing.

Baseboard. The board that is applied along the base of a wall to cover the joint where wall and floor come together. May be of wood or plastic.

Base Molding. Molding used to trim the upper edge of interior baseboard.

Base Shoe. Molding used next to the floor on interior baseboard. Sometimes called a carpet strip.

Bat. A type of insulation that comes in relatively short lengths.

Battens. Narrow wood strips used to cover the joints between boards.

Batten Door. A door made of boards or planks that are secured by boards nailed vertically and often diagonally.

Bay Window. A window that projects outward from a wall. A bay window is straight in the center and angled at each end. A bow window curves outward.

Beading. Fine wood molding.

Beam. Any heavy piece of structural lumber or timber used to support a load.

Bearing Partition. The same as a "load-bearing" partition or wall. One that supports a vertical load, such as joists, beams, girders, or floor trusses.

Bearing Wall. A wall that supports any vertical load in addition to its own weight.

Bed. To set a material onto a surface that has been especially prepared; or the material used to prepare the surface, for example, a "bed" of putty for window glass or a "bed" of mortar for brick or masonry block.

Bed Molding. A molding at an angle, as between the overhanging eaves of a building and the sidewalls.

Bevel. A cut on an angle that is greater or smaller than a right angle.

Bevel Siding. Wood siding that is similar in shape to clapboard.

Bleed. When saps and resins in a piece of painted wood come through the paint, the wood is said to be bleeding.

Blind-nailing. Nailing in such a way that the nailheads are not visible on the face of the work.

Blind Stop. A rectangular molding, usually ¾ by 1⅜ inches or more in width, used in the assembly of a window frame. Serves as a stop for storm and screen or combination windows and to resist air infiltration.

Board Foot. The standard unit of measurement for lumber. A piece of lumber that is 1 by 12 by 12 inches.

Boiled Linseed Oil. Linseed oil in which enough lead, manganese, or cobalt salts have been incorporated to make the oil harden more rapidly when spread in thin coatings.

Bolts, Anchor. Bolts to secure a wooden sill plate to concrete or masonry flooring or a wall or pier.

Bond. To fasten together. Also, to use brick, stone, block, or timber as a connection in a structure.

Boston Ridge. A method of applying asphalt on wood singles at the ridge or at the hips of a roof as a finish.

Bow Window. See BAY WINDOW.

Brace. A piece of framing lumber applied to a wall or floor on an incline to provide temporary stiffening or bracing for a structure.

Brad. A small nail.

Btu. Abbreviation for British thermal unit, the standard measurement for heat. One Btu is equal to the amount of heat needed to raise the temperature of one pound of water one degree Fahrenheit.

Built-up Roof. Roofing composed of layers of asphalt felt impregnated with pitch, tar, or asphalt. The top is finished with crushed stone or minerals. Used generally on flat or slightly pitched roofs.

Butt Joint. The junction at which the

ends of two timbers or other members meet in a square-cut joint.

BX Cable. Electric wires in a flexible metal covering. The same as armored cable.

Cantilever. Any structure or part of a structure, or beam supported at one end only.

Cap. The concrete covering that is applied to the top of a masonry wall or chimney.

Casement Windows. Windows with one or two sashes hinged at the sides so that they open and close like a door.

Casing. The wood trim around doors and windows.

Casing Nails. Nails with small heads used to fasten casing in place. The heads are set below the wood surface and the holes filled with putty or spackling compound.

Caulk. To fill a seam or crack with a waterproof material.

Caulking Compound. Material used for caulking joints where window and door frames join the siding, and for other areas where there is an open seam.

Clapboard. A type of siding similar to bevel siding, where one edge of the board is thicker than the other.

Collar Beam. 1- or 2-inch-thick members connecting opposite roof rafters; they serve to stiffen the roof structure and also act as the framework for a ceiling.

Combination Doors or **Windows.** Doors or windows that have both glass and screen inserts, often removable. They provide insulation in winter and insect protection in summer.

Concrete. A mixture of Portland cement, sand, gravel, and water.

Condensation. Beads of moisture or frost forming on the inside of any wall or window that is considerably colder than the air around it.

Conduit, Electrical. A pipe in which wire is installed.

Corner Braces. Diagonal braces at the corners of a frame structure, to stiffen and strengthen the wall.

Cornice. The crowning horizontal member of a structure.

Counter Flashing. A flashing used on chimneys at the roof line to cover shingle flashing and prevent moisture from entering.

Countersink. To set the head of a nail or screw below the surface of the material that is being fastened in place.

Cove Molding. Molding with a concave face, used as trim.

Crawl Space. A shallow space below a porch or below the floors of a house with no basement.

Detail Drawing. A separate drawing or plan to show the exact construction or design of a certain element in a structure.

Dimension Lumber. Lumber from 2 inches thick to 5 inches thick and up to 12 inches wide. Most of the materials used to frame a house are dimension lumber.

Dormer. A vertical window that is built into a sloping roof.

Double-Hung Window. A window with a movable sash, both upper and lower.

Downspout. A pipe that carries off rain water from roof gutters.

Drain Tile. Tile pipe laid in a ditch to carry surface water away from the foundation, or connected to the downspouts to carry away water from the roof.

Drip Cap. A molding placed on the top of an exterior door to divert rain beyond the frame.

Dry Rot. A type of wood decay caused by fungi.

Dry Wall Construction. A wall or ceiling material in sheets or panels that is applied dry, as opposed to a plaster wall.

Dry Well. A large hole, often filled with stone or gravel, used to collect water from the house gutters and downspouts or from the overflow of a septic tank.

Ducts. In a house, usually round or rectangular metal pipes for distributing warm air from a conditioning device, or as cold air returns. Ducts are also made of asbestos and composition materials.

Dutch Door. A type of door that is separated horizontally at about the midpoint so that the upper half can be opened while the lower half remains closed.

Eaves. The portion of the roof that extends beyond and overhangs the exterior wall.

End-Matched Lumber. Boards that have the ends as well as the side tongued and grooved so that these ends can be joined together without the need of a support under the joint.

Escutcheon. The metal or shield plate used around the keyhole on doors.

Expansion Bolt. A type of bolt used for fastening materials to masonry. Similar to an anchor bolt.

Facade. The exterior front of a building.

Face Nailing. Driving a nail perpendicular to the surface.

Facia or **Fascia.** A flat board, band, or face, used sometimes by itself but usually in combination with moldings, often located at the outer face of the cornice.

Fire Brick. A special brick used on the inside of a fireplace and designed to withstand higher temperatures than ordinary brick.

Flashing. Sheet metal or other material used in roof and wall construction to protect a building from seepage of water.

Flat Paint. An interior paint that contains a high proportion of pigment and dries to a flat or lusterless finish.

Flue. The space or passage in a chimney through which smoke, gas, or fumes, ascend. Each passage is called a flue, which, together with any others and the surrounding masonry, making up the chimney.

Flue Lining. Fire clay or terra-cotta pipe, round or square, usually made in all the ordinary flue sizes and in 2-foot lengths, used for the inner lining of chimneys with brick or masonry work around the outside. Flue lining in chimneys runs from about a foot below the flue connection to the top of the chimney.

Fly Rafter. End rafters of the gable overhang supported by roof sheathing and lookouts.

Footing. A masonry section, usually concrete, in a rectangular form wider than the bottom of the foundation wall or pier it supports.

Foundation. The supporting portion of a structure below the first-floor construction, or below grade, including the footings.

Framing, Balloon. A system of framing a building in which all vertical structural elements of the bearing walls and partitions consist of single pieces extending from the top of the foundation sill plate to the roofplate and to which all floor joists are fastened.

Framing, Platform. A system of framing a building in which floor joists of each story rest on the top plates of the story below or on the foundation sill for the first story, and the bearing walls and partitions rest on the sub-floor of each story.

Frieze. In house construction, a horizontal member connecting the top of the siding with the soffit of the cornice or roof sheathing.

Frost Line. The depth of frost penetration in soil. This depth varies in different parts of the country. Footings should be placed below this depth to prevent movement.

Furring. Strips of wood or metal applied to a wall or other surface to even it and usually to serve as a fastening base for finish material.

Gable. The triangular portion at the end of a building, formed by the eaves and ridge of a sloped roof.

Galvanized Iron. Steel coated with zinc to prevent rusting.

Galvanized Nails. Zinc-coated nails used on exterior work and where maximum holding power is required.

Gambrel Roof. A roof with two pitches, with the lower slope steeper than the upper.

Girder. A large or principal beam of

wood or steel used to support concentrated loads at isolated points along its length.

Glazing. Fitting and puttying a pane of glass into a window sash.

Grade. The slope of the ground.

Grading. Changing the natural slope of the grounds.

Grout. A prepared type of cement mortar or plastic used for filling the joints between ceramic and clay tile.

Gusset. A member made of flat wood, plywood, or similar material used to provide a connection at the intersection of wood members. Most commonly used at joints of wood trusses. They are fastened by nails, screws, bolts, or adhesives.

Gutter Eave Trough. A shallow channel or conduit of metal or wood set below and along the eaves of a house to catch and carry off rainwater from the roof.

Hardboard. A composition material made of wood fibers and a binder. Very dense but flexible, and used for interior as well as exterior work.

Hardware. All the metal portions of the house, such as locks, hinges, and pulls.

Header. (*a*) A beam placed perpendicular to joists and to which joists are nailed in framing for chimney, stairway, or other opening.

(*b*) A wood lintel.

Hearth. The portion of a fireplace that extends into the room at floor level.

Hip Roof. A roof that rises by equally inclined planes from all four sides of the building as opposed to a pitched roof, where only two surfaces raise to form a gable at each end.

Hot Wire. An electric wire that is alive, i.e., current is flowing through it.

I Beam. A steel beam made into the shape of the letter *I* and used as a girder.

Insulation Board, Rigid. A structural building board made of wood or cane fiber in ½-inch and 25⁄32-inch thicknesses. It can be obtained in various-sized sheets, in various densities, and with several treatments.

Insulation, Thermal. Any material high in resistance to heat transmission, which, when placed in the walls, ceilings, or floors of a structure, will reduce the rate of heat flow.

Jack. A device used for lifting a heavy weight.

Jack Posts. The same as adjustable posts. Steel posts with a jack at the top. Once they have been put into place, the jack is turned to lift and support the structure above.

Jack Rafter. A rafter that spans the distance from the wallplate to a hip, or from a valley to a ridge.

Jamb. The side and head lining of a doorway, window, or other opening.

Joint. The space between the adjacent surfaces of two members or components joined and held together by nails, glue, cement, mortar, or other means.

Joist. One of a series of parallel beams, usually 2 inches thick, used to support floor and ceiling loads, and supported in turn by larger beams, girders, or bearing walls.

Joist Hanger. A metal strap used to carry the ends and support floor joists.

Kiln-Dried. Lumber that has been dried in a kiln—an oven—rather than by air.

Lag Screw. A heavy wood screw.

Lath. Strips of wood nailed to studding as a base for plaster or stucco. May also be of metal or composition material.

Lavatory. A washbasin. A small area with two plumbing fixtures—usually a washbasin and toilet.

Leader. Also **down-spout.** The pipe running from the gutters at the eaves of the roof to the ground.

Lean-To. A small structure that is built against another structure, usually a larger one.

Light. A single pane of glass, or the space in a windor or door to accommodate a single pane.

Lintel. A horizontal structural member that supports the load over an opening such as a window or door.

Lot. A plot or portion of land subdivided from a larger area.

Louver. A slatted panel or series of panels fitted into a door or window frame for light and ventilation.

Lumber, Board. Yard lumber less than 2 inches thick and at least 2 or more inches wide.

Lumber, Dimension. See DIMENSION LUMBER.

Lumber, Matched. Lumber that is grooved on one edge and tongued on the other.

Lumber, Yard. Various grades and sizes of lumber for use in ordinary construction such as framework and rough coverage.

Masking Tape. Adhesive tape used in painting and decorating to protect an area, such as woodwork, from being smudged or smeared.

Masonry. Stone, brick, concrete, or concrete block, bonded with mortar to make such items as walls, foundations, chimneys.

Mastic. A paste compound used with application of various flooring materials.

Matched Boards. Tongue-and-groove cuts in boards.

Members. The parts of the whole, as in a building.

Millwork. Various finished and manufactured wooden building components made at a millwork plant or planing mill. Includes doors, windows, kitchen-cabinet work, and moldings, but usually does not include flooring or siding. Finished wood.

Miter Joint. A joint made by cutting the ends of two matched pieces at a 45-degree angle so that when they are joined together they form a right angle.

Molding. Decorative or functional strips of wood, usually rounded, used as trim for woodwork, or to conceal joints.

Mortar. A mixture of sand and cement used in masonry.

Mortise. A hole, slot, or recess cut into a piece of wood.

Mullion. The bar, or pier, between the lights of screens or windows. A division, comprised of stone, metal, or wood.

Natural Finish. A transparent finish, such as shellac, varnish, or other sealer, that does not seriously change the color of the wood. It allows the grain to show through.

Newel Post. The main post at the foot of a stairway, into which the stair rail is fitted.

Non-Load-Bearing Wall. A wall supporting no load other than its own weight.

Notch. A crosswise rabbet at the end of a board.

Oakum. A caulking material of hemp fiber.

O.c. Also **On Center.** In a building, the measurement of spacing of stubs, rafters, joists, and the like from the center of one member to the center of the next.

Paper, Building. Large rolls of paper or felt used in wall and roof construction as insulation. Also useful as temporary floor covering to avoid getting paint on them or to protect the finish.

Partition. A wall that subdivides spaces within a building.

Penny. A term denoting the length of nails. Abbreviated by the letter *d*.

Pier. A masonry column used to support other structural members.

Pitch. The slope of a roof.

Plane. A tool for smoothing or leveling. To make smooth or level.

Plank. A thick, heavy board.

Plaster. A coating for walls and ceilings. It is a mixture of lime, sand, and water, applied wet, and hardens when dry.

Plate. Sill plate: a horizontal member anchored to a masonry wall. Sole plate: bottom horizontal member of a frame wall. Top plate: top horizontal member of a frame wall supporting ceiling joists, rafters, or other members.

Plumb. Exactly perpendicular; vertical.

Plumb Line. A line or string weighted at one end, used to check verticality.

Plywood. A piece of wood made of three or more layers of veneer joined with glue and usually laid with the grain of adjoining plies at right angles. Almost always an odd number of plies is used to provide balanced construction.

Pointing. The mortar between joints in masonry. Also, the process of filling mortar between the joints with a trowel and then smoothing it to give a neat effect.

Portland Cement. A type of cement mixed with sand, gravel, and water to form concrete.

Post. An upright piece of wood, steel, or masonry that serves as a support.

Prime Coat. The initial coat of paint or varnish that serves as a filler and preparation for additional or finished coats.

Putty. A pliable compound used for glazing, filling small holes, and similar construction and repair jobs.

Quarter Round. A small molding that has the cross section of a quarter circle.

Rabbet. A groove cut in wood so that another piece of wood can be fitted into the first piece.

Rafter. One of a series of structural members of a roof designed to support roof loads. The rafters of a flat roof are sometimes called roof joists.

Rafter, Hip. A rafter that forms the intersection of an external roof angle.

Rafter, Valley. A rafter that forms the intersection of an internal roof angle. The valley rafter is normally made of doubled 2-inch-thick members.

Rail. Cross members of panel doors or of a sash. Also the upper and lower members of a balustrade or staircase extending from one vertical support, such as a post, to another.

Rake. The inclined edge of a gable roof (the trim member is a rake molding).

Rake Joint. A joint between bricks where the mortar is raked out slightly before it sets.

Random Work. A masonry term describing stonework that is not laid in courses.

Rasp. A coarse type of file for rough surfaces.

Reinforced Concrete. Concrete that is strengthened internally with steel or wire mesh.

Rendering. A drawing, usually done by an architect, to show how a projected building will look when finished.

Return. The continuation, usually at a right angle, of the molding on the face of a building.

Reveal. The side of the opening of a window or door between the frame and the wall.

Ridge. The horizontal line at the junction of the top edges of two sloping roof surfaces.

Ridge Board. The board placed on edge at the edge of the roof into which the upper ends of the rafter are fastened.

Rise. In stairs, the vertical height of a step or flight of stairs.

Riser. Each of the vertical boards closing the spaces between the treads of stairways.

Roll Roofing. Roofing material, composed of fiber and saturated with asphalt, that is supplied in rolls.

Roof Sheathing. The boards or sheet material fastened to the roof rafter on which the shingle or other roof covering is laid.

Rout. See MORTISE.

Sash. The frame of a window that contains the pane of glass. A sash is usually movable.

Sash Weight. The metal piece attached to a window-sash cord.

Scribing. To trim, fit, or shape woodwork so that it will fit into an uneven space.

Sealer. A finishing material, either clear or pigmented, that is usually applied directly over uncoated wood for the purpose of sealing the surface.

Section. A cutaway drawing, as in a blueprint, showing the heights, openings, and thicknesses, of the various openings and materials.

Shake. A thick hand-split shingle, resawed to form two shakes; usually edge grained.

Sheathing. The structural covering, usually wood boards or plywood, used over studs or rafters of a structure. Structural building board is normally used only as wall sheathing.

Shim. A shallow strip of wood, metal, or stone, used to level or fill in a small depression.

Shingles. Roof covering of asphalt, asbestos, wood, tile, slate, or other material cut to stock lengths, widths, and thicknesses.

Shingles, Siding. Various kinds of shingles, such as wood shingles or shakes and nonwood shingles, that are used over sheathing for exterior sidewall covering of a structure.

Shiplap. Boards with edges shaped in such a way that when placed together they form a half-lap joint. Used for sheathing and siding.

Shoe Mold or **Base Shoe.** A strip of wood, usually a quarter-round, that is used to cover the joint where floor and baseboard meet.

Shore. A post, plank, or other support used to brace a wall during alterations, set obliquely, as a buttress.

Siding. The finish covering of the outside wall of a frame building, whether made of horizontal weatherboard, vertical boards with battens, shingles, or other material.

Siding, Panel. Large sheets of plywood or hardboard that serve as both sheathing and siding.

Sill. The lowest member of the frame of a structure, resting on the foundation and supporting the floor joists or the uprights of the wall. The member forming the lower side of an opening, as the sill of a door, or window.

Sizing. A coating of varnish or shellac applied to plaster or wallboard to smooth and cover small imperfections, and to

act as a seal before applying paint or wallpaper.

Sleeper. A piece of stone, timber, or steel laid on or close to the ground to receive floor joists.

Soffit. Usually the underside covering of an overhanging cornice.

Soil Cover or **Ground Cover.** A light covering of plastic film, roll roofing, or similar material used over the soil in crawl spaces of buildings to minimize moisture permeation of the area.

Soil Stack. A general term for the vertical main of a system of soil, waste, or vent piping.

Spackle. A joint cement used to fill in and cover joints and small cracks and holes. especially in wallboard.

Span. The distance between structural supports such as walls, columns, piers, beams, girders, and trusses.

Specifications. The exact dimension, materials, types of work and quality of work to be incorporated into a building as stated by the architect, or in the working drawings, or in the agreement with the contractor.

S.s. Glass. Windowpane glass, single strength.

Storm Sash or **Storm Window.** An extra window usually placed on the outside of an existing window as additional protection against cold weather.

Story. That part of a building between any floor and the floor or roof next above.

Straightedge. A wood or metal bar with a straight edge, used for drawing and checking straight lines.

String or **Stringer.** A timber or other support for cross members in floors or ceilings. In stairs, the support on which the stair treads rest; also called stringboard.

Stud or **Studding.** The 2-inch-by-4-inch stock used to frame the sides of a building in walls and partitions. Lath, plaster board, and gypsum board are nailed to the studs.

Sub-Floor. Boards or plywood laid on joists over which a finish floor is laid.

Sump Pump. An electric pump placed at the lowest point in a cellar to pump out water that might collect.

Template. A guide, pattern, or mold, usually cut out of thin plate, or cardboard. Also, a beam supporting joists, or a short piece of timber placed under a beam to help distribute pressure.

Tenon. A notched projection cut to fit into a mortise to make a joint.

Termites. Subterranean insects that superficially resemble ants except that their bodies are straight-sided rather than "waisted" like the body of an ant. They live in underground nests and enter buildings by tunneling inside woodwork or timbers in contact with the earth. They also can enter through small cracks in foundations or by means of small earthen tunnels that they construct over various obstacles to reach their food supply. If not checked, they can completely destroy sound wood, leaving only a shell. They thrive in warm, moist ground.

Termite Shield. A shield made of sheet copper, which is placed between the top of a masonry foundation wall and the wood sill above. It is extremely effective in keeping termites from entering the woodwork.

Threshold. A strip of wood or metal with beveled edges used over the finished floor and the sill of exterior doors.

Toenailing. Driving a nail at a slant with the initial surface in order to permit it to penetrate into a second member.

Tread. In a stairway, the horizontal board on which the foot is placed.

Trim. The finish materials in a building, such as moldings, applied around openings (window trims, door trim) or at the floor and ceiling of rooms (baseboard, cornice, picture molding).

Trimmer. A beam or joist to which a header is nailed in framing for a chimney, stairway, or other opening.

Truss. A frame or jointed structure designed to act as a beam of long span, while each member is usually subjected to longitudinal stress only, either tension or compression.

Undercoat. A coating applied prior to the finishing or top coats of a paint job. It may be the first of two or the second of three coats. In some usages of the word, it may become synonymous with priming coat.

Valley. The trough formed where two opposing slopes of a roof meet.

Valley Rafter. The timber that forms the intersection of a roof slope.

Vapor Barrier. Material used to retard the movement of water vapor into walls and prevent condensation in them.

Vent. A pipe or duct that allows flow of air as an inlet or outlet.

Vermiculite. A mineral closely related to mica, with the faculty of expanding on heating to form lightweight material with insulation quality. Used as bulk insulation and also as aggregate in insulating and acoustical plaster and in insulating concrete floors.

Wainscoting. Paneling on the lower portion of an interior wall.

Wallboard. Sheets of gypsum or other board nailed to studding to provide a surface wall or finish.

Wall Curtain. A wall surface that carries no load other than its own weight.

Wall, Retaining. A wall, usually of stone or large timbers such as railroad ties, to hold back or terrace a bank of earth.

Water-Repellent Preservative. A liquid designed to penetrate into wood and impart water repellency and a moderate preservative protection. It is used for millwork, such as sash and frames, and is usually applied by dipping.

Weatherstrip. Narrow or jamb-width sections of thin metal or other material to prevent infiltration of air and moisture around windows and doors.

Weep Hole. A small opening in a masonry wall to drain off rainwater.

Index

Index

About the Author

Hubbard H. Cobb, author of *The Dream House Encyclopedia*, has been an expert in the field of home building, remodeling, decorating, and maintenance for most of his working career.

For seventeen years he was with *The American Home* magazine, for seven years as Editor-in-Chief and for ten years as Building Editor. He is the author of five previous books in the home field, one of which sold more than one million copies. For more than twenty years he conducted the syndicated column "Fix It Yourself" in more than fifty newspapers and also conducted a radio program about home-building, remodeling, and maintenance over the Columbia Broadcasting System network.

Mr. Cobb does not just talk and write about homes. He has remodeled five Connecticut homes himself, has personally performed operations as complicated as installing electric wiring and plumbing pipes, and is therefore intimately familiar with all the pitfalls that face do-it-yourselfers.

He lives in New York City and East Haddam, Connecticut, and is married to the former Elizabeth Youngblood Simon. A former magazine writer and newspaper columnist, Mrs. Cobb is an enthusiastic co-worker in her husband's remodeling adventures. She recently supervised the remodeling of a ninety-year-old Federal home for her mother.

A former Air Force combat flier, Mr. Cobb now devotes himself to writing.